Becoming a

Foodservice Professional

YEAR I

National Restaurant Association
EDUCATIONAL FOUNDATION

ACKNOWLEDGMENTS

The production of this book would not have been possible without the expertise of our many advisors and manuscript reviewers. The National Restaurant Association Educational Foundation is pleased to thank the following professionals for their time and efforts during the development of this curriculum:

GINI LA FLEUR	La Fleur and Associates, South Holland, IL
KAREN REINHARD	Woodstock High School, Woodstock, IL
NANCY STEWART	Stewart and Associates, Laguna Niguel, CA

The ProStart program was developed with a gift from the American Express Foundation.

DISCLAIMER

The information presented in this book has been compiled from sources and documents believed to be reliable and represents the best professional judgment The Educational Foundation of the National Restaurant Association. However, the accuracy of the information presented is not guaranteed, nor is any responsibility assumed or implied by The Educational Foundation of the National Restaurant Association for any damage or loss from inaccuracies or omissions.

Inventory Code: PSST1

ISBN Number: 1-883904-87-0

November 1998

10 9 8 7 6 5 4 3

Dedicated to

Virginia La Fleur,

whose spirit lives on in our hearts and in the pages of this book.

Thanks, Gini
1949-1997

Table of Contents

YEAR I

INTRODUCTION: PREPARING FOR A SUCCESSFUL CAREER

Unit 2 176

Unit 3 282

Unit 4 374

INTRODUCTION

Preparing For A Successful Career

Dave Thomas

Founder and Senior Chairman of the Board
Wendy's

I never knew my birth parents. Rex and Auleva Thomas, a couple from Kalamazoo, Michigan, adopted me when I was six weeks old. Auleva died when I was five, and my early years included numerous moves from state to state as my father sought work. These frequent moves were challenging. I felt like I had no roots or sense of belonging. Always the new kid on the block, I sought refuge in work. One of the things I enjoyed most during my childhood was going to restaurants to eat. I'd see families eating together and enjoying the friendly atmosphere. I decided at an early age that I was going to have my own restaurant with great food that families would visit again and again.

I started working at age 12, delivering groceries in Knoxville, Tennessee, but I was fired after a misunderstanding with my boss about my vacation. My second job was as a soda jerk at Walgreen's, but I was fired again when my boss found out I wasn't 16. While applying for my next job, still 12 years-old, I landed a job at the counter at the Regas Restaurant in Knoxville. I worked hard, putting in 12-hour shifts, constantly afraid I'd lose yet another job.

The Regas brothers treated me like one of their family, providing me with encouragement and a caring mentorship that has had a positive and lasting effect. By the time I was 15, I'd moved again and was working full-time at The Hobby House Restaurant in Ft. Wayne, Indiana. As my family prepared for another move, I decided to stay in town and took a room at the local YMCA. Then I made the biggest mistake of my life: I dropped out of high school to work full-time. I thought I could learn more about the restaurant business with a hands-on education than I could learn in school.

When I was 18, I joined the Army, eventually becoming one of the youngest soldiers to manage an enlisted men's club. After my service, I returned to The Hobby House, where I met my future wife, Lorraine, a waitress, whom I married in 1954.

In 1956, my boss, Phil Clauss, and I opened a barbecue restaurant called The Ranch House. There, I met the man who became one of the greatest influences in my life—Colonel Harlan Sanders, founder of Kentucky Fried Chicken. Clauss bought a KFC franchise from the Colonel, and, all of a sudden, I was in the chicken business. In 1962, Clauss offered me a chance to turn around four failing KFC carryouts he owned in Columbus, Ohio. If I could turn the carry-outs around and pay off a big debt, Clauss would give me 45 percent of the business. Although daunting, this was the kind of challenge I liked.

After a lot of hard work, the restaurants began to prosper, and I added four more restaurants. I'm grateful and lucky to say, I was a millionaire at age 35. I opened the first Wendy's Old Fashioned Hamburgers restaurant on November 15, 1969, in Columbus. I named the restaurant after my 8-year-old daughter, Melinda Lou, nicknamed "Wendy" by her older brother and sisters. The first Wendy's menu included fresh, made-to-order hamburgers, chili, french fries, soft drinks, and a Frosty Dairy Dessert. The decor was homey, with bentwood chairs and tiffany-style lamps. I planned to open several restaurants around Columbus, giving my children a place to work during the summers. Wendy's grew and prospered.

In 1973, I began franchising the Wendy's concept, pioneering the idea of selling franchises for entire cities and parts of states, rather than single units. Wendy's grew rapidly, with more than 1,000 restaurants opening in its first 100 months. That rapid growth continues: Wendy's and its franchisees now operate more than 4,800 restaurants in the U.S. and 34 countries.

In early 1989, I agreed to appear in Wendy's commercials as the company spokesman. I guess because of those commercials, most people recognize me now. In 1990, I became a national spokesman for the White House initiative on adoption, called "Adoption Works For Everyone." Since then, I've been a national adoption advocate, working to raise awareness for the tens of thousands of children who need permanent homes and loving families.

While dropping out of school was my biggest mistake, it led to one of my proudest accomplishments. In 1993, 45 years after leaving school, I earned my GED certificate and received my high school diploma from Coconut Creek High School in Ft. Lauderdale, Florida. I was voted Most Likely to Succeed by the graduating class, and attended the prom with my wife Lorraine, where we were named Prom King and Queen.

I think the hospitality industry is one of the most exciting fields to work in. We need young people who are creative and innovative, and ready to meet the challenges of a business that's always on the move. With a good education and work experience (and if you're lucky, a good mentor), you can go as far as your dreams take you.

From my early days as a soda jerk and short order cook, to becoming an entrepreneur and TV spokesman, I've been recognized for my work in the restaurant industry and for children. I've received lots of restaurant industry honors and Entrepreneur and Man of the Year awards. The adoption community has honored me with a variety of awards, and I've attended special receptions at the White House in recognition for my work for adoption. I've also testified before Congress in support of tax credits for adoptive parents.

On the rare occasions when I'm not in the studio making commercials or traveling the country for interviews or speeches, you might find me on the golf course, perfecting my game.

There are a million opportunities in our industry. If you're willing to work hard and have a burning desire to succeed, you will succeed. That's what makes the difference. That's the true recipe for success.

Intro.1

SECTION i.1

Working in the Hospitality Industry

AFTER STUDYING SECTION i.1, YOU SHOULD BE ABLE TO:

- State in your own words the importance of service to success in the hospitality industry.
- List the elements of excellent service and give examples.
- State the difference between school and workplace environments.
- Develop a list of workplace guidelines.
- Identify and give examples of positive work attitudes.

This is an exciting time to begin a career in the hospitality industry. More new restaurants are opening each year, and many restaurant chains are ranked among the nation's top corporations. Many jobs and opportunities exist in the foodservice industry for people who possess the right combination of interests, skills, education, and training. Job opportunities in this industry are varied and unique.

People choose careers in the hospitality industry for a variety of reasons.

"No matter what segment of the industry you choose," agrees Rosalyn Mallet, FMP*, a vice president of franchise development, "you can be sure that hospitality is an industry where, if you're willing to work hard and network, you can do almost anything."

**An FMP is a Foodservice Management Professional certification earned through educational experience in the industry.*

"There is no bigger thrill than talking to happy customers who let you know all your hard work and creativity has paid off," says Darlene Tegtmeier, an assistant bar manager/bartender in a fine-dining restaurant.

Attracted to the fast pace of the foodservice industry, Steven Hartenstein, General Manager of a fine-dining restaurant, says he does "everything from A to Z. I'm responsible for purchasing and receiving food supplies, and managing the finances of the restaurant. I enjoy all of the daily challenges, and the fact that every day is different from the last."

A unique element of the foodservice industry is that the customer and the manufacturer of the product are in direct contact. Food is prepared and served, then purchased directly by customers, who are the guests that you serve.

When you work in the foodservice industry you have daily contact with guests and often receive immediate feedback about the quality of food and service. So the quality must be right the first time!

More than anything else, people who work in food service must love to serve others. They must also enjoy working with food, be efficient, flexible, able to work cooperatively, and remain calm under pressure in a fast-paced environment.

A Commitment to Service

Before you begin a career in the hospitality industry, it's important to understand what service is all about. Working in a service industry means that it's your job to serve people directly. People who work in a service industry don't spend much of their time in an office by themselves (as accountants, advertising copywriters, and clerks do), and they don't make things that are to be sold to the public in stores (those are manufacturing industries, and people who work in them produce shoes, computer parts, or cars, for example). Service professionals include police officers, restaurant and hotel workers, nurses, retail salespeople, teachers, theater ticket-takers, lawyers, landscapers, and nutritionists.

People who serve the public are people with a special commitment to others as well as the skills and knowledge to perform their jobs. People who work in the hospitality or foodservice industry must enjoy serving others, because service is the most important element of their jobs.

Serving customers means making them feel like they're special guests in your home. Good service comes from a natural desire to serve, but it can be improved through training, effort, stamina, and commitment. Serving people all day is not always easy. Think about the last time you were at a restaurant or in your school cafeteria or at a ball park. Did you notice how busy the servers were? Were there customers who were rude to them or were demanding? To be successful in the hospitality industry, you have to be able to give people what they want, and make them feel they are getting good value for their money. Pleasing others will make you feel good about your job as well as help you earn money.

> **Think About It**
>
> **The more you know about yourself, the easier it will be to make choices about your career. Following are some suggestions to help you choose a career that will be right for you.**
>
> - **What are some of your favorite classes, activities, and interests? Why do you enjoy them?**
> - **What special skills, talents, and abilities do you possess?**
> - **What ideas, values, goals, and causes are important to you?**
> - **Remember, many people change careers during their lifetime. Never be afraid to investigate an opportunity that sounds more interesting and challenging than what you are doing.**

Service with a Smile

In any foodservice operation, customers must be served pleasantly, correctly, and in a timely manner. Customers expect the people who serve them to be pleasant, helpful, and friendly. What does this mean for you? The following are some tips for anyone working in food service or hospitality.

Exhibits i.1 and i.2
Knowing how to serve people is the key to success in the hospitality industry.

- Always greet customers. Smile and look people in the eye when you speak to them.
- Fulfill guests' requests pleasantly, without appearing irritated or annoyed.
- Always say "thank you."
- Cooperate with coworkers who request food, equipment, or help in better serving customers.

From the moment you are hired for a job you can begin planning for your first day of work. Employers do not expect you to know all the procedures and responsibilities of your new position immediately. However, you can become familiar with the guidelines for professionalism and business courtesy, so that on your first day on the job you will know what is expected.

Welcome to the "Real World"

The world of work is very different from the world of school that you've been living in. Sure, you may not get a grade based on how well you do a job, but your performance at work will determine whether or not you get a raise or promotion. Employers will be watching closely to see if you are the kind of employee they want to give additional responsibilities (and money) to.

Another difference between the classroom and the "real world" is that if your performance or attitude is poor, an employer can terminate (fire) you. If this happens, you will need to find another job, but it will be difficult without a good reference from your last employer.

When you enter the world of work, even as a part-time employee, you are expected to follow guidelines of professional, adult behavior. These guidelines help all employees work well together and contribute to the success of the organization. Qualities that employers expect to find in successful employees are really a matter of common sense.

Exhibit i.3
Employers will expect you to follow their workplace guidelines.

Workplace Guidelines

Attendance—Always call if you are going to be out sick or arriving late. Your managers expect you to be available and on time—they count on you to be there as promised.

Teamwork—Teamwork is vital to any foodservice operation. Employees must be willing to do their assigned work and sometimes more if necessary. Cooperation with coworkers is a must for getting the job done.

Promptness—When someone tells you to do something, do it right away.

Positive Attitude—Having a positive attitude means being enthusiastic about your work and your coworkers. A positive attitude increases your self-confidence, helping you deal with challenges as well as the daily routine.

Dependability—Dependability is important in any career. It means that you will meet your job commitments effectively and on time.

Ask questions—If you don't know or don't understand something, ask. Your employer or supervisor will be more than happy to answer your questions or direct you to the person who can.

Fairness and honesty—It is important to be fair and honest with your employer. No one has to give you a job. A job is an agreement between you and your employer to perform a day's work for a day's pay.

Exhibit i.4
Teamwork is one of the most important guidelines you'll need to practice every day.

Intro.2

SECTION i.2

Career Opportunities in Food Service

AFTER STUDYING SECTION i.2, YOU SHOULD BE ABLE TO:

- Give examples of career opportunities in the foodservice industry.
- Make a list of qualities of successful foodservice employees.

It's never too early to begin thinking about your career. A **career** is a profession or work in a particular field, such as food service, that you choose for yourself. Even though you're in school, you can still be thinking about how your interest in food, for example, experimenting with recipes, preparing meals, or organizing parties, could someday lead to a career in food service.

For organizational purposes, jobs in the foodservice industry are divided into two categories: front-of-the-house and back-of-the-house. **Front-of-the-house** employees serve guests directly. Front-of-

KEY TERMS

- **Back-of-the-house**
- **Career**
- **Career ladder**
- **Entry-level job**
- **Entrepreneur (ON-trah-prah-NOOR)**
- **Foodservice management**
- **Front-of-the-house**

the-house positions include managers, assistant managers, hosts/hostesses, cashiers, bar staff, wait staff, and buspersons.

Exhibit i.5
Cooks and chefs are considered back-of-the-house employees because they don't usually have direct customer contact.

Back-of-the-house employees work outside the public space. Back-of-the-house positions include chefs, line cooks, pastry chefs, dishwashers, bookkeepers, storeroom clerks, purchasers, dietitians, and menu planners. While these employees don't ordinarily serve guests directly, they are service professionals because they serve the people who serve the guests. They are said to serve their "internal customers," which includes the servers and other front-of-the-house employees.

Entry-Level Jobs

Whether your interest is in a job in the front- or the back-of-the-house, you can expect to begin your career in an entry-level position. An **entry-level job** is one that requires little or no previous experience. Such jobs are an important starting point in your career. Entry-level jobs usually lead to other positions with more responsibility. The foodservice industry has many entry-level positions to offer, and the industry as a whole is expected to generate more new jobs than any other service industry during the next decade.

Entry-level jobs in the foodservice industry include busperson, assistant cook, server, and dishwasher. It is easy to see why these jobs are important to the foodservice operation. Each role is key to the success of the operation as a whole. The operation can only be as good as its team.

Following are brief descriptions of the responsibilities you can expect in some popular entry-level jobs in food service.

Busperson—The work that a busperson does makes an impression on customers as soon as they are seated. Seeing that their table is set properly and then having the table cleared quickly allows guests to relax and enjoy themselves, knowing that their needs are being taken care of. Guests will often ask buspersons for water, condiments, fresh silverware, and other extras. A quick and polite response to such requests further enhances a guest's enjoyment.

Dishwasher—Clean, sparkling, sanitary tableware is essential to an enjoyable meal and it is the responsibility of the dishwashers to see that this function is fulfilled. Although the dishwashers work in the back-of-the-house, their work is very visible in the front-of-the-house, helping determine the guests' overall impression of the operation. The dishwasher also keeps an eye on service areas, making certain that supplies do not run out.

Host/hostess or entrance employee—The very first impression of an operation that guests receive is from the host/hostess or employee who meets them at the entrance. If that impression is a friendly, hospitable, and gracious one, guests will feel relaxed and ready to enjoy themselves. In addition to greeting customers, hosts assist guests with coats or other things they wish to check; take reservations; seat customers; ask whether departing customers enjoyed their meals; thank customers for their visit; and answer customers' questions about hours of the operation, types of credit cards accepted, and what menu items are available.

Server—Whether in a full-service or quick-service operation, servers spend more time with the guests than any other employee. The server's attitude and performance has a tremendous impact on the guest's enjoyment of the dining experience. In a full-service operation servers greet customers; take their order; serve the order; check on customers' needs after serving the meal; and continue to provide service until customers have left the table.

Exhibit i.6
Service with a smile brings customers back again and again.

Counter servers in a quick-service operation usually have only brief contact with each customer. This means that servers have only a few moments to make a good first impression. Counter servers greet customers; take their order; accept payment; and thank customers for their patronage.

Assistant cooks help the more experienced cooks and chefs prepare and cook guests' orders. Often assistant cooks prep meals—which means to portion out food, precook it, or get it ready ahead of time—so everything is ready to assemble when guests order it.

A Selection of Foodservice Careers

Already you can see that jobs in food service can be varied and unique. Higher level jobs include planning menus, developing recipes, managing a foodservice operation, writing about food, developing marketing and advertising strategies, teaching others about food and nutrition, and supplying food to restaurants.

Following are some careers in the foodservice industry.

Foodservice management is the running of a foodservice operation. It includes the coordination of people, resources, products, and facilities related to the design, preparation, and presentation of food outside the home.

Restaurant manager—Managers are responsible for both front-of-the-house and back-of-the-house operations. They are responsible for service; staff training; maintaining the restaurant and its property; keeping food safe; keeping guests and employees safe; marketing and promoting the operation; ensuring profits; keeping costs down; purchasing and storing food; and supervising employees. In short, the manager oversees everything that happens in the foodservice operation.

Assistant managers—Assistant managers are responsible for helping the manager oversee all aspects of operations. Assistant manager is the usual training position for future managers.

Exhibit i.7
Managers are responsible for overseeing all aspects of the operation.

Executive chef—The executive chef oversees the entire kitchen, from supervising all kitchen employees, to purchasing food supplies and making decisions about menu items. Chefs and executive chefs must be trained and educated in the culinary arts and are certified by a professional organization.

Chefs and cooks—An assistant executive chef is responsible for the kitchen team in the executive chef's absence and also lends his or her cooking expertise to overall food preparation. Other chef positions include pantry cook, who is responsible for cold food trays and buffet arrangements; roast cook, who prepares all meat, poultry, and fish; sauce and stock cook, who prepares all sauces and stocks; vegetable cook, who prepares all vegetables and soups; and pastry chef, who prepares all desserts and specialty baked goods. These positions are typically found only in fine-dining restaurants.

Home economists have degrees in food and nutrition and are employed by schools, county or regional health services, and government agencies where they educate consumers about food preparation and healthy food choices.

Exhibits i.8 and i.9
Strong writing skills are important in foodservice marketing.

Communication writers—People with strong communication skills are needed to write books, magazine articles, and brochures, providing consumers with information about food and related matters. Writers may also contribute their talents to the development of training and instructional materials for both restaurants and foodservice companies.

Food stylists arrange food attractively for photographs to be included in magazines and brochures, and to be used by government agencies, associations, and food producers and distributors.

Food service marketers are active in sales, management, and distribution of food products and services. An enormous variety of food items and products must be marketed and sold to foodservice operators.

Research and development—Opportunities in research and development involve the development and testing of new products in test kitchens and laboratories. The government, food producers, universities, and manufacturers of kitchen appliances all need people with these interests and skills.

Food science—Food scientists study the composition of foods. They develop new food products as well as new ways to process and package them. In addition, they test foods for quality, purity, and safety to ensure that they meet government standards.

Dietitians—Dietitians are trained in the principles of food and nutrition. They help people make wise food choices and help develop special diets when needed. Dietitians typically work in universities, restaurants, schools, hospitals, and institutional cafeterias developing nutritious menus.

Food production and food processing—Careers in this area include everything from farming, to running a food processing facility, to distributing food products to restaurants. The production of food and delivering it to consumers requires a large network of dedicated people.

Accounting—Accountants in the foodservice industry are knowledgeable about trends in the industry, give financial advice, and handle payroll and financial procedures.

Exhibit i.10
Accounting requires a good understanding of mathematics.

Entrepreneur—**Entrepreneurs** (ON-trah-prah-NOOR) own and run their own businesses. Successful entrepreneurs must dedicate themselves to their business, be well-organized, committed to working long hours, and have a general knowledge of business practices. Entrepreneurs are generally risk-takers who work well without supervision.

Trainers are teachers who conduct training sessions for groups of employees or managers. Typically, trainers work for large foodservice companies that own many units. Training managers are responsible for ensuring that all employees and managers receive the right kind of training for their job.

Grocery store and deli managers are increasingly finding that their jobs are like those of restaurant managers. Many stores sell foods that are ready to eat, so managers and employees must know how to prepare food, understand and apply food safety standards, and promote what they have to their customers. This area of the industry is growing rapidly, and many employees and managers will be needed in years to come to supply this demand.

What Brings Success?

If you have had a part-time or summer job, you might already know the kind of work you enjoy doing. You also know that working helps you develop such essential skills as responsibility, self-confidence, and decision making, while you earn a paycheck. If you haven't had a job yet, don't worry. You've already made the most important first step toward a good career by taking classes in school that will help build your skills.

People advance in their careers by mastering the skills needed for their jobs and by showing that they are qualified to take on new responsibilities. Training and experience are important, but employers are also looking for certain skills that you can develop while you are still in school. Training and additional education can help motivated individuals

Exhibit i.11
Sample career ladder.

move higher up the career ladder. A **career ladder** is a series of jobs through which a person can advance to further their career, as shown in Exhibit i.11.

The ability to communicate effectively is one of the top skills that employers look for. Communication skills include writing, speaking, reading, and listening. Speaking to coworkers and customers; writing reports; reading company guidelines; and listening to supervisors, customers, and coworkers are essential in any job.

How can you develop good listening skills?

- **Avoid the tendency to finish another person's sentence—in your mind or aloud.**
- **Focus immediately on the first few words the other person is saying.**
- **Stay focused on what the person is saying.**
- **Repeat the message—put what the person is saying in your own words.**
- **Ask questions if you don't understand something.**
- **Remain calm if someone says something that you strongly disagree with; react to the message, not the messenger.**
- **Concentrate on key ideas and phrases.**
- **Read between the lines. Often it's not what someone says but how the person says it.**
- **Spend more than 50 percent of your time listening. Become a better listener than talker.**

Computer skills are also valuable in the foodservice industry. Most jobs today require some knowledge of computers. For example, in many restaurants servers place orders on computers; cashiers and counter servers in quick-service operations use computerized cash registers. Math skills are also essential, even though computers may be used. For example, if a customer tells a server to keep 15 percent of the payment as a tip, the server needs to know how to calculate that percentage.

Critical thinking and problem solving are also important skills to develop. Employers value employees who can think of fresh solutions to problems.

Maintaining a positive attitude is a key attribute of any employee. Employers, customers, and coworkers value a person who is enthusiastic and optimistic. Another related quality is the ability to work as part of a team. Employees, especially in food service, must be team players, doing their share of the work load—and more if that's what it takes to get the job done.

Willingness to learn new technology and new ways of doing things is important to career success. Employees who advance are the ones who are willing to learn new skills and techniques and not think that the way they know is the only way to do something.

Exhibit i.12
Computer skills are important in the hospitality industry.

How can you develop these skills now?

- Make a commitment to put forth your best effort, both in your studies and in your favorite school activities.
- Be active in school clubs and activities that interest you.
- Volunteer your time in the community—help out in your local library, hospital, nursing home, or pet shelter.
- Take some time to read and learn on your own.
- If you can use a computer in school, the library, or your home, become familiar with basic computer functions and software programs, including word processing, the Internet, and CD-Roms.

Take advantage of every opportunity to improve your learning and work habits while you're still in school and working part time. The more you practice these habits now, the farther you will be able to advance in your career.

Intro.3

SECTION i.3

Starting Your Career in Food Service

AFTER STUDYING SECTION i.3, YOU SHOULD BE ABLE TO:

- Outline a plan for an effective job search.
- Given a list of effective cover letter elements, write a cover letter.
- Demonstrate networking skills.

KEY TERMS

- **Cover letter**
- **Networking**

Now that you've focused on your interests and career goals, it's time to consider the continuing education you will need to achieve those goals. Most careers in the foodservice industry require at least a high school diploma or the equivalent. Admission to a college or trade school also requires a high school diploma. No matter what careers interest you, completing high school and continuing your education are the first steps to a successful future.

Although not all foodservice careers require a college education, today many do. For instance, to become a professional chef, dietitian, nutritionist, food stylist or scientist, marketer, home economist, or accountant, you will most likely need to complete additional classes and training.

Choosing a College or Trade School

You will need to consider the following questions when you decide which college or trade school to attend.

Does the school have a program in your chosen field that fits your needs? Do they offer the certification, associate's degree, or bachelor's degree in which you are interested? What is the reputation of the program? If class times or schedules conflict with your other priorities, find out if the school offers evening classes or correspondence classes through video, satellite, or Internet broadcasts.

What are the entrance requirements or fees for applying? Several schools place just as much emphasis on motivation and interest in succeeding as they do on grades and test scores.

Where is the school? Can you live at home or must you live on campus? Will you need your own car? If the school's main location is not convenient for you, remember that many colleges offer classes in several locations. If you are interested in visiting campuses, colleges offer tours for prospective students and their families.

How much does it cost? What kind of financial aid is available? Are scholarships available for which you would qualify? Many colleges have private and federally funded financial aid programs, including grants, loans, scholarships, and work-study programs. Be sure to ask about them.

What is the success rate of the graduates of the school? Does the school assist former students in their job search? Several schools actually have their own placement offices that help link graduates directly with employment opportunities.

What other activities are available at the school? What kinds of clubs and organizations are available for you to explore your interests and develop skills? Participation in college organizations can also contribute to an impressive résumé.

To find the answers to these questions, begin with your high school guidance office or local library. Don't be afraid to make some phone calls. You can also find college application and financial aid information, as well as phone numbers, on the Internet.

The Job Search

Do you have a part-time job? The skills you used to find that job are the same skills you will need to advance your professional career. If you learn how to find a job now, you'll have a head start when you're ready to work full time. Finding and keeping a job will help you develop both personal and career skills.

Job hunting can be exciting and fun. The job market is the ideal place to tell others about your abilities, talents, and dreams. As the average age of people in today's workplace grows older, younger people have even more opportunities before them.

People find jobs in a wide variety of ways. Some employers recruit graduates from a particular high school, and many recruit from colleges and universities. Others print employment ads in local newspapers. Other sources include school placement offices, employment agencies, community agencies, local Yellow Pages, and web pages on the Internet.

Job ads in newspapers are listed alphabetically by job title or job category. For example, if you're looking for a position as a busperson, there may be an ad under "B" for busperson, or there may be an ad under "R" for restaurant. Most ads will specify how you are to apply for the job—in person, by mail, or by phone. Sometimes foodservice operations state a designated time for prospective employees to apply in person. Others will request that you send a cover letter with a résumé or that you phone them directly.

Give it a try!

Try it: get a classified section of your local newspaper and find the restaurant job listings. How many different headings can you find? How much do the jobs pay? How does one apply? What are the hours?

What Is a Cover Letter?

When you send your résumé to a potential employer, you should send a cover letter along with it. A **cover letter** is a brief letter in which you introduce yourself to the employer. The letter highlights your strengths and confirms your interest in the position being offered. In a cover letter, you can explain your qualifications with a more personal touch.

Keep your cover letter brief, to the point, and straightforward. It should be typewritten, using correct grammar and punctuation. Make sure the company name, address, and person's name are all correct. If you use a computer, remember to use the spellcheck function. Always read letters carefully before you send them. Remember, first impressions are critical, and many employers who see a sloppy cover letter will get the feeling that your work might be sloppy too.

Following are tips for writing a cover letter:

Attention. Grab your reader's attention in the first paragraph to make sure the person keeps on reading. State why you're writing the letter.

Interest. Hold the reader's interest by telling how you got their name or found out about the company or the job.

Ms. Louise Brown
Manager
Blue Parakeet Café
82 South Pleasant Street
Funtown, USA 50094

July 28, 2002

Dear Ms. Brown:

I would like to schedule an appointment to meet with you regarding a position as part-time server.

Your advertisement in the *Anytown Daily News* for servers at the Blue Parakeet Café offers a great opportunity for me to begin my career in foodservice. I'm a junior at Anytown High School where I'm currently enrolled in a new program that includes food preparation classes as well as business management courses.

For your review, I'm enclosing a copy of my résumé that shows my qualifications. I:

- Am hard-working, dependable, and honest
- Have a pleasant disposition and outgoing personality
- Enjoy being with people
- Have an excellent memory for names and faces

I am sure that once you've had a chance to look over my résumé and meet with me, you'll agree that my enthusiasm and willingness to learn will make me an ideal server at the Blue Parakeet Café. You can reach me after 3:00 p.m. at 123-456-7890. I look forward to hearing from you at your earliest convenience. Thank you for your consideration.

Sincerely,

Rose J. Hernandez

Rose J. Hernandez
2340 East 83rd Street
Anytown, USA 85467

Exhibit i.13
Here is an example of a good cover letter.

Desire. Tell the reader what you want to do for their company. List your qualifications and the reasons why you want the job.

Action. End your letter by saying that you look forward to meeting them in an interview.

Always keep a copy of your cover letter and the ad to which you responded. This will help you follow up your request for an interview with a phone call. A follow-up phone call proves that you're serious about wanting the job.

Here is an example of a follow-up phone call.

1. Call the manager and introduce yourself. Be friendly, yet businesslike.

   "Good afternoon, Ms. Brown. My name is Rose Hernandez. How are you today?"

2. State the purpose for your call.

   "Ms. Brown, I'm calling to follow up on the letter and résumé I sent you last week responding to your ad for servers. I wanted to be sure that you received it."

3. Ask for the interview.

   "Would it be possible for us to meet and discuss a part-time server position? Do you suppose you might have time Thursday or Friday afternoon this week?"

4. Stay calm, truthful, and expect the unexpected.

   "I guess I'm a little nervous because I've never called a manager before about a job. You were about to call me for an interview? That's great!"

5. Politely end the conversation and confirm the interview date and time.

   "Thanks so much, Ms. Brown. I look forward to meeting you at 3:30 on Thursday afternoon."

How Networking Works

An important tool for your job search is networking. **Networking** means contacting people who can give you information about job openings. For example, your teachers may know of job openings; your friends who are working may provide job leads; your parents, relatives, or neighbors may also know of employment opportunities. The more people who know about your job search, the better your chances of finding a position.

The following is an example of networking:

Say you have a friend whose sister is a server at a local family restaurant. You could call that server, identify yourself as a friend of her brother, and ask her if she knows of any openings.

The conversation might sound like this:

> *"Hi, Kyana. This is Aaron. You don't know me, but I'm a friend of your brother's from school. Bryan said you're working at the Blue Parakeet Café these days, and you said it's pretty decent over there. I need a favor and I was wondering if you could help. I'm looking for a job as a busperson or a kitchen helper. Do you know if the manager is hiring anyone? Or could you give me the manager's name so I could call myself?"*

If the person knows of an opening, ask for a recommendation. For example:

> *"So, Kyana, when I call Mr. Ramirez (the manager), would you mind if I said that you recommended that I give him a call?"*

Be sure to thank the person, and if you have an interview, call the person to let him or her know how you did. For example:

> *"Hi, Kyana. It's me, Aaron. Guess what?! I just wanted to let you know we're going to be working together Tuesday and Thursday nights. Mr. Ramirez hired me for that kitchen helper spot—and he said I could help out with that little league baseball party Saturday afternoon for some extra cash. Very cool—thanks for your help!"*

Intro.4

SECTION i.4

Preparing Your Portfolio and Résumé

AFTER STUDYING SECTION i.4, YOU SHOULD BE ABLE TO:

- Compile the best examples of your work into a portfolio.
- Write a résumé that lists your skills and competencies.

KEY TERMS

- **Portfolio**
- **References**
- **Résumé (RE-zoo-may)**

Just as you need the proper kitchen tools for food preparation, you need the appropriate tools for your job search. These tools are your portfolio and résumé. Creating your portfolio and résumé will make you feel more confident and they will present a clear picture of your interests, abilities, and talents to a prospective employer.

A Winning Portfolio

A **portfolio** is a collection of samples that showcase your interests, talents, contributions, and studies. A portfolio displays your finest efforts and is a good self-marketing tool to show potential employers. Exhibit i.14 provides a list of things a portfolio may include.

Portfolios should be complete, neat, and well-organized. Include a cover page that gives your full name, address, phone number; your career objectives; and a brief description of the contents. Select

Exhibit i.14
Portfolios can include a variety of items.

- A list and samples of your skills and abilities (such as the list of competencies you will be learning at your worksites)
- Samples of your work (for example, if you decorated a cake that you're especially proud of, take a picture of it and include it as a sample; or describe how you decorated it or what inspired you)
- Examples of problems you solved (at school, in your community, with your friends)
- Examples demonstrating your teamwork
- Examples that show your leadership and responsibility
- Important experiences and what you learned from them
- Certificates of recognition and reward (the certificate you will receive upon successful completion of this program and your high school diploma are two examples)
- Newsletters or announcements (with your name or group highlighted)
- Essays, reports, and papers that you're proud of (and those with high grades or positive teacher remarks)
- Letters of thanks
- Your résumé
- Audio or video tapes that display your abilities
- Test scores
- Original recipes that you created
- Letters of recommendation from past employers or groups you have worked with. (These can be from the sponsors of a charity walk-a-thon in which you participated, or a school event, for example.)

samples that clearly highlight your best talents. Each sample should be accompanied by a brief explanation of why it is important. Type information whenever possible. Include clean photocopies of letters and other important documents or certificates.

Your portfolio is best displayed in a three-ring binder or folder. It's a good idea to use three-ring, clear plastic sheets to hold your samples. Your portfolio should be about ten pages in length and easy to carry to interviews. A portfolio that is sloppy, too long, or too big does not make a good impression.

Start collecting materials for your portfolio now, while you're still in school. Creating a complete and accurate portfolio is an ongoing process. Think about what would impress you if you were a potential employer. Ask friends and family for advice.

An Effective Résumé

A key ingredient in your portfolio is your résumé. A **résumé** (RE-zoo-may) is a written summary of your experience, skills, and achievements that relate to the job you're seeking. A résumé is not your life story; rather, it is like a sales brochure that tells an employer why you are the best person to hire for the job. When looking at your résumé, ask yourself, "If I were the employer, would I hire this person?"

Your résumé should be short—no more than one page—and contain only the most important information. Include relevant work experience on your résumé. If you do not have any work experience, concentrate on the activities that show your skills and abilities and how they relate to the job for which you are applying. Following is a sample résumé format.

Name (first name first)

Home street address

City, State, Zip code

Phone number where you can be reached

Objective:

What job are you seeking?

Qualifications:

What are your skills/capabilities?

Experience:

How have you demonstrated these skills/capabilities in the past? List all jobs here, beginning with the most recent.

Education:

Name of your high school; your status (junior, senior); the courses you are taking

References available on request.

References are people who aren't related to you but who know you well and can provide information about you—your character, work ability, or academic standing. Some people to consider as references are teachers, previous employers, church leaders, and neighbors. It is considerate to ask these people first before you use them as job references. Be sure to have their full names, addresses, and phone numbers with you when you apply so you can give this information to the potential employer.

Notice how this student emphasized his current job. The other work experience is important as well. As you gain more work experience, you can eliminate less important items. When you graduate from high school, you would state on the education line:

Education:
1998; Diploma, Your High School, Your Town, Your State

Courses:
Pre-Management and Foods Courses
ProStart certificate from the National Restaurant Association

Your résumé will change as you do, as you gain more experience, training, and education. Like your portfolio, developing a résumé is an ongoing process. No matter how much experience you have, your résumé should be an easy-to-read outline of your successes and achievements.

Harvard Lippman
1234 Main Street
Funtown, USA 12345
Phone: 123.456.7890

Objective: Server, part-time

Qualifications:
- Ability to use a computer
- Received high grades in food classes
- Know how to organize work
- Work well with others
- Would like to manage a restaurant

Work Experience:
1996-present, Busperson, First-Class Café, Funtown, USA
- Clear tables quickly and set correctly
- Refill water and other beverages during dinner service
- Assist servers in serving food, as needed
- Received certificate for annual "Smile Award"

Other Experience:
- Help serve food at high school café (sponsored by Foodservice Class)
- Organized annual junior class bake sale (sponsored by Foodservice Class)
- Developed new recipe for lowfat brownies sold at annual bake sale
- Used computer program to type recipes for class cookbook
- Volunteer kitchen worker at community Thanksgiving dinner

Education:
- Junior at Funtown High School
- Currently taking food and management classes in Foodservice school-to-career program

References available on request

Exhibit i.15
Here is how a résumé looks when it is completed.

Intro.5

SECTION i.5

Completing Application Forms

AFTER STUDYING SECTION i.5, YOU SHOULD BE ABLE TO:

- Read and complete a college application form.
- Read and complete a job application form.

KEY TERMS

- **Application form**
- **College application**
- **Job application**
- **Trade school application**

Whether you apply to a college, a trade school, or for a job, you will have to complete an application form. An **application form** asks basic personal information about you and your background.

College Applications

In addition to asking for your name and address, **college** or **trade school applications** require education information. The application may also require that you state the program or course of study you are applying for and ask you to complete a short essay. You will be asked to have your high school transcript sent to the college also. The admissions office at the school will look at your application and transcript to see the courses you took and your grade point average. This information helps determine whether or not you will be accepted into the program.

It is *not* illegal for college applications to ask about your race, national origin, or birth date. However, you may choose not to answer these questions. Schools do not use this information to decide who gets accepted. Rather, they use the information to gather statistics about their student population.

Job Applications

The **job application** is important because it gives general information and it reveals some insights about you to the employer. It shows how well you can follow instructions, your ability to read and write, as well as your employment history. Treat the application seriously and take time to fill it out carefully and completely. It is illegal for a job application to ask about marital status, height, weight, age, handicaps, race or national origin, religion, or political information. The job application form usually asks you to state your work experience and list references.

Completing a Job Application Form

When you are filling out the job application, be sure to write or print clearly. Use correct grammar and punctuation, and organize your thoughts before you write them on the form. If your responses on an application are unclear or messy you will not make a good impression on the interviewer.

If there is something on the form that you don't understand, leave the space blank or write *please see me* in the space. Write *n/a* if a question is *not applicable* (doesn't apply) to you. Later, you can ask the person who handed you the application to explain any questions you have, or you can discuss them with the interviewer.

When answering questions about money on the application, write *Open*. You first need to learn about the job before you can make any decisions about the salary. You will be asked to state how much money you earned on any previous jobs. Be honest; don't exaggerate.

Even if you have no work experience, you still have qualities and skills that are needed in the workplace. List any volunteer work, baby-sitting jobs, or school or church activities that show that you have had experience contributing your efforts to projects.

You will be asked to sign your name on the application form to state that you have

Let's Try it!

Stop at a local business that interests you and ask for a job application. Bring it to class and complete it. Ask classmates to review your application for spelling errors. Then turn it in to the employer. Follow up with the employer and see what happens!

answered all questions and given information that is true and accurate to the best of your knowledge. Being dishonest on a job application can be a reason for immediate termination (firing). Employers do check on your educational and work background, as well as contact your references.

All job applications are basically the same, so once you have completed one form, you will know what to expect on others. Exhibit i.16 lists some terms that will likely appear on the job application.

Exhibit i.16
Words commonly found on job application forms.

WORD	MEANING
Employment	Work; a job
Personal information	Facts about yourself
Social security number	Numbers assigned by the government to all people who apply; everyone with a job is required to have a social security number
Related	From the same family
Employment desired	The kind of job you want
Position	Job; area you want to work in
Salary desired	Wage or salary you will accept to do a job
Inquire	Ask
Education	School experience
Location	Where something is
Permanent address	The location of your permanent home
Date graduated	The day, month, and year you finished school; if you are still in school, you can write your expected graduation date
Activities	Things you do, especially for relaxation or fun
Former employers	People for whom you used to work
References	People who know you and will tell an employer about you
Business	The kind of work a person does
Years acquainted	How long you have known someone
Physical conditions	State of health or fitness
Injured	Hurt
Detail	A small item or piece of information
Emergency	An unexpected situation calling for fast action
Notify	To inform

Intro.6

SECTION i.6

The Job Interview

AFTER STUDYING SECTION i.6, YOU SHOULD BE ABLE TO:

- List the steps to an effective job interview.
- Explain the follow-up steps for a job interview.

KEY TERMS

- **Etiquette (EH-tah-kit)**
- **Job interview**

If an employer likes your cover letter and résumé, you may be asked for a job interview. At the **job interview,** you'll meet with the employer to discuss your qualifications for the job. This is your opportunity to "show your stuff" in person to a potential employer, and you want to do everything possible to make the interview a success.

This first impression to your potential employer will make the strongest statement about you. Make sure that you make your first impression a great one! Your résumé and cover letter will be remembered if the person interviewing you likes what he or she sees in the office. The following key points will help you make a great first impression.

Appearance—If you look neat and clean, you give the impression that your work will also be neat and clean. You don't have to wear expensive clothes to have a good appearance. Wear clothes that are clean and appropriate for the job for which you are interviewing. The key is to avoid wearing anything in excess.

Good personal hygiene is a must. The most important point to remember is that you will be working with food and people—preparing, serving, and removing food or greeting guests in a foodservice operation. In the foodservice industry, cleanliness and neatness are absolutely essential.

Just a note: *Employers expect you to be clean and neat in your appearance every day on the job, too.*

Positive attitude—If you smile and are enthusiastic, it suggests that you will do your work with that same attitude. Remember, the ability to smile and stay calm under pressure is necessary for a successful career in food service. Don't worry if you're a little nervous during your interview. Most interviewers will see that you are a person who takes a serious attitude toward work.

Good manners—Good manners are the basis for business **etiquette** (EH-tah-kit). Saying *please, thank you,* and *excuse me* all show good manners. If you are considerate and thoughtful, your behavior implies that you will also act that way around coworkers and customers—and excellent customer service is expected in the foodservice industry. The first rule of business etiquette is to arrive at the interview on time. Punctuality for the interview indicates that you will be punctual on the job.

Exhibit i.17
Proper etiquette will help you in several business and professional situations.

When you meet the person who will interview you, smile, extend your hand, and exchange a friendly greeting. Always call the interviewer *Mr.* or *Ms.* unless the person asks you to use his or her first name. Wait until the interviewer invites you to sit down, and then sit up straight in the chair—don't slouch or sprawl out. Avoid nervous fidgeting, such as playing with your hair, drumming your fingers, or tapping your pen. It's best to sit still, look alert, and pay attention to what the interviewer is saying. Practice effective listening skills (as discussed in Section i-2). If you bring someone with you to the interview, have that person wait outside.

It is a good idea to learn basic facts about the company before the interview. It shows you are serious about working for the company and are interested in the job. Also, the potential employer may ask you what you know about the company. Information you should know includes the company size and reputation, its key products and services, and names of its competitors. This information can be found in your school library/media center, your community library, and local chambers of commerce and business associations.

WHAT MATERIALS DO YOU NEED TO BRING WITH YOU TO THE INTERVIEW?

What materials do you need to bring with you to the interview?

- *Portfolio, including your résumé*
- *Names, addresses, and phone numbers of three people you plan on using as references*
- *Birth certificate or valid passport; social security card; or proof that you are able to work in the United States*

If you're unsure about what work documents to bring, call the person who will be interviewing you. A potential employer will be impressed by your preparedness and attention to detail.

Some key business publications that are helpful for finding company information include *Fortune Magazine*, *The New York Times*, *The Wall Street Journal*, *Barron's*, *Forbes*, *Dun & Bradstreet* and the *Thomas Register*. Your community newspapers are also good sources for information about local businesses. There are also many computer on-line sources of information. Your school or community librarian can help you access these services.

INTERVIEW QUESTIONS AND ANSWERS

Most job interviews last about an hour, depending on the job level. Most interviewers try to help you relax and feel comfortable. Your potential employer will ask questions to get to know you better and to see if your talents would be a suitable match for the job available. The potential employer has a job position to fill and wants to hire someone capable of doing the job or learning it quickly. The interviewer also wants to know whether you will fit in with the foodservice team and the organization as a whole.

Think of the interview as a chance to visit a workplace, to learn more about an interesting job, and an opportunity to meet new people. It's important to make a good impression, but it's also important to be yourself. Practicing your interviewing skills with a friend is a good way to prepare yourself for the real interview. A friend, family member, or teacher can play the role of the employer and ask you sample interview questions. Give each question serious thought and come up with an answer that is honest and complete. Practicing before an interview will help you answer questions quickly and accurately during the actual interview.

While there are no correct or incorrect answers to interview questions, some responses are more appropriate than others. The first question the interviewer may ask is, *Why don't you tell me a little about yourself?* The appropriate response is to talk about your accomplishments, experience, and qualifications. Practice a three-minute statement that presents your capabilities. Here is an example:

"My name is Ira Levin, and I'm looking for a job that will get me started in my professional foodservice career. Currently, I'm a junior at Funtown High School where I'm enrolled in a program that teaches both food preparation and business management skills. For the past two years, I've been a server in our school cafeteria, the Jazzy Café, where I also work as a kitchen helper—the chef has even used some of my original low-fat dessert recipes. I'm a good team player and I'm dependable. My grades are above average, and I really enjoy working with people. My goal is to be a restaurant manager some day. That's why I thought this position as a part-time server at the Blue Parakeet Café would be a great opportunity to move up the career ladder."

Now for practice, take a few minutes to write a "Tell me about yourself" statement on a separate sheet of paper.

Exhibit i.18
Interviews vary in length and formality. Be prepared for anything!

"My name is ______________________. Currently, I'm a _____________________ at

___________________________ high school where I'm enrolled in/studying courses in

____.

(Mention key skills/accomplishments/experiences/areas of strength here)

____

____

____

____

____.

That's why I thought this position as ____________________________________ at

______________________________________ would be a great opportunity for me."

Exhibit i.19
Here are some examples of personal characteristics that you could use to describe yourself during an interview.

accurate	enthusiastic	like people
able to remain calm under pressure	good attitude	responsible
communicate well	hard worker	sense of humor
dependable	know computer skills	tolerant
energetic	high standards	trustworthy
entertaining	leader	willing to learn and take instructions

Here are examples of typical interview questions you may be asked to answer on your job interview.

Why do you want to work for this company? Why do you want to be a __________ in this company?

Reply: Talk about why the job or the company interests you. Avoid any reference to money.

What contributions can you make to this company?

Reply: Talk about your qualifications and skills and how they will benefit the company.

How did you hear about us?

Reply: Through the newspaper, a friend, a relative, or a teacher.

The next three questions are relevant if you have previous work experience:

How many jobs have you had during the past three years?

Reply: State how many jobs you've had.

What exactly did you do on your last job/current job?

Reply: Talk about your responsibilities, duties, and achievements.

Why are you leaving your present job? Why did you leave your last job?

Reply: Be honest, but don't speak ill of your previous employer or job responsibilities. Appropriate responses depend on your situation. You could say that the previous/current job allowed you to work part time, and you're now ready to commit to full-time employment. You could also say that you are now ready to take on more responsibilities, but those opportunities were not available with your current/previous employer. Other reasons include layoffs, reduction in work hours, or the employer was not able to accommodate your school schedule.

If we hire you, how long do you think you would be able to work here?

Reply: If you're looking at a part-time job for one semester, say so. If you're looking for full-time permanent employment, say you hope to stay with the organization for a long time.

What are your favorite subjects in school? Why?

Reply: Name your favorite subjects and tell why.

What subject do you find most difficult?

Reply: Here is one example: *World history was my worst subject—it really bored me, and my grades showed it. But I knew a 'D' would hurt my overall grade average, so I found a senior to tutor me in exchange* *for typing her term papers. By the end of the semester, I was able to pull a 'B'.* The interviewer is trying to determine your ability to persevere under less than favorable circumstances. Everyone has difficulty learning things sometimes, but a person with ambition will find a workable solution. That's what the potential employer is looking for in a good employee.

Did you participate in any school activities? Why or why not?

Reply: Name the activities. Joining school activities shows that you're a sociable person. If you had to work after school and for this reason you were not able to join any activities, say so. Be sure your answer reflects that you do work well with others.

Do you plan to continue your education?

Reply: Continuing your education is not limited to college. It can include taking additional courses in food preparation, for example, or a willingness to participate in on-the-job training. Your answer should reflect that you want to gain as much knowledge and training as possible to advance in your foodservice career.

How many days of school or work did you miss during the last year?

Reply: While regular attendance and punctuality are extremely important in any workplace, foodservice operators in particular depend on employees who show up for work every day and on time. Someone who is absent for several days at school or work may not be dependable on the job. If you have been absent for many days at school or work, have a reasonable explanation prepared.

Other questions you may be asked include questions about salary, what motivates you to do a good job, and whether you have ever been fired from a job. For questions regarding salary on previous jobs, tell the truth. If the interviewer asks you what salary you are looking for in this job, be diplomatic. You should say that you have no set figure in mind, or ask the person what salary is usually offered to someone with your qualifications. If you've ever been fired from a job, don't panic. Reply that while you usually can work with everyone, this particular boss and you just weren't a good match, in spite of your efforts to work out the problems.

Before ending the interview, the potential employer will ask you if you have any questions. This is your chance to show that you have confidence in yourself and also want to be sure the job is a good match for your personal and professional goals.

Here are some questions you might consider asking the interviewer:

- Is this a new position or would I be replacing someone?
- Was the person who previously had this job promoted? (This is very important for a full-time job. The object is to discover whether the company is promoting employees or if there is a high rate of employees leaving the company because they are unhappy.)
- Could you please describe a typical work day for me?
- If you hired me, when would you expect me to start working?
- How long would it take for me to be trained for the job?
- When do you plan on filling the position? If the interviewer says a decision will be made within one or two weeks, ask if you may call to inquire about the decision.

Avoid asking questions about salary, vacation, bonuses, or holidays. Salary is a sensitive issue. Wait for the interviewer to bring up the subject. Ask the interviewer what the standard salary is for someone with your qualifications. It's a good idea to have a general idea of the salary range for the job before you go to the interview. You can find this information at your school or community library. While you should not be the one to begin the discussion, you should leave the interview knowing the overall salary range.

When the interview is ended, smile, shake the person's hand, and thank the interviewer for taking the time to explain the job to you. If you do want the job, this is the time to say so. For example, you might say, *This would be a great opportunity for me—I hope you give my qualifications serious consideration. I know I'd work well with your foodservice team.* Even if you know you don't want the job, it is important to observe business courtesy.

Follow Up After the Interview

A simple thank-you note can make you stand out from the crowd of job seekers. It's a good idea to write the thank-you note as soon as you arrive home. This proves to the employer that you really want the job.

The note should be short, confirm that you want the job, reinforce your qualifications, give a time you will follow up with a phone call, and offer to meet with the potential employer again to answer any additional questions. Ending the letter with a sentence that encourages the potential employer to call you is a good marketing idea. Most people read the beginning few sentences and the last sentence before reading the body of any letter. Here is a sample thank you letter.

Ms. Louise Brown
Manager
Blue Parakeet Café
82 South Pleasant Street
Funtown, USA 50094

August 3, 2002

Dear Ms. Brown:

Thank you for meeting with me on Thursday afternoon to explain the part-time server position at the Blue Parakeet Café. The responsibilities of the server position, along with the training and flexible hours, would give me a head start in my foodservice career. I definitely want to be a member of your team!

I'm confident that I can quickly learn the service techniques and become a productive member of your staff. My teachers have told me that I am a fast learner and I'm willing to attend your weekend training classes.

If I may, I'll call you next Thursday to see if you've made a decision and to answer any additional questions you may have. Please don't hesitate to call me at 123-456-7890 if you have any new questions in the meantime. Once again, thank you for considering me for the position.

Sincerely,

Rose J. Hernandez

Rose J. Hernandez
2340 East 83rd Street
Anytown, USA 85467

Exhibit i.20
Sample thank you note.

The follow-up phone call should be on the day you promised. Here is a sample follow-up phone call.

1. **Remind the person who you are.**

   "Good afternoon, Ms. Brown. This is Rose Hernandez. How are you today?"

2. **State the reason for your call—what position you applied for.**

   "Ms. Brown, I'm calling to follow up on our meeting last Thursday regarding the part-time server position. It sounded like the ideal job for me."

3. **Find out if the potential employer made a decision.**

   "I was wondering if you had made a decision yet."

4. **If you got the job, write down the answers to the following questions:**

   "When would you like me to start working and what time should I be there?"

   "What should I bring with me?"

   "Where should I go on my first day?"

   "Who should I see?"

   "I just need to coordinate my bus schedule—do you know how many hours I'll be working on my first day?"

5. **If the employer has not made a decision, don't panic.**

   "I understand. Could you please tell me if you're still considering me for the position?"

If you are a candidate:

"Are there any questions I can answer that will show you I'm really the server you're looking for?"

If there are no questions:

"Thanks again, Ms. Brown. I hope you'll call me if you do have any questions, and I look forward to hearing from you soon."

If you didn't get the job:

"Oh, I'm sorry to hear that. Thank you for taking the time to explain the position to me. I hope you'll think of me if you have other openings."

If you did not get the job, it is acceptable to ask the person for constructive feedback on your interviewing skills, or ask the interviewer what you could do to get more experience or training. Sometimes interviewers can refer you to other jobs that would be more suitable for your abilities. Don't be afraid to ask the person. Even if you didn't get the job, don't be too disappointed. Every interview is an opportunity to sharpen your communication skills and meet foodservice professionals. It also helps you find out your strengths and weaknesses and gives you the chance to do better next time.

Before, During, and After the Interview

Before the interview:

- *Know the route to the job. Take a preview trip to the interview site. Make sure you consider traffic.*
- *If you're taking public transportation, bring enough money.*
- *Know what materials to take with you.*
- *Review important interview questions and how you will respond.*
- *Practice aloud what you will say to the interviewer about yourself.*
- *Bring a pen that writes clearly and a clean notebook.*
- *Write down the name, address, and telephone number of the person you're meeting, and bring it with you.*
- *Give yourself enough time to get ready.*
- *Get a good night's sleep.*
- *Arrive at the interview 15 minutes before your appointment.*
- *If you are going to be late, call the interviewer.*
- *Good luck and relax!*

During the interview:

- *Smile, look interested, and pay attention.*
- *Sit with your back straight; lean back in the chair.*
- *Practice good listening skills.*
- *Never say unkind or bad things about your previous boss or coworkers.*
- *Be an interactive participant. Avoid answering questions too quickly—it looks like you're not giving the answers enough thought.*
- *Ask questions.*
- *Look confident (and you'll feel confident).*
- *Sell yourself! Explain how your skills and abilities make you the ideal person for the job.*

After the interview:

- *Write a brief thank-you note to the interviewer as soon as possible.*
- *Follow up with a phone call to the interviewer.*
- *Congratulate yourself on doing your best!*

Intro.7

SECTION i.7

Working on the Job

AFTER STUDYING SECTION i.7, YOU SHOULD BE ABLE TO:

- State your interpretation of a first day on the job.
- Outline the steps to resigning a job.

KEY TERMS

- **Employee manual**
- **Orientation**

Congratulations! You're about to go to your first day in your new job. What can you expect your first day to be like? Orientation and training will fill most of your first day. **Orientation** is the process that helps new employees learn about the procedures and policies of the operation and introduces them to their coworkers. Your employer wants to give you a positive impression of the operation, the management, and all other staff members. The purpose of orientation is to make you feel comfortable in your new job, to know what your responsibilities are, and to make you feel part of the team.

The type of orientation you receive depends on the size of the organization. If you're working in a large operation, you may see a video, hear lectures, and receive printed manuals. Smaller operations might give you a typed employee manual, an individual tour of the operation, and introduce you to coworkers.

Exhibit i.21
Orientaion is a process to help new employees learn about the organization and what is expected of them.

The type of training you receive depends on your job and the size of the organization. Some training may be accomplished by watching videos and reading workbooks, similar to your high school classroom experience. Other training may be hands-on, similar to working in your classroom kitchen or cafeteria kitchen. The purpose of training is to be sure that you know how to do the job on your own. Remember to ask questions.

DURING ORIENTATION YOU CAN EXPECT TO LEARN:

- *The history of the foodservice operation.*
- *Key company goals that are important to your job.*
- *How the company is organized; who reports to whom.*

It shows that you are serious about doing a good job.

Your supervisor will give you whatever tools you need on your first day. These might include:

- **Name tag**
- **Locker or other personal space**
- **Uniform**
- **Office, cubicle, desk, or work area**
- **Telephone**
- **Employee manual (containing general information concerning employment)**
- **Training materials to help explain the work you will be doing**
- **First week's schedule**

An **employee manual** is a written booklet containing general information about employment, including company policies, rules and procedures, employee benefits, and other topics related to the company. It is similar to a high school student manual. When you receive the employee manual, you will be asked to sign a form stating that you have received it. Your signature means that you have read the information and agree to follow the rules and policies it contains. Exhibit i.22 lists some items a typical employee manual may contain.

Exhibit i.22
Contents of a typical employee manual.

Employment Policies
- Absence from work
- Schedule substitutions and trading work shifts
- Paid holidays
- Overtime
- Tips
- Pay periods
- Shift changes
- Time cards
- Performance appraisals
- Wage and salary reviews
- Work breaks

Rules and Procedures
- Dress Code
- Illegal activities (drinking alcohol, drugs)
- Grievances (complaints or problems at work)
- Disciplinary procedures
- Probationary policies
- Causes for dismissal
- Emergencies (injuries, fires, natural disasters, robberies)
- Safety rules
- Off-duty time at the operation
- Friends visiting the operation
- Personal telephone use

Employee Benefits
- Medical and dental insurance coverage
- Sick leave and disability
- Meals
- Pension, retirement, and/or death benefits
- Profit sharing
- Retirement

Other Topics That May Be Included
- Employee and locker areas
- History and mission of the organization
- How the company is organized (the chain of command)
- Job description
- Where to enter and leave the facility
- Smoking and nonsmoking areas
- Restrooms
- Breakage (accidents, broken dishes or equipment)
- Parking
- Training opportunities
- Employee assistance programs
- Job openings and postings

Moving On

There will probably be a time when you will leave your job because of a better opportunity, change in school schedule, or any number of reasons. It is standard business practice to give your current employer a two-week notice before you leave. You can inform your employer in person or you can write a letter of resignation.

Take care in writing a letter of resignation. You may include your reasons for leaving, but always be polite. Avoid any negative comments, and always thank your employer for giving you the opportunity to work for the company. As you learned from filling out a job application, prospective employers ask about your work record and request references from previous employers. If you show anger or negativity when you resign, you may be hurting yourself in the future.

A good guide to follow throughout your working career is always to leave on a positive note. If you keep your long-term goals in mind, you will be able to rise above any negative words and attitudes of others. You will have the patience and persistence to see your career vision to its ultimate goal. Possessing excellent skills and having good education and training are only part of the equation for a successful career in food service: commitment to service, a positive attitude, and perseverance are also needed to take you to the top!

Ms. Louise Brown
Manager
Blue Parakeet Café
82 South Pleasant Street
Funtown, USA 50094

March 10, 2003

Dear Ms. Brown:

As much as I have enjoyed working as a server at the Blue Parakeet Café, I must resign effective March 20, 2003.

I have been offered a position as assistant manager in a full-service restaurant in Anytown that will enable me to continue to pursue my long-term goals in food service. Working at the Blue Parakeet Café has been a wonderful training experience for me. I know I'll be more considerate of all servers in my new position!

Thank you personally for setting such a great example as a manager. I hope you'll visit me at the Anytown Grand Café at your earliest convenience.

Thank you again for giving me the opportunity to work at the Blue Parakeet Café.

Sincerely,

Rose J. Hernandez

Rose J. Hernandez
2340 East 83rd Street
Anytown, USA 85467

Exhibit i.23
An example of a resignation letter.

Flashback

INTRODUCTION

SECTION i.1: WORKING IN THE HOSPITALITY INDUSTRY

- The hospitality and foodservice industry is unique because it is the only type of business where the customer and the manufacturer of a product are in direct contact.
- People who work in hospitality and food service must be committed to service. They must be efficient, flexible, a team player, and able to remain calm under pressure in a fast-paced environment.
- Hospitality and foodservice professionals view customers as guests, try to make their dining experience enjoyable, and serve them nutritional, safe food.
- It is essential to treat everyone—customers, coworkers, and supervisors—with respect and consideration.
- Working in the hospitality and foodservice industry means serving people directly. Service professionals include hotel workers, nurses, sales people, lawyers, and landscapers, just to name a few.
- Good service requires first of all that you like people; then training, stamina, effort, and commitment also come into play. Hospitality professionals enjoy their jobs of helping people get what they want.
- Customers expect anyone who serves them to have a pleasant, helpful, and friendly manner.
- The world of work is *very different* from the school environment. When you enter the world of work, even as a part-time employee, you are expected to follow guidelines of professional, adult behavior.
- Attendance, team work, promptness, a positive attitude, dependability; asking questions when necessary; and fairness and honesty on the job are essential for your success in a foodservice profession.

SECTION i.2: CAREER OPPORTUNITIES IN FOOD SERVICE

- A **career** is a profession or work in a certain field that usually begins with an **entry-level job.**

- Whatever career you choose, you can expect to begin your career in an entry-level job, which is an important starting point in your work experience.
- Examples of entry-level jobs in the foodservice industry include busperson, kitchen helper, server, and dishwasher.
- Training and additional education are ways by which motivated individuals can move higher up the **career ladder.** A career ladder is a series of jobs through which a person can advance in a career.
- Even though you are still in school, you can start planning for a foodservice career that you will enjoy.
- Foodservice jobs range from serving food, preparing food, developing recipes, managing a foodservice operation, writing articles about food, developing marketing and advertising strategies, to teaching and educating others about food and nutrition.
- There are two categories of personnel necessary to run a foodservice establishment: front-of-the-house positions, which are involved with guest service, and back-of-the-house positions, which are those jobs in all areas outside the public space.
- **Front-of-the-house** foodservice professionals include restaurant manager and assistant manager.
- **Back-of-the-house** professionals include executive chef, assistant chef, and other specialized chef positions.
- Other career opportunities related to food service are varied. These include home economics; communication and writing; foodservice marketing; research and development; food science; dietetics; food production and food processing; accounting; training; grocery and deli managers; and **entrepreneurs.**
- A part-time or summer job helps you develop skills such as responsibility, self-confidence, and decision making; however, you can acquire other essential skills while you are still in school. These include communication skills—writing, speaking, reading, and effective listening; computer competency; and math skills.
- Critical thinking and problem solving are also important on the job. Employers value employees who can think of new solutions to problems.
- Other personal qualities viewed favorably by employees include a positive

attitude, team spirit, and a willingness to learn new technology and new ways of doing things.

SECTION i.3: STARTING YOUR CAREER IN FOOD SERVICE

- Preparing for a career means deciding where your interests lie, what your career goals are, and the type of continuing education you will need to be successful.
- No matter what careers interest you, completing high school and continuing your education are steps to a successful future.
- You must consider your own goals and individual requirements before deciding which college or trade school to attend.
- Your job search might very likely begin in the high school guidance office.
- Other useful sources for your job search include: employment ads in local newspapers; community college bulletin boards; vocational school placement office; state or regional job service offices; counseling services of community agencies; local telephone directories (yellow pages) to contact employers directly; and on-line computer services.
- It is customary to send a typed **cover letter** with a résumé to the potential employer.
- To ensure that your cover letter is read, keep the copy brief and stick to the point. Write in a straightforward manner, and use correct grammar and punctuation.
- A good cover letter should capture the reader's attention, interest, and desire, concluding with a call to action. Follow up all cover letters with a phone call to the potential employer.
- **Networking,** which means contacting people who can give you information about job openings, is an effective job hunting technique.

SECTION i.4: PREPARING YOUR PORTFOLIO AND RÉSUMÉ

- A **portfolio** is a collection of samples that highlight your interests, talents, contributions, and studies.
- Types of items included in a portfolio depend on you and the job you desire. Portfolio samples include lists of your skills and abilities; examples of problem-solving abilities, teamwork, leadership, and responsibility; certificates or awards; newspaper clippings; essays or reports; résumé; test scores; letters of recommendation; or other samples that present your achievements.

- Portfolios should be complete, neat, and well organized.
- A **résumé** is a written summary of your past experience, education, previous jobs, skills, and achievements related to the job you're seeking.
- Résumés and portfolios will change as you gain more experience, training, and education.
- **References** are those people who know you well and can provide information about your character, work ability, or academic standing.

SECTION i.5: COMPLETING APPLICATION FORMS

- **Application forms** ask basic personal information about the applicant's background.
- **College** or **trade school applications** require that you give your education background. The application may also require that you state the program or course of study you are interested in and ask you to complete a short essay.
- You will be asked to have your high school transcript sent to the college also.
- The **job application** form usually asks about your work experience and for references.
- Always check with people before you use them as job references.
- Use correct grammar and punctuation, and organize your thoughts before you write them on the form.
- Leave blank or indicate *n/a* on questions that you do not understand or that do not apply to you.
- Avoid giving salary amounts, except when asked how much money you earned on any previous jobs. Be honest.
- If you have no prior work experience, list any volunteer work or other activities that show you know what is expected at the workplace.
- Dishonesty on a job application can result in immediate termination of your employment. Employers check on educational and work background. They also contact references.

SECTION i.6: THE JOB INTERVIEW

- To create a good first impression at a **job interview,** remember three key points: present a well-groomed personal appearance, have a positive attitude, and use good manners, which are the basis for business **etiquette.**
- Check with the potential employer if you are unsure about what materials you should bring.

- Research basic information about the company before the interview, including the company size and reputation, key products and services, and names of competitors.
- The potential employer will ask questions to see if your talents would be a suitable match for the job available and how you would work with the existing foodservice team.
- There are no correct or incorrect answers to interview questions; however, some responses are more appropriate and impressive than others.
- To break the ice, the interviewer will ask you to talk about yourself. The appropriate response is to discuss your accomplishments, experience, and qualifications in a three-minute summary.
- Other interview questions will attempt to get your view of the company, how you could improve the organization, previous work experience, personal goals, education, work ethic and attitude, dependability, ability to handle pressure, and salary.
- Be prepared to ask questions about the position, advancement opportunities, description of an average work day, starting date, and training.
- Avoid asking questions about money, vacation, bonuses, or holidays. Allow the potential employer to initiate the discussion; however, you should not leave the interview without knowing the salary range.
- Follow up after the interview with a brief note to potential employers thanking them for their time, confirming that you want the job, reinforcing your qualifications, and giving a time when you will follow up with a phone call.
- During the follow-up phone call: remind the person who you are, state the reason for your call, and find out if the potential employer has made a decision.
- If the employer has not made a decision, offer to answer any further questions the interviewer may have about your qualifications.
- Every interview is an opportunity to sharpen your communication skills and meet foodservice professionals.

SECTION i.7: WORKING ON THE JOB

- While your employer won't expect you to learn all procedures your first day on the job, there are certain workplace guidelines that all employees should know.

- You can expect orientation and training the first day of your new job.
- **Orientation** is the process that helps new employees learn about the procedures and policies of the operation and introduces them to their coworkers.
- Training may be done through instruction, as you're used to in the classroom, by viewing videos accompanied by workbooks, or through hands-on training.
- One of the most important items is the **employee manual.**
- A typical employee manual contains information on employment policies; rules and procedures; employee benefits; and other topics, including company history, employee personal space, and job opportunities.
- When you leave a job, for whatever reason, standard business practice recommends you notify your current employer two weeks before you leave, either in writing or in person.
- Write a letter of resignation carefully; you may include your reasons for leaving, but always be polite.
- Avoid negative remarks, and always thank your employer for giving you the opportunity to work for the company.

Throughout the next two years you will be working in a variety of foodservice operations. This unit covers the basic skills and competencies that you will need to prepare for your first experience in a foodservice operation.

UNIT I

Ted Balestreri

Co-owner and President
The Sardine Factory, Monterey, California

I was 14 when I got my first restaurant job. I washed dishes and bused tables during my teen years, sometimes holding down three jobs as well as going to school. The people were good, the money was good, and it was a lot of fun. By the time I was 19, I was General Manager of my own restaurant.

At 27, a partner and I opened our own restaurant, The Sardine Factory, in Monterey, California, the most beautiful place where land meets water. We owed a lot of money when we first opened. I didn't know if the place would fly, but we all poured our hearts and souls into it. Soon, word spread that The Sardine Factory was the place to go for the best food and service in town. We had a great desire to please our customers. We were sincere, and it paid off for us.

Personal touches are what make service memorable. We try to instill a sense of pride in serving people in everyone who works at The Sardine Factory and the other restaurants I own. The motto at our restaurants is, "If we made you feel at home, we made a million-dollar mistake" because people don't go out to eat so they can feel like they're at home. They want to be treated better than at home. Our job is to make going out special.

Everyone who works for The Sardine Factory knows never to challenge customers. We try to hire people who appreciate working with people, who like making people happy, and who have a lot of enthusiasm for their work and positive attitudes.

Every day here is different from the next. It's fun, it's exciting, and it's a great feeling to know you helped somebody have a great time out.

CHAPTER 1

Successful Customer Relations

SECTION 1.1

The Importance of Customer Service

AFTER STUDYING SECTION 1.1, YOU SHOULD BE ABLE TO:

- Recognize and state the importance of customer service to food service.
- List the reasons and the ways to make a positive first impression in the food-service industry.
- Describe a variety of customers that may have special needs.
- Distinguish between effective and ineffective communication with customers by giving examples.

KEY TERMS

- **Comp**
- **Customer service**

Today's foodservice patrons have high expectations when they eat out. As a result, competition for customers has never been greater. To keep customers coming back for more, excellent service is essential. Even if the food is great, customers will be disappointed if the service is poor.

Before we talk about the mechanics of waiting on tables, it is important to focus on service attitude. In any type of food-service operation, customers must be served pleasantly, correctly, and in a timely manner. All employees are responsible for providing good service, even if they don't interact directly with guests. For instance, kitchen staff also provides good customer service when they work together with the wait staff to meet customer needs.

Serving Customers

Customers expect the people who serve them to be pleasant, helpful, and friendly. Exhibit 1.1 shows what employees should do to provide this kind of service.

Exhibit 1.1
Steps to providing friendly, helpful service.

- Greet customers with a smile and make eye contact.
- Fulfill customers' requests pleasantly, without appearing irritated or annoyed.
- Thank customers sincerely and express pleasure in helping them.
- Be cooperative when coworkers ask for assistance.

Timing in food service is important to successful customer service. Customers want to be served at their own pace. In full-service operations, especially expensive ones, customers often want to dine leisurely. If guests do not look at the menu when it is first offered, they should not be rushed. In general, a course should be served within five minutes after the preceding one is finished. Another course should not be served until customers have completed the previous one.

Guests in quick-service operations should always be greeted and served as quickly as possible. However, a customer just walking in might need a moment to think about the menu before ordering and may even want help deciding what to order.

Timing is also important when presenting the check to guests. Servers should present the check after the meal has been finished and there is nothing more that the guest wants or needs. Traditionally, servers waited until guests asked for the check. However, many customers did not know that they were supposed to ask for it.

There will be times when guests arrive just before closing. These customers should never be rushed. They are entitled to the same service as other guests.

Apply It Now

What other timing issues might a foodservice employee need to consider?

Making a Good First Impression

All foodservice employees must make a good impression on customers by presenting themselves professionally. This does not mean that everyone has to look alike; there are many opportunities for individual style and appearance. Follow the steps in Exhibit 1.2 to make a good impression on guests.

Exhibit 1.2
Making a good impression.

- Dress appropriately.
- Practice good hygiene.
- Wear clean, wrinkle-free uniforms or clothing that is in good condition.
- Maintain clean hair, held back or up.
- Have clean hands and nails.
- Do not wear strong fragrances.
- Do not drink, eat, smoke, or chew gum in front of customers.

Exceeding Customers' Expectations

Foodservice employees and managers must create an environment that satisfies and pleases customers. If guests do not receive a basic level of service, they will be disappointed, irritated, annoyed, and even angry.

The foodservice industry has become very competitive, and customers are more sophisticated than ever before. In order to attract and keep customers, establishments must stand out from their competitors. This can be done by:

- **Focusing completely on customers.** If you are thinking about the plans you have after work, you are not focusing on the customer.
- **Showing a sense of urgency.** All customer questions, requests, and complaints should be responded to or resolved immediately. If a customer asks where a pay phone is, for example, take time to direct him to the phone.
- **Saying *hello* and *goodbye* to every customer you come in contact with.** Customers deserve to be greeted warmly and sincerely the minute they walk through the door. And when

Exhibit 1.3
To make a favorable impression, employees must dress appropriately.

guests leave, employees should thank them and say goodbye. In addition, employees who pass customers or come in contact with them in any way should acknowledge them with a smile or a greeting.

Employees should try to anticipate customers' needs and accommodate them *before* being asked. This requires watching and listening to customers carefully for clues about their needs. Employees must do whatever is necessary to please customers and think creatively when serving them.

Customers' special requests, for example, should be honored gladly. They provide you and your operation with an opportunity to shine. Never say *no* to a guest. If you cannot accommodate an exact request, suggest something else that might be acceptable.

Let's Try It!

You are walking through the restaurant and notice a guest with an empty coffee cup. Even though the guest is at another server's station, what would you do to anticipate her needs?

Teamwork

Teamwork is an essential part of any successful operation. In addition to anticipating customers' needs, employees should be aware of coworkers' needs as well. If all employees work together as a team, they can ask each other for help when they need it instead of letting a customer receive poor service.

When walking by another server's table with empty hands, for example, an employee should stop to pick up any dirty dishes. A manager who's not afraid to roll up her sleeves and bus a table can be an example to others. By helping each other, everybody's job becomes a little easier. Employees who work together and support one another have less job-related stress, happier customers, and increased job satisfaction.

Serving Customers with Special Needs

In addition to following the previous guidelines for providing excellent service, employees must be particularly aware of and sensitive to customers with special needs. Among these guests are:

- **Older customers.** Employees should help customers who have difficulty seeing, hearing, walking, or carrying food to a table, as well as those who must count money slowly. Always be respectful and have patience when serving older customers.

- **Customers with disabilities.** Without calling special attention to people with disabilities, employees should help and accommodate them in every possible way, such as seating them in areas with plenty of space. Guests with temporary disabilities, such as a broken arm or leg, should also be appropriately accommodated.

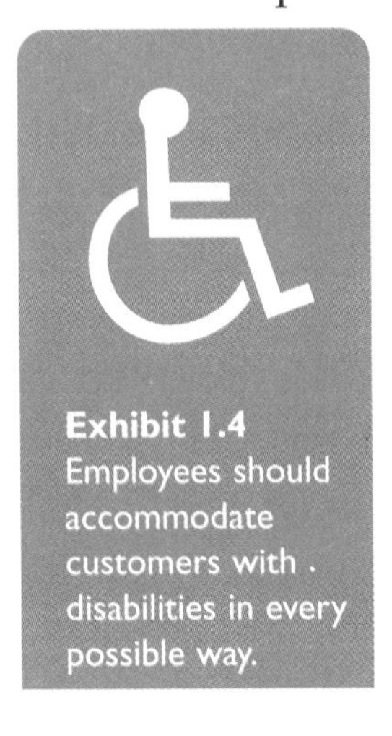

Exhibit 1.4
Employees should accommodate customers with disabilities in every possible way.

- **Families with children.** Servers should know about children's menu items and where to find high chairs and booster seats. Children often get restless when they are hungry. Providing a quick snack (such as crackers or rolls), or crayons and some paper, will be greatly appreciated by both parents and children.
- **Customers on special diets.** Guests on special diets often ask that menu items be changed in some way. Employees should try to give customers exactly what they order, even if their requests seem strange or picky.
- **Customers with food allergies.** Food allergies can be severe and, sometimes, fatal. Servers must know exactly what is in every menu item. If you don't know the answer to a customer's specific question about menu ingredients, ask someone who does. Don't ever take the chance of serving something that may cause an allergic reaction; instead, take the time to find out for sure.

Communicating with Customers

Good communication is important to providing excellent customer service. Customer service consists of employees' and managers' attitudes, skills, and policies that allow a foodservice operation to meet its customers' needs and wants. Always speak clearly and

Exhibit 1.5
Servers should be aware of children's special needs, like high chairs or booster seats.

politely to guests. Even if you're tired or having a bad day, it is important to keep a pleasant and cheerful attitude. Exhibit 1.6 lists some guidelines for communicating positively and politely with customers.

Enforcing Rules and Policies

All employees must understand an operation's rules and policies and know when and where to apply them. Rules created for safety and legal reasons should always be enforced and followed. Sometimes servers will have to explain the operation's rules to customers. When a rule cannot be changed, simply suggest another solution to the customer.

Some rules are made to ensure better customer service or smoother operations, such as dress codes and **comping** (not charging for) menu items. An operation's upper-level management usually decides how rules are to be applied in order to best take care of customers.

Sometimes servers and other employees are allowed, or given the authority, to make decisions and to bend rules. Management, however, still has the responsibility of establishing clear but flexible guidelines for these situations.

Apply It Now

Describe a rule or policy that an operation may establish for each of the following:

- **Safety reasons**
- **Legal reasons**
- **Customer service reasons**

Exhibit 1.6
Guidelines for communicating with customers.

- Avoid inappropriate topics with guests, such as your personal life, unpleasant events, or tip amounts.
- Speak courteously and in full sentences. "What may I get for you?" is much more professional than "Ready to order?"
- Replace tired, overused phrases, such as "Have a nice day" with fresher ones like "Thanks for stopping in today."
- Describe menu items in appetizing terms and recommend items you like.
- Avoid slang and informal phrases. Terms like *nope*, *yeah*, *beats me*, and *how ya' doin'* are unprofessional, and such words as *ain't* and *yous* are simply incorrect.
- Don't speak too quickly. If you list the types of available salad dressings too quickly, for example, you may need to repeat the information. Even if you've heard the list many times before, remember that your guests have not.
- Listen. Good, active listening means actually understanding what a person is saying rather than daydreaming or planning what you will say next. Be careful not to interrupt a customer who hasn't finished talking.
- Use positive nonverbal communication. Facial expressions, tone of voice, gestures, and posture often indicate the way you feel about yourself, your job, the operation, and customers.

Review Your Learning 1.1

1. Compare and contrast the timing involved in full-service and quick-service operations.
2. Identify the first-impression mistakes in the description below.

> *A female server is waiting on a customer. She is wearing a dirty, sloppy uniform, has long hair that is worn down, and is blowing a bubble with her gum.*

3. Explain how you might help customers in the following situations.
   a. A parent with three small children is becoming upset while trying to keep them quiet and occupied.
   b. A man on crutches is waiting to be seated.
   c. An older woman cannot see well enough to read the menu.
   d. A customer tells you that he is allergic to all kinds of nuts.
4. List the eight guidelines for effectively communicating with customers.
5. Not charging for menu items is known as:
   a. crediting
   b. empowering
   c. bargaining
   d. comping

1.2

SECTION 1.2

The Manager's Role in Customer Service

AFTER STUDYING SECTION 1.2, YOU SHOULD BE ABLE TO:

- Explain how customer satisfaction directly affects a restaurant's success.
- Outline the service planning process.

In the foodservice industry, customers have many dining options. If the food at many nearby, comparable restaurants is similar, people will base their decisions about where to eat primarily on one thing—service. Money spent on advertising, promotions, state-of-the-art kitchen equipment, and research about the latest food trends will not keep customers coming back if they do not receive exceptional service from everyone in an operation.

KEY TERMS

- Comment cards
- Focus group
- Human resources
- Internal customer
- Long-term goal
- Material resources
- Mission statement
- Mystery shopper
- Profit
- Service encounter
- Service guarantee
- Service plan
- Short-term goal
- Word-of-mouth advertising

Service Encounters

Customers get an overall impression of a foodservice operation from its employees. Every time a guest comes in contact with an employee—or the work performed by an employee—the operation has an opportunity to win that customer's loyalty. A foodservice manager might invest a lot of money and time creating an appealing menu, perfecting recipes, and choosing the right decor. But if customers are treated rudely by employees or receive incomplete food orders, the bad service is what will be remembered.

Customers' opinions of a lot of foodservice operations are formed by their **service encounters**—or contacts—with an operation's workers. Managers and employees have hundreds of customer service opportunities every day—opportunities to help customers form positive opinions of the entire operation. All employees are crucial to the customer service effort. Front-of-the-house employees, such as servers, hosts and hostesses, and buspeople, meet and talk directly to guests; back-of-the-house employees, such as chefs, cooks, and

Exhibit 1.7
Customers' opinions are formed by their service encounters with employees.

dishwashers, impress customers with the cleanliness of the operation and the quality of the food.

Back-of-the-house employees don't see customers on a regular basis. Instead, they aim to serve **internal customers**—their coworkers who come in direct contact with guests—and contribute to the excellent service that customers receive. Among these back-of-the-house employees, the person who maintains the parking lot or cleans the operation's windows and entrance is responsible for the customer's first—and often lasting—impression. Others serve guests by cleaning floors and dishes or purchasing and cooking excellent food.

The Impact of Dissatisfied Customers

Because competition in the foodservice industry is so intense, customers can be picky about what restaurant they choose to visit. Studies have shown that the most important factor in the customer's mind when choosing a restaurant is the quality of service provided. One bad experience can mean the loss of a customer forever.

Losing just one customer may not seem significant at first glance. But over time, the loss of just one customer can have a serious impact on the future success of the foodservice operation. Let's consider an example:

Did You Know?

- **More than 80 percent of the customers who do not return to a foodservice operation say that they were unhappy with employees' attitudes, not with bad food.**
- **Only 4 percent of dissatisfied customers let management know that they are unhappy.**
- **Dissatisfied customers tell an average of 10 people about their bad experience.**

Joan Smith eats at the So-So Café twice a month, each time spending $25. Last week she was treated rudely by her server, but didn't tell an employee about her dissatisfaction; instead, she decided not to return.

Losing Joan as a regular customer means a loss of $50 a month, or $600 a year, for the operation. Over 10 years, the So-So Café will lose $6,000 in business from Ms. Smith. In addition, any negative word-of-mouth advertising will result in even more lost business. If 100 customers a year are dissatisfied, the So-So Café will lose hundreds of thousands of dollars annually.

Let's Try It . . .

Will Walker and his wife Wanda have dinner at The Lone Star Eatery three times a month, each time spending $50. After being treated rudely by an employee, the Walkers vow never to return. How much has the restaurant lost as a result of the Walkers' bad dining experience?

It's important to remember that it costs five times more to advertise and attract new guests than it does to keep current ones coming back. Word-of-mouth advertising, however, is free and tells a lot of potential customers what kind of service an operation provides. All managers and employees must work to ensure that **word-of-mouth** advertising, or the opinions customers share with their friends and acquaintances about the establishment, are positive ones.

It should now be clear that customer service is the greatest factor in a guest's decision to either return to a restaurant or never come back. A satisfied customer is an establishment's greatest asset, returning repeatedly, bringing friends, and telling others about the excellent service. Customers who have problems that are solved quickly and to their satisfaction will also come back again and again.

Planning for Customer Service

Excellent customer service does not happen by chance; it is the result of sound planning. Managers of excellent customer service must establish goals, design and implement systems to meet them, and maintain service excellence once it is reached.

Profiting from Excellent Customer Service

Excellent customer service leads to increased revenue for a foodservice operation. As a direct result, employees also benefit by enjoying higher tips, job security, and career advancement opportunities.

Suppose that an establishment serves 3,000 guests per week, or 156,000 per year, and the average check is $6 per guest. The operation can achieve a 2 percent increase in customer count—or the addition of 3,120 guests (156,000 x 0.02)—by delivering excellent customer service. This translates into an $18,720 (3,120 x $6) increase in annual sales.

As shown below, a 5 percent increase in customer count results in an increase in annual sales of $46,800:

156,000 x 0.05 = 7,800
7,800 x $6 = $46,800

And a 10 percent increase in the number of customers served means additional sales of $93,600 each year:

156,000 x 0.1 = 15,600
15,600 x $6 = $93,600

A good **service plan** is an organized, systematic method of handling customer service. Planning involves analyzing a goal, situation, assignment, or problem and then developing a step-by-step method for addressing it. Exhibit 1.8 lists the five major steps involved in developing a service plan.

Exhibit 1.8
Developing a service plan.

1. Identify problems and their causes.
2. Set goals.
3. Consider available resources.
4. Develop policies and procedures.
5. Obtain feedback and monitor results.

Managers who create an effective service plan can positively shape the future by developing systems and policies that result in excellent customer service, rather than merely reacting to past policies and unexpected crises.

Setting Goals and Considering Resources

The second and third steps in developing an excellent customer service plan are setting goals and considering available resources. The ultimate goal of all businesses is to make a profit. A **profit** is the dollar amount left when revenues are greater than costs. With increased profits, managers can expand an operation, increase employee wages, and continually improve customer service. Making an operation as profitable as possible is a key to success.

An operation's objectives should include both short-term and long-term goals. **Short-term goals** usually cover periods of one day, one week, one month, several months, or one year. **Long-term goals** ordinarily cover two to five years, or longer. Managers must be able to continually revise and change goals to fit the growing foodservice operation.

An operation's goals are defined in its mission statement. A **mission statement** describes an operation's philosophy of doing business. A mission statement also gives a business focus and profoundly affects its profitability. A 200-year-old historic inn, for example, will probably do well by providing old-world charm and a caring staff, rather than live entertainment and in-room conveniences like fax machine, cable, and a television. Exhibit 1.9 describes what a mission statement should accomplish.

Exhibit 1.9
A mission statement.

A mission statement should do the following:

- Highlight and identify the establishment's food. In addition to new recipes, specialty and homemade items should be emphasized.
- Define the company's service policies and standards.
- Describe the atmosphere.
- Identify prices.
- State how the operation differs from the competition.

Here are three examples of mission statements:

> Our mission is to offer the highest form of service and hospitality and to provide the freshest, best-prepared Italian food in a family-style, mid-priced setting.

❧

> Our mission is to attract and keep customers by offering friendly and courteous service, a variety of high-quality foods, and affordable prices in a quick-service environment.

❧

> Our mission is to provide patrons with helpful, friendly, and prompt service, as well as the most appealing and nutritious meal choices possible, in a comfortable atmosphere for a reasonable price.

❧

Managers use the mission statement to help them plan and manage daily operations. They also communicate the mission statement to their employees so that the entire service team remains focused. In addition to using the mission statement, managers should gather information from customers, employees, trade publications, educational resources, and other related operations. They can send out surveys, distribute comment cards, and talk to customers directly to get valuable information to serve customers well.

After an operation's service goals have been identified, managers should consider the resources needed to achieve them. There are two basic types of resources: the people who work for an operation and help achieve its service goals **(human resources)** and the equipment and materials used to operate the business **(material resources)**. Managers must use all available resources to achieve operational goals.

Implementing Plans and Monitoring Results

Once a plan for improving customer service has been designed, it is not enough to simply post a notice, send out a memo, or hold a meeting. Managers and employees must do whatever is necessary to put the plan into action.

Suppose that a restaurant's tables are not being cleaned and set up properly at the end of the night and customers are arriving in the morning to find sticky surfaces and crumbs on seats. Since the manager doesn't have the resources to pay opening employees to arrive earlier, she posts a notice that says closing servers will be responsible for cleaning and resetting all tables before leaving in the evening. After two weeks, there is no improvement. Why not? Since this shift had not previously been responsible for cleaning, they needed a step-by-step procedure on how tables should be cleaned and reset at the end of the shift—including the cleaning solution to use and specific cleaning instructions—as well as a tool for monitoring, or checking, results. Exhibit 1.10 discusses steps to implementing a good service plan.

Exhibit 1.10
Implementing a service plan.

To help implement plans and achieve goals, these steps should be followed:

1. Identify in detail exactly what must be done and who will be responsible.
2. Communicate information to employees and train them properly.
3. Develop a tool for monitoring employees' performance.
4. Monitor the entire plan continuously over the long term.

Apply It Now

Apply the four steps in Exhibit 1.10 to the table cleaning and set-up scenario described earlier.

One effective way to monitor how well the service plan is working is through feedback. Feedback from customers can be collected through comment cards, mystery shoppers, and focus groups.

Comment cards are quick surveys that customers complete telling how satisfied they were with the food and service. They should be kept short and simple. Pencils placed on tables may encourage customers to fill out the cards. General results should be circulated so that every manager and employee is aware of customer concerns.

All problems mentioned in comment cards should be taken seriously and corrected whenever possible. Employees who are complimented by customers should be praised; those whom customers complain about must be instructed on what they are doing wrong and on the correct actions that they should take.

Mystery shoppers are hired by an operation to visit and report on their experiences and impressions of a particular foodservice operation. They provide more in-depth feedback than comment cards, especially if mystery shoppers have been trained on an establishment's systems and procedures.

Exhibit 1.11
The identity of a mystery shopper is kept a secret

When beginning a mystery shopper program, managers should present it as an opportunity for all employees to see how they are viewed by customers. Everyone should be encouraged to take criticism constructively and be willing to improve performance based on mystery shopper reports. Managers may want to develop a reward system for employees who receive positive feedback.

Surveys should include service questions like "How can we improve our service?" and "What would make you come back?" rather than "How was your meal?" In addition to written questionnaires, managers can also call a sample of guests the day after their visit to get feedback over the telephone.

Focus groups consist of customers that meet together regularly to talk with managers on how service can be improved. Many successful service managers use weekly or monthly focus groups to learn about needed customer service improvements.

Employee feedback is an important part of giving great customer service. Employees are a source of many excellent ideas. Managers may want to hold focus groups with employees from each area of the foodservice operation. At the focus group meeting, these employees should feel free to say anything about the operation without fear of angering management and with the assurance that no one will repeat outside the meeting anything that was said. Varying the employees in the group once in a while gives everyone an opportunity to contribute.

The Service Guarantee

Foodservice establishments use a variety of **service guarantees**, or guarantee of customer satisfaction. Some, for example, guarantee that a meal will be served within a specified time or the next meal is free. Guarantees help improve an operation's image as an excellent business and often encourage people to try a restaurant for the first time.

Establishing a service guarantee is one of the last steps in the customer service planning process. After managers have established an operation's service goals, considered resources, and implemented plans, the guarantee may uncover unexpected challenges. Handling these challenges will set into motion again the process of planning and managing customer service.

Guarantee

If your lunch is not delivered to your table within 20 minutes of ordering, your next lunch is free.

Exhibit 1.12
Sample service guarantee.

Review Your Learning 1.2

1. Customers' opinions are formed by:
   a. feedback.
   b. their service encounters.
   c. an operation's mission statement.
   d. comment cards.
2. Colette's Café serves 1,800 guests per week, and the average check is $7.50 per guest. If the establishment increases its customer count by 4 percent, by how much will annual sales increase?
3. Explain the difference between the following:
   a. Front-of-the-house employees and back-of-the-house employees
   b. Service plan and mission statement
   c. Short-term goals and long-term goals
   d. Human resources and material resources
   e. Mystery shoppers and focus groups
4. You manage The Pizza Pie, a family-style restaurant specializing in providing quality service to parents bringing in children for birthdays and other special occasions. Your prices are lower than the competition's, and you offer a fun atmosphere for kids, including games, toys, and rides.
   a. Write a mission statement to communicate your philosophy of doing business to employees and customers.
   b. Write a short plan for achieving the goals established in your mission statement.
   c. Develop a service guarantee for your operation.

Flashback

CHAPTER 1

SECTION 1.1: THE IMPORTANCE OF CUSTOMER SERVICE

- To provide excellent service, employees should greet customers with a smile and make eye contact; fulfill customers' requests pleasantly, without appearing irritated or annoyed; thank customers sincerely; express pleasure in helping customers; and be cooperative when coworkers ask for assistance.
- Timing in foodservice is important to successful customer service. Customers want to be served at their own pace. In full-service operations guests often want to dine leisurely.
- Customers in quick-service operations should always be greeted and served as quickly as possible.
- To make a good impression on guests, employees should dress appropriately; practice good hygiene; wear clean, wrinkle-free uniforms or clothing that is in good condition; maintain clean hair, held back or up; have clean hands and nails; not wear strong fragrances; and not drink, eat, smoke, or chew gum in front of customers.
- In order to attract and keep customers, establishments must stand out from their competitors by focusing completely on customers, showing a sense of urgency, and saying *hello* and *goodbye* to every customer.
- Employees should try to anticipate customers' needs and accommodate them *before* being asked.
- Employees should also be aware of coworkers' needs. Working together as a team, employees can ask each other for help when they need it instead of letting a customer receive poor service.
- Customers with special needs include older guests, those with disabilities, families with children, customers on special diets, and those with food allergies.
- Good communication is key to providing excellent **customer service.** To communicate positively and politely with customers, employees should avoid inappropriate topics; speak courteously and in full sen-

tences; replace tired, overused phrases with fresher ones; describe menu items in appetizing terms; avoid slang and informal phrases; not speak too quickly; listen; and use positive nonverbal communication.

- Employees must understand an operation's rules and policies and know when and where to apply them. Rules created for safety and legal reasons should always be enforced and followed. Some rules, such as dress codes and **comping,** are made to ensure better customer service or smoothe operations. An operation's upper-level management usually decides how rules are to be applied in order to best take care of customers.

SECTION 1.2: THE MANAGER'S ROLE IN CUSTOMER SERVICE

- Customers' opinions of a foodservice operation are formed by their **service encounters**—or contacts—with an operation's workers.
- All employees are important to the customer service effort. Front-of-the-house employees meet and talk directly to guests; those who work in the back-of-the-house impress customers with the cleanliness of the operation and the quality of the food.
- The most important factor in the customer's mind when choosing a restaurant is the quality of service. One bad experience can mean the loss of a customer forever.
- It costs five times more to advertise and attract new guests than it does to keep current ones coming back. **Word-of-mouth** advertising, however, is free and lets a lot of potential customers know what kind of service an operation provides.
- Excellent customer service leads to increased revenue for a foodservice operation. As a direct result, employees also benefit by enjoying higher tips, job security, and career advancement opportunities.
- Excellent customer service is the result of sound planning.
- A good **service plan** is an organized, systematic method of handling customer service. Planning involves analyzing a goal, situation, assignment, or problem and then developing a step-by-step method for addressing it.
- The ultimate goal of all businesses is to make a **profit.**
- An operation's objectives should include both **short-term** and **long-term** goals.

- An operation's philosophy of doing business is defined in its **mission statement,** which describes an operation's philosophy of doing business. A mission statement should highlight and identify the establishment's food, define service policies and standards, describe the atmosphere, identify prices, and state how the operation differs from the competition.
- The two basic types of resources are **human resources** and **material resources.**
- Once a plan for improving customer service has been designed, managers must identify exactly what must be done and who will be responsible for putting the plan into action; communicate information to employees and train them properly; develop a tool for monitoring employees' performance; and monitor the entire plan continuously over the long term.
- Feedback is a way to monitor how well the service plan is working.
- Feedback from customers can be collected through **comment cards, mystery shoppers,** and **focus groups.**
- **Service guarantees** improve an operation's image and often encourage people to try a restaurant for the first time.
- Establishing a service guarantee is one of the last steps in the customer service planning process.

Susan M. Olenek, RS

Coordinator of Environmental Health
Will County (Illinois) Health Department

After graduating from Illinois State University with a Bachelor of Science degree in Biology, I started as a field sanitarian for the local health department. My responsibilities included inspections of restaurants, beaches, and private water (wells) and waste (septic) systems. I continued my training and became certified as a Registered Sanitarian, concentrating in foodservice safety. Currently, I am supervising the training of new field sanitarians. We train between 150 and 200 foodservice managers a year in foodservice safety. We inspect restaurants, as well as schools, hospitals, convenience stores, nursing homes, grocery stores, hotel food service, day care, soup kitchens, bars, and business foodservice. It is our responsibility to inspect any of the more than 1,600 operations that serve food to the public in this county.

A typical day starts with a meeting with all the field sanitarians. We review the previous day's inspections and determine the goals of the inspectors and the department. I then conduct opening inspections (an inspection that all new foodservice establishments must pass before they receive food products) and review plans for new or remodeled foodservice operations.

The inspections vary depending on the type of operation. Operations are divided into three categories: low risk, like convenience stores, and other operations where there is a minimum of food preparation and human contact with food; mid risk, like fast food establishments where there is more food preparation and more contact between employees and the food; and high risk, operations like family and upscale restaurants and large grocery stores that have a great deal of food preparation and employee food contact. Inspections at the low risk operations take less than an hour and are conducted every 5 to 6 months. Inspections are conducted at mid risk operations every 3 to 4 months and last about an hour. At high risk establishments, inspections occur every 2 to 3 months and can last 2 or more hours.

The most important piece of information I can pass on to people beginning to work in this industry is the need for good personal hygiene. Humans are the primary cause of food contamination. Employees need to be taught the importance of washing their hands, bathing regularly, and wearing clean clothes.

CHAPTER 2

Preparing and Serving Safe Food

2.1

SECTION 2.1

The Importance of Food Safety

AFTER STUDYING SECTION 2.1, YOU SHOULD BE ABLE TO:

- List reasons why it is important to keep food safe.
- Describe good personal hygiene and how it affects food safety.
- List the steps to proper handwashing.
- Give examples of potentially hazardous foods.
- Categorize and describe the microorganisms that cause foodborne illnesses.
- Identify and list ways chemical and physical hazards can contaminate food.
- Distinguish between situations in which contamination and cross-contamination occur.

KEY TERMS

- Bacteria
- Contamination
- Cross-contamination
- Foodborne illness
- Foodborne outbreak
- Microorganism
- Mold
- Parasite
- pH
- Potable water
- Potentially hazardous foods
- Temperature danger zone
- Toxic metal contamination
- Toxin
- Virus
- Water activity (a_W)
- Yeast

- List the conditions under which bacteria multiply rapidly and use the letters FAT-TOM.
- Explain how time and temperature guidelines can reduce growth of micro-organisms.
- Define the food temperature danger zone and list temperatures that fall within that zone.
- Differentiate between different types of thermometers and demonstrate how to use them.

Serving Safe Food

Dining out is an experience people enjoy. Restaurants offer more than good food; they can also be the perfect place for talking to friends, celebrating special occasions, doing business, or relaxing after a hard day. When people dine out, they expect to have a good time. But even more important, they expect to eat good, wholesome, and safe food in a clean environment, served by a pleasant waitstaff.

Think About It...

Have you ever gotten sick after eating a meal at a restaurant? Did you wonder if you had been served unsafe food or if someone hadn't handled your food properly? How would you feel if, by accident, you spread harmful bacteria that caused someone to get seriously ill?

Exhibit 2.1
Service, presentation, and atmosphere are important, but serving safe food is a *must*.

All foodservice establishments, from four-star restaurants to hospital cafeterias, share the same concern for food safety. An otherwise pleasurable dining experience can be ruined by eating food that makes you sick. Illness caused by eating unsafe food also results in loss of business to the foodservice establishment. Some foodborne illnesses can even lead to death. The reputation of a foodservice establishment can be destroyed by a single case of food-related illness. So serving safe food is good business.

Consider the following cases.

- A once-popular restaurant in the Midwest was forced into bankruptcy after a serious foodborne illness outbreak, caused by contaminated onions, resulted in the death of a 73-year-old woman. Lawsuits filed against the restaurant reached well into millions of dollars.
- At an East Coast school, over 400 children became ill after they were served lunch. Later it was discovered that the source of the illness was the egg salad sandwiches that the students ate.

Did You Know?

A foodservice establishment can be held legally responsible for the food it serves. It might be ordered to pay money to the person(s) who suffered illness caused by their food. An operation may be required to prove that they have done everything that could be reasonably expected to prevent foodborne illness by ensuring that safe food was served.

As you can see, foodborne illness can tragically affect many innocent people and be very expensive. Look at Exhibit 2.2 to see the many ways foodborne illness can hurt a restaurant.

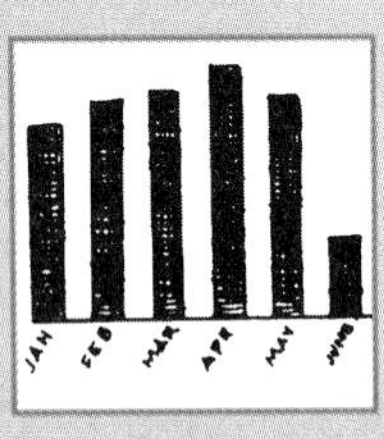

Loss of Customers and Sales

Loss of Prestige and Reputation

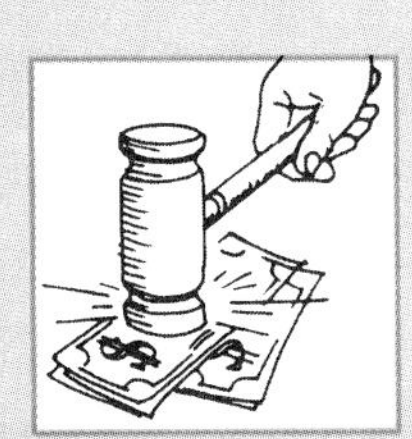

Legal Suits Resulting in Lawyer and Court Fees

Increased Insurance Premiums

Lowered Employee Morale

Absenteeism of Employees

Need for Retraining Employees

Embarrassment

Exhibit 2.2
Foodborne illness can quickly ruin any restaurant, costing people their jobs.

Overall, the foodservice industry has done an excellent job of providing safe food to the public. But food safety is still the most important concern for everyone, from the person who receives and stores food shipments, to the people who prepare and serve the food, to the chef who plans the menu. If you know and understand the basics of food safety you can do your share in preventing food-related problems.

Basics of Good Personal Hygiene

Most living things, including humans, carry bacteria on, or in, their bodies. **Bacteria** refers to invisible, single-celled organisms that often cause disease. Bacteria can be transferred from one thing to another. When bacteria is transferred to food, it can result in illness when the food is eaten. If you are careful to work only when you're healthy and if you practice good hygiene, you can help prevent many illnesses that result from food contaminated with bacteria. You see, food safety really does begin with you.

The first step toward keeping food safe is good personal hygiene. Personal cleanliness is essential for anyone working in the foodservice industry. Good personal hygiene includes bathing daily and washing hands thoroughly. It also means wearing clean clothing and not wearing jewelry, fingernail polish, or false fingernails. Keep your hair clean, neat, and restrained with hats, caps, hair clips, or hair nets. Do not work when you are ill. Employees who are ill can transmit micro-organisms that cause illness to their coworkers and their customers. Exhibit 2.3 outlines some tips for healthy working.

Let's Try It!

There's no doubt about it—washing your hands is very important to good hygiene! We all know how to wash our hands, right? *Wrong.* **Most people don't wash long enough or carefully enough to kill many germs. Experts say you should scrub your hands long enough to sing "Happy Birthday" twice. Try it next time you wash your hands—and don't forget to rinse thoroughly.**

Exhibit 2.3
Tips for healthy working.

- Stay at home if you are suffering from fever, vomiting, jaundice, or excessive coughing or sneezing.
- Let your supervisor know if you do not feel well.
- If you are taking medicine, keep it in your employee changing area, away from food.
- If you have a cut or burn, you should:
  - Let your supervisor know. He or she may have you work at a non-foodhandling task.
  - Wash your hands frequently.
  - Clean and bandage the cuts, scrapes, burns or sores.
  - Wear disposable plastic gloves over bandages on hands and forearms.

Proper Handwashing Techniques

Turn on the water and let it run to a temperature as hot as hands can comfortably stand.

Allow hot water to run over hands and apply soap to them (antibacterial soap is recommended, and dispenser soap is preferred over bar soap). Lather well beyond the wrists, up to the elbows if wearing short sleeves, to remove soil and dirt.

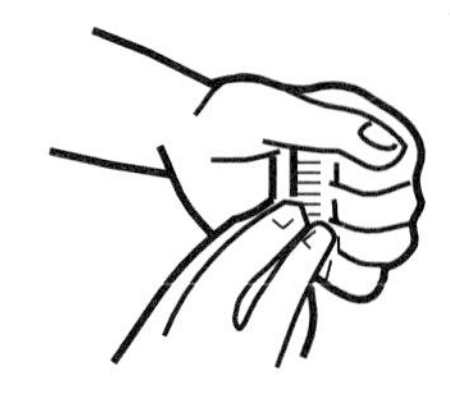

Pay extra attention to the areas between fingers and around and under fingernails.

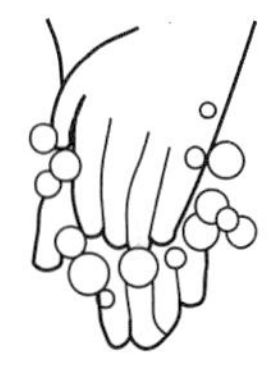

Rub hands together in a rotating motion using friction for at least 20 seconds.

Rinse hands thoroughly under running water, allowing water to flow from the elbows down to the fingertips. This action will rinse away contaminants. Turn water faucet off using a sanitary, single-use disposable paper towel or your elbow.

Dry hands thoroughly with a hot-air hand dryer or with a fresh, single-use disposable paper towel.

What Causes Foodborne Illness?

How does food become unsafe? Foods may become accidentally unsafe by contamination. **Contamination** means that harmful things have gotten into food, making it unsafe to eat. Foods can be contaminated by **microorganisms**, organisms such as bacteria or viruses that are so small they can only be seen through a microscope. Some contaminants occur naturally in foods, such as toxins that are found in fish or plants. **Cross-contamination** occurs when harmful microorganisms are transferred to food by other foods, human hands, utensils, equipment, or other work surfaces.

Exhibit 2.4
When should you wash your hands?

- **Before starting work**
- **While at work, after:**
  - Using the restroom
  - Working with raw food
  - Eating or drinking
  - Touching your hair, face, or body
  - Cleaning
  - Taking out garbage
  - Sneezing or coughing
  - Touching anything that may contaminate hands
  - Smoking and chewing tobacco
- **Before putting on gloves or when changing gloves**
- **When switching from working with one food to another food**
- **When going from a nonfood preparation task to a food preparation task**

Food can also be contaminated by chemicals, such as cleaning materials, and by physical objects, such as glass or metal, that accidentally get into food. There are also natural physical hazards in food, such as bones found in chicken or fish.

All these types of contamination can cause foodborne illness. A **foodborne illness** is an illness that is carried or transmitted to people by food. Foodborne illness can range from a mild stomach irritation to, in some cases, death. A foodborne illness that affects two or more people who have eaten the same food is called a **foodborne outbreak.**

It is important to remember that any food, even water and ice, can cause foodborne illness. Most often, however, moist, high-protein foods, such as meat, poultry, fish, eggs, and dairy products, are the cause of foodborne illness. These foods are classified as **potentially hazardous foods**. This is because micro-organisms tend to grow easily in these foods.

Bacteria and Viruses

Bacteria and viruses are the greatest concern to food safety. Bacteria can cause illness in two ways:

Exhibit 2.5
It is important to follow proper procedures when handling potentially hazardous foods.

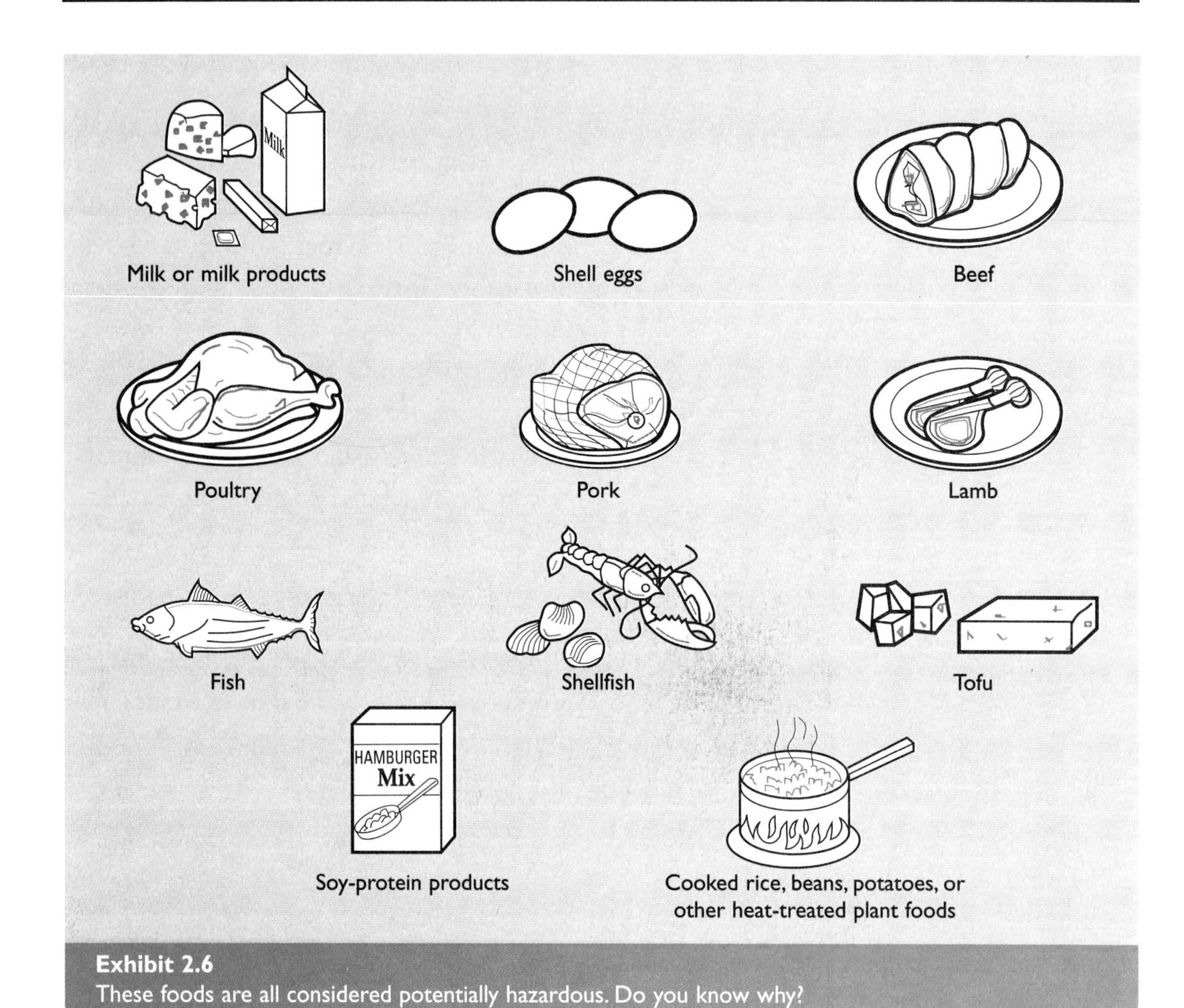

Exhibit 2.6
These foods are all considered potentially hazardous. Do you know why?

1. Bacteria in food can multiply rapidly to disease-causing levels at favorable temperatures.
2. Bacteria can produce toxins in food that can poison humans when the food is eaten.

Most foodborne illnesses are caused by bacteria. Exhibit 2.7 on the next page shows a list of illnesses caused by harmful, disease-causing bacteria.

Many food items, including ice and water, can transport a virus. Like bacteria, a **virus** is a small, simple microorganism that causes disease. Unlike bac-

Exhibit 2.7 Some common foodborne illnesses caused by bacteria.

	Salmonellosis infection	Shigellosis infection	Staphylococcal intoxication	Clostridium perfringens toxin-mediated infection	Bacillus cereus intoxication	Botulism intoxication
Bacteria	Salmonella	Shigella	Staphylococcus aureus	Clostridium perfringens	Bacillus cereus	Clostridium botulinum
Symptoms Appear Within	6-72 hours	1-7 days	1-6 hours	8-22 hours	½-5 hours; 8-16 hours	12-36 hours
Illness Lasts	2-3 days	Indefinite, depends on treatment	24-48 hours	24 hours	6-24 hours; 12 hours	Several days to a year
Symptoms	Abdominal pain, headache, nausea, vomiting, fever, diarrhea	Diarrhea, fever, chills, fatigue, dehydration	Nausea, vomiting, diarrhea, dehydration	Abdominal pain, diarrhea	Nausea and vomiting, diarrhea, abdominal pain	Dizziness, visual disturbances, inability to swallow, respiratory paralysis
Source	Domestic and wild animals; also humans, especially as carriers	Human feces, flies	Humans (skin, nose, throat, infected sores); also animals	Humans (intestinal tract), animals, soil	Soil, dust	Soil, water
Potential Carriers	Poultry and poultry salads, meat and meat products, milk, shell eggs, egg custards and sauces, other protein foods	Potato, tuna, shrimp, turkey, and macaroni salads, lettuce, moist and mixed foods	Warmed-over foods, ham and other meats, dairy products, custards, potato salad, cream-filled pastries, other protein foods	Meat that has been boiled, steamed, braised, stewed, or roasted at low temperature for a long period of time, or cooled slowly before serving	Rice and rice dishes, custards, seasonings, dry food mixes, spices, puddings, cereal products, sauces, vegetable dishes, meat loaf	Improperly processed canned goods of low-acid foods, garlic-in-oil products, grilled onions, stews, meat/poultry loaves
Prevention	Avoid cross-contamination, refrigerate foods, cool cooked meats and meat products properly, avoid fecal contamination from foodhandlers by practicing good personal hygiene	Avoid cross-contamination, avoid fecal contaminaton from foodhandlers by practicing good personal hygiene, use sanitary food and water sources, control flies	Avoid cross-contamination, exclude sick foodhandlers from food preparation and serving, practice good personal hygiene, practice sanitary habits, proper heating and refrigeration of food	Use careful time and temperature control in cooling and reheating cooked meat dishes and products	Use careful time and temperature control and quick chilling methods, hold hot foods above 140°F (60°C), reheat leftovers to 165°F (73.9°C)	Do not use home-canned products, do not use cans that are damaged, use careful time and temperature control for sous-vide items and all large, bulky foods, keep sous-vide packages refrigerated, purchase garlic-in-oil in small quantities for immediate use, cook onions only on request

Reprinted with permission from *Overview of Food and Beverage Operations Management Skillbook.*

teria, viruses need living cells in order to grow and multiply. Once a virus gains access to cells in humans or other living organisms, it kills the cells and forces them to produce more viruses. Also unlike bacteria, viruses do not grow in food, but they can be carried by food items. It takes only a small number of viral agents to cause illness.

One of the most common foodborne viral diseases is hepatitis A. Hepatitis A causes inflammation of the liver, fever, nausea, abdominal pain, fatigue, and jaundice. A mild case of hepatitis A lasts for several weeks; a severe case may cause a person to be bedridden for months.

Exhibit 2.8
Believe it or not... even water and ice can transport a virus.

Viruses can be found in drinking water that is not potable. **Potable water** is water that is drinkable. It has been filtered and disinfected so it is safe to drink. Another source of viruses can be contaminated foods like shellfish (especially oysters, mussels, and clams) that have been illegally harvested in polluted water.

Remember!

The most effective way to prevent foodborne or waterborne viral illnesses is to buy shellfish from approved suppliers and avoid food contamination by practicing proper personal hygiene, especially thorough handwashing.

Parasites

Parasites are organisms that need to live inside a host to survive. A well-known parasite is *Trichinella spiralis*, commonly known as roundworms. Roundworms attach themselves to the stomach of animals such as pigs, deer, and bear. Roundworm larvae (newly hatched offspring) can cause trichinosis in humans.

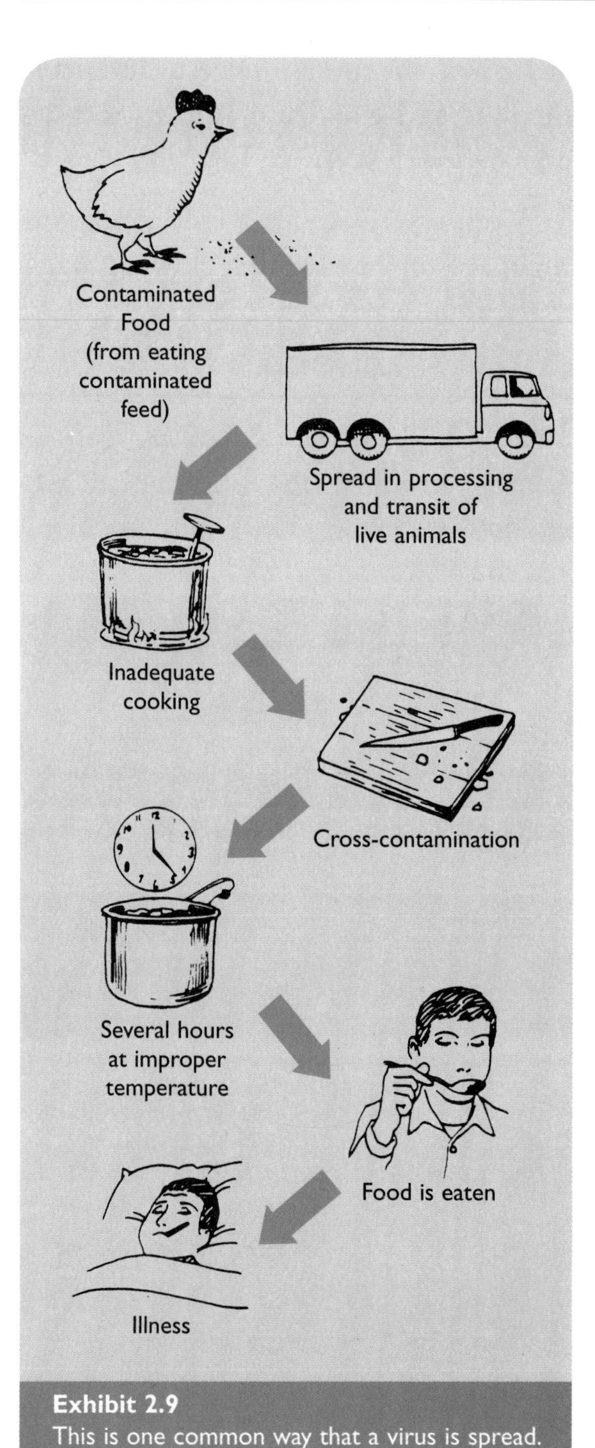

Exhibit 2.9
This is one common way that a virus is spread.

People most often become infected by *Trichinella spiralis* by eating raw or undercooked pork or game meat. Symptoms usually appear within 8 to 15 days and include diarrhea, nausea, abdominal pain, swelling around the eyes, and eventually fever and muscular stiffness. Exhibit 2.10 outlines steps for preventing a trichinosis outbreak.

Exhibit 2.10
To prevent a trichinosis outbreak:

- Always cook wild game products until they reach an internal temperature of at least 155°F (68.3°C) in a conventional oven, 165°F (73.9°C) in a microwave oven.
- Never serve uninspected meats.
- Freezing at 5°F (-15°C) for 30 days can inactivate roundworms in a piece of meat that is less than six inches thick.
- Always wash, rinse, and sanitize equipment and utensils after working with wild game meats.

Remember!

Never serve raw or undercooked pork.

Fungi

Molds are highly adaptable organisms that grow quickly. The mold that is visible to the human eye is actually a tangled mass of thousands of tiny mold plants. It was once thought that food mold was not dangerous to humans, but it is now known that certain molds can cause serious illnesses, infections, and allergies. Other molds can produce toxins (poisons) that cannot be destroyed by cooking methods.

Molds commonly grow on cheese and are sometimes used to produce cheese. Molds that are a natural part of the cheese-making process (such as the molds in Gorgonzola, Bleu, Brie, and Camembert) present no health risk but can be very hard to tell apart from other molds. Other molds might cause illness, and they should be discarded.

Rule of Thumb

Always throw out foods with molds.

A **yeast** is a type of fungus that needs sugar and moisture in order to survive. Yeasts can grow in sugar-based food products, such as jellies and honey, spoiling the food in the process. Yeast cells can also grow in cottage cheese and fruit juices. It is wise to discard any food contaminated with yeast.

When a yeast spoils a food item, you might see any or all of the following signs on the food.

- Alcohol smell or taste
- Bubbles
- Pink discoloration
- Slime

Exhibit 2.11
Always purchase seafood from a reputable and certified seafood dealer.

Toxins

Certain fish may carry a **toxin,** or poison. Some predatory marine fish, such as barracuda and snapper, collect toxins from eating other smaller fish that have eaten algae carrying *ciguatoxin.* When people eat fish with a lot of *ciguatoxin,* they can develop an illness called *ciguatera.* Symptoms include vomiting, itching, nausea, dizziness, hot and cold flashes, temporary blindness, and sometimes hallucinations.

Exhibit 2.12
Guidelines to guard against toxins in fish.

- Purchase fish from a reputable and certified seafood dealer.
- Refuse fish that has been delivered thawed and refrozen. Signs of refrozen fish include dried or dehydrated appearance, excessive frost or ice on the package, and freezer burn.
- Fresh fish must be received at a temperature of 32°F to 40°F (0°C to 4.4°C) and immediately placed in refrigerated storage at 40°F (4.4°C) or lower.
- When ready to use, thaw frozen fish quickly at refrigeration temperatures below 40°F (4.4°C).

Certain fatty fishes, such as tuna, bluefish, mackerel, and mahi-mahi (dolphin fish), that have been mishandled can cause *scrombroid intoxication.* Symptoms of *scrombroid intoxication* include flushing and sweating, a burning peppery taste in the mouth, dizziness, nausea, vomiting, and headache. Most toxins are odorless. They may not be destroyed by cooking or freezing. Exhibit 2.12 outlines some things you can do to guard against toxins in fish.

Mushrooms are a type of fungus, and certain mushrooms are poisonous to eat. Since poisonous and nonpoisonous mushrooms often look alike, avoid using any mushrooms that are not purchased from a reliable, approved source.

Chemical and Physical Hazards

There are many foreign substances, such as chemical cleaning supplies, pesticides, and poisonous metals from improper equipment, that can contaminate food. To prevent contamination from foodservice chemicals:

- Follow the manufacturers' label directions for safe handling of chemicals.
- Never use food containers to store chemicals.
- Never use chemical containers to store food.
- Keep chemicals in a dry and locked cabinet or area, separate from food surfaces, utensils, or equipment where food is stored, held, or prepared.

- If a chemical is transferred to a smaller container, the smaller container must be labeled appropriately, with the contents.
- Foodservice employees who use chemicals must wash their hands before returning to food preparation duties.

Toxic metal contamination can occur when high-acid foods, such as sauerkraut, fruit gelatin, or lemonade, are prepared using utensils or stored in containers made of metals such as copper, brass, or galvanized zinc. To prevent accidental toxic metal contamination:

- Do not use enamelware, lead, or any lead-based product for food production.
- Use containers for their intended purpose only. For example, do not use galvanized metal garbage cans to store foods.
- Use metallic items for their intended purpose only. For example, do not use a refrigerator shelf as a makeshift grill.
- Use only appropriate sanitary foodservice brushes for basting.

Physical objects, such as broken glass and crockery, packaging materials, or jewelry can also cause accidental contamination. Some physical hazards are naturally part of food; for example, bones in chicken or fish.

To prevent food contamination by physical objects:

- Never scoop ice with a glass.
- Check and replace worn can openers.
- Do not use unfrilled toothpicks for garnishes or on sandwiches. All toothpicks and non-edible garnishes should be stored away from food storage and preparation areas.
- Put shields on lights over food-storage and food-preparation areas.
- Remove and properly dispose of nails, staples, and any other objects from boxes and crates when food is received.
- Avoid wearing dangling jewelry when working with food.
- Discard dishes, glasses, and tableware that are chipped or cracked.

How Can You Keep Food Safe?

If micro-organisms are invisible to the human eye, how can you prevent them from entering and contaminating food? To prepare and serve safe food, you must know the facts about contaminants and food safety techniques that help prevent harmful micro-organisms, chemicals, and physical objects from contaminating food.

Barriers to Bacterial Growth

Since bacteria are the most common causes of foodborne illnesses, you must know and recognize the conditions in which they thrive and multiply. Once you know these conditions, you can control them to prevent foodborne illnesses from occurring.

Bacteria multiply quickly when there are six conditions present. An easy way to remember these six conditions is by memorizing the letters *FAT-TOM*. Exhibit 2.13 gives you a quick overview of what FAT-TOM stands for. It will be discussed in more detail in the following pages.

Food. High-protein foods are more likely than other foods to enter a foodservice operation carrying bacteria. And once there, they can be more easily contaminated than other foods. To control bacterial growth in potentially hazardous foods, there are specific guidelines for you to follow.

Acidity. The **pH** level of a food is the measure of its acidity or alkalinity. The pH is measured on a scale from 0 to 14. Foods with a pH below 7.0 are acidic. Foods with a pH above 7.0 are alkaline. A solution with a pH of 7.0 is exactly neutral—neither acidic nor alkaline. Distilled water is neutral.

Exhibit 2.13
FAT-TOM.

F — **Food.** Like humans, bacteria need food to live. Bacteria thrive on moist, high-protein foods, such as beef, eggs, and shellfish. These foods are the potentially hazardous foods that must always be handled with care.

A — **Acidity.** In order to grow, bacteria need an environment that has a moderate acidity level, or in other words, a pH level between 4.6 and 7.0.

T — **Time.** Bacteria can multiply very quickly in a very short amount of time. Also, the more time they spend in the temperature danger zone, the more of them there will be.

T — **Temperature.** Temperature is a major influence on bacteria growth. Bacteria prefer an environment that is not too hot and not too cold. The temperature danger zone for potentially hazardous foods is between 40°F and 140°F (4.4°C and 60°C).

O — **Oxygen.** Most bacteria need oxygen to live, but many that cause foodborne illness can live either with or without oxygen.

M — **Moisture.** Bacteria thrive in moist environments.

Many bacteria can survive in the pH range between 4.6 and 7.0. This means that chicken and beef, which have a natural pH level around 5.0, are more likely to have bacterial growth than fresh fruits, which have a pH level below 4.6. A pH level below 4.6 inhibits the growth of disease-causing foodborne bacteria. Exhibit 2.14 shows pH levels for some common foods.

Time and temperature. These are two of the most important factors in keeping food safe from harmful micro-organisms. Why? Because micro-organisms grow best on foods when they are in the **temperature danger zone,** which is between 40°F and 140°F (4.4°C and 60°C). That is why three of your most important tasks in keeping foods safe involve time and temperature. Always:

1. Measure the temperature of food.
2. Make sure food is kept at proper food temperatures (below 40°F and above 140°F).
3. Record temperatures.

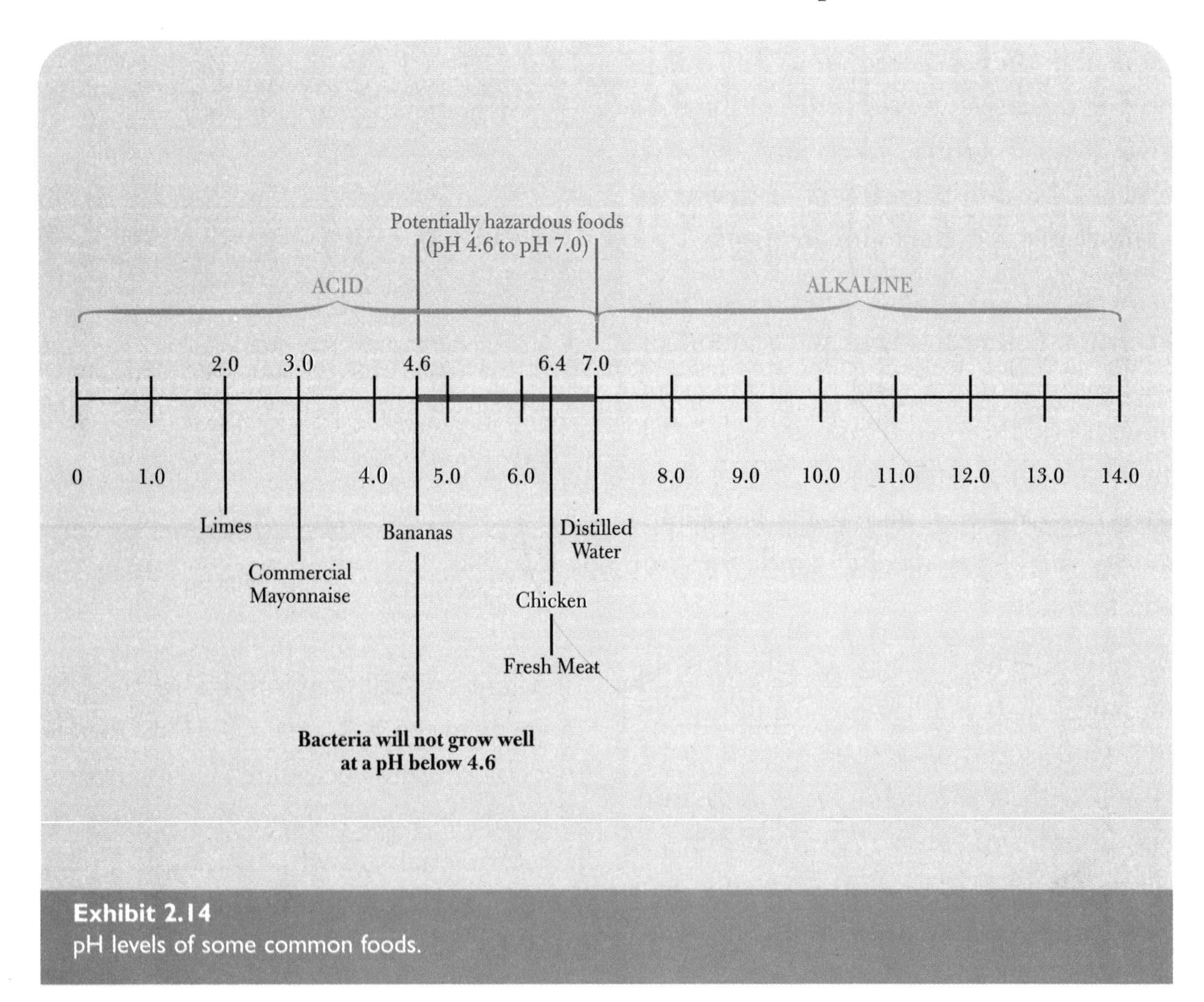

Exhibit 2.14
pH levels of some common foods.

Food should not be within the dangerous temperature range for more than four hours during the food preparation process.

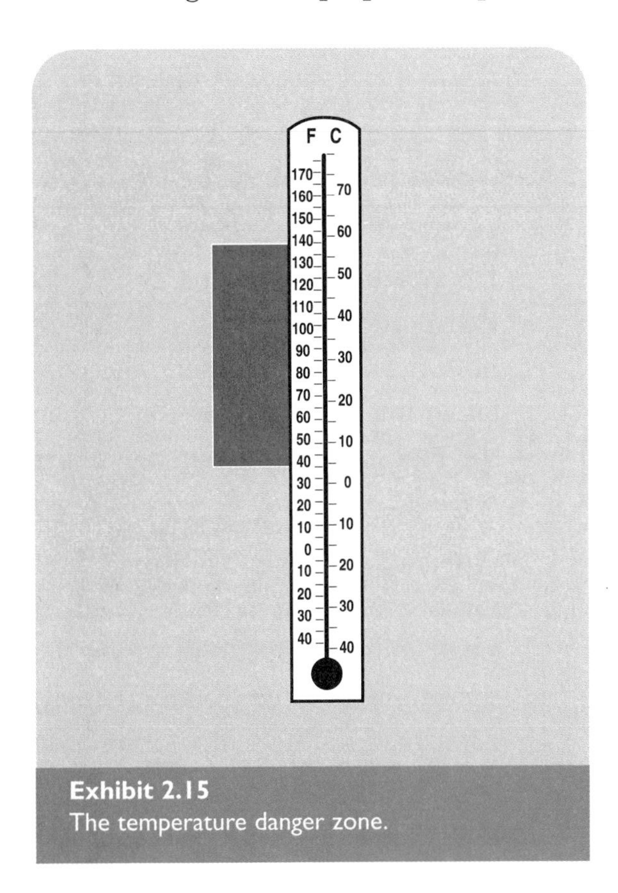

Exhibit 2.15
The temperature danger zone.

How do you take a food's temperature? There are several different types of food thermometers available. Food thermometers should be metal, not mercury-filled or glass. They should be able to measure internal temperatures of 0°F to 220°F (-17.8°C to 104.4°C); and should be accurate to ±2°F or ±1°C.

Thermocouple

- Measures temperature electrically through a sensor in the tip.
- Shows the temperature on a digital readout panel.

Bi-metallic Stemmed Thermometer

- The most common food thermometer.
- Measures temperature through a metal stem.

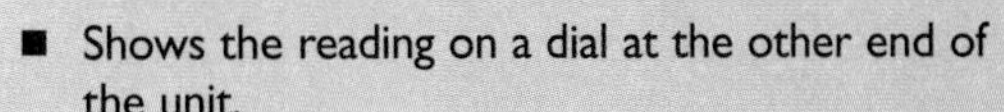

- Shows the reading on a dial at the other end of the unit.
- Has a calibration nut (a nut for adjusting the temperature reading) just below the dial.
- WARNING: Never leave a bi-metallic stemmed thermometer in food that is cooking in an oven or a microwave, or on a stove top.

Digital Thermometer

- Measures temperature through a metal tip.
- Shows the temperature on a readout panel.

Time Temperature Indicator (TTI)

- Looks like a label.
- Usually found on packages.
- Has liquid crystals that change color if foods reach an unsafe temperature.

Candy, Meat, and Deep-fry Thermometers

- Used for only one type of food (candy, meat, or deep-fried foods).
- WARNING: Never use mercury-filled or glass thermometers because they may break!

Exhibit 2.16
Thermometers used to measure food temperatures.

Exhibit 2.16 illustrates several different types of food thermometers.

Built-in thermometers and hang-type thermometers are usually found inside refrigerators or freezers and tell the temperature of the air in the unit. Thermometers are also often built into hot-holding equipment and dishwashing machines. It is important to take the temperature of foods stored in a refrigerator or held for service. This will help you decide whether the proper temperature is actually being maintained. Exhibit 2.17 lists some common temperature guidelines for storage and holding equipment.

Exhibit 2.17
Common temperatures for storage and holding equipment.

- Refrigerator air temperature:
  35° to 38°F (1.7° to 3.3°C)
- Freezer air temperature:
  -10° to 0°F (-23.3° to -17.8°C)
- Hot-holding equipment:
  140°F (60°C) or above

Do not keep the doors of refrigerators or freezers open any longer than you need when taking out or putting away food. Why not? Because doing this raises the air temperature in the unit, and stored foods may be exposed to the temperature danger zone. Never cool hot foods in the refrigerator or freezer units, either. This can bring the temperature in the unit up to dangerous levels.

Follow these important steps when measuring food temperatures and reading thermometers:

1. Insert thermometer.
   - Stick the sensing tip of a clean and sanitized thermometer into the center and/or thickest part of the food.
   - Do not let the sensing tip of the thermometer touch the sides or bottom of the container. The container may be hotter or colder than the food, and you could get a false reading.
   - Open a single package from a carton of individual packages, such as small milk cartons, and insert the thermometer (see Exhibit 2.18). After reading the temperature, discard the open package or use it immediately for cooking.
   - Stick the sensing area of the thermometer between packages of frozen foods or tightly packed boxes.
   - For soft bulk dispensers of milk or flexible packages of meat or entrées, fold the package around the sensing tip of the thermometer. Do not poke a hole in the package.

2. Wait for the needle or readout to stop. Wait 15 more seconds to make sure the temperature is correct.
3. Check the temperature—especially of large items such as roasts or batches of stew—in at least two places.
4. Carefully record the time you measured the temperature and the temperature of the food in your temperature log. This is a very important step. You may need this information later to make sure food hasn't spent more than four hours in the temperature danger zone. If you notice something unusual, such as if the food in hot-holding has fallen below 140°F (60°C), let your manager know immediately.
5. Wash, rinse, sanitize, and air-dry thermometer stems before and after each use. Remember to use a sanitizing solution that is safe for food-contact items.

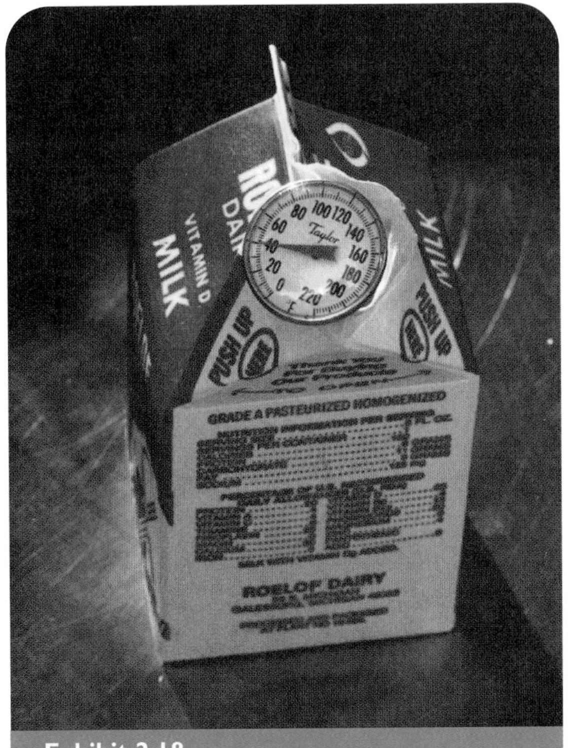

Exhibit 2.18
When testing the temperature of a delivery of individual packages, open a single package and insert the thermometer.

Food Safety Tip:
Before measuring the temperature of microwave-cooked foods, let them stand for at least two minutes to even out the product's temperature.

Oxygen. Time and temperature are factors that easily can, and must, be controlled to keep food safe. Oxygen is a more difficult factor to control. This is because most bacteria that cause foodborne illness can grow either with or without the presence of oxygen.

Moisture. Bacteria need water to grow. The amount of water or moisture in foods is known as its **water activity (a_w)**. Bacteria grow quickly when the water activity level is between 0.9 and 0.99. Most fresh foods have water activity levels close to this range. Any food with a water activity value above 0.85 is considered potentially hazardous.

How can you control water activity? Water activity in foods can be lowered by freezing, dehydrating, or mixing the food with a dissolved substance, such as sugar or salt. Some food products, such as sugar and flour, are stored and handled dry. Other dry foods, such as rice, pasta, and dried beans, become potentially hazardous in the cooking process once water is added.

Now that you know the factors that allow bacteria to grow quickly, you can prevent the growth of bacteria and keep food safe.

Remember!

The more ways you can create barriers to bacterial growth, the lower the risk for contamination and illness.

Review Your Learning 2.1

1. Potentially hazardous foods are:

   a. moist, high-protein foods.
   b. foods with a high pH level.
   c. dry, sugary foods.
   d. fresh, salty foods.

2. What are signs that food has been spoiled by yeast?

   a. Blue discoloration.
   b. Bubbles.
   c. Crusty surface.
   d. Sticky.

3. What does the term *potable water* mean?

4. What are some ways you can prevent foodborne illness?

5. What are the six letters used to describe the conditions in which bacteria multiply rapidly?

6. What is the range of temperatures from 40°F to 140°F (4.4°C to 60°C) also known as?

2.2

SECTION 2.2

Establishing a Food Safety System

AFTER STUDYING SECTION 2.2, YOU SHOULD BE ABLE TO:

- List the seven major steps in a Hazard Analysis Critical Control Point (HACCP) food safety system.

A HACCP Food Safety System

With all the potential problems of keeping food safe and preventing foodborne illness, what can foodservice establishments do? One of the best ways they can prevent foodborne illness is by developing and following a food safety system that involves all members of their operation. One such food safety system is a **Hazard Analysis Critical Control Point** system or **HACCP** (pronounced HASS-ip). The HACCP system pays close attention to potentially hazardous foods and how they are handled in the foodservice environment.

In a HACCP system, **hazards** are defined as biological, chemical, or physical properties that might make food unsafe. Some examples of hazards include:

- Micro-organisms that can grow during preparation, storage, and/or holding.
- Micro-organisms that can survive cooking or freezing.

KEY TERMS

- **Critical control point**
- **Dry lab**
- **Flow of food**
- **Flowchart**
- **Hazard**
- **Hazard Analysis Critical Control Point (HACCP)**
- **Risk**

- Chemicals that can contaminate food or food-contact surfaces.
- Physical objects that can accidentally enter food.

Did you know?

The HACCP system was developed for the National Aeronautics and Space Administration (NASA) to make sure food served to astronauts traveling in outer space was absolutely safe. Its purpose was to ensure that no mistakes were made at any point in the foodhandling process that could lead to an outbreak of foodborne illness. At that time, most methods of checking for food safety only tested the finished food product for contamination. The HACCP system was different because it followed the flow of food throughout the entire process to identify and correct any errors before they could become a problem. Because the HACCP system was so successful in preventing foodborne illness in food manufacturing, foodservice operations began to adapt the system for their own use.

A foodservice establishment can prevent such hazards by taking special care during the entire process of preparing and serving food. The HACCP system identifies certain **critical control points**—points where specific action can be taken to eliminate, prevent, or minimize a hazard (or hazards) from happening.

A HACCP system identifies points at which:

- Food can become contaminated.
- Contaminants can increase.
- Contaminants can survive.

You will learn the seven major steps of a HACCP system. These steps should be followed in order to control food safety.

- **Steps 1, 2, and 3** help you design your system.
- **Steps 4 and 5** help you put your system to use.
- **Steps 6 and 7** help you maintain your system and test its effectiveness.

Step 1—Assess Hazards

Before you choose menu items, you must know of any risks that are involved in serving those foods. A **risk** is the chance that a condition or set of conditions will lead to a foodservice hazard. By controlling risks, you can lower the chances of foodborne illness.

Remember!

Potentially hazardous foods may be served as separate items *and* as ingredients in recipes. For example, meat is often served as an ingredient in chili or sauces as well as as an entrée.

❑❑❑❑
Dinner
St. Andrew's Hospital
❑❑❑❑

(Please Check ✔ Your Selections)

Soup
❑ *Hearty Beef Noodle*
❑ *New England–style Clam Chowder*

Salads
❑ Great Garden Salad—mixed greens, green and black olives, tomatoes, chives, and *hard–boiled egg*
❑ Fresh Seasonal Fruits—strawberries, green grapes, and apples slices

Dressings
❑ Raspberry Vinaigrette
❑ Peppered Ranch*
❑ Spicy French
❑ Oil and Vinegar

Entrées (Select one)
❑ *Baked Pork Chop* with Hot Apple Compote
❑ *Swiss Steak* with *French–cut Green Beans*
❑ *Poached Salmon* with *Lemon Butter Sauce*
❑ *Vegetarian Lasagna* with Garlic Bread

Breads and Spreads
❑ White Bread
❑ Whole Wheat Bread
❑ Challah
❑ *Whipped Butter*
❑ Margarine
❑ Apple Butter

Sweet Treats
❑ *Frozen Strawberry Yogurt*
❑ Apple Crumb Cake
❑ *Vanilla Ice Cream*
❑ Lemon Sherbet

Beverages
❑ Coffee
❑ *Whole Milk*
❑ Hot Tea
- ❑ Orange Pekoe
- ❑ Black

❑ Decaffeinated coffee
❑ *Low-fat Milk*
❑ Herbal Tea
- ❑ Apple Spice
- ❑ Chamomile

❑ Iced Tea
❑ Non–dairy Creamer
❑ Sparkling Water

Seasonings
❑ Salt
❑ Ketchup
❑ Pepper
❑ Mustard
❑ Sugar
❑ Mayonnaise*
❑ Lemon

Name____________________ **Room**__________

*Commercially-prepared sauces and dressings that are prepared for food service use generally are made to have a high acidity and are not considered potentially hazardous.

Exhibit 2.19
Sample institutional menu. Potentially hazardous foods are italicized.

The first task of step 1 is to identify potentially hazardous foods. These foods are the greatest risks to food safety. Review your menus and recipes to identify the potentially hazardous foods you serve. Look at the menu in Exhibit 2.19. Why are the italicized foods considered potentially hazardous?

The next task in step 1 is to recognize the flow of food through your operation. It's important to know this **flow of food:** it is the route food takes on its way to being served. It begins with the decision to include an item on your menu and ends with the food being served to the customer. Recognizing the flow of food allows you to see all the places where food safety hazards might exist. Exhibit 2.20 is a chart that shows the flow of food through an operation.

As Exhibit 2.20 shows, the flow of food begins well before the food is prepared and cooked. At every step along the way, potential for hazards exists. The next section in this chapter, Section 2.3 will walk you through the flow of food in greater detail.

The third task in step 1 is to identify hazards. Once you've selected the foods you plan to serve, you need to pinpoint hazards that could occur during the flow of food.

Remember, there are three kinds of food hazards.

1. Biological hazards are micro-organisms or naturally occurring toxins contaminating food.
2. Chemical hazards are chemical substances such as pesticides, detergents, additives, and toxic metals that contaminate foods.

Exhibit 2.20
Flow of food in a foodservice operation.

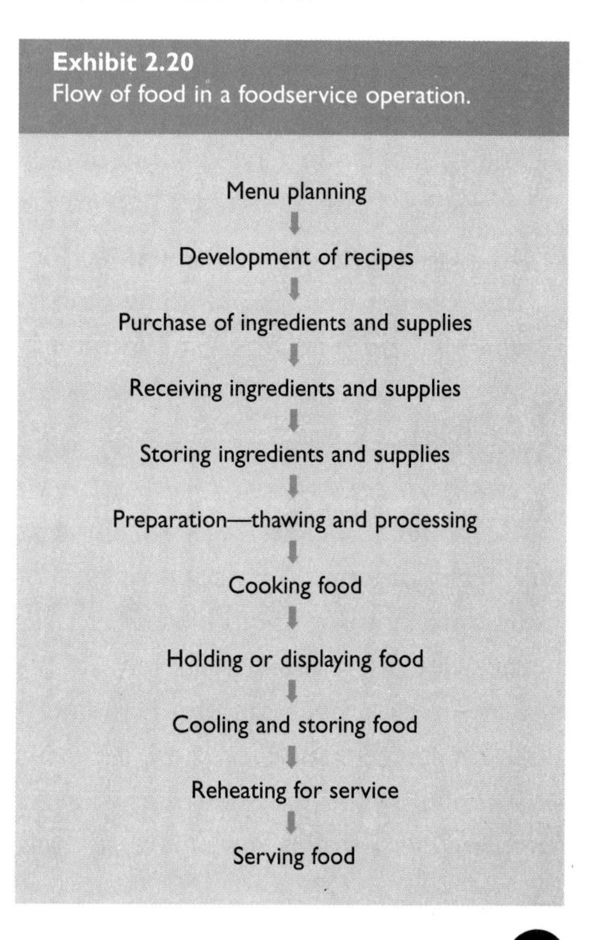

3. Physical hazards are particles or fragments of items that are not supposed to be in foods, such as chips of glass, metal shavings, and toothpicks.

To help you determine the hazards you need to control:

- *Study your recipes.* What are the potentially hazardous foods? At which points can you control contamination, survival, and growth of disease-causing micro-organisms?
- *Observe employees in action.* Do employees practice proper hygiene procedures? Is food being prepared and processed in ways that might increase the risk of contamination?
- *Measure temperatures and test foods.* Improper storing, cooking, holding, cooling, and reheating temperatures are common reasons for outbreaks of foodborne illness.

The final task of step 1 is to estimate risk. Different foodservice establishments will have different kinds of risks. For example, a hot dog stand has fewer risks because its operation is relatively simple and it serves a small variety of foods. A 24-hour coffee shop, which serves a greater variety of items and has a larger kitchen, has greater risks. Greater risk means that more conditions need to be controlled in order to prevent foodborne illness.

Exhibit 2.21
Foodborne illness can be especially dangerous to children, older people, or sick people.

What other factors increase risk of foodborne illness?

- *Customers*—Children, older people, and sick people have a lower resistance to foodborne illness. Hospitals and long-term care centers, especially those serving older patients and patients with weak immune systems, have to be especially careful with the food they serve.

- *Suppliers*—Always choose reputable, and in some cases certified, suppliers for all potentially hazardous items.
- *Size and type of operation*—Complicated or multi-step recipes require proper equipment and facilities. For example, a small family restaurant may find it difficult to safely monitor all the steps needed to serve Chicken Cordon Bleu. It might be better able to serve Baked Turkey Breast.
- *Employees*—Employees need to be trained in the proper preparation and service of food. They must also have the proper equipment and materials to do their job well.

Step 2—Identify Critical Control Points

The next step in developing a HACCP system is to identify the critical control points in the flow of food and in your recipes. You know that a critical control point (CCP) is a point where specific control measures can be taken to:

- Prevent foods from becoming contaminated.
- Prevent contaminants from surviving.
- Prevent further growth of contaminants.

A good way for you to understand the flow of a specific food or menu item through a restaurant is to draw a diagram called a flowchart. A **flowchart** follows a menu item from the point when the ingredients are received to the moment the item is served to the customer. When you create a flowchart, identify where hazards exist at each step in

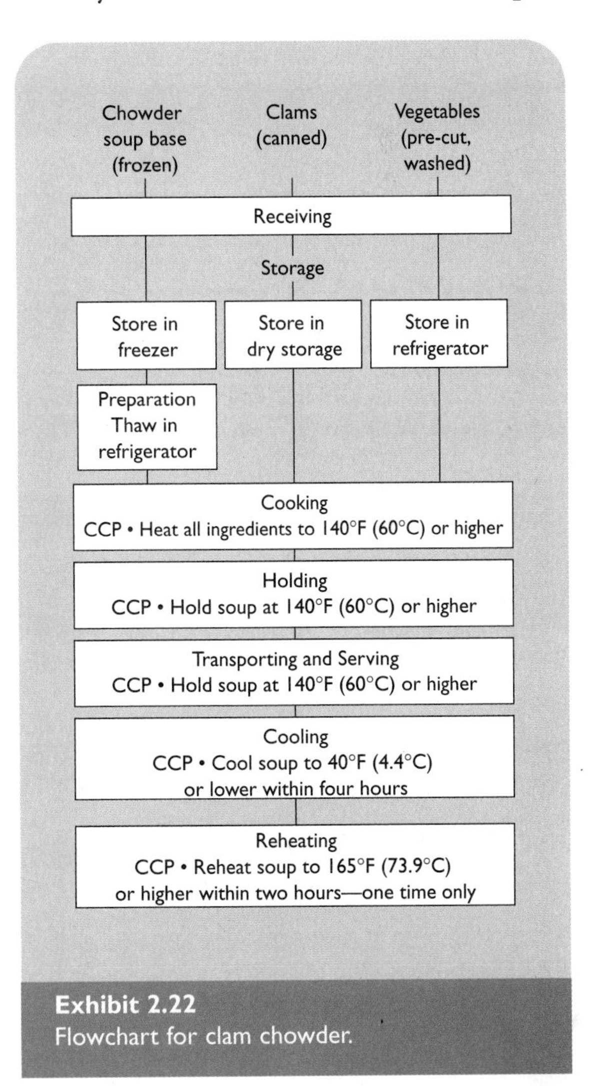

Exhibit 2.22
Flowchart for clam chowder.

the flow of food. Then identify where procedures can prevent, reduce, and eliminate the risk of contamination. These are your critical control points, and require special attention. A flowchart should be a one-page drawing, much like the one shown in Exhibit 2.22, that it is easy to read and follow. Once you know the critical control points, include them in your recipe.

Step 3—Set Up Procedures for Critical Control Points

Determine the requirements, using such factors as time and temperature, that must be met at each critical control point to keep food safe. Make sure the directions are very specific and clear. Requirements should be easy to observe and measure.

Exhibit 2.23
Clam chowder recipe with critical control points (CCPs).

Yield: 3 gallons (11.36 l)

Ingredients	**Weights**	**Measures**
Chowder soup base (frozen)	2 1/4 gal	8.52 l
Clams (canned)	4–15 oz cans	4–25 g cans
Vegetables (pre-cut, washed)	6 lbs	2.72 kg

Preparation

1. Thaw base under refrigeration.
2. Drain clams.
3. Combine thawed base, clams, and vegetables in a stockpot.

Cooking

CCP 4. Simmer ingredients until a final product temperature of 140°F (60°C) is reached. Stir frequently and skim surface as necessary.

Serving and Holding

CCP 5. Serve immediately, or hold for service at 140°F (60°C) or higher. Do not mix new product with old.

Transporting

CCP 6. Hold for transporting at 140°F (60°) or higher for no longer than 30 minutes.

Cooling

CCP 7. Cool to 40°F (4.4°C) or lower within four hours in shallow pans with a product depth of two inches or less.

8. Store at a product temperature of 40°F (4.4°C) or lower in refrigerated unit. Cover.

Reheating

CCP 9. Reheat chowder to a product temperature of 165°F (73.9°C) or higher within two hours.

Sanitation Instructions: Measure all temperatures with a thermocouple. Wash hands before handling food, after handling raw foods, and after any interruption that may contaminate hands. Wash, rinse, and sanitize all equipment and utensils before and after use. Return all ingredients to refrigerated storage if preparation is interrupted.

CCPs are highlighted in boldface.

You should also develop procedures to prevent cross-contamination of foods. For example, when you check the temperature of your clam chowder, make sure the thermometer you use is clean and sanitized. As many requirements as possible should be included in your recipes and flowcharts.

Example of requirements include all of the following steps.

- Wash hands.
- Wash, rinse, and sanitize food-contact surfaces and utensils.
- Thoroughly cook food to appropriate internal temperatures.
- Hold cooked foods at temperatures above 140°F (60°C).
- Rapidly cool, and keep food below 40°F (4.4°C).
- Reheat food to 165°F (73.9°C) for 15 seconds within two hours.

Exhibit 2.23 shows a clam chowder recipe including critical control points.

Step 4—Monitor Critical Control Points

Monitoring, or checking to see that the requirements are met, is one of the most important activities in the HACCP system. Why? Monitoring lets you know when and where your requirements for critical control points are not being met. All employees should be involved in monitoring critical control points.

> **Let's try it!**
>
> **One of your requirements to keep food safe at a critical control point might be to keep the food at a certain temperature. To check (monitor) if that requirement is being met, measure the product's temperature with a clean, sanitized thermometer and record times when temperatures are taken. Then, record your observations and measurements in log books.**

Step 5—Take Corrective Action

What do you do when you find out a critical control point hasn't been met? Corrective action must be carried out immediately. Many corrective actions are very simple and limited, such as continuing to heat food to a specified temperature. Other corrective actions may be more involved, such as rejecting a shipment of food. Exhibit 2.24 shows how corrective action should be taken if a critical control point isn't met for holding baked chicken breasts.

Exhibit 2.24
Sample requirements for holding baked chicken breast, including corrective action.

Requirement: Hold baked chicken breast at 140°F (60°C) or higher until served. Do not hold longer than two hours.

Corrective action: If it has been held for more than two hours, discard. If it has been held for less than two hours and temperature falls below 140°F (60°C), reheat it to 165°F (73.9°C) or higher for at least 15 seconds within two hours.

Step 6—Set Up a Record-keeping System

Accurate records have at least two important benefits. First, they provide a source of information about daily operations and long-term trends. Second, by showing that criteria are being met and that your operation is addressing problems, you create a record that may be valuable if a foodborne illness should occur. Steps for a thorough record-keeping system include:

- Using organized, bound notebooks or written logs.
- Monitoring times and temperatures regularly.
- Keeping HACCP system flowcharts and recipes up-to-date and easily available for review.

Step 7—Verify that the System is Working

Retrace the flow of food and check how well your controls and procedures are working. Check to make sure that all the controls are in place. Observe employees and check log books regularly to make certain that everyone is following proper safety procedures. Test the information in the log against your own food temperature measurements to make sure that dry lab does not occur. **Dry lab** occurs when someone enters temperatures in the record book without actually measuring the temperature.

Remember!

No HACCP system is written in stone. Flowcharts, recipes, procedures, control measures, and corrective actions can always be changed to better suit the needs of customers and the operation.

Review Your Learning 2.2

1. What is a critical control point (CCP)?

   a. Point in a recipe when ingredients are added.
   b. Point where measures can be applied to prevent hazards.
   c. Point in the cooking process where food is tasted.
   d. Point when chemically contaminated food is found.

2. Ways to identify hazards include all the following except:

   a. Measure temperatures and test foods.
   b. Observe employees in action.
   c. Keep a personal food diary.
   d. Study your recipes.

3. What does a HACCP flowchart show?

   a. Specific job tasks of employees.
   b. Corrective actions to be taken.
   c. Flow of food through an establishment.
   d. Key food preparation skills.

4. What are the seven major steps in a HACCP system?

5. What are the three types of food hazards identified in a HACCP system? Give an example of each type.

2.3

SECTION 2.3

The Flow of Food

AFTER STUDYING SECTION 2.3, YOU SHOULD BE ABLE TO:

- Outline proper procedures for receiving, storing, preparing, cooking, holding, cooling, reheating, and serving food that includes use of proper tools and equipment.
- Compare different types of storage areas found in a foodservice operation.

As we discussed in the last section, the flow of food begins well before the food is prepared for service. At each step in the flow of food, various risks for contamination exist. Let's talk about the importance of the stages food must go through before it is served to the customer.

KEY TERM

- **First in, first out (FIFO)**

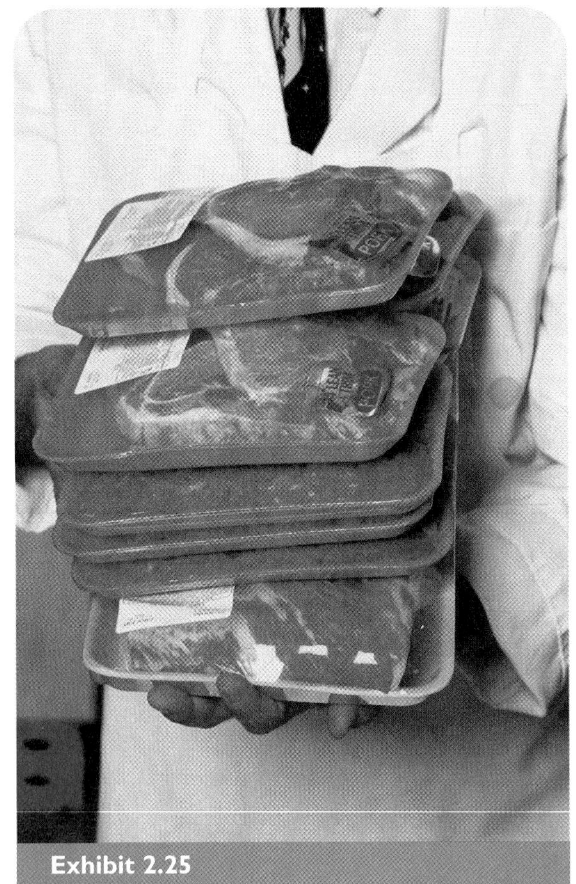

Exhibit 2.25
When receiving fresh ingredients, move them quickly into storage and keep them at the proper temperature.

Receiving

Why is receiving important to food safety? Receiving is the first time you get to examine food. Before you accept any delivery, you need to follow some very important food safety rules:

- Measure food temperatures and make sure the temperature is correct for each type of food. Reject food if the temperature is not correct.
- Reject any food past the use-by or expiration date.
- Look for any signs of possible contamination, such as damage or spoilage.
- Label and date all incoming foods.
- Limit the time food spends in the temperature danger zone (40°F to 140°F [4.4°C to 60°C]). Move foods quickly into storage, and do not leave goods on the dock or in hallways.
- Keep the receiving area clean, well-lit, and free of pests.
- Arrange to accept/schedule deliveries during non-busy times when you have time to inspect shipments carefully.
- Check to be sure delivery trucks are clean.

Reject any damaged cans. Check for:
- Swelled top or bottom.
- Rust.
- Leakage.
- Missing or unreadable labels.
- Flawed or dented seals or seams.

Never use homemade canned goods in foodservice.

Exhibit 2.26
Receiving canned goods.

Storage

Food can become contaminated or spoiled if stored improperly. Different kinds of foods have different storage requirements. However, there are a number of general storage rules you should follow to keep foods safe. Following are some tips for storing foods:

- Practice the **first in, first out (FIFO)** method of stock rotation. For example, if a can of peaches has a packaged date of June 8, 2002 and another can of peaches comes in with a packaged date of August 20, 2002, put the August 20 can behind the June 8 can. This way the older can will be used first.

- Store cooked food and food that will receive no further cooking above and away from raw food.
- If food is removed from its original packaging, it should be stored in clean, sanitized containers. These containers should be moisture- and pest-proof with tight-fitting lids. Label and date the containers. Throw away the original packaging.
- Store foods only in areas designed for food storage. Do not overload shelves or store food on floors or against walls. It is easy for pests to get into food if it is stored on the ground.
- Use foods before their use-by or expiration dates. Otherwise discard them.
- Do not line refrigerator or freezer shelves with paper or aluminum foil. This blocks the circulation of cold air.
- Keep storage areas and food-transporting carts and trays clean and dry. Clean up spills immediately.
- Check for signs of insects and rodents in storage areas and products. Dispose of all trash and garbage properly.
- Check the unit temperatures of freezers and refrigerators frequently to make sure they are operating properly.

Storage freezers are designed to keep frozen foods at or below 0°F (-17.8°C). Refrigerators are designed to keep chilled foods at 40°F (4.4°C) or below. Dry storage areas are used for storing dry goods such as flour, rice, and sugar. Maintain temperatures of 50°F to 70°F (10°C to 21.1°C). Humidity in dry storage areas should be kept at 50 to 60 percent.

Remember to store raw meat, poultry, seafood, and shellfish in the refrigerator on the lowest shelves. This will keep their juices from dripping on cooked or ready-to-eat foods and contaminating them.

Preparation

The greatest risk for contamination and temperature abuse occurs during preparation. Thawing food is often the first step in the preparation process. Exhibit 2.28 shows methods for thawing foods safely.

Never thaw food at room temperature!

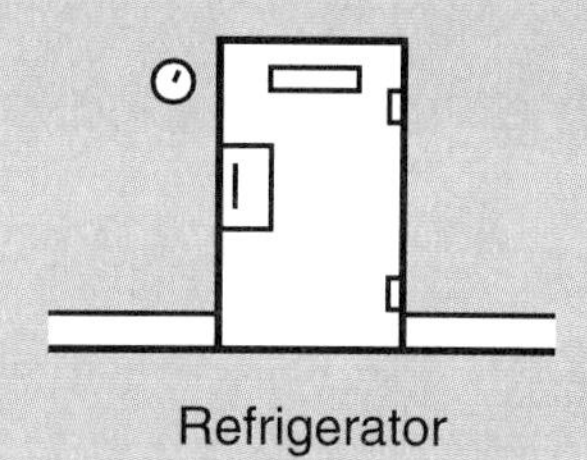

Refrigerator

In refrigerator units at temperatures below 40°F (4.4°C)—Always thaw foods in pans on shelves below ready-to-eat and cooked foods. For large items such as turkeys and roasts, be sure to save space in advance. They may take one to three days to thaw. Leave enough space for air to circulate around thawing foods.

Under potable running water at a temperature of 70°F (21.1°C) or below—This process can be continued only for a period of time during which any part of the food product does not have a temperature above 40°F (4.4°C) for more than four hours. Use a clean and sanitized food prep sink. Do not let water used for thawing splash on any other food or on anything that will touch food. After thawing is complete, wash and sanitize the sink and utensils used.

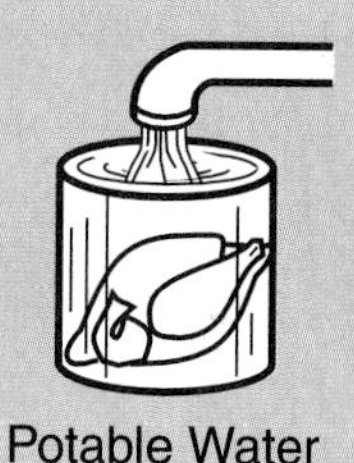

Potable Water

Microwave Oven

In a microwave oven—Use this method only when foods will be cooked immediately or if you plan to finish cooking them in the microwave. This method is not effective for thawing large items.

As a part of the cooking process—Foods such as hamburger and shrimp are often cooked while still frozen. This method is not effective for thawing large items.

Cooking

Exhibit 2.28
Methods of thawing food safely.

Cooking Food

Cooking foods to their proper internal temperatures is a way to control the risk of bacteria surviving. When cooking food, check the internal temperature with a clean, sanitized thermometer. Remember to check the temperature in several places, especially in the thickest part. Exhibit 2.30 is a chart listing some minimum safe cooking temperatures for food.

Holding and Displaying

When holding or displaying food, keep foods out of the temperature danger zone, or bacteria may begin to grow. Avoid preparing food any further in advance than necessary. This will decrease the chance of food remaining in the temperature danger zone for too long. Exhibit 2.31 outlines the general guidelines for holding hot and cold foods.

Exhibit 2.29
Foods must be cooked to their proper internal temperatures.

All raw animal food cooked in a microwave—165°F (73.9°C)

Poultry and stuffed meats—165° F (73.9°C) for 15 seconds; cook stuffing and meat first, then stuff the food

Ground beef, pork, ham, sausage, and bacon—155°F (68.3°C) for 15 seconds

Beef roasts—145°F (62.8°C) for three minutes; 140°F (60°C), temperature maintained for 12 minutes; or 130°F (54.4°C), temperature maintained for 121 minutes

Fish—145°F (62.8°C) for 15 seconds

Exhibit 2.30
Minimum safe cooking temperatures.

Exhibit 2.31
Guidelines for holding hot and cold foods.

Holding *Hot* Foods

- Hold hot foods at 140°F (60°C) or higher.
- Measure the temperature of hot foods at least once every two hours in more than one place. Be sure to check the temperature of the food itself, not just the holding unit. Record the temperature in a log.
- Do not add newly cooked food to food already in hot holding.
- Do not add raw food to cooked food.
- Stir foods regularly.
- Only use hot-holding equipment to keep food hot. This equipment is not designed to cook or reheat food.

Holding Both *Hot* and *Cold* Foods

- Use long-handled serving spoons or tongs, so hands are kept away from the food. When not in use, the serving end of each utensil should be in the food with the handle pointed away from the food, or it should be rinsed under clean running water.
- Keep serving containers covered.
- Transport food at proper temperatures in covered containers or packages to prevent contamination. Dollies, carts, and trays should be clean and sanitized.

Holding *Cold* Foods

- Hold cold food at 40°F (4.4°C) or lower.
- Measure the temperature of cold foods at least once every four hours. Be sure to check the temperature of the food itself, not just the holding unit.
- Do not mix fresh food with food already in cold holding.
- Arrange lighting on the unit to keep heat from the lamp away from the cold food.
- Wash vegetable garnishes and replace them if they become soiled by food.
- Ice is a food and must be made with drinkable water. Replace ice if it becomes soiled by food.
- Do not place packaged food, such as creamers, directly on ice. Prechill them, then place them in a metal pan and place the pan on the ice.

COOLING

Leftovers or previously cooked foods that are to be refrigerated need to be rapidly cooled to a product temperature of 40°F (4.4°C). The Food and Drug Administration recommends cooling foods from 140°F (60°C) to 70°F (21.1°C) in two hours and from 70°F (21.1°C) to 40°F (4.4°C) in an additional four hours, for a total cooking time of six hours. Exhibit 2.32 outlines how to cool food quickly and safely.

Never use refrigerators and freezers to cool large pots of hot food. This will not safely or thoroughly cool the hot food. Plus, it will make the air in the unit too warm to keep other foods at safe cool temperatures. Don't forget to label and date foods in the refrigerator!

REHEATING

Leftover and previously prepared foods must be reheated quickly and thoroughly before they are served again. The rule? Reheat food to 165°F (73.9°C) or higher for at least 15 seconds within two hours. If the food cannot be reheated within two hours, you must discard it.

Exhibit 2.32
Cooling food quickly and safely.

- Divide food into smaller amounts in one of the following ways.

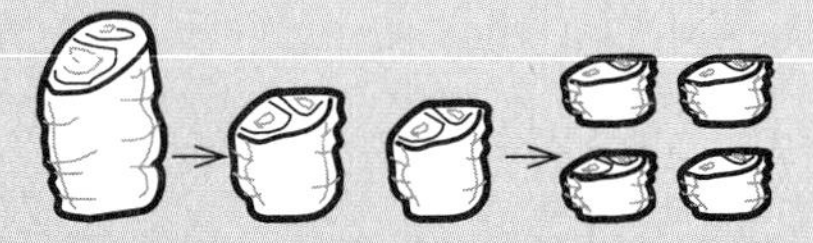

  - Cut large pieces of meat into smaller pieces.
  - Use pre-chilled, stainless steel shallow pans. Pour thick food, such as chili, to a product depth no more than two inches deep. Pour a thin food, such as chicken broth, to no more than three inches deep. Put pans on the top shelves of the refrigerator. Cover the pans after the food has cooled.

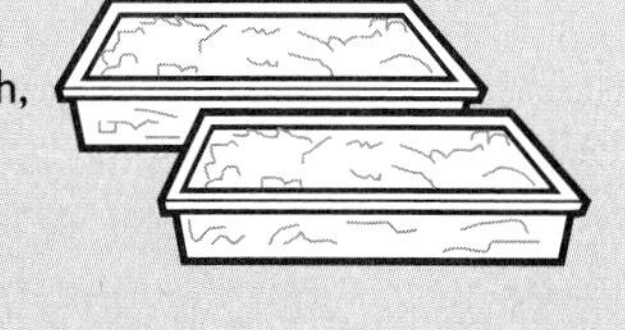

- Use an ice-water bath to cool a batch of food. Place the pot of hot food into a larger container. Surround the sides of the hot food pot with ice and water. Make sure you stir both the food and the ice. Add more ice when necessary.

- Stir food regularly.
- Place pans of food in a quick-chill unit such as a blast chiller (if your restaurant has one) for quick cooling.

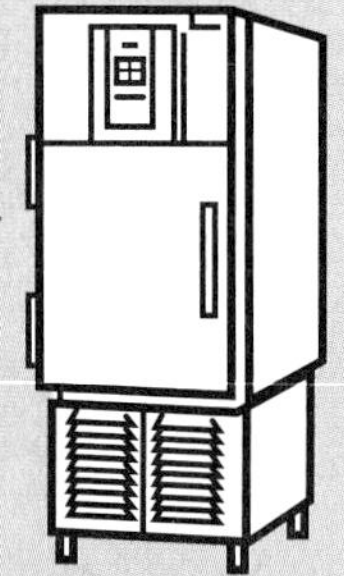

When reheating food:

- Use thermometers to measure the inside temperatures of foods as they reheat. Check the temperature in at least two different parts of the food.
- Never mix leftovers with fresh food.
- Keep food only two days before reheating, and reheat it only once. (This is not a regulation, but is a practice that many foodservice operations follow.)

IMPORTANT! Never use hot-holding equipment to reheat foods. Hot holding equipment will not heat the food quickly enough or hot enough to kill disease-causing micro-organisms.

Serving Food Safely

Self-service areas, such as salad bars, present particular challenges to food safety. These areas should be monitored regularly to discourage customers from unsanitary practices (such as tasting foods and serving foods without using the proper utensils). Here are some tips for monitoring self-service areas:

- Measure food temperatures at least every two hours.
- Be sure food protectors are in place during service.
- Take used plates and utensils from guests and give them clean ones when they return to the food bar.
- Replace all food and utensils that customers may have contaminated by touching them by the wrong ends, dropping them on the floor, or coughing or spilling on them.

- When in doubt, throw it out!
- Keep hot foods hot, cold foods cold!

Rule of Thumb:

When serving food to a customer, do not touch any part of the utensils, glasses, or dishes that food or the customer's mouth will touch.

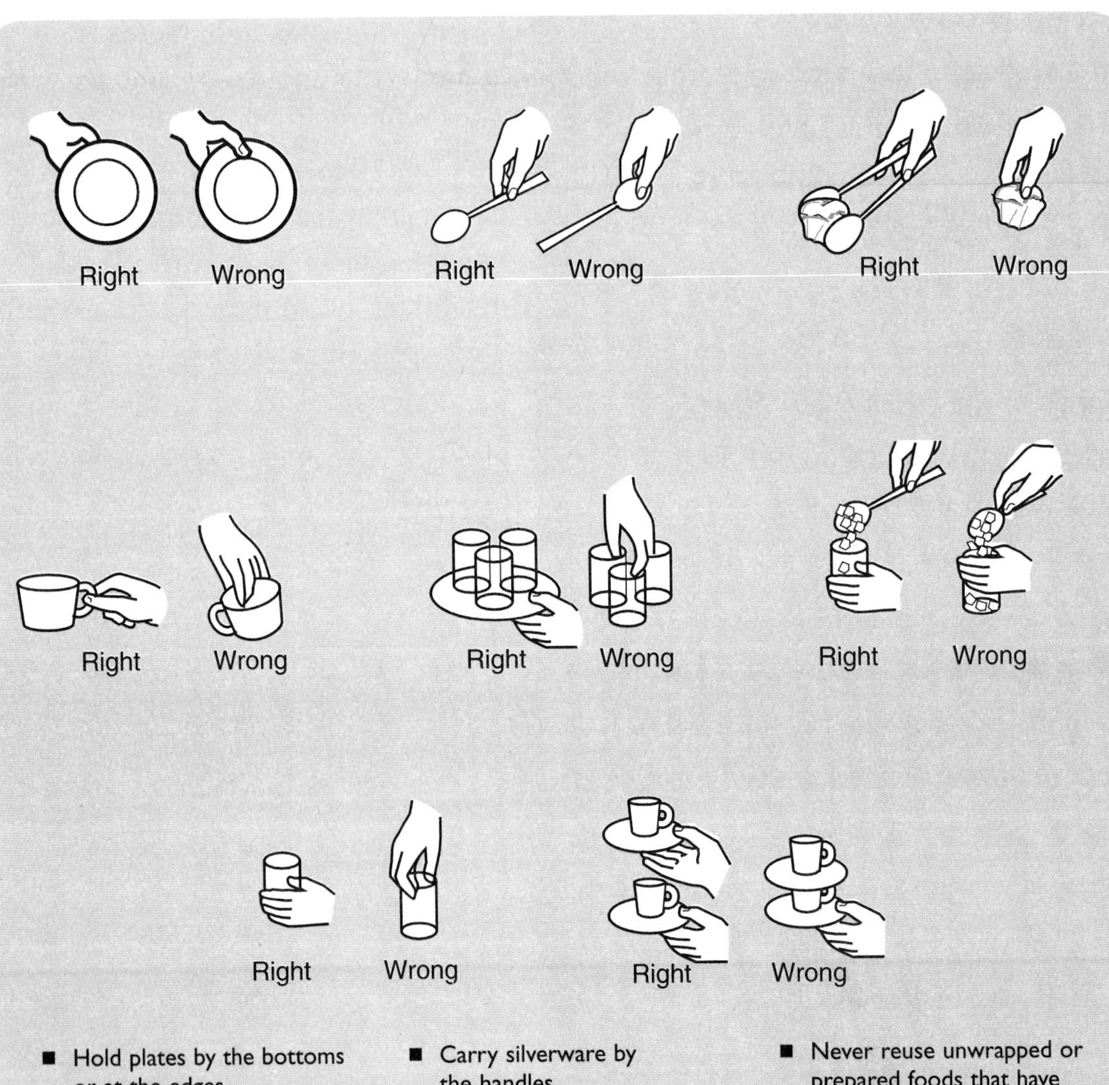

- Hold plates by the bottoms or at the edges.
- Grasp cups by the bottoms or by the handles.
- Never stack cups and saucers on top of each other.
- Carry silverware by the handles.
- Scoop ice with long-handled, non-breakable utensiles—never with a glass, cup, bowl, or a scoop without a handle.
- Never reuse unwrapped or prepared foods that have already been served to customers, including breads, rolls, relishes and sauces.

Exhibit 2.33
Serving food safely.

Review Your Learning 2.3

1. Which of the following is *not* proper procedure for receiving food?
   a. Check the temperature.
   b. Check for signs of damage or spoilage.
   c. Check for taste.
   d. Check that the delivery trucks are clean.

2. First in, first out (FIFO) is a:
   a. Method of stock rotation.
   b. Method of record keeping.
   c. Method for controlling temperature.
   d. Method of pest control.

3. Ways to chill hot foods quickly include all the following *except:*
   a. Divide food into smaller amounts.
   b. Place it immediately in the freezer unit.
   c. Use an ice water bath.
   d. Stir food regularly.

4. Ways to thaw frozen food safely include all the following *except:*
   a. Under running potable water at 70°F (21.1°C) or below.
   b. In a microwave oven.
   c. In refrigerator units at temperatures below 40°F (4.4°C).
   d. On the countertop.

5. If food is stored out of its original container, how should it be labeled?
   a. With the chef's name.
   b. With the contents and date.
   c. With the time and temperature.
   d. With your name and the date.

2.4

SECTION 2.4

A Clean and Sanitary Kitchen

AFTER STUDYING SECTION 2.4, YOU SHOULD BE ABLE TO:

- Define the difference between clean and sanitary.
- State procedures for cleaning and sanitizing tools and equipment.

Cleaning and Sanitizing

In a clean and sanitary kitchen, food moves quickly and efficiently, and has few chances of becoming contaminated, cross-contaminated, or kept too long in the temperature danger zone. A **clean** kitchen means it is free of visible soil, such as dirt and dust, and food waste. That's why the first requirement for any kitchen equipment is cleanability. Cleanability means that all surfaces and equipment are able to be cleaned quickly and easily.

Areas that come into contact with food must also be sanitary. **Sanitary** means free of harmful levels of disease-causing microorganisms and other harmful contaminants. Because such contaminants are often invisible, all surfaces that come into contact with food must be thoroughly washed, rinsed, and sanitized using very hot water or a chemical sanitizing solution. All dishes, glasses, flatware, pots, pans, utensils, and equipment must be cleaned and sanitized after every use to avoid possible cross-contamination.

KEY TERMS

- Clean
- Integrated pest management (IPM)
- Master cleaning schedule
- Sanitarian
- Sanitary

WHEN SHOULD YOU CLEAN AND SANITIZE FOOD-CONTACT SURFACES?

- *When beginning to work with another type of food*
- *After an interruption of service*
- *At least every four hours for equipment in constant use*
- *Once a day for grill surfaces and griddles*

REMEMBER! Cleaning and rinsing must be done before sanitizing. Sanitizing is NOT a substitute for cleaning.

Tableware, equipment (including cutting boards), and utensils can be cleaned and sanitized by hand in a three-compartment sink. Many high-volume kitchens prefer to use a dishwashing machine. Exhibit 2.34 lists the proper steps for both the manual and machine methods of cleaning and sanitizing.

There are a number of cleaning and sanitizing solutions that will help you do your job. Exhibit 2.35 shows some common cleaners and their qualities.

Sanitizing can be done either by chemical sanitizing or by immersing the object in hot water at 171°F (77°C) for 30 seconds (water in a dishwashing machine must be at least 180°F [82.2°C]). Chemical sanitizing is done by immersing an object in a specific concentration of sanitizing solution. You can also sanitize larger objects by rinsing, swabbing, or spraying them with sanitizing solution.

The three most common chemicals used for sanitizing are described in Exhibit 2.36. Each is relatively non-irritating. All chemicals must be mixed with water. Each requires the use of test kits to determine the proper amount of solution and water to mix.

Exhibit 2.34
Steps for cleaning and sanitizing.

Cleaning and sanitizing manually:

- Clean and sanitize sinks and work surfaces.
- Scrape and presoak items, then sort.
- In the first sink, wash in clean, hot (at least 110°F to 120°F [43.3°C to 48.9°C]) detergent solution.
- In the second sink, rinse in clear, hot (at least 110°F to 120°F [43.3°C to 48.9°C]), potable water.
- In the third sink, sanitize items using either a chemical sanitizing solution or hot water (171°F, or 77°C) for 30 seconds. Use a dip basket to allow complete rinsing of items.
- Air-dry all items. Do not towel dry.

Cleaning and sanitizing by machine:

- Flush, scrape, or soak items.
- Load the machine so all sides of an item are sprayed by wash and rinse water.
- Run machine following the manufacturer's instructions.
- Air dry all items. Do not towel dry.

Exhibit 2.35
Common cleaners.

Detergents
- Designed to clean almost anything
- Rinse easily
- High- or low-sudsing

Acid Cleaners
- Designed to clean scaling, rust stains, and tarnish
- Must be applied carefully

Solvent Cleaners
- Degreasers, used on greasy soil
- Alkaline (low-acidity)

Abrasive Cleaners
- Used for scouring
- Must be applied carefully to avoid damaging smooth surfaces

Exhibit 2.36
Chemical sanitizers include:

- Chlorine
- Iodine
- Quats (Quaternary Ammonium Compounds)

When using chemical sanitizers, read and follow the manufacturer's directions carefully. Always store chemical cleaners and sanitizers in a locked cabinet away from food preparation and food storage areas. This is to avoid any chances of foods becoming contaminated by chemicals.

WARNING: Read the material safety data sheet (MSDS) on each chemical that you use before you use it. (The MSDS is an informational sheet provided by chemical suppliers or manufacturers listing hazards and necessary precautions for safe use and storage of their products.) Carefully follow all directions when using cleaners and sanitizers. Never mix chemicals.

Follow these safety guidelines for storing chemical cleaning supplies:

- Store chemicals in their original containers or other sturdy, clearly labeled containers.
- If a chemical is put into a smaller container, label it with the contents and store it properly.
- Never store chemicals in food containers or use chemical containers to store food.
- Store chemicals away from food preparation and food storage areas.
- Never allow chemicals to touch or get into food. Discard any food that may become contaminated accidentally.
- Clean up any spills promptly.
- Properly wash your hands and, if necessary, change your uniform before returning to work.

Equipment

When selecting equipment, it is important to consider safety. Foodservice equipment should:

- Be easy to clean.
- Be made from non-toxic and non-absorbent materials.
- Have rounded edges or corners.
- Have smooth surfaces.
- Be resistant to cracking and chipping.

Fixed equipment, such as slicers, grinders, and cutting machines, comes with manufacturers' instructions for disassembling and cleaning that you should carefully follow. See *Chapter 5: Foodservice Equipment* for more detailed information on selecting and cleaning equipment.

Organizing a Cleaning and Sanitizing Program

A cleaning program refers to the system that organizes all the cleaning and sanitizing tasks in the kitchen. Foodservice organizations need an organized and well-planned cleaning program to make sure that clean and sanitary conditions are maintained at all times. Effective cleaning programs should be based on a master cleaning schedule for the entire foodservice establishment, from the dining room to the garbage area. Exhibit 2.37 shows a sample of a master cleaning schedule.

A **master cleaning schedule** includes the following information:

- What needs to be cleaned.
- Who is to clean it.
- How it is to be cleaned.
- How often it is to be cleaned.

Waste Management

How can garbage be a hazard to food safety? Garbage is wet waste, usually from

Item	What	When	Use	Who
Floors	Wipe up spills	As soon as possible	Cloth, mop and bucket, broom and dustpan	
	Damp mop	Once per shift, between rushes	Mop, bucket	
	Scrub	Daily, closing	Brushes, squeegee, bucket, detergent (brand)	
	Strip, reseal	January, June	See procedure	
Walls and ceilings	Wipe up splashes	As soon as possible	Clean cloth, detergent (brand)	
	Wash walls	February, August		
Work tables	Clean and sanitize tops	Between uses and at end of day	See cleaning procedure for each table	
	Empty, clean and sanitize drawers, clean frame, shelf	Weekly, Sat. closing	See cleaning procedure for each table	
Hoods and filters	Empty grease traps	When necessary	Container for grease	
	Clean inside and out	Daily, closing	See cleaning procedure	
	Clean filters	Weekly, Wed. closing	Dishwashing machine	
Broiler	Empty drip pan; wipe down	When necessary	Container for grease; clean cloth	
	Clean grid tray, inside, outside, top	After each use	See cleaning procedure for each broiler	

Exhibit 2.37
Sample master cleaning schedule.

food. If it isn't handled properly, garbage can attract pests. It can also contaminate food, equipment, and utensils.

Exhibit 2.38
Handling garbage.

- Remove garbage often to prevent odors and pests. Never allow garbage to accumulate inside or outside the establishment.
- Remove any garbage as quickly as possible from food preparation areas.
- Use clear plastic bags, or wet-strength paper bags that resist pests and leakage.
- Store bags of garbage inside leak-proof, water-tight metal or plastic containers with tight-fitting lids.
- Store outside containers on or above a smooth surface.
- Keep all containers tightly covered.
- Clean and sanitize garbage containers frequently and thoroughly within designated areas.

Recycling

Recycling preserves natural resources because used materials are not just thrown away, but are made into other usable products. Recycling also reduces the amount of trash found in our nation's landfills. Many communities now have programs to recycle solid waste. Solid waste is dry, bulky trash, such as steel cans, glass bottles, plastic wrappers, and cardboard boxes.

Common recyclables found in foodservice operations include:

- Steel food cans.
- Glass bottles.
- Plastic containers.
- Aluminum beverage cans.
- Paper.
- Grease or oil.
- Milk cartons.
- Food waste.

Recyclables are usually rinsed, crushed, and then placed in a separate and enclosed container. A waste hauler picks them up and they are processed for shipment back to steel mills, paper mills, and glass and plastics companies, which turn them into usable products. Even food waste can be recycled into mulch and fertilizer!

Check with your local recycling coordinator to find out what types of materials are recycled in your area. Your local government can provide you with requirements

Did you know?

About one and a half pounds of waste are produced for each restaurant meal served? A good recycling program can help control solid waste disposal costs, demonstrate a commitment to your local community, and provide resources for your local recycling industry.

for sanitary handling and storage of recyclables and for other ways to reduce solid waste. If you store items for recycling, make sure they are clean so they don't attract pests. Store all recyclables as far away from the kitchen and building as possible.

Controlling Pests

How do you prevent pests, such as rodents, cockroaches, and other insects, from entering your kitchen? Good housekeeping and sanitation are the first steps in pest control. However, often pest control requires greater effort or a system of integrated pest management. **Integrated pest management** is a system to prevent, control, or eliminate pest infestation in the foodservice establishment.

There are three rules of integrated pest management:

1. Do not provide food, water, or shelter for pests—follow good sanitation and housekeeping practices, such as those outlined here.
   - Use only reputable and reliable suppliers. Check all incoming shipments for roaches, ants, and roach egg cases.
   - Dispose of garbage properly and promptly. Keep recyclables as far away from the kitchen and building as local ordinances permit.
   - Properly store all food and supplies.
   - Keep cleaning equipment dry.
   - Wipe up all spills immediately and dispose of mop and cleaning water properly.
   - Keep food and soiled clothing out of employees' lockers.
2. Keep pests out in the first place by repairing, maintaining, and remodeling facilities. Here are some tips to prevent pests from entering a foodservice facility.
   - Use screens on all outside doors, windows, and other openings.
   - Check arches or framing around doors and windows regularly for cracks. Fill with caulking when necessary.
   - Be sure to close off spaces under large, immobile equipment that is fitted to its base or to the floor.
   - Cover basement and other floor drains with a perforated metal cap with a removable hinge.
   - Maintain exterior grounds by keeping the grass cut. Eliminate any

standing water on the property.

3. Work with a licensed Pest Control Operator (PCO) to get rid of pests that do enter the establishment. Foodservice operators must take necessary steps to prevent pests from entering the building or multiplying once they're inside. There are a number of things a foodservice operator can do to control pests before calling an exterminator. However, the actual process of pest extermination should be turned over to a licensed pest control operator.

Government Regulation of the Foodservice Industry

Governments became interested in food safety a long time ago. The first health laws in the Western world were written more than 400 years ago. The first health officer in this country was appointed when the United States was just a small group of British colonies.

Today, many government departments monitor food safety. These departments operate on the federal (national), state, and county or municipal levels. All offer guidance to the foodservice industry about food safety. Some of these agencies are also responsible for enforcing health regulations and safety standards set for the foodservice industry.

Federal agencies include:

- U.S. Department of Health and Human Services (HHS), which includes the U.S. Food and Drug Administration (FDA)
- U.S. Department of Agriculture (USDA)
- U.S. Centers for Disease Control and Prevention (CDC)
- U.S. Environmental Protection Agency (EPA)
- National Marine Fisheries Services (NMFS)

Foodservice Inspections

A foodservice operator's contact with health officials will most often be on the local (county or municipal) level. In general, federal agencies, such as the FDA, conduct research and determine minimum sanitation standards. Local agencies use these standards and monitor foodservice operations to make sure they are followed.

Foodservice managers should get a copy of local health codes and be very familiar with them. By knowing the requirements of the local health code, a

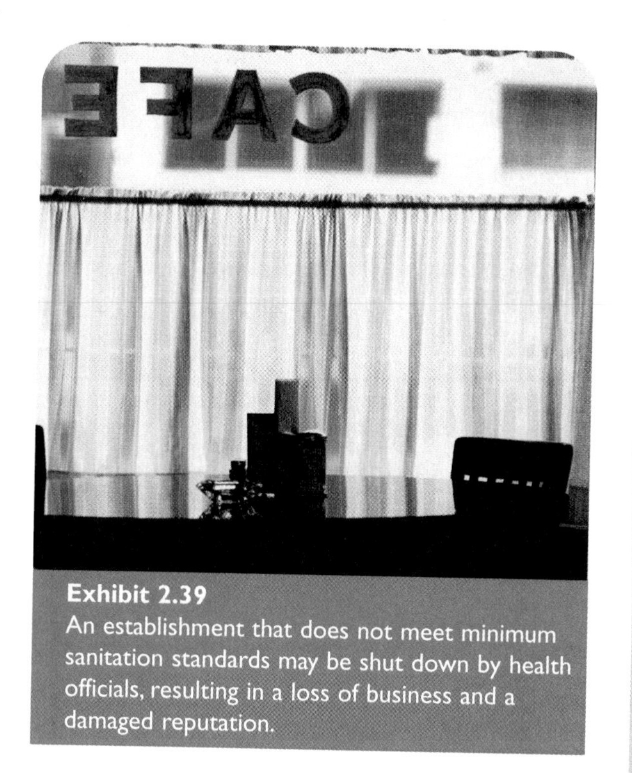

Exhibit 2.39
An establishment that does not meet minimum sanitation standards may be shut down by health officials, resulting in a loss of business and a damaged reputation.

manager can develop appropriate procedures to meet them. These codes are the guide that the sanitarian follows when inspecting a kitchen. Exhibit 2.40 shows a sample inspection form.

The FDA recommends that local governments inspect foodservice establishments at least once every six months. Inspections are done by a sanitarian, sometimes known as a health official or health inspector. The **sanitarian** is a person trained in sanitation principles and methods as well as public health. Sanitarians are employees of the state and local heath departments. Having a good relationship with a sanitarian ensures that you continue to learn and improve your food safety procedures.

HAZARD ANALYSIS CRITICAL CONTROL POINT MONITORING PROCEDURE REPORT

COUNTY	DIST.	EST. NO.	MONTH	DAY	YEAR

Establishment Name ______ Operator's Name ______
Address ______ County ______
(T)(C)(V) ______ Zip code ______
Food ______

Critical Control Point	Priority	Process (Step)	Monitoring Procedure	Name or Title of Responsible Person
YES ☐ NO ☐		CONDITION AT DELIVERY	☐ Approved source (inspected) ☐ Temperature check less than 45°F ☐ Not spoiled ☐ Shellfish tag complete	
YES ☐ NO ☐		STORAGE	☐ Refrigeration: Product temperature less than 45°F ☐ Raw/Cooked/Separated	
YES ☐ NO ☐		DEFROST	Methods ☐ Under refrigeration ☐ Running water less than 70°F ☐ Microwave ☐ Less than 3 lbs., cooked frozen	
YES ☐ NO ☐		COOK	☐ Greater than or equal to 165°F ☐ Greater than or equal to 150°F ☐ Greater than or equal to 140°F ☐ Greater than or equal to 130°F How determined ______	
YES ☐ NO ☐		HOT HOLD	☐ Product greater than or equal to 140°F Temperature checks every ____ minutes	
YES ☐ NO ☐		COOL	120°F to 70° in 2 hours; 70° to 45° in 4 additional hours by the following methods: (Check all that apply.) ☐ Shallow pans ☐ Ice water bath and stirring ☐ Reduce volume by ______ ☐ Rapid chill refrigeration Temperature checks every ____ minutes	
YES ☐ NO ☐		PREPARE AND SERVE	Maximum total time between preparation and service ____ hours ____ minutes	
YES ☐ NO ☐		SLICE, DEBONE, MIX, ETC.	☐ Wash hands ☐ Use gloves, utensils ☐ Workers' health ☐ Wash and sanitize equipment and utensils ☐ Minimize quantity of food at room temperature ☐ Use pre-chilled ingredients	
YES ☐ NO ☐		REHEAT	☐ Rapidly heated to 165°F How determined ______	
YES ☐ NO ☐		HOLD FOR SERVICE	☐ Hot product greater than or equal to 140°F ☐ Cold product less than or equal to 45°F Temperature checks every ____ minutes	

Actions that will be taken when the monitoring procedures are not met: ______

I have read the above food preparation procedures and agree to follow and monitor the critical control points and to take appropriate corrective action when needed. If I want to change any monitoring procedure, I will notify the Health Department prior to such a change.

Signature of person in charge ______ Signature of inspector ______

Source: New York State Department of Health

Exhibit 2.40
Sample HACCP inspection form.

Review Your Learning 2.4

1. Explain the difference between *clean* and *sanitized.*

2. How often should you clean food contact surfaces?

3. What should a good cleaning program cover?

4. How is garbage a hazard to food safety?

5. How can you prevent pests from entering a facility?

6. What is a sanitarian?

Flashback

CHAPTER 2

SECTION 2.1: THE IMPORTANCE OF FOOD SAFETY

- Serving safe, wholesome food that has been prepared by healthy workers in a clean and sanitary environment is one of the most important parts of a foodservice worker's and manager's job.
- All foodservice establishments share a common concern for food safety.
- Serving safe food is more than good business, it's required by law.
- An operation may be required to prove that they have done everything that could be reasonably expected to prevent foodborne illness by ensuring that safe food was served.
- Often, the foodservice establishment is ordered to pay monetary damages if a customer contracts a foodborne illness.
- A **foodborne illness** is one that is carried or transmitted to people by food.
- A **foodborne outbreak** is an incident of foodborne illness that affects two or more people.
- Food can become contaminated by micro-organisms such as bacteria, viruses, parasites, and fungi; food can become accidentally contaminated by chemicals or physical objects.
- High-protein foods are considered **potentially hazardous** foods and must be handled carefully to prevent bacterial growth.
- Bacteria require six conditions for optimal growth: food, acidity, temperature, time, oxygen, and moisture. These can be remembered by the letters *FAT-TOM*. By controlling these six conditions, you can help prevent bacterial growth.

SECTION 2.2: ESTABLISHING A FOOD SAFETY SYSTEM

- Many foodservice establishments follow a Hazard Analysis Critical Control Point (HACCP) food safety system to prevent foodborne illness.
- A **HACCP system** follows the entire flow of food to identify and correct food safety hazards before they happen. It does this through establishing critical control points.
- **Critical control points** are points where specific control measures can

be applied to:

- Prevent foods from becoming contaminated.
- Prevent contaminants from surviving.
- Prevent further growth of contaminants.

■ There are seven steps to design, implement, and maintain a HACCP system.

- Step 1—Assess Hazards
- Step 2—Identify Critical Control Points
- Step 3—Set Up Procedures for Critical Control Points
- Step 4—Monitor Critical Control Points
- Step 5—Take Corrective Action
- Step 6—Set Up a Record-keeping System
- Step 7—Verify that the System is Working

SECTION 2.3: THE FLOW OF FOOD

■ The **flow of food** is the path that food travels through a foodservice organization. It begins with the decision to include an item on the menu and ends with the food being served to the customer.

■ At every step in the flow of food, the potential for contamination of food exists.

■ Practice the **first in, first out (FIFO)** method of stock rotation. For example, if a can of peaches has a packaged date of June 8, 2002 and another can of peaches comes in with a packaged date of August 20, 2002, put the August 20 can behind the June 8 can. This way the older can will be used first.

■ One of the best ways to control biological hazards is to maintain proper temperatures of foods at all times.

■ You should follow proper procedures for receiving, storing, preparing, cooking, holding, cooling, reheating, and serving potentially hazardous foods.

SECTION 2.4: A CLEAN AND SANITARY KITCHEN

■ Kitchens should be designed for good sanitation and easy cleanability. Food areas must always be clean and sanitary.

■ **Clean** means free of visible soil and food waste.

■ **Sanitary** means that the number of harmful bacteria on surfaces and equipment has been reduced to safe/acceptable levels by using very hot water or a chemical sanitizing solution.

- **Integrated Pest Management (IPM)** is a system to prevent, control, or eliminate pest infestation in the food-service establishment.
- The three rules of IPM include good sanitation practices, repair and maintenance of facilities to keep pests out, and teamwork with a licensed Pest Control Operator (PCO) to exterminate pests.
- There are several government departments that monitor food safety.
- The Food and Drug Administration of the U.S. government recommends that local health departments inspect foodservice establishments at least once every six months to be certain that proper sanitation and food safety codes are followed.
- Foodservice managers should get a copy of local health codes and be very familiar with them.
- Inspections are done by a sanitarian, also known as a health official or health inspector. The **sanitarian** is a person trained in sanitation principles and methods as well as public health.

PROFILE

Herman Cain

Chief Executive Officer and President
National Restaurant Association

When I was in high school, I started thinking about going to college, and I asked my favorite teacher what I should major in. "Math," my teacher told me. I asked why, and he told me, "Because it's hard."

I took that excellent advice, and since then, I've done things not because they're easy or safe, but because they're challenging and difficult. I graduated from Morehouse College with a degree in mathematics, and went on to earn a master's degree in computer science from Purdue University. Then I found the restaurant industry.

After serving in the U.S. Navy, I worked for the Coca-Cola Company, the Pillsbury Company, and Burger King. In three years, I helped make my group of Burger King restaurants in Philadelphia some of the best-performing in the entire company. So I was offered the job of President of the Godfather's Pizza chain, which was suffering financial losses at the time. In less than two years, I helped turn the company into a success, and I led a group of managers in buying the company from Pillsbury.

This is the greatest industry in the world. It's exciting, it's always changing, and there are countless opportunities for people who are willing to work hard.

Keeping yourself and other people free from accidents and injuries is crucial in restaurants. You can work hard and still be careful. It's a matter of working smart, keeping your mind on the job, and remembering everything you've learned about your work. Accidents are expensive, and they can hurt people for life. There's never a reason not to keep yourself and others safe.

It might be hard, but working carefully and safely is a crucial part of the job.

CHAPTER 3

Preventing Accidents and Injuries

3.1

SECTION 3.1

Introduction to Workplace Safety

AFTER STUDYING SECTION 3.1, YOU SHOULD BE ABLE TO:

- State who is legally responsible for providing a safe environment and ensuring safe practices.
- Define the role of Occupational Safety and Health Administration (OSHA) regulations.
- State in your own words the Hazard Communication Standard requirements for employers.

SAFETY AND THE LAW

The safety of all customers and employees is the responsibility of every foodservice establishment. Customers have a legal right to expect safe food served in a safe environment on safe premises. **Premises** encompass all the property around the restaurant.

KEY TERMS

- **Carcinogenic (CAR-sin-oh-JEN-ick)**
- **Corrosive**
- **Hazard Communication Standard (HCS)**
- **Health hazard**
- **Liability**
- **Material Safety Data Sheet (MSDS)**
- **Occupational Safety and Health Administration (OSHA)**
- **Physical hazard**
- **Premises**
- **Toxic**
- **Workers' compensation**

Employees also have a legal right to work in a safe environment that is free of hazards. Restaurants that fail to provide safety for their customers or employees can be sued, and can lose their good reputation as well as large amounts of money.

Foodservice operators have become more aware of their responsibility—and possible liability—for their customers and employees. **Liability** means the legal responsibility that one person has to another. These responsibilities, or liabilities, are serious because they are enforceable by law in court.

Restaurant managers are expected to know about hazards, do whatever is necessary to correct them, and be sure there are proper warnings where everyone can see them. If an accident does happen, restaurants may be held legally responsible by the court.

Workers' Compensation

You may have heard the term **workers' compensation**, which is a state-administered program designed to help employees who are injured in accidents that occurred at work, or who become sick because of job-related reasons. Workers' compensation provides payments for lost work time, payments for medical treatment, and payments for rehabilitation and retraining for the injured employee.

Government Regulations

There are government rules and regulations that are strictly enforced to ensure that all employees in a foodservice establishment (or any establishment) are working in a place that emphasizes safety.

The **Occupational Safety and Health Administration (OSHA)** is the federal agency that creates and enforces safety-related standards and regulations in the workplace. OSHA has specific standards and forms for investigating and reporting

Exhibit 3.1
OSHA poster No. 2203.

accidents, injuries, and illnesses. Employers are required by law to inform employees of the job safety and health protection provided under the Occupation Safety and Health Act of 1970. Every foodservice operation must display an up-to-date version of the OSHA poster No. 2203 (or state equivalent), "Job Safety and Health Protection," where employees can easily see it when they report to work. This poster is so important that it can't be reduced in size or altered in any way from the original. Exhibit 3.1 shows a sample of this poster.

One of the most common OSHA violations found in restaurants is the lack of a hazard communication program. The **Hazard Communication Standard (HCS)** is also called Right-to-Know and HAZCOM. This safety standard requires that all employers notify their employees about chemical hazards present on the job, and train employees to use these materials safely.

Chemicals may be considered either physical hazards, health hazards, or both. **Physical hazards** are chemicals that are flammable, explosive, highly reactive to air or water, or stored under pressure that could cause damage to property and immediate injury (most commonly burns). **Health hazards** are chemicals that cause long- or short-term injuries or illnesses. Health hazards include chemicals that are **toxic** (poisonous), **carcinogenic** (cause cancer), irritating, or **corrosive** (cause a material to be eaten away or dissolved). Exhibit 3.2 lists some chemicals commonly found in foodservice operations.

Exhibit 3.2
Common foodservice chemicals.

CHEMICAL CLEANERS
- Ammonia (Quats)
- Brass and silver cleaners
- Chlorine bleach
- Coffee pot cleaners
- Degreasing agents
- Disinfectants
- Drain cleaners
- Floor cleaners
- Dishwashing machine detergent

FUELS
- Propane
- Butane

OTHERS
- Carbon dioxide gas cylinders
- Nitrogen dioxide gas cylinders
- Fire extinguishers
- Floor treatments
- Herbicides and fungicides
- Pesticides

Material Safety Data Sheets (MSDSs) describe the hazards of the chemicals in a foodservice operation. Each product has its own MSDS. Employees should be trained to check the MSDS for each of the products they use. MSDSs are usually supplied by the chemical manufacturer or supplier. The following information is what you can find on an MSDS.

Manufacturer Information.

The name, address, phone number, and emergency phone number of the manufacturer of the product.

Section 1—Product Identification.

The chemical and common or trade name of the product.

Section 2—Hazardous Components.

The chemical and common or trade name of each hazardous ingredient that makes up more than one percent of the product. Any product that is carcinogenic must be listed. There may be a U.S. Environmental Protection Agency (EPA) number if the product is regulated by them.

Section 3—Physical Data.

The product's appearance, odor, boiling point, pH, solubility in water, and other characteristics of the chemical.

Section 4—Fire and Explosion Data.

Special fire hazards, such as the flash point, flammability, and unusual fire and explosion hazards. Type of extinguisher and special firefighting procedures will also be included here.

Section 5—Reactivity Data.

Chemical stability and certain conditions that should be avoided, such as mixing the chemical with air, water, or other chemicals.

Section 6—Spill or Leak Procedures.

How to clean up spills and leaks, dispose of used chemicals, and store and handle chemicals properly.

Section 7—Health Hazard Data.

How the chemical enters the human body, such as by breathing or skin absorption, as well as the physical effects of exposure. A chemical that is cancer-causing will be identified here.

Section 8—First Aid.

Emergency procedures to follow if you come into contact with the chemical are explained here.

Section 9—Special Protection Information.

Personal protective equipment, such as gloves or eye goggles, will be described, as well as requirements for ventilation and work/personal hygiene practices.

Section 10—Additional Information/Precautions.

Any additional instructions for the product will be listed here.

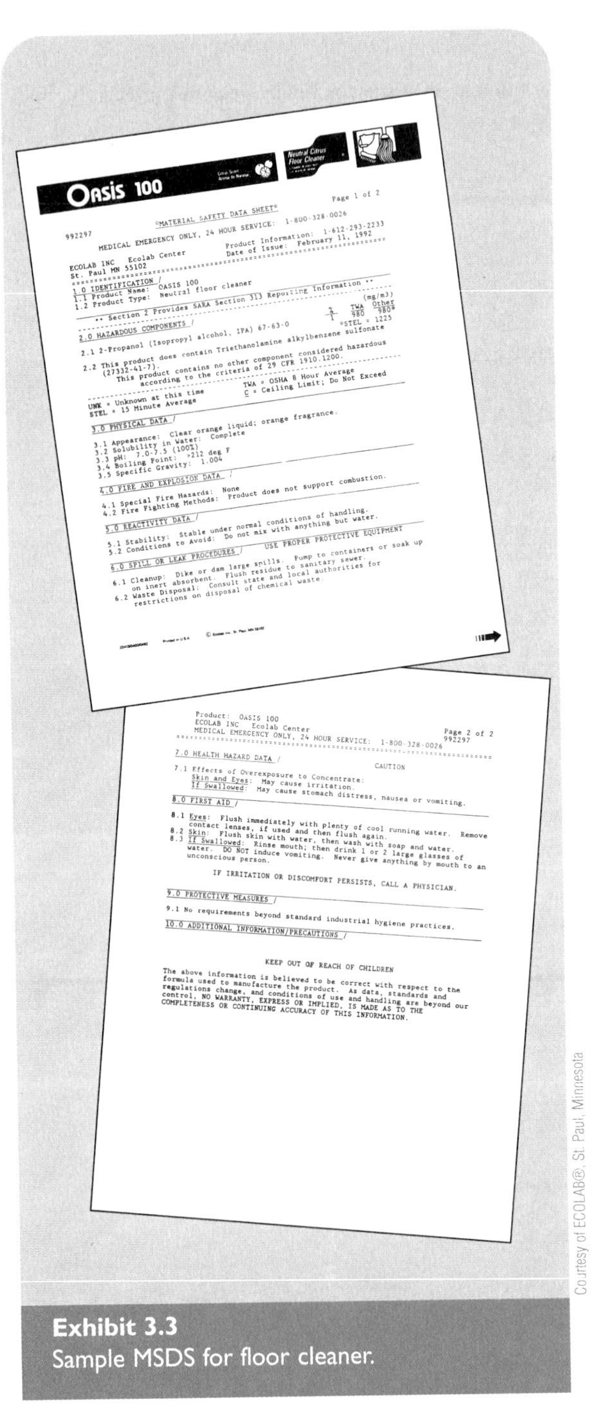

OASIS 100

Neutral Citrus Floor Cleaner

Page 1 of 2

992297

MATERIAL SAFETY DATA SHEET

MEDICAL EMERGENCY ONLY, 24 HOUR SERVICE: 1-800-328-0026

ECOLAB INC Ecolab Center
St. Paul MN 55102

Product Information: 1-612-293-2233
Date of Issue: February 11, 1992

1.0 IDENTIFICATION /

1.1 Product Name: OASIS 100
1.2 Product Type: Neutral floor cleaner

** Section 2 Provides SARA Section 313 Reporting Information **

2.0 HAZARDOUS COMPONENTS /

	%	TWA (mg/m3)	Other (mg/m3)
2.1 2-Propanol (Isopropyl alcohol, IPA) 67-63-0	1	980	980*

*STEL = 1225

2.2 This product does contain Triethanolamine alkylbenzene sulfonate (27332-41-7).
This product contains no other component considered hazardous according to the criteria of 29 CFR 1910.1200.

UNK = Unknown at this time
STEL = 15 Minute Average
TWA = OSHA 8 Hour Average
C = Ceiling Limit; Do Not Exceed

3.0 PHYSICAL DATA /

3.1 Appearance: Clear orange liquid; orange fragrance.
3.2 Solubility in Water: Complete
3.3 pH: 7.0-7.5 (100%)
3.4 Boiling Point: >212 deg F
3.5 Specific Gravity: 1.004

4.0 FIRE AND EXPLOSION DATA /

4.1 Special Fire Hazards: None
4.2 Fire Fighting Methods: Product does not support combustion.

5.0 REACTIVITY DATA /

5.1 Stability: Stable under normal conditions of handling.
5.2 Conditions to Avoid: Do not mix with anything but water.

6.0 SPILL OR LEAK PROCEDURES / USE PROPER PROTECTIVE EQUIPMENT

6.1 Cleanup: Dike or dam large spills. Pump to containers or soak up on inert absorbent. Flush residue to sanitary sewer.
6.2 Waste Disposal: Consult state and local authorities for restrictions on disposal of chemical waste.

Printed in U.S.A.

Product: OASIS 100
ECOLAB INC Ecolab Center
MEDICAL EMERGENCY ONLY, 24 HOUR SERVICE: 1-800-328-0026

Page 2 of 2
992297

7.0 HEALTH HAZARD DATA /

CAUTION

7.1 Effects of Overexposure to Concentrate:
Skin and Eyes: May cause irritation.
If Swallowed: May cause stomach distress, nausea or vomiting.

8.0 FIRST AID /

8.1 Eyes: Flush immediately with plenty of cool running water. Remove contact lenses, if used and then flush again.
8.2 Skin: Flush skin with water, then wash with soap and water.
8.3 If Swallowed: Rinse mouth; then drink 1 or 2 large glasses of water. DO NOT induce vomiting. Never give anything by mouth to an unconscious person.

IF IRRITATION OR DISCOMFORT PERSISTS, CALL A PHYSICIAN.

9.0 PROTECTIVE MEASURES /

9.1 No requirements beyond standard industrial hygiene practices.

10.0 ADDITIONAL INFORMATION/PRECAUTIONS /

KEEP OUT OF REACH OF CHILDREN

The above information is believed to be correct with respect to the formula used to manufacture the product. As data, standards and regulations change, and conditions of use and handling are beyond our control, NO WARRANTY, EXPRESS OR IMPLIED, IS MADE AS TO THE COMPLETENESS OR CONTINUING ACCURACY OF THIS INFORMATION.

Courtesy of ECOLAB®, St. Paul, Minnesota

Exhibit 3.3
Sample MSDS for floor cleaner.

To see how this information is shown on an MSDS, look at Exhibit 3.3, which shows an example of an MSDS for floor cleaner.

Some of this information may seem complicated, yet safety for guests and employees is very important for any restaurant's success. An effective safety program helps managers provide reasonable care, and can be used as written evidence that reasonable care was provided. A safety program can raise the overall quality of the dining experience of a restaurant's customers, lower operating costs, and increase profitability.

The following things are required in a restaurant's Hazard Communication Program:

- A written policy stating the establishment's intention to comply with OSHA requirements.
- An up-to-date, written inventory of every hazardous chemical product stored and used at the establishment, including the product name, the amount stored on site, and its location in the establishment.
- A Material Safety Data Sheet (MSDS) for each hazardous chemical on the written chemical inventory list. MSDSs must be stored in a central location that is accessible to all

Exhibit 3.4
Material Safety Data Sheets (MSDSs) must be stored in a central location that is accessible to all employees at all times.

employees all the time, for example, in the employee break room. MSDSs can be obtained from the manufacturer or supplier of a chemical product.

- Easy-to-read labels on each chemical container. The label must contain the name of the product, its hazards, and the name and address of the manufacturer.
- A written copy of the establishment's training program for employees.
- A written copy of the establishment's Hazard Communication Plan.

Review Your Learning 3.1

1. What is liability?
2. OSHA poster No. 2203, or the state equivalent, is required by law to be displayed. What type of information does it contain?
3. What does the Hazard Communication Standard require of employers?
4. What is a Material Safety Data Sheet (MSDS)?

3.2

SECTION 3.2

Preventing Fires and Burns

AFTER STUDYING SECTION 3.2, YOU SHOULD BE ABLE TO:

- Identify electrical hazards that contribute to accidental fires.
- Classify different types of fires and fire extinguishers.
- Outline proper actions to take in the event of a fire at a foodservice operation.
- Describe the ways to prevent burns.

KEY TERMS

- **Arson**
- **Heat detector**
- **Smoke detector**

Fire Hazards

Because fire is a major hazard, everyone should know how to protect themselves and their customers. Installing fire safety equipment, developing and publicizing evacuation routes, maintaining exit routes, and training and drilling employees are the main parts of a fire safety plan.

One-third of all accidental fires in restaurants are due to either faulty electrical wiring and equipment, or to improper use of equipment. Check for any of the hazards shown in Exhibit 3.5 before using any electrical appliance. Also, check for discharged or damaged fire extinguishers. Replace any that are not working properly.

Grease fires can be prevented by following a regular cleaning schedule for walls and work surfaces; ranges, fryers, broilers, microwave and convection ovens; heating, air conditioning, and

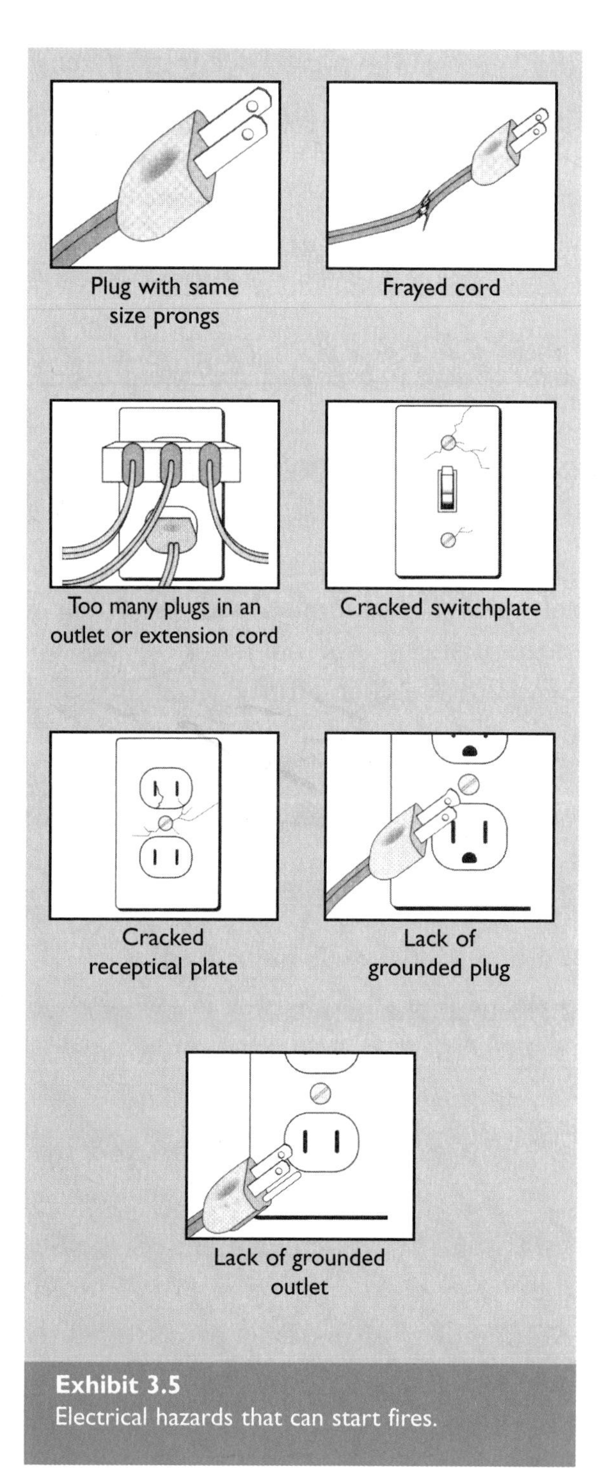

Exhibit 3.5
Electrical hazards that can start fires.

ventilation units; and hoods and filters. Keep all flammable items and materials away from heat sources, such as ranges and hot-water heaters. In addition, all linens, food in dry storage, boxes, and paper goods should always be stored away from corrosive materials, such as acid cleaners or bleaches. **Arson**, the deliberate and malicious burning of property, is very difficult to stop, but good overall fire safety and building security are ways to eliminate many of the opportunities for an arsonist.

Fire Detection Devices

Smoke and heat detectors should have a dependable battery-powered supply or hard-wiring hook-up, a loud alarm, and a test button. Exhibit 3.6 describes some of the different types of smoke and heat detectors. Most detectors work by reacting to heat, smoke, or flame. **Smoke detectors** require a flow of air in order to work well; they must not be located in "dead" spaces, such as the ends of halls, or between ceiling beams. Smoke detectors should not be used in food preparation areas. **Heat detectors** are able to detect fires where there is no smoke and are activated by a significant increase of temperature associated with fire. A fire safety expert should install and maintain all fire detection devices.

Exhibit 3.6
Common fire detection devices.

Smoke Detectors	
Ionization detectors	Use a small electric current to attract combustion particles from smoke, heat, or flames.
Photoelectric detectors	Use a beam of light located inside the device to react to smoke or flame.
Heat Detectors	
Thermostats	Contain a metal strip or disk that closes against an electric contact and starts the alarm when a preset temperature is reached.
Rate of rise detectors	Trigger an alarm when the temperature rises faster than a preset number of degrees per minute.
Flame detectors	Use infrared and ultraviolet sensors that respond to the movement of flame, or to its radiant energy.

Classes of Fires and Fire Extinguishers

All restaurant fires are classified as *A, B,* or *C.* Class A fires usually involve wood, paper, cloth, or cardboard and typically occur in storage rooms, dining areas, garbage areas, and restrooms. Class B fires usually involve flammable liquids and grease and typically occur in kitchens and maintenance areas. Class C fires usually involve live electrical equipment and typically occur in motors, switches, cords, circuits, and wiring. Different types of fires often require different types of fire extinguishers. Examples of the three classes of fires and the extinguishers that should be used on them are described in Exhibit 3.7.

Let a fire safety expert help you choose the right type of fire extinguishers for your restaurant. Automatic and mechanical extinguishers, sprinklers, and alarms need to be kept fully charged and inspected regularly. Extinguishers should be located near possible fire hazards, as well as along convenient exit routes. All types of extinguishing systems focus on four ways to put out a fire.

1. Remove the fire's fuel supply.
2. Deny it oxygen.
3. Cool the fire's fuel below its combustion point.
4. Disrupt the flame's chain reaction by using a dry chemical extinguisher.

Automatic systems operate whether the restaurant is open or closed. Automatic sprinklers provide early response to fire. Special kitchen sprinkler systems are required by the National Fire

Protection Association (NFPA) for deep-fat fryers, ranges, griddles, and broilers. These systems usually include a type of heat detector that releases dry or wet chemicals, carbon dioxide, or inert gases.

Hand portable fire extinguishers can be used for small fires, but the person using them must know the correct way to

Exhibit 3.7
The three classes of fires and the extinguisher types that should be used on them.

Ordinary

Combustibles

Class A (Ordinary combustibles)

- Wood, paper, cloth, and cardboard
- Most often occur in food storage rooms, dining areas, restrooms, and refuse storage areas
- Type A, or A/B/C extinguishers may be used on a class A fire
- Examples:
  - Fire in trash can
  - Cigarette igniting a tablecloth
  - Plastic container that comes in contact with a range burner or hot griddle

Flammable

B

Liquids

Class B (Flammable liquids)

- Flammable liquids, gases, grease, oil, shortening, pressurized cans
- May occur in kitchens (deep-fat fryers) and maintenance areas
- Only B/C extinguishers containing the dry chemicals sodium bicarbonate or potassium bicarbonate should be used on deep-fat fryer fires
- If a class B fire does not occur in a deep-fat fryer, any A/B or B/C extinguisher can be used
- Examples:
  - Flames from a grill igniting grease deposits on a hood filter in the kitchen
  - Aerosol cans stored near a heat source exploding

Electrical

Equipment

Class C (Electrical equipment)

- Live electrical equipment, cords, circuits, motors, switches, wiring
- Only those B/C and A/B/C extinguishers containing nonconductive materials, such as carbon dioxide, should be used on electrical fires
- Examples:
  - Fire in a toaster
  - Frayed cord igniting while a machine is operating
  - Fire in the motor of a grinder

use them. Fires only up to three feet tall and wide (or less) may be put out with a portable extinguisher. Larger fires are a job for the fire department. Hand portable fire extinguishers are marked with the type of fire they fight. Fire extinguishers should be stored securely in an easy-to-see location. When using any extinguisher, remember the PASS system, which is illustrated in Exhibit 3.9.

Exhibit 3.8
Types of hand portable extinguisher materials.

Water-based Extinguishers

- Rechargeable from a clean water source (all recharging and testing should be done by an approved fire extinguisher servicing company)
- Use on class A fires only

Aqueous Film-forming Foam Extinguishers

- Reduces temperature and supply of oxygen to fire
- Must be protected from freezing
- Use on class A or A/B fires
- Do not use on deep-fat fryer fires

Carbon Dioxide Extinguishers

- Gas-based mixture leaving no residue
- Limited in range
- May deplete user's oxygen supply
- Use on class B or C fires

Dry Chemical Extinguishers

- Interrupt chemical action that sustains fire
- Available in A/B/C and B/C
- Only B/C type should be used on deep-fat fryer fires

Exhibit 3.9
Use the PASS system.

Evacuation

To protect employees and customers if there is a fire, a well-designed and practiced emergency plan should be ready—in advance. Place the fire department and emergency rescue team telephone numbers on every phone along with a floor plan with escape routes, exits, and assembly points clearly marked.

Evacuation routes are usually planned to give everyone at least two ways out of the building to a safe meeting place. Be sure everyone knows the routes, exits, and meeting points. Keep routes and exits clear and unlocked; do not use them for storage or trash. Knowing and practicing fire safety procedures will help everyone remain calm if a fire should occur.

Plan for an evacuation:

- Mark each route with signs and lights.
- Provide emergency lighting (battery-powered).
- All exit doors should open outward without keys.
- Exit steps and ramps should be marked, kept clear, and repaired as needed.

What should you do if a fire occurs? First, *remain calm* and then:

- Start evacuating people *immediately*.
- Call the fire department. Do not assume someone else has called.
- Shut off the gas valve.
- Meet at the designated assembly point.
- Inform a firefighter if someone is missing.

Should You Fight a Fire?

The most important rule for fighting a fire is to *ask yourself if you are in danger*. The only fires that you may be able to handle are small, such as a fire in a single pan or a fire in a trash can. It is possible to smother a fire in a pan by turning off the heat source, covering the pan, and removing the pan from the source. For a fire in a trash can, you may use a fire extinguisher.

Use an extinguisher only after you have been trained, and always follow the instructions on the extinguisher.

Remember: If you have any doubt that you can fight a fire safely, *the best response is to set off an alarm and evacuate immediately*. If you decide to fight a fire, always leave a way to escape. If the fire is electrical or from an unknown source, notify the fire department, even if you think it is out.

Preventing Burns

Hot pans, dishes, food, and beverages can burn both customers and employees.

Correct uniforms and protective equipment (pot holders, gloves, and mitts) can protect employees against spattering, escaping steam, and hot equipment. Keep hand protectors dry; wet materials transfer heat quickly and can cause steam burns. If gloves are worn, they should fit snugly and must be made of nonflammable materials. Never wear rubber or disposable plastic gloves when handling hot items because they can melt and burn hands.

Exhibit 3.10
Call the fire department for assistance if you discover a fire.

Where there's smoke, there's FIRE!

According to the National Fire Protection Association (NFPA), **do not** *fight a fire if:*

- *There is thick smoke.*
- *The fire is so hot that you can't get close to it.*
- *The fire is more than three feet in diameter.*
- *The fire could spread to highly-combustible materials or to materials that could give off toxic gases.*
- *The proper type of fire extinguisher is not available.*
- *You have not been trained to use a fire extinguisher.*

Heat-resistant, knee-length aprons can also prevent burns from hot liquids.

Traffic patterns are especially important in the kitchen and serving areas. When carrying hot food or other hot items, warn others who may not see you that you are coming through. To prevent accidents from traffic patterns:

- Set patterns so, wherever possible, traffic is one-way.
- Maintain adequate travel and working space around heating and cooking equipment.

The best way for employees to avoid burns is to respect heat, and to always assume a heat source is on and hot.

- Keep all aisles and doorways clear of obstacles. Doors should swing freely and not be in the way of work areas.

When using deep-fat fryers:

- Dry off food or brush off excess ice crystals with a clean paper towel before placing it in the fryer basket.
- Fill fryer baskets no more than half full.
- Follow manufacturer's directions for cleaning, filtering, and adding new fat or oil.

When using steam equipment, check steamer and steam table contents carefully, always keeping your face away from escaping steam. Wear protective aprons and gloves. If steam tables are used in the dining area, post signs as necessary, and provide long-handled serving utensils so customers do not have to get close to hot equipment. Dishwashers should be careful removing dishes from hot water or a dishwashing unit that releases steam. Just-washed dishes are often too hot to handle, so other employees should also

Warn customers if plates, food, or beverages are hot. This includes items like soup and coffee. For coffee service, servers should hold the cup themselves or set it on the table to avoid spills and splashes. For the same reason, coffee cups or bowls of hot soup should not be filled to the rim. Always let customers know if the interior filling of a food is hot.

Exhibit 3.11
10 Steps for avoiding burns.

1. Be sure equipment is in good working condition.
2. Avoid overcrowding the range top.
3. Set pot handles away from burners, and make sure they don't stick out over the edge of the range top.
4. Adjust burner flames to cover only the bottom of a pan.
5. Check hot foods on stoves carefully, by standing to one side of the pot or kettle and lifting the edge of the lid farthest from yourself.
6. Place sealed pouch bags in boiling water carefully to avoid splashing.
7. Never leave hot fat unattended.
8. Ask for help when moving or carrying a heavy pot of simmering liquid off burners to storage or hot-holding areas.
9. Metal containers, foil, or utensils should never be used in microwave ovens.
10. Use hot pads and be careful removing food and food containers from the microwave.

Exhibit 3.12
Check pots of hot food carefully—avoid escaping steam.

Review Your Learning 3.2

1. What is the PASS system?
2. What are the three classes of fires? What materials burn in each fire?
3. What is arson?
4. What three things do detectors detect in the presence of a fire?
5. Name some basic traffic principles that can help prevent burns.
6. Name two safety guidelines for using a deep-fat fryer.

3.3

SECTION 3.3

Preventing Slips, Trips, and Falls

AFTER STUDYING SECTION 3.3, YOU SHOULD BE ABLE TO:

- List hazards that contribute to injury due to slips, trips, or falls.
- Outline proper procedures for cleaning up spills on floors.
- Demonstrate how to safely use ladders.

There are many ways you can help prevent common slips, trips, and falls. Most slips, trips, and falls occur on three types of surfaces: steps, floors, and pavement outside the building. These types of accidents usually occur while people are doing something else—walking, carrying objects—or simply daydreaming. The best way to safeguard customers and your coworkers is by anticipating what might happen. While prompt service is important, hurrying can cause accidents. Watch for chairs or tables sticking into aisles. For the safety of everyone, all aisles in serving and dining areas should be at least four feet wide.

Exterior areas should also be checked for weather hazards, such as snow, ice, flooding, standing puddles, or oil slicks. Debris, such as garbage or tree branches, should be removed, especially after storms or high winds. The parking lot should have adequate lighting to see possible hazards. Potholes or other damage to the pavement should be repaired as soon as possible. Sidewalks and ramps leading to the entrances of the restaurant

Never store items on steps or at the top of the stairs. A tumble down a flight of stairs can cause severe injuries.

should be clean and free of trash. Stairways should always be kept clear of boxes, bags, and equipment.

Grease and oil on floors is a major cause of slips and falls and can occur anywhere. To prevent grease buildup, floors should be thoroughly cleaned at least once a day, usually after closing. Floor coverings—carpets, rugs, mats, and runners—should be kept in good repair and regularly cleaned. They should fit smoothly and tightly to the floor. Rug and runner edges should be unfrayed, securely bound, and without any holes or tears, especially at the seams. Non-skid floor mats should be used in areas that often get wet or slippery, such as entrances, aisles, and food-preparation and serving areas.

Spills should be cleaned up immediately. While one employee is in charge of the clean-up, another employee should:

- Verbally warn nearby customers and employees.
- Block the area. Post a sign, such as "Caution—Wet Floor," while clean-up is happening.
- Leave the sign in place until the area is safe. If the spill is liquid and can't be cleaned immediately, use an absorbent compound to soak up the liquid.
- Direct people around the spill.

Stairs, ramps, and raised dining areas could cause people to trip because they often take people by surprise. Tell employees to remind guests of steps and raised dining areas, and to help those customers who may need assistance.

To prevent slips and falls in these areas:

- Provide adequate lighting.
- Clearly mark stairs and ramps.
- Be sure handrails are sturdy and secure.
- Check stair coverings for tears or ragged edges.
- Keep stairs clear of obstacles. Never use them for storage areas.

What would you do?

A young couple is seated in a booth near the kitchen door. They place an infant in a baby carrier on the floor because the carrier doesn't fit on the seat bench next to them. It sticks only about a foot into the aisle. What danger does this pose to employees and the customers? Based on what you know about both customer service and safety, what would *you* do?

Using Ladders Safely

Employees should always use a ladder or step stool to reach racks and shelves that are higher than shoulder level. Three common ladders used in storage areas are straight ladders, step ladders, and step stools. A straight ladder should reach three feet above the spot where you will rest the top of the ladder. Step ladders and step stools should be long enough so that you do not have to stand on the top step or reach above your shoulder to reach or place a load on a rack or shelf. Exhibit 3.14 shows different types of ladders you might use.

A ladder must be inspected to see that it is right for the job and is in good condition. Ladders are rated by the weight they can safely carry, and each ladder should be labeled with this information. All parts of the ladder should be in good condition. All ladders should have nonskid feet and should be long enough for safe support.

The safest way to use a ladder is for two employees to work together: one person should hold the bottom of the ladder, and the other person should pass or receive items. Here is how to use a ladder safely.

- Always work with someone who can hold the bottom of the ladder and pass or receive items. Be very careful if you must work alone.
- Set the ladder away from overhead obstacles. If you are working outside, keep the ladder out of strong gusts of wind.
- Rest the ladder feet on a firm, flat, and clean surface. Do not try to make it taller by placing it on boxes or other objects.
- The ladder should be within easy reach of the items you need or the place where you will store items.

Exhibit 3.13
Ways to safeguard customers and coworkers from trips and falls.

- Check for places where customers and employees might run into equipment, furniture, or each other.
- Watch for tables or chairs sticking into aisles, and for food or standing water on the floor or on mats in front of salad bars and buffets.
- Remind guests to step up or down for raised dining areas and help those who may have difficulty walking, have poor eyesight, or are talking to their friends and not paying attention.
- Be careful during rush hour periods to avoid running into coworkers or customers.
- Never run or become involved in horseplay with other employees. Safety is one of your most important responsibilities.

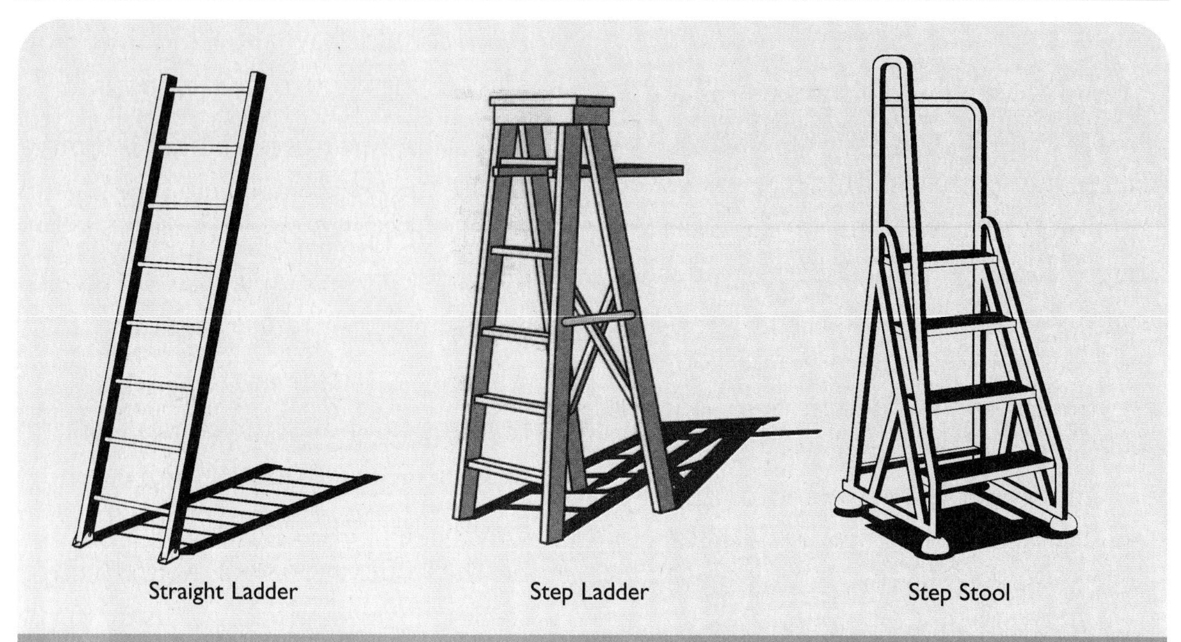

Exhibit 3.14
Different types of ladders.

- Lock the folding bar of a step ladder or step stool in place.
- Test the ladder's balance before climbing.
- Never put a metal ladder on, or near, electrical wiring, service boxes, or equipment.
- Lock doors near the ladder or do not use the ladder near unlockable doors that someone may open.
- Use at least one hand to steady yourself as you climb. If an object cannot be carried easily in one hand, get help from someone, or leave the object where it is until you can get help.
- Be careful not to lean too far to one side to reach an item. Move the ladder closer.
- Do not stand on the top two rungs of a straight ladder or the top step of a step ladder or step stool.
- When the job is completed, chain or secure the ladder to prevent it from falling on anyone.

Exhibit 3.15
Working together on a ladder.

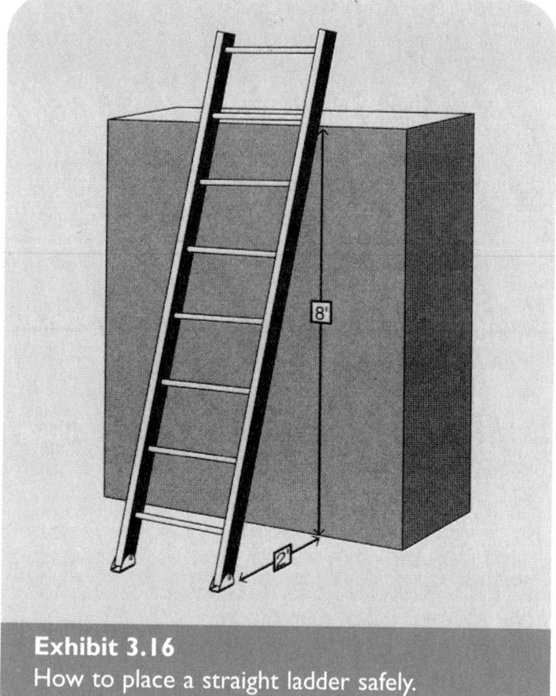

Exhibit 3.16
How to place a straight ladder safely.

Review Your Learning 3.3

1. True or false: You can use stairways for storage as long as items are against the wall.
2. True or false: It is safe to stand on the top step of a ladder if someone is holding it steady for you.
3. Name three things you should do when there is a spill being cleaned up.
4. What can you do to prevent slips and falls on stairs and ramps?
5. What information should be on the label of a ladder?

3.4

SECTION 3.4

Lifting and Carrying Safely

AFTER STUDYING SECTION 3.4, YOU SHOULD BE ABLE TO:

- Demonstrate proper lifting and carrying procedures to avoid injury.

Even though your back has some of the strongest muscles in your body, you need to use them carefully each time you lift. Athletes do warm-up exercises to protect their muscles and backs from injury. It's a good idea to do some warm-up exercises for a few minutes to prepare muscles for lifting. As always, you should check with a doctor for exercises that are right for you.

Good storage practices and special lifting techniques are needed to prevent back injuries. Heavy loads can be stored on waist-level shelves and racks. Lighter items should be stored on the top shelves. Extra heavy loads should be marked.

Think about it...

When you see Olympic weight lifters, you can see much of their strength is in their legs. For the first part of the lift, they bend at the knees and lift with their legs. That's why their leg muscles are so strong and developed.

Safe Lifting Practices

Before you lift anything, think out each step from beginning to end for safe lifting. Never take a risk with your back. Take the following precautions before lifting anything.

- Wear sturdy, non-skid shoes and be sure the laces don't trail on the ground.
- Don't wear loose clothes that might catch on the load or on a nearby object and throw you off balance.

- Check the weight of the load. If you don't know the weight of the load, test it carefully while it is still on the floor or shelf by lifting a corner and setting it down again.
- Look for hand holds that can be gripped with the whole hand. Wear gloves if the load is slippery or has sharp edges.
- Check the balance of the load. The contents of a box might have moved to one side, or a piece of equipment may be much heavier at one end. You don't want any surprise shifts in weight during the lift.
- Ask for help if the load seems too heavy or hard to move.
- Use hand trucks, dollies, or carts for moving heavy loads.
- Use proper lifting techniques.

Exhibit 3.17
Safe lifting practices.

1. **Establish solid footing**. Check the conditions of the floor. Stand close to the load, with your feet shoulder-width apart. Put one foot slightly in front of the other.
2. **Align your body**. Stand straight. Face the load. Bend at your knees—not at the waist—and lower yourself—with the leg muscles—to reach the load.
3. **Make the lift**. Grip the load with your whole hand—*not* just your fingers. Keep your wrists as straight as possible. Tighten your stomach muscles and align your back. Arch your lower back by pulling your shoulders back and sticking out your chest. When getting a load off a lower rack, set your grip and check the weight before pulling the load off a rack. Transfer the weight immediately to your legs. Lift with your legs taking the weight. Smoothly and slowly take the load up. Do not twist as you stand up. If the load is too heavy, slowly bend your knees and carefully set down the load on the floor.
4. **Set down the load**. Keep your lower back pulled in by tightening stomach muscles. Keep the weight of the load on the legs. Bend at the knees and smoothly go down. Set down a corner of the load, slide your hand out from under it, and settle the rest of the load.

Carrying Safely

The principles of good lifting are also true for safe carrying. Servers and busers should plan their route to keep their body and load in balance while they are moving. In foodservice operations, people with heavy objects always have the right of way. The proper way to carry a tray is with one hand in front, and one hand in the middle, under a balanced load. It is helpful to have a tray stand already set up, or to have another employee set it up for the one carrying the tray. Employees should carry loads using the steps outlined in Exhibit 3.20.

Sometimes it is necessary to move large pieces of equipment for cleaning. Here are some ways to move large items safely when they have wheels or are on casters.

- Spread feet wide apart, with one foot in front of the other; bend the knee on the front leg.
- Keep back straight.
- Get a firm grip on the item.
- Use body weight to slowly lean into the load; use leg strength to push in a smooth manner.
- Move loads on wheels carefully, pushing—instead of pulling or jerking.

Exhibit 3.18
Always carry trays with one hand in the middle under a balanced load.

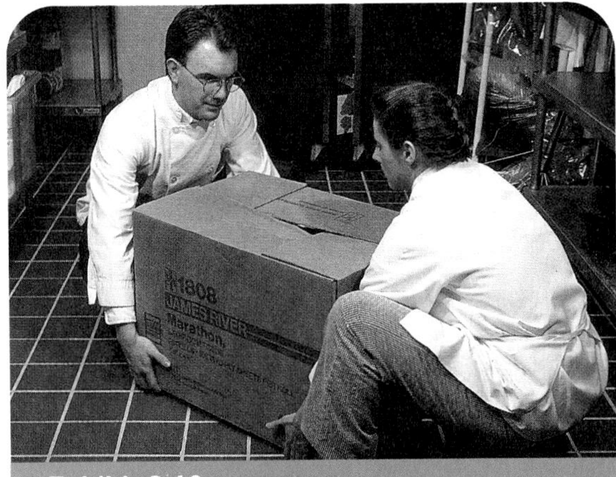

Exhibit 3.19
Lifting and carrying loads together.

Exhibit 3.20
Steps for carrying loads.

1. Look for any hazards, such as slippery floors, people, pieces of furniture or equipment out of place, spills, sharp corners, carpeting tears, narrow hallways, and stairs. Check also for safe places to set down the load if necessary.
2. Use the whole hand to grip the load, *not* just the fingers.
3. Keep the load close to the body for good balance. Keep elbows against sides of the body to prevent bumping into anything.
4. Keep stomach muscles firm and tuck in the lower back. The load should be carried by the legs, not the back.
5. Move your feet instead of twisting at the waist when turning.

Review Your Learning 3.4

1. What precautions should be taken before lifting anything?
2. Describe the proper way to lift heavy objects.
3. Name three hazards to look for in planning your route for carrying.
4. Following safe lifting and carrying guidelines helps prevent injury to what important part of the body?
5. Always lift with you legs and not just your ______________ .

3.5

SECTION 3.5

Preventing Cuts

AFTER STUDYING SECTION 3.5, YOU SHOULD BE ABLE TO:

- Locate and list hazards that can cause cuts.
- Demonstrate correct and safe use of knives.

Cuts can happen more frequently to kitchen employees, but other employees and customers could be hurt from broken glass or sharp tableware. Some sharp hazards are:

- Cans, can lids, and can openers
- Cutting strips on boxes of aluminum foil and plastic wrap
- Wooden crates (splinters and nails or staples)
- Box openers and utility knives
- Steak and chef knives; single-use plastic knives
- Broken bottles, glasses, and dishes
- Machinery with blades: slicers, grinders, choppers, blenders

One Rule is Essential

Always concentrate and focus on the task at hand. This is one of the best ways to prevent injuries from knives or machinery.

To avoid cuts, follow these kitchen safety tips:

- Use gloves or a towel to protect hands while removing lids from glass bottles or jars.
- Use proper openers on bottles and cans; never use knives.
- Use plastic or metal scoops and ladles to handle food and ice; never use drinking glasses for these tasks.

- Cover food with plastic wraps or lids instead of glass.
- Never cool glasses, bottles, or carafes in ice intended for food or beverages.
- Throw out nearby food or ice when glass is broken.
- Glasses, bottles, and dishware should not be stored above or near ice machines or food preparation areas. If something breaks, pieces of glass may get into the ice that is served to customers. If glass is broken in an ice machine, the ice has to be melted and drained. After this is done, the glass can be taken out and the machine cleaned and sanitized thoroughly.

How should you clean up and discard glass and cans? Rinse empty glass containers and metal cans and store them in properly marked containers. Broken glass should be cleaned up immediately. If possible, provide a container that is used only for broken glass and is clearly marked. This will help reduce injuries to employees taking out the trash. Wear protective gloves when cleaning up glass. For large broken glass pieces, use a dust pan and brush. Never throw broken glass any distance into a waste bin or put it down a drain. If glass is broken in areas where there are customers, instruct the customers to stay seated, and not to help with the clean up.

Exhibit 3.21
Protect your fingertips when chopping and slicing.

It's important to be careful with other sharp edges as well. Keep your hands away from the metal cutting strip or serrated edge when using plastic wrap or foil, and keep it covered when not in use. Pull the plastic wrap or foil straight out and hold onto the edge, using pressure on the plastic or foil, rather than your hands, to pull it against the metal strip and cut it.

Using Knives Safely

Knives are a standard tool in the kitchen, but they can very be dangerous if not handled properly. Each type of knife has a specific use. Sharp knives are much safer than dull ones. They cut more evenly and with less work. Because sharp knives give you more control, knives should be sharpened regularly and safely. Knife skills will be covered in more detail in *Chapter 4: Kitchen Basics*.

Cleaning Equipment Safely

It is important to keep hands, the equipment, and the floor as clean and dry as possible. Never operate equipment for which you have not received training. By law, employees under age 18 are not allowed to operate or clean large electrical equipment with blades, such as slicers.

Before using machinery, check the cords, plugs, and belts for wear or cracking, and check that all guards and safety devices are in place. All settings must be correct for operation. When equipment is running, keep your hands and eyes away from moving parts. Wear gloves, goggles, and sleevelets or arm protectors when necessary—food may be thrown back out before it is mixed in. Never stir or add food to a mixer while it is running. Equipment safety information is discussed in more detail in *Chapter 5: Foodservice Equipment*.

Exhibit 3.22
10 safe knife handling practices.

1. Keep knives sharpened. A sharp blade cuts more evenly and with less force than a dull blade.
2. Never touch knife blades.
3. Use a knife only for its intended purpose.
4. Place a damp cloth under a cutting board to help prevent slipping of the board.
5. Stop cutting and place knife down on a flat and secure surface if an interruption occurs.
6. Never leave knives soaking under water.
7. Never try to catch a falling knife; step out of its way.
8. Carry knives with the cutting edge angled slightly away from your body.
9. To pass a knife, place it down on a sanitized surface, and let the other person pick it up by the handle.
10. Store knives properly in racks, scabbards, or sheaths.

Exhibit 3.23
You should be properly trained before using any piece of foodservice equipment.

Review Your Learning 3.5

1. Name three sharp hazards you are likely to find in a kitchen.
2. Where should you avoid storing glasses, bottles, and dishware? Tell why.
3. Name four kitchen safety tips.
4. What should you tell customers if glass is broken in areas where they are seated?
5. What is the proper way to pass a knife to another person?
6. What should you do when a knife falls?

3.6

SECTION 3.6

Safe Driving and First Aid

AFTER STUDYING SECTION 3.6, YOU SHOULD BE ABLE TO:

- List safe driving techniques.
- Outline basic first aid concepts and procedures.

Safe Driving

Safe driving techniques are important not only for making deliveries, but also for running work-related errands or going on catering jobs. Employers should develop a defensive driving program that provides overall guidelines and training. Managers should also check the driving records of employees hired to drive. Safe driving requirements include the following.

- Wear seatbelts at all times.
- Lock all doors.
- Obey traffic laws, posted warning signs, and speed limits.
- Do not smoke while driving, since lighting and extinguishing cigarettes or smoking materials can be a distraction.

KEY TERMS

- **Cardiopulmonary resuscitation (CPR) (CAR-dee-oh-PULL-man-air-ee ree-SUHS-i-TAY-shun)**
- **First aid**
- **Heimlich maneuver (HIME-lick mah-NOO-ver)**

Remember...

Drivers must never drink or use drugs before or during their shift!

First Aid

First aid refers to medical treatment given to an injured person either for light injuries or until more complete treatment can be provided by emergency service or other health care providers. Effective first aid meets the injured person's emotional as well as medical needs, and helps diffuse the shock, anger, and resentment an injured person may feel toward your operation. A good first aid program requires equipment, training, a concerned attitude for the injured, and thorough follow-up. To ensure employee and customer safety, always remember:

- Accidents can be prevented.
- Accidents have serious results.
- You have a large responsibility to keep yourself safe.
- You have a large responsibility to keep your customers and other employees safe.

First aid kits are required by some state and local agencies. Kits should be located within easy reach of possible accident sites inside the restaurant, and also placed in delivery or catering vehicles if employees often work away from the establishment. Exhibit 3.24 shows a standard first aid kit.

Most foodservice injuries requiring first aid are limited to minor heat burns, chemical burns, cuts, sprains, and muscle cramps. The need for cardiopulmonary resuscitation (CPR) and Heimlich maneu-

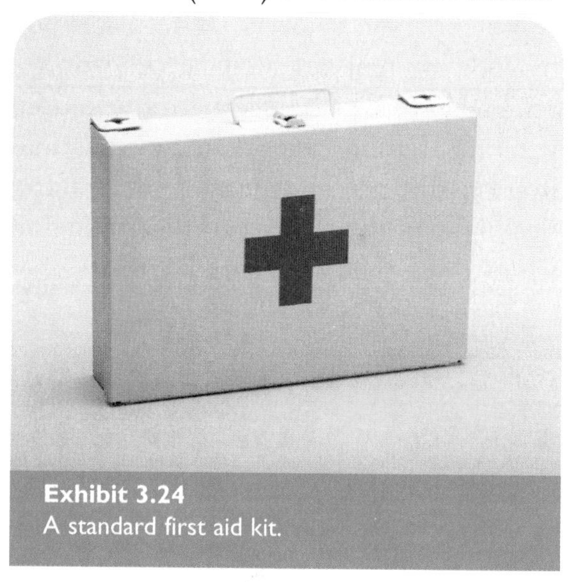

Exhibit 3.24
A standard first aid kit.

ver training should be carefully assessed. **Cardiopulmonary resuscitation (CPR)** (CAR-dee-oh PULL-man-air-ee ree-SUHS-i-TAY-shun) restores breathing and heartbeat to injured persons who show no signs of breathing or pulse.

The **Heimlich maneuver** (HIME-lick mah-NOO-ver) removes food or other obstacles from a person's airway if someone is choking. Some states require either employee training in the Heimlich maneuver, or displaying posters in the restaurant that describe the steps in the procedure. Exhibit 3.25 illustrates the two steps to the Heimlich maneuver.

Training and certification for CPR and the Heimlich must be renewed every year. There should be at least one trained and certified person on every shift. In addition to knowing first aid medical procedures, remember to show concern for the injured person. Training should include instruction on staying calm in emergencies and dealing with the shock and disorientation felt by those who are injured.

CPR and the Heimlich maneuver can save lives, but they are difficult to do and may cause harm to the injured person if not done properly. CPR should not be administered unless an employee has a current certification from a recognized provider of first aid training.

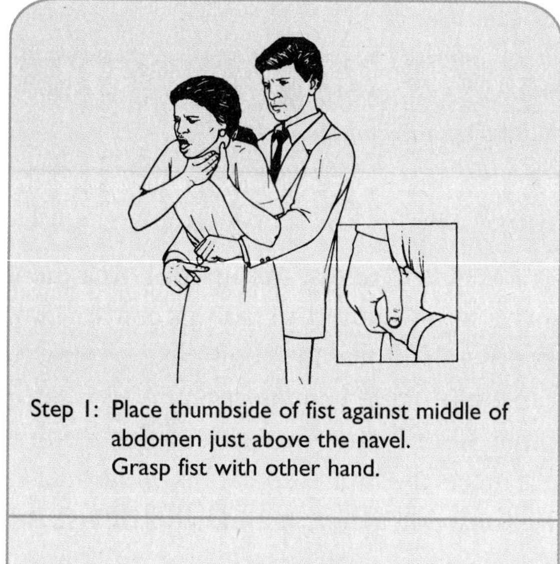

Step 1: Place thumbside of fist against middle of abdomen just above the navel. Grasp fist with other hand.

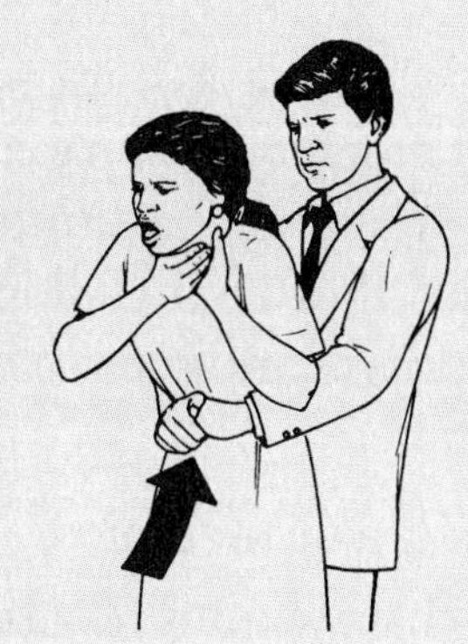

Step 2: Give quick, upward thrusts.

Exhibit 3.25
The Heimlich maneuver should be repeated until the object is coughed up or the person becomes unconscious.

It is recommended that all employees be trained in handling emergencies that could happen at your operation. These emergencies might include:

- Foodborne illness outbreaks.
- Employees with contagious illnesses.
- Customer or employee injuries on site.
- Accidents involving restaurant vehicles.
- Loss of power, water, or other utilities.
- Fires.
- Floods, storms, earthquakes, and other dangerous weather conditions.
- Armed robberies and other criminal assaults.

Review Your Learning 3.6

1. True or false: It is important for employees to receive special instruction and training before performing the Heimlich maneuver and CPR.
2. True or false: Good first aid can meet injured persons' immediate emotional needs as well as their medical needs.
3. Name three emergencies that are likely to occur in a restaurant.
4. When is the Heimlich maneuver performed?
5. What is first aid?
6. When is CPR performed?
7. Where should first aid kits be located?

3.7

SECTION 3.7

Safety as an Ongoing Process

AFTER STUDYING SECTION 3.7, YOU SHOULD BE ABLE TO:

- Explain the importance of the general safety audit.
- Explain the importance of completing standard reports for any accident or illness at the operation.
- List ways to use protective clothing and equipment to prevent injuries.

KEY TERMS

- **Accident**
- **General safety audit**
- **Near miss**

THE SAFETY AUDIT

Is your restaurant safe? Safety program guidelines should be based on the operation's existing safety practices and the insurance carrier's requirements. Any safety program must meet the operation's specific needs. It should also include other items, depending upon the geographic location, such as snow and ice removal, flood water drainage, or earthquakes.

The purpose of a general safety audit is to give you an overview of the level of safety in the establishment. A **general safety audit** is a safety inspection of an operation's facilities, equipment, employee practices, and management practices. In a general safety audit, any areas or practices that might be hazardous to employees and customers are identified.

The safety audit is in the form of a checklist. A *no* response to any item requires follow up. Regular safety self-inspections can help make sure safety practices are used throughout the operation. Exhibit 3.26 shows an example of a general safety audit. The general areas covered in a safety audit are:

- *Facilities*—The building (exterior and interior) and major systems, such as electricity and plumbing. Outside areas, such as drive-through windows, parking lots, and outdoor eating areas, must not be overlooked. Furnishings (booths, tables, and chairs) and fixtures (sinks, lights, and doors) are also part of the facilities.
- *Equipment*—All equipment (cooking and cutting equipment, refrigerators, tools, vehicles, fire extinguishers, and alarms) must be maintained and kept in acceptable working condition.

Exhibit 3.26
A general safety audit sample.

Yes	No	
FACILITIES		
☐	☐	Do all exit doors open from the inside—without keys—to allow rapid escape when necessary?
☐	☐	Are ground fault circuit interrupters (GFCI) installed wherever equipment and floors may become damp from cleaning?
☐	☐	Does the cooling system in the kitchen achieve the industry standard of 85°F (29.4°C) or lower?
EQUIPMENT		
☐	☐	Are machines properly guarded with covers, lids, and other devices?
☐	☐	Are hot pads, spatulas, and other equipment provided for use with ovens, stoves, and other heat-generating equipment?
EMPLOYEE PRACTICES		
☐	☐	Do employees make use of goggles, hair restraints, gloves, tampers, hot pads, safe knife storage devices, machine guards, and other personal protective equipment?
☐	☐	Do employees lift boxes and equipment properly?
MANAGEMENT PRACTICES		
☐	☐	Do managers follow all safety rules that apply to employees?
☐	☐	Do managers introduce new employees to the safety program?
☐	☐	Is senior management involved in creating safety policies?

- *Employee practices*—Employees must be trained in safe practices, and monitored to see that they use these practices on the job.
- *Management practices*—Evaluate the level of commitment to protecting employees and customers.

Accident Investigation

An **accident** is an unplanned, undesirable event that can cause property damage, injuries or fatalities, lost time from work, and disruptions of work. A **near miss** is an event in which property damage or injury is narrowly avoided. Any event that compromises customer or employee safety should be investigated and recorded—even if an actual injury did not occur.

A foodservice establishment is required to report to OSHA within eight hours any accident resulting in death, or the hospitalization of three or more employees. Other employee injuries and illnesses must be recorded within six working days. In addition, an establishment must maintain a year-long log of occupational injuries and illnesses. OSHA form No. 200, which is shown in Exhibit 3.27, is a log all operators must use to record occupational injuries and illnesses for a one-year period. This log must be displayed in an accessible place for employee viewing every February, and must be posted for one month.

In addition, each establishment should have their own forms that are used to report injuries or illnesses involving both customers and employees. Exhibits 3.28 and 3.29 show samples of these forms. Accident investigation involves the following six procedures.

1. Record information as soon as possible after the event occurs, within one hour. Use OSHA required forms and appropriate corporate or company forms.
2. Collect physical evidence or take pictures at the site.
3. Interview all people involved and any witnesses.
4. Determine as clearly as possible the sequence of events, the causes and effects, and the actions taken.
5. Submit reports to OSHA, insurance carrier, lawyer, and corporate headquarters, as appropriate. Keep copies of all reports and photographs for your files.
6. Keep all employees informed of procedures and hazards.

Promoting Safety

Encouragement and incentives motivate people much more strongly than punishment and criticism. Praise others for fol-

Remember...

The goal of a safety program is to prevent accidents—not just respond to them. Make safety improvements a normal part of the everyday procedures.

lowing the right procedures as you see them in action. A recognition or award system for employees, such as thanking them for offering safety suggestions, is another good way to encourage safety practices.

When violations or accidents occur, they are signals that the safety program may need improvement. People should only do jobs for which they have been trained, and which they are physically able to complete. Training should be updated whenever major aspects of the operation change and when you purchase new pieces of equipment.

Protective Clothing and Equipment

Supplying good-quality tools, utensils, equipment, and protective clothing shows management's commitment to employee safety. Personal protective equipment, such as gloves and goggles, will protect employees from potential hazards on the job. Employees should not wear loose or baggy shirts that could get caught on

Exhibit 3.27
OSHA form No. 200.

U.S. DEPARTMENT OF LABOR

For Calendar Year 19____ Page____ of ____

Company Name

Establishment Name

Establishment Address

Form Approved
O.M.B. No. 1220-0029
See OMB Disclosure
Statement on reverse.

Extent of and Outcome of INJURY						Type, Extent of, and Outcome of ILLNESS												
Fatalities	Nonfatal Injuries					Type of Illness							Fatalities	Nonfatal Illnesses				
Injury Related	Injuries with Lost Workdays				Injuries without Lost Workdays	CHECK Only One Column for Each Illness *(See other side of form for terminations or permanent transfers.)*							Injury Related	Illnesses with Lost Workdays				Injuries without Lost Workdays
Enter DATE of death. Mo./day/yr.	Enter a CHECK if injury involves days away from work, or days of restricted work activity, or both.	Enter a CHECK if injury involves days away from work.	Enter number of DAYS *away from work.*	Enter number of DAYS of *restricted work activity.*	Enter a CHECK if no entry was made in columns 1 or 2 but the injury is recordable as defined above.	Occupational skin diseases or disorders	Dust diseases of the lungs	Respiratory condition due to toxic agents	Poisoning (systemic effects of toxic material)	Disorders due to physical agents	Disorders associated with repeated trauma	All other occupational illnesses	Enter DATE of death. Mo./day/yr	Enter a CHECK if injury involves days away from work, or days of restricted work activity, or both.	Enter a CHECK if injury involves days away from work.	Enter number of DAYS *away from work.*	Enter number of DAYS of *restricted work activity.*	Enter a CHECK if no entry was made in columns 8 or 9.
(1)	(2)	(3)	(4)	(5)	(6)	(a)	(b)	(c)	(7) (d)	(e)	(f)	(g)	(8)	(9)	(10)	(11)	(12)	(13)

INJURIES

ILLNESSES

Certification of Annual Summary Totals By ____________ Title ____________ Date ________

OSHA No. 200 **POST ONLY THIS PORTION OF THE LAST PAGE NO LATER THAN FEBRUARY 1.**

machinery, catch on fire, or interfere with lifting. Jewelry, especially necklaces and bracelets, should not be worn because they can get caught in machinery. Scarves or neckties can also get caught or catch on fire, so they should not be worn by kitchen employees. Cooks and other kitchen employees who work around heat should wear long-sleeves to protect their arms, and an apron or chef's jacket for added protection from burns. Dishmachine operators should wear water-resistant aprons and rubber gloves.

Shoes should have skid-resistant soles and low heels. They should lace up tightly or have no laces. Shoes should be heat-, water-, and grease-resistant, and be a closed-toe style to protect feet from falling objects or spills from hot water or food.

Different types of gloves can be worn to protect the hands from cuts or burns. Steel mesh gloves protect hands from

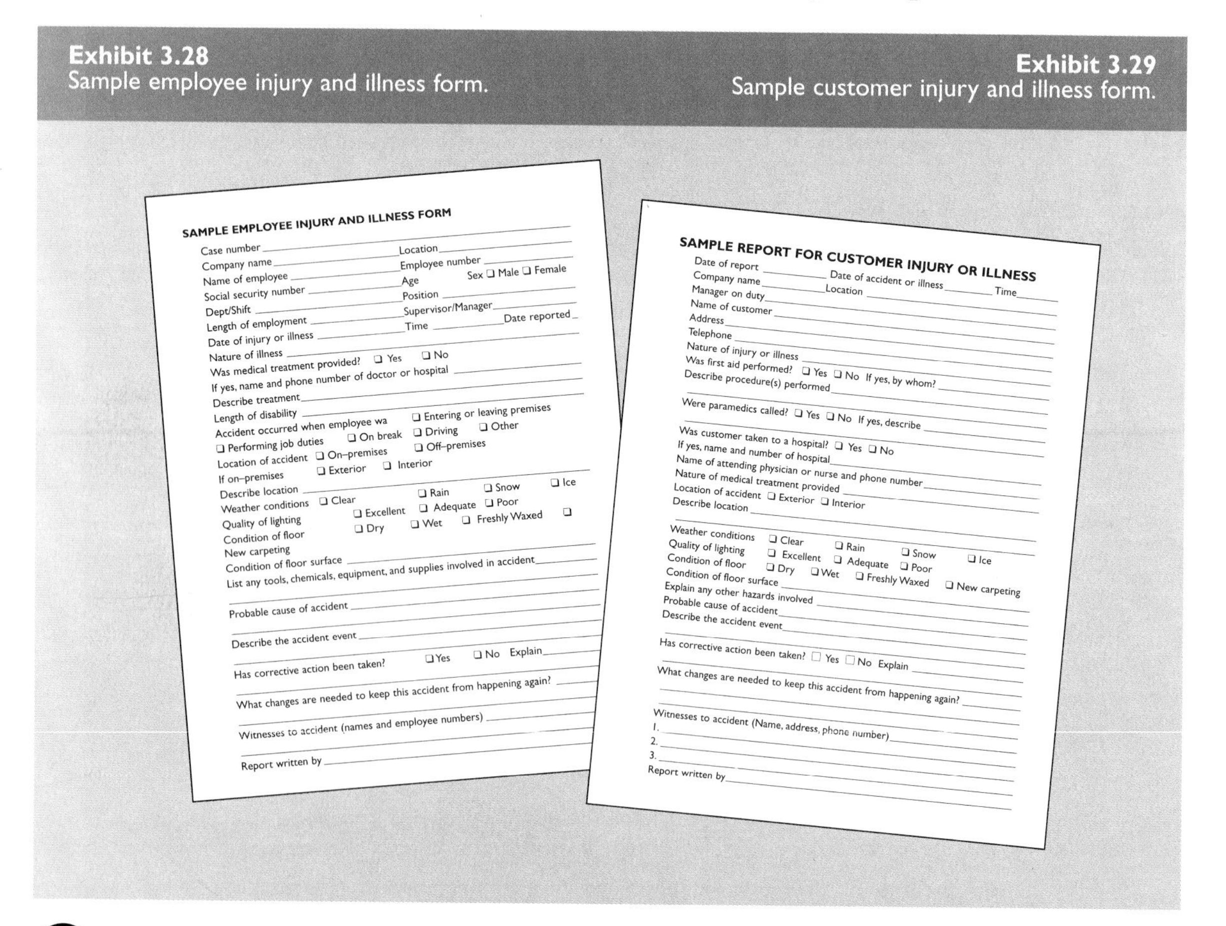

Exhibit 3.28
Sample employee injury and illness form.

SAMPLE EMPLOYEE INJURY AND ILLNESS FORM

Case number ______ Location ______
Company name ______ Employee number ______
Name of employee ______ Age ______ Sex ❑ Male ❑ Female
Social security number ______ Position ______
Dept/Shift ______ Supervisor/Manager ______
Length of employment ______ Time ______ Date reported ______
Date of injury or illness ______
Nature of illness ______
Was medical treatment provided? ❑ Yes ❑ No
If yes, name and phone number of doctor or hospital ______
Describe treatment ______
Length of disability ______
Accident occurred when employee wa ❑ Entering or leaving premises
❑ Performing job duties ❑ On break ❑ Driving ❑ Other
Location of accident ❑ On–premises ❑ Off–premises
If on–premises ❑ Exterior ❑ Interior
Describe location ______
Weather conditions ❑ Clear ❑ Rain ❑ Snow ❑ Ice
Quality of lighting ❑ Excellent ❑ Adequate ❑ Poor
Condition of floor ❑ Dry ❑ Wet ❑ Freshly Waxed ❑
New carpeting
Condition of floor surface ______
List any tools, chemicals, equipment, and supplies involved in accident ______
Probable cause of accident ______
Describe the accident event ______
Has corrective action been taken? ❑ Yes ❑ No Explain ______
What changes are needed to keep this accident from happening again? ______
Witnesses to accident (names and employee numbers) ______
Report written by ______

Exhibit 3.29
Sample customer injury and illness form.

SAMPLE REPORT FOR CUSTOMER INJURY OR ILLNESS

Date of report ______ Date of accident or illness ______ Time ______
Company name ______ Location ______
Manager on duty ______
Name of customer ______
Address ______
Telephone ______
Nature of injury or illness ______
Was first aid performed? ❑ Yes ❑ No If yes, by whom? ______
Describe procedure(s) performed ______
Were paramedics called? ❑ Yes ❑ No If yes, describe ______
Was customer taken to a hospital? ❑ Yes ❑ No
If yes, name and number of hospital ______
Name of attending physician or nurse and phone number ______
Nature of medical treatment provided ______
Location of accident ❑ Exterior ❑ Interior
Describe location ______
Weather conditions ❑ Clear ❑ Rain ❑ Snow ❑ Ice
Quality of lighting ❑ Excellent ❑ Adequate ❑ Poor
Condition of floor ❑ Dry ❑ Wet ❑ Freshly Waxed ❑ New carpeting
Condition of floor surface ______
Explain any other hazards involved ______
Probable cause of accident ______
Describe the accident event ______
Has corrective action been taken? ❑ Yes ❑ No Explain ______
What changes are needed to keep this accident from happening again? ______
Witnesses to accident (Name, address, phone number) ______
1. ______
2. ______
3. ______
Report written by ______

All mitts and gloves should be kept dry, because wet materials can conduct heat quickly and cause steam burns.

blades and knives, and leather work gloves can protect hands when opening crates or lifting objects or boxes. Hot pads, mitts, or thermal gloves protect hands from burns. Rubber gloves can protect hands from hot dishwashing water and cleaning chemicals. Disposable plastic gloves, like the kind used for foodhandling, should never be used around heat because they can melt. Gloves should fit snugly on the hand so they do not interfere with gripping or moving. Sleeves may also be worn to protect wrists and arms from splashing grease or other hazards.

Exhibit 3.30
Safety mitts protect hands from burns.

Reprinted with permission from Tucker Industries, Incorporated, Burn Guard® products, Colorado Springs, Colorado.

Goggles or safety glasses can be worn to protect employees from splashing chemicals in their eyes, or from food flying out of grinders, choppers, or mixers. Protective clothing and equipment should be checked frequently for worn spots, defects, or any damage that would make them less effective. Damaged items should be replaced as soon as possible.

Employees also have a responsibility to use the equipment properly and to wear the protective clothing. In the most successful safety programs, employees recognize safety hazards and remove them on their own initiative.

Let's Try It!

You have been asked to go into the kitchen right now and start cooking. How would you need to change your shoes, your clothes, or your hairstyle to be able to work safely and protect yourself from injury?

Review Your Learning 3.7

1. What is a general safety audit?
2. What are the four general areas to check during a safety audit?
3. What does OSHA's Form No. 200 show?
4. What is the best way for managers to get employees to comply with safety standards?
5. Why are loose or baggy shirts unsafe?

Flashback

CHAPTER 3

SECTION 3.1: INTRODUCTION TO WORKPLACE SAFETY

- Customers have a legal right to expect safe food served in a safe environment on safe premises.
- **Premises** encompass all the property around the restaurant.
- **Liability** means the legal responsibility that one person has to another.
- A foodservice operator's liability includes safe premises, a safe environment, and safe food.
- Restaurant managers are expected to know about hazards, do whatever is necessary to correct them, and be sure there are proper warnings where everyone can see them.
- If an accident does happen, restaurants may be held legally responsible by a court of law.
- **Workers' compensation** is a state-administered program designed to help employees who were injured in accidents that occurred at work, or who became sick because of job-related reasons.
- The **Occupational Safety and Health Administration (OSHA)** is the federal agency that creates and enforces safety-related standards and regulations in the workplace.
- OSHA has specific standards and forms for investigating and reporting accidents, injuries, and illnesses.
- **The Hazard Communication Standard (HCS)** requires that all employers notify their employees about chemical hazards present on the job, and train employees to use these materials safely.
- **Physical hazards** are chemicals that are flammable, explosive, highly reactive to air or water, or stored under pressure that could cause damage to property and immediate injury (most commonly burns).
- **Health hazards** are chemicals that cause long- or short-term injuries or illnesses. Health hazards include chemicals that are **toxic** (poisonous), **carcinogenic** (cause cancer), irritating, or **corrosive** (cause a material to

dissolve or be eaten away).

- **Material Safety Data Sheets**, or **MSDSs,** describe the hazards of the chemicals in a foodservice operation. Each product has its own MSDS.

SECTION 3.2: PREVENTING FIRES AND BURNS

- Because fire is a major hazard, everyone should know how to protect themselves and customers.
- One-third of all accidental fires in restaurants are due to either faulty electrical wiring and equipment, or to improper use of equipment.
- Grease fires can be prevented by following a regular cleaning schedule for walls and work surfaces; ranges, fryers, broilers, microwave and convection ovens; heating, air conditioning, and ventilation units; and hoods and filters.
- Keep all flammable items and materials away from heat sources, such as ranges and hot-water heaters.
- **Arson,** the deliberate and malicious burning of property, attempts are very difficult to stop, but good overall fire safety and building security are ways to eliminate many of the opportunities for an arsonist.
- **Smoke detectors** require a flow of air in order to work well; they must not be located in "dead" spaces, such as the ends of halls, or between ceiling beams.
- **Heat detectors** are activated by a significant increase of temperature associated with fire.
- Extinguishers should be located near possible fire hazards, as well as along convenient exit routes.
- All types of extinguishing systems focus on four ways to put out a fire.
  - Remove the fire's fuel supply.
  - Deny it oxygen.
  - Cool the fire's fuel below its combustion point.
  - Disrupt the flame's chain reaction by using a dry chemical extinguisher.
- Portable fire extinguishers are marked with the type of fire they fight.
- There are three classes of fire in a restaurant environment:
  - Class A—Wood, paper, cloth, or cardboard
  - Class B—Flammable liquids, gases, and greases
  - Class C—Live electrical equipment and circuits

- To protect employees and customers if there is a fire, a well-designed and practiced emergency plan should be ready in advance.
- The best way for employees to avoid burns is to respect heat, and to always assume the heat source is on and hot.
- Hot dishes, food, and beverages present a hazard to both customers and employees.
- Servers need to warn customers if plates, food, or beverages are hot.
- In addition, servers need to alert customers if the interior filling of a food is hot.

SECTION 3.3: PREVENTING SLIPS, TRIPS, AND FALLS

- While prompt service is important, hurrying can cause accidents.
- Slips and falls usually occur while people are doing something else—walking, carrying objects—or simply daydreaming.
- Never store items on steps, landings, or areas leading to steps. A tumble down a flight of stairs can cause severe injuries.
- Keeping floors clean and free of grease is one of the most important ways to prevent slips and falls indoors.
- Follow safety precautions when using ladders.

SECTION 3.4: LIFTING AND CARRYING SAFELY

- Even though your back has some of the strongest muscles in your body, you need to use them carefully each time you lift.
- Good storage practices and proper lifting techniques are needed to prevent back injuries.
- Before you lift anything, think out each step from beginning to end, for safe lifting. Never take a risk with your back.
- The principles of good lifting are also true for carrying.
- People with heavy objects always have the right-of-way.
- The proper way to carry a tray is with one hand in front, and one hand in the middle, under a balanced load.

SECTION 3.5: PREVENTING CUTS

- Cuts can happen more frequently to kitchen employees, but other employees and customers could be hurt from broken glass or sharp tableware.

- Glasses, bottles, and dishware should not be stored above or near ice machines or food-preparation areas.
- Broken glass should be cleaned up immediately.
- Sharp knives are safer than dull ones, because they cut more evenly and with less work.
- One rule is essential: always concentrate and focus on the task at hand. This is one of the best ways to prevent injuries from knives or machinery.
- By law, employees under age 18 are not allowed to operate, or clean, large electrical equipment with blades, such as slicers.
- Before using machinery, employees need to check the cords, plugs, and belts for wear or cracking, and check that all guards and safety devices are in place.

SECTION 3.6: SAFE DRIVING AND FIRST AID

- Safe driving techniques are important not only for making deliveries, but also for running errands or going on catering jobs.
- Employers should develop a defensive driving program that provides overall guidelines and training.
- Drivers must never drink or use drugs before or during their shift.
- **First aid** refers to medical treatment given to an injured person either for light injuries or until more complete treatment can be provided by emergency service or other health care providers.
- Effective first aid meets the injured person's emotional as well as medical needs, and helps diffuse the shock, anger, and resentment an injured person may feel toward your operation.
- First aid kits are required by some state and local agencies.
- **Cardiopulmonary resuscitation (CPR)** and the **Heimlich maneuver** can save lives, but they are difficult to do and may cause harm to the injured person if not done properly.
- CPR should not be administered unless an employee has a current certification from a recognized provider of first aid training.

SECTION 3.7: SAFETY AS AN ONGOING PROCESS

- In a **general safety audit**, any areas and practices that might be hazardous to employees and customers are identified.

- The purpose of a general safety audit is to give you an overview of the level of safety in the establishment.
- An **accident** is an unplanned, undesirable event that can cause property damage, injuries or fatalities, lost time from work, and disruptions of work.
- A **near miss** is an event in which property damage or injury is narrowly avoided.
- Any event that compromises customer or employee safety should be investigated and recorded—even if an actual injury did not occur.

The next step in getting ready to work in a professional foodservice operation is a basic understanding of what goes into food production. After this unit, you will be ready for your first foodservice experience.

UNIT 2

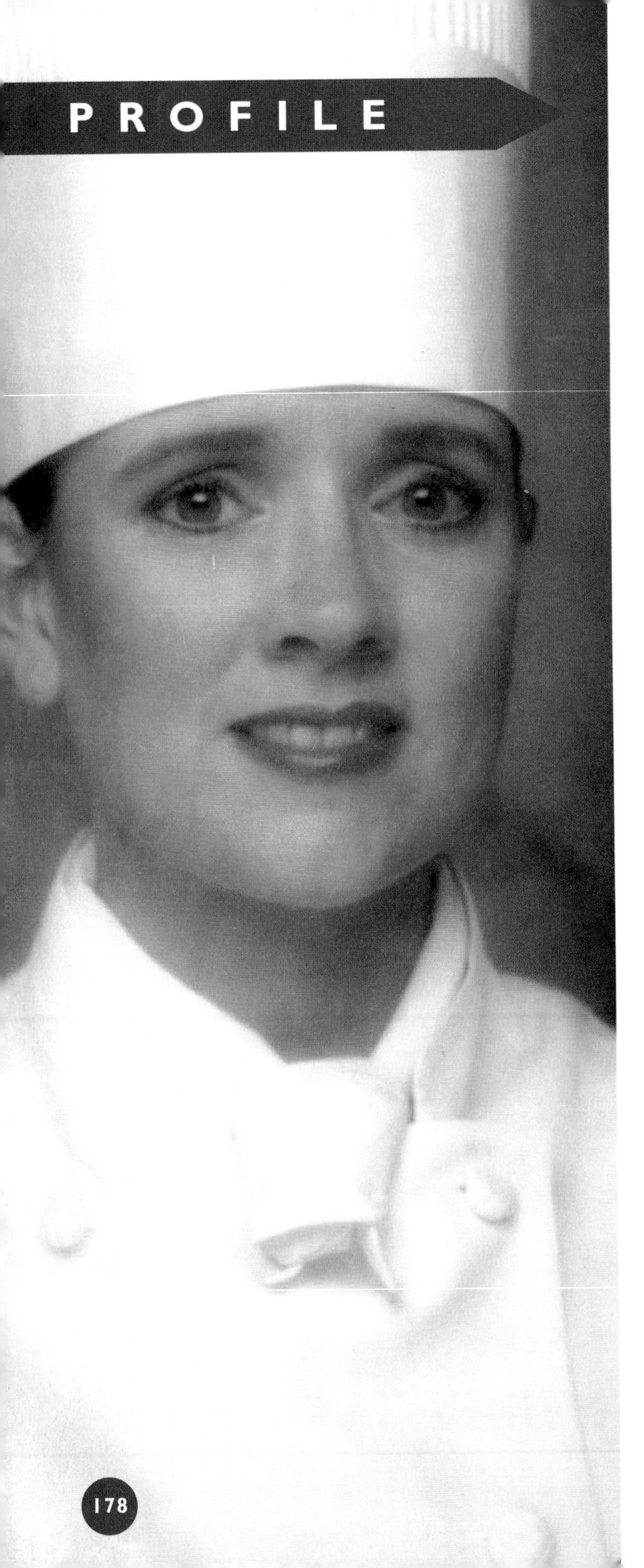

Denise Murray

Sous Chef, Garde Manger
The Signature Room at the Ninety-Fifth
Chicago, Illinois

All I ever wanted to be was a chef. My parents were great entertainers, and when they had dinner parties, I'd hang out in the kitchen, which was where I thought all the fun was: getting everything ready, helping put things together. I loved it!

I went to school for six years to become a chef. I was a chef's apprentice for three years, and I spent the next three years specializing in garde manger, or the preparation of appetizers, hors d'oeuvres, and other cold foods. It was hard, and working in a kitchen is often hot, loud, and busy. You have to put in long hours and lift heavy things. And you never run out of new things to learn. But I love what I do. I'm constantly called on to use my creativity, put new foods together, and put foods together in new and fun ways. Every dish I send out to a customer is a personal representation of who I am.

When you get into a rhythm with your tasks and with your teammates, the adrenaline really flows. You have to be in sync with the people you work with. In order to do that, you have to know what you're doing. You have to know the basics. Your tools are your building blocks for everything you do. You're quicker, more efficient, and more creative if you know how to use your knives and your other tools well. It's like any other job. You wouldn't try to build a house if you didn't know how to use a hammer. Well, you can't cook if you don't know how to use tools in the correct and safe way.

I love being the sous chef at a five-star restaurant. Customers expect the best, and that's exactly what I give them.

CHAPTER 4

Kitchen Basics

SECTION 4.1

Using Standardized Recipes

AFTER STUDYING SECTION 4.1, YOU SHOULD BE ABLE TO:

- Identify the components and functions of a standardized recipe.
- Convert recipes to yield smaller and larger quantities.
- Describe the use of common liquid and dry measure tools.
- Explain the difference between customary and metric units of measure.

KEY TERMS

- **Customary unit**
- **Metric unit**
- **Standardized recipe**
- **Volume**
- **Yield**

When you think of your favorite recipes, what comes to mind? Do you think of your grandmother's oatmeal raisin cookies or your dad's spicy fried chicken? Where can you find those recipes? Are they scribbled on scraps of paper or note cards tucked away in a recipe box? Or do they exist only in someone's memory?

Recipes used at home can follow any format that helps the cook prepare the dish. But recipes for institutional use, or **standardized recipes,** must follow a format that is clear to anyone who uses them. A standardized recipe lists the ingredients first, in the order they are to be used, followed by assembly directions or the method for putting the ingredients together.

As you will see in this chapter, standardized recipes are an important part of a successful professional kitchen.

Exhibit 4.1 shows an example of a standardized recipe for brownies. A standardized recipe includes the following information.

- ***Ingredients***—the foods needed to make the recipe, usually listed in the order in which they are used. This makes it easier to follow the recipe and not forget any ingredient. Amounts needed for each ingredient are also given.
- ***Yield***—number of servings or the amount the recipe makes.
- ***Temperature, time,*** and ***equipment***—includes size and type of pans and other equipment needed, the oven

Exhibit 4.1
Standardized recipe for brownies.

Yield: 9 lb (4 kg)

Ingredient	Customary (U.S.) Measure	Metric Measure
Unsweetened chocolate	1 lb	450 g
Butter	1 lb 8 oz	675 g
Eggs	1 lb 8 oz	675 g
Sugar	3 lb	1350 g
Salt	1½ tsp	7.5 ml
Vanilla	1 oz	30 g
Cake flour	1 lb	450 g
Chopped walnuts or pecans	1 lb	450 g

1. Melt chocolate and butter together in a double boiler. Stir so that the mixture is smooth. Let it cool to room temperature.
2. Blend the eggs, sugar, and salt until well mixed, but do not whip. Add the vanilla.
3. Blend in the chocolate mixture.
4. Stir the flour and fold it in.
5. Fold in the nuts.
6. Grease and flour the pans or line them with parchment. Quantity of basic recipe is enough for one full 18x26 inch (46x66 cm) sheet pan, or two half-size sheet pans, or four 9x13 inch (23x33 cm) pans, or six 9-inch (23 cm) square pans.
7. If desired, batter may be sprinkled with additional 50% (8 oz/224 g) chopped nuts after panning.
8. Baking: 325° (162.8°C), about 60 minutes. For 2-inch (5 cm) square brownies, cut sheet pan 8x12, to yield 96 pieces.

Reprinted from *Professional Cooking,* Third Edition, by Wayne Gisslen. New York, NY: John Wiley & Sons, Inc., 1995.

temperature, cooking time, and any preheating instructions.

- ***Step-by-step directions***—how and when to combine the ingredients. Some recipes include both a conventional oven method and a microwave oven method.
- ***Nutrition information***—not essential, but useful. Nutrition information may include any of the following: amounts of fat (saturated and unsaturated), carbohydrates, protein, fiber, sodium, vitamins, and minerals.

Measurement Methods

Before you can begin to prepare a recipe, you must understand the two basic systems of measurement and know how to use liquid and dry measurement tools. The most commonly used system of measurement in the United States is based on **customary units.** You may be familiar with such customary units as ounces, teaspoons, tablespoons, cups, pints, and gallons. Most American recipes are written using the customary system. Exhibit 4.2 lists customary units used in recipes. Often they are abbreviated, as shown in parenthesis.

The metric system is the standard system used in many parts of the world. It is also used by scientists and health professionals. **Metric units** are based on multiples of 10 and include milliliters, liters, milligrams, grams, and kilograms. For example, just as there are 100 pennies in one dollar, there are 100 milligrams in one gram. Exhibit 4.3 lists the most common metric units used in recipes. Often they are abbreviated, as shown in the parenthesis.

Exhibit 4.2
Customary (U.S.) units of measure

Volume	Weight
teaspoon (tsp)	ounce (oz)
tablespoon (Tbsp)	pound (lb)
cup (c)	
fluid ounce (fl oz)	**Temperature**
pint (pt)	degrees Fahrenheit (°F)
quart (qt)	
gallon (gal)	**Length**
inches (in)	inches (in)

Exhibit 4.3
Metric units of measure

Volume	Temperature
milliliter (ml)	degrees Celsius (°C) (or centigrade)
liter (l)	
Weight	**Length**
milligram (mg)	millimeters (mm)
gram (g)	centimeters (cm)
kilogram (kg)	meter (m)

It's important to be very familiar with both systems of measurement. As long as you have the correct measuring equipment, it's not necessary to convert measurements from one system to the other. If a recipe is written using metric units, use metric measuring tools.

You can express the same amount in different ways by using different units of measure. This is called an *equivalent.* For example, 4 tablespoons of flour is equivalent to 1/4 cup of flour, or about 60 milliliters. Exhibit 4.4 on the next page lists some common equivalents between customary and metric units of measure.

In a recipe, amounts of ingredients can be measured in several ways. Most ingredients are measured by volume. **Volume** is the amount of space an ingredient takes up. A salad recipe might list one cup cooked pasta or 1/2 teaspoon of pepper. Some ingredients are measured by weight or heaviness, such as one pound of fish filets or two ounces of butter. Other ingredients may be measured by the count, or number, of items, such as one medium banana or three egg whites. No matter how an ingredient is measured, careful, accurate measurement is necessary for quality and quantity control.

Dry ingredients are usually measured by leveling them off evenly at the rim of the spoon or cup. Sometimes, however, a recipe calls for a *heaping* measure. This means that you scoop up the ingredient with your measure but do not level it off. Sometimes a heaping measure will give almost twice the amount of a leveled-off measure.

Dry measures usually come in a set of several sizes. A typical customary set of measuring cups includes 1/4c, 1/3c, 1/2c, and 1c measures. A metric set includes 50 ml, 125 ml, and 250 ml measures. Even smaller amounts of dry ingredients can be measured as a dash or a pinch—the amount that can be held between the thumb and forefinger. Herbs and spices are often measured this way.

Measuring Tips:

- *Some recipes call for you to sift ingredients such as flour, powdered sugar, and granulated sugar. Sifting is a process that removes lumps from an ingredient and gives it a smoother consistency. Be sure to sift an ingredient before measuring it.*
- *Never measure an ingredient while holding the measuring cup over the bowl in which you are mixing! If you overpour, your entire recipe may be ruined.*

Exhibit 4.4
Equivalent measures.

Volume

Customary Measure	Customary Equivalent	Metric Equivalent
1 tsp		5 ml
1 Tbsp	3 tsp	15 ml
1 fl oz	2 Tbsp	30 ml
1/4 c	4 Tbsp	60 ml
1/3 c	5 1/3 Tbsp	80 ml
1/2 c		120 ml
2/3 c		160 ml
3/4 c		180 ml
1 c	8 fl oz	240 ml
	16 Tbsp	0.24 l
1 pt	2 c	470 ml
	16 fl oz	0.47 l
1 qt	2 pt	950 ml
	4 c	0.95 l
	32 fl oz	
1 gal	4 qt	3.8 l

Weight

Customary Measure	Customary Equivalent	Metric Equivalent
1 oz		28 g
1 lb	16 oz	450 g
2 lb	32 oz	900 g
		0.9 kg
2.2 lb		1 kg

Temperatures

Customary Measure	Customary Equivalent	Metric Equivalent
0°F		-17.8°C
32°F	(freezing point)	0°C
212°F	(boiling point)	100°C

Exhibit 4.5
Measuring dry ingredients.

When measuring dry ingredients:

- Fill the cup with the ingredient. Some ingredents (such as flour and sugar) must be spooned into the cup lightly. Other ingredients, like brown sugar, must be packed down, but only if specified in the recipe.
- Level off the top of the cup using the straight edge of a spatula.
- Pour the ingredient into the mixture. If needed, use a rubber scraper to make sure all the ingredient has been emptied out of the cup.

Liquid measuring cups are see-through and have measurement markings on the side. They are typically marked in fractions of a cup, fluid ounces, and milliliters. A spout makes pouring easier.

A TIP FROM THE PROFESSIONALS:

If you need 1/8 tsp of a dry ingredient and you don't have a 1/8 tsp measuring spoon, fill the 1/4 teaspoon measure and level it off. Then, using the tip of a straight-edged spatula or table knife, remove half the ingredient.

Common customary sizes are 1 cup and 2 cups. Metric cups usually come in 250 ml and 500 ml sizes. Measuring spoons generally come in a set of four or five. Most customary sets include these sizes: 1/4 tsp, 1/2 tsp, 1 tsp, and 1 Tbsp. Metric sets include 1 ml, 2 ml, 5 ml, 15 ml, and 25 ml measures. Measuring pitchers are used for measuring liquids and are generally available in pint, quart, gallon, milliliter, and liter sizes.

Measuring Temperature

As you learned in *Chapter 2: Preparing and Serving Safe Food,* thermometers are used to measure foods' internal temperatures. The stem, inserted in the food, gives an instant reading. Thermometers measure degrees of temperature in either Fahrenheit (°F), which is the customary measure, or Celsius (°C), which is the metric measure. You can convert between the two measurements easily by following the formulas outlined in Exhibit 4.7.

Exhibit 4.6
Measuring liquids.

When measuring liquid ingredients:

- Set the measuring cup on a level surface.
- Carefully pour the liquid into the cup.
- Bend down to check the measurement at eye level for an accurate reading.
- Add more liquid, or pour off excess, until the top of the liquid is at the desired measurement mark.
- Pour the ingredient into the mixing container. If needed, use a rubber scraper to empty the cup completely.
- For small amounts of liquids, use measuring spoons.

Exhibit 4.7
Temperature conversion.

- **Fahrenheit (F°) to Celsius (C°):** Subtract 32 from the Fahrenheit number, multiply by 5, and then divide by 9.
- **Celsius (C°) to Fahrenheit (F°):** Multiply the Celsius number by 9, divide by 5, and then add 32.
- **Temperature at which water boils:** 212°F (100°C)
- **Temperature at which water freezes:** 32°F (0°C)

Measuring Fats

Fats, such as butter, margarine, or shortening, can be measured in several ways.

- *Stick method*—used for fat that comes in 1/4 pound sticks, such as butter or margarine. The wrapper is marked in tablespoons and in fractions of a cup. Simply cut off the amount you need.
- *Dry measuring cup method*—pack the fat down into the cup, pressing firmly to remove air bubbles. Level off the top. Using a rubber scraper,

empty as much of the fat as possible. Use the same technique when using measuring spoons to measure fat.

- *Water displacement method*—this method involves combining fat with water in a liquid measuring cup. First, subtract the amount of fat to be measured from one cup. The difference is the amount of water to pour into the measuring cup. For example, to measure 2/3 cup of shortening, start with 1/3 cup of water in a measuring cup. Next, spoon the fat into the cup, making sure it all falls completely below the level of the water. When the water reaches the one cup level, you have the right amount of fat. Pour off the water and remove the fat with a rubber scraper. Although this method may seem complicated, it is found to be the most accurate when measuring solid fats.

It is sometimes difficult to be exact with the dry measure cup method because air bubbles can make the measurement inaccurate. Using the water displacement method also makes the fat easier to scrape out of the measuring cup because it isn't packed tightly.

Measuring by Weight

Think of the difference between a cup of popcorn and a cup of water. Both take up the same amount of space—eight fluid ounces—but they do not weigh the same; the water is heavier. To find out how much each cup weighs, you would use a kitchen scale, not a measuring cup. Weight is often measured in ounces, while volume is measured in fluid ounces.

> **Let's try it!**
>
> **If you need 1/2 cup of shortening, how much water should you start with in the measuring cup? When you add the correct amount of fat to the water, what will the water level then be?**

Exhibit 4.8
Look at the different ingredients in this picture. Can you tell which ones are measured by count? By weight? By volume?

Remember:

Ounces of weight are not the same as fluid ounces. Never use a dry or liquid measuring cup to measure an ingredient when the amount is given by weight. The measurement will not be accurate.

A food scale is helpful for measuring ingredients by weight. Scales are used to weigh ingredients for preparation and portion control. Ounce/gram and pound/kilo scales both should be available. Scales may be spring-type, balance beam, or electronic. When using a food scale:

- Decide what container you will weigh the food in. Place the empty container on the scale.
- Adjust the scale until it reads zero.
- Add the food to the container until the scale shows the desired amount.

Understanding units of measure is one of the keys to successful food preparation. The measurements given in recipes must be followed exactly. This is especially important in baking and pastry recipes. Professional foodservice recipes have a large yield. **Yield** means the number of servings or portions a recipe makes. Mistakes in measurement can ruin more than just one loaf of bread—they can ruin as many loaves as you were planning to make at one time!

Converting Recipes

Sometimes you may need to change a recipe if the yield is not the amount you need. Using basic math skills, it's easy to increase or decrease many recipes. Most recipes, even those for baked goods, can be doubled successfully. Keep in mind that larger equipment may be needed for mixing and cooking, and cooking times will often need adjustment.

Unless otherwise indicated, recipes are intended to be used at altitudes of 3,000 feet (about 1,000 m) or below. If they are used at higher altitudes, they may not turn out as desired. Why not? As the altitude gets higher, the air pressure gets lower. This affects food preparation in two ways:

1. **Water boils at a lower temperature.**
2. **Bubbles of gas may form more readily in liquids and escape. Baked goods are likely to rise less and be too heavy.**

Sometimes reducing the amount of baking powder or soda and sugar and increasing the liquid can help. Always look for recipes with special directions for preparing at high altitudes.

Many recipes for casseroles and soups can be doubled, and even halved, tripled, and so on. Exhibit 4.9 shows a basic formula for both increasing and decreasing recipe yields.

Exhibit 4.9
Formula for increasing or decreasing recipe yields.

1. Decide how many servings you need (Desired yield).
2. Use the following formula:
   $\frac{\text{Desired yield}}{\text{Original yield}}$ = Conversion factor (Number to multiply ingredients by)
   For example, if your chili recipe serves eight and you need to serve four:
   4/8 or 4 ÷ 8 = 0.5 The conversion factor is 0.5.
3. Multiply each ingredient amount by the conversion factor. This keeps all the ingredients in the same proportion to each other as they were in the original recipe.
4. As needed, convert answers to logical, measurable amounts. Think about the equipment you will use for measuring. For example: 6/4 c flour = 1 1/2 c
   12 Tbsp brown sugar = 3/4 c
5. Make any necessary adjustments to equipment, temperature, and time. The depth of food in a pan affects how fast it will cook. Use pans that are the right size for the amount of food—neither too large nor too small.

Review Your Learning 4.1

1. Look through various cookbooks and read a selection of recipes. Which recipes are easy to read? Which give the most complete directions? How many give nutrition information or low calorie substitutions?

2. What is a recipe's yield?

3. Convert the following recipe ingredients from customary units to metric units of measurement.
   a. 1 c milk
   b. 1 lb butter
   c. 2 Tbsp vinegar
   d. 1 oz parsley

4. One cup (c) is equivalent to how many:
   a. fluid ounces (fl oz)?
   b. milliliters (ml)?
   c. tablespoons (Tbsp)?

5. What is the difference between fluid ounces and weight ounces?

6. At what temperatures Fahrenheit and Celsius does water boil?

4.2

SECTION 4.2

Getting Ready to Cook

AFTER STUDYING SECTION 4.2, YOU SHOULD BE ABLE TO:

- Apply effective mise en place through practice.
- Identify different functions of several types of knives and demonstrate their proper uses.
- List common spices and herbs and describe their uses.
- Describe and demonstrate several basic prepreparation techniques, including clarifying butter, separating eggs, whipping egg whites, and making parchment liners.

So, you understand the importance of standardized recipes, the measurement systems, and why it's important to measure carefully. Are you ready to begin to cook? Before you can begin to cook you must know how to prepare to cook. The saying, "Well begun is half done" applies doubly in cooking, because getting ready to cook plays a major part in the success of your recipe. Even if you prepare only one short recipe, you must first do *pre*preparation. Only then are you ready to begin the actual cooking.

MISE EN PLACE

In the foodservice industry, getting ready for the cooking you're about to do is called mise en place. **Mise en place**

KEY TERMS

- **Bain marie (bayn muh-REE)**
- **Clarify**
- **Herbs (urbs)**
- **Mise en place (meez ahn PLAHS)**
- **Spices**

Exhibit 4.10
Important prepreparation steps.

- Assemble your tools.
- Assemble your ingredients.
- Wash, trim, cut, prepare, and measure your ingredients.
- Prepare your equipment (preheat oven, line baking sheets, etc.).

(meez ahn PLAHS) is French for "to put in place" and it means the preparation and assembly of ingredients, pans, utensils, and equipment or serving pieces needed for a particular dish or service.

Mise en place solves two basic problems facing the professional chef.

Problem #1: There is too much work to do in a kitchen to leave everything until the last minute; some work must be done ahead of time.

Problem #2: Most foods are at their best quality immediately after preparation. They deteriorate as they are held, and they begin to lose their nutritional value.

There is only one way to solve these problems: plan ahead by following the suggestions listed in Exhibit 4.11.

Exhibit 4.11
Planning ahead.

1. Break each menu item down into its stages of production.
   - Determine which stages may be done in advance.
   - Assembling and preparing ingredients are important parts of advance preparation. This includes cleaning and cutting produce, cutting and trimming meats, and preparing breadings and batters for frying.
   - Some steps of a recipe can be done in advance if they do not result in loss of quality.
   - Final cooking should be done as close to service time as possible.
2. Determine the best way to hold the item at its final stage of prepreparation.
   - Sauces and soups are frequently kept hot, above 140°F (60°C), in steam tables or other holding equipment. Many foods, such as vegetables, should be kept hot for only short periods because they quickly become overcooked.
   - Refrigerator temperatures below 40°F (4.4°C) are best for preserving the quality of most foods, especially perishable meats, fish, and vegetables, before final cooking or reheating.
3. Determine how long it takes to do each step in a recipe. Plan a production schedule beginning with the preparations that take the longest.
   - Many tasks can be carried on at once because they don't require your complete attention the entire time. For example, it may take six to eight hours to prepare a stock, but you don't have to stand and watch it the entire time.
4. Examine recipes to see whether they can be revised for better efficiency and quality. For example, instead of preparing a full batch of green peas and holding them for service in the steam table, you might blanch and chill them, and then heat portions to order in a sauté pan, steamer, or microwave oven. (These cooking methods will be described in greater detail in *Section 4.3: Cooking Methods.*)

Remember:

The goal of prepreparation is to do as much of the work that you can in advance without any loss in ingredient quality.

Knife Basics

Usually, the cleaning and cutting of raw foods is one of the first steps of mise en place. Fresh vegetables, fruits, and meats often require trimming and cutting. Basic knife skills and chopping techniques are very important for this prepreparation step. Exhibit 4.13 lists several different types of knives and their most common uses.

Exhibit 4.12
It's important to choose the right knife for the task at hand.

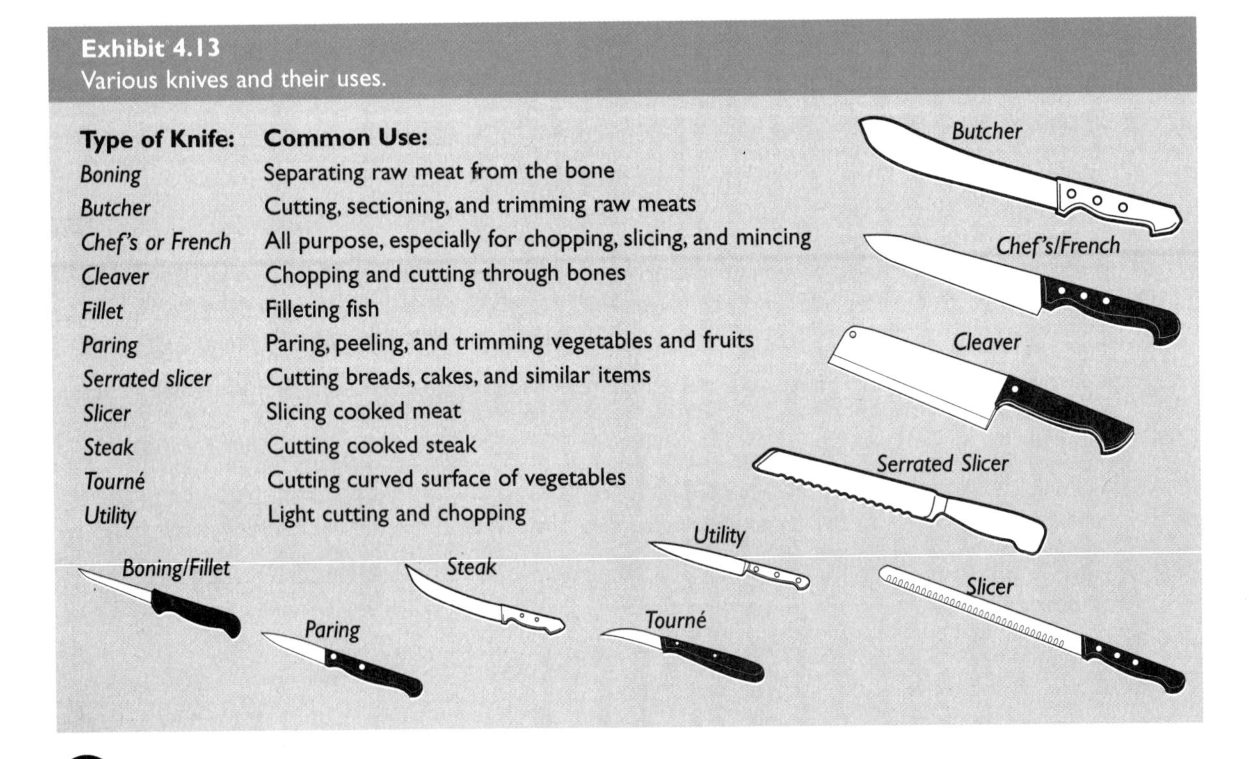

Exhibit 4.13
Various knives and their uses.

Type of Knife:	Common Use:
Boning	Separating raw meat from the bone
Butcher	Cutting, sectioning, and trimming raw meats
Chef's or French	All purpose, especially for chopping, slicing, and mincing
Cleaver	Chopping and cutting through bones
Fillet	Filleting fish
Paring	Paring, peeling, and trimming vegetables and fruits
Serrated slicer	Cutting breads, cakes, and similar items
Slicer	Slicing cooked meat
Steak	Cutting cooked steak
Tourné	Cutting curved surface of vegetables
Utility	Light cutting and chopping

Exhibit 4.14
Three basic knife grips.

1. Grip the handle with four fingers. Hold the thumb against the side of the blade.

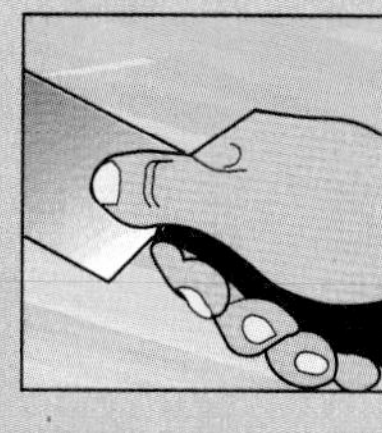

2. Grip the handle with three fingers. Rest the index finger flat against the blade on one side, and hold the thumb on the opposite side to give additional stability and control.

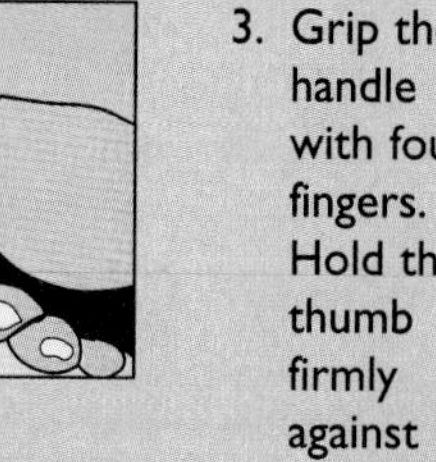

3. Grip the handle with four fingers. Hold the thumb firmly against the blade's back.

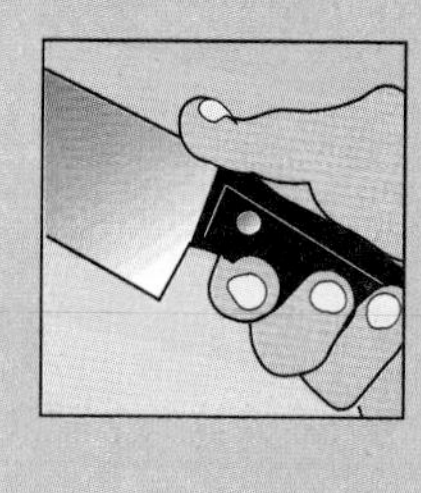

Knives can be dangerous when not handled carefully. Always focus on the task at hand to avoid injury to yourself and others around you. Remember these knife safety tips:

- A sharp knife is safer than a dull one. Dull knives are more likely to slip and cause an accident.
- When using a knife, keep your fingers away from the sharp edge of the blade.
- Never hold food in your hand while cutting.
- If a knife falls, step away from it. NEVER try to catch a falling knife.

To use most knives, you will hold the food on the cutting board with one hand and hold the knife by its handle with the other. There are three basic knife grips, as shown in Exhibit 4.14.

In every grip, the hand that is not holding the knife, called the *guiding hand*, prevents slippage and helps to control the size of the cut. Proper placement of the guiding hand is shown in Exhibit 4.15. The fingers of the guiding hand (left) are bent inward toward the palm, and the thumb is held well back.

Exhibit 4.15
Proper placement of the guiding hand.

Batonnet (ba-tun-AY)
Cut slightly thicker than julienne

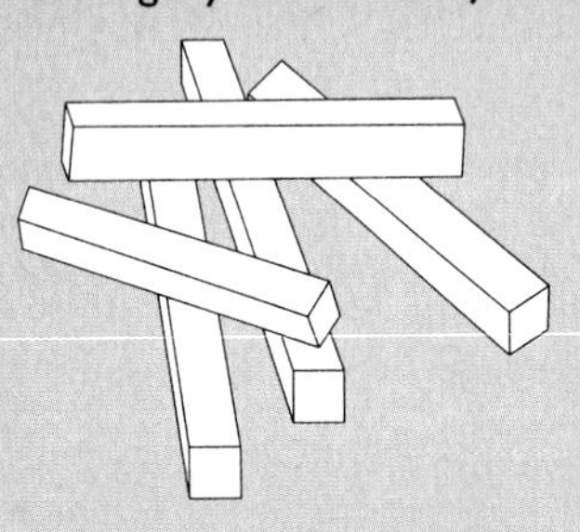

Dice
Cut into cube-shaped pieces

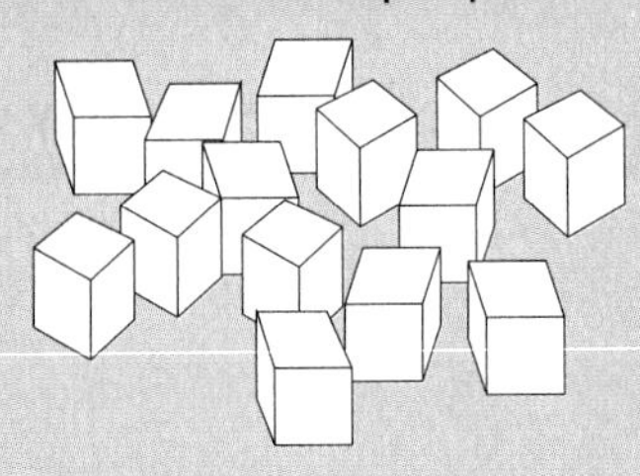

Brunoise (broon-WAHZ)
Very small dice

Julienne (jew-lee-EN)
Cut into long, thin, rectangular pieces

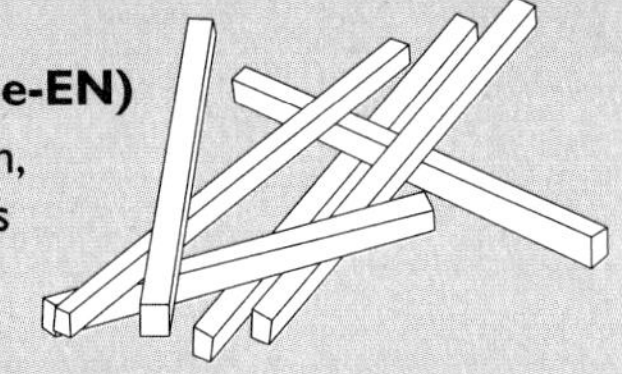

Coarse chop
Chopped into rather large, uniform pieces; used for mirepoix

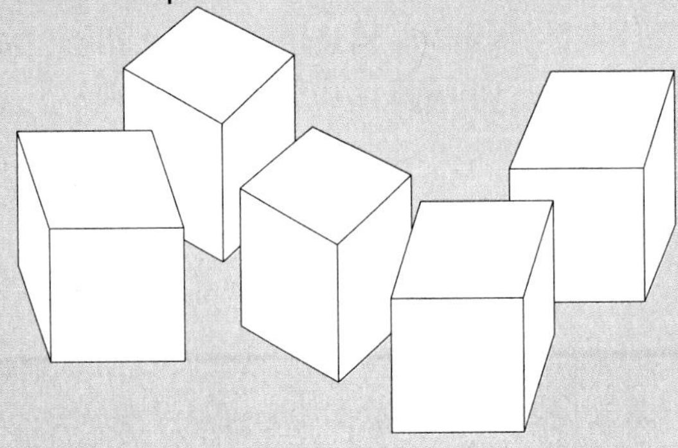

Mince
Cut very fine and evenly; used for herbs, shallots, and garlic; the tip of the knife is held against the cutting board while the blade is brought down to cut the food

Diagonal
Cut into pieces with diagonal edges; often used for stir-fried dishes

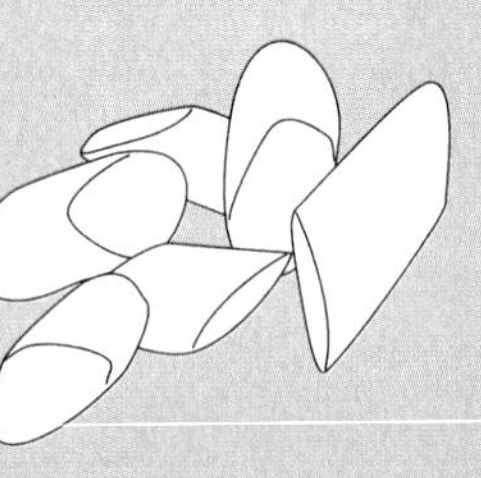

Slice
Cut into large, thin, flat pieces

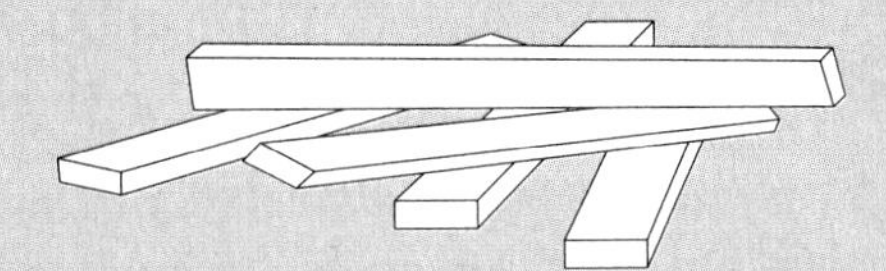

Exhibit 4.16
Basic knife cuts.

When using a knife, use a back-and-forth sawing motion while pressing down gently at the same time. With practice, you will be able to cut foods in many different ways. Some basic knife cuts you should be familiar with are described in Exhibit 4.16.

Beware of cross-contamination! When cutting and trimming raw meats and poultry, always clean and sanitize knives and cutting boards before using them to prepare another food item.

Herbs and Spices

Herbs and spices are important ingredients used to enhance and add to the flavor of foods. **Herbs** (urbs) are the leaves, stems, or flowers of an aromatic plant. Herbs are available fresh or dried. Dried herbs are much stronger than fresh herbs because the herbs' flavorful oils are concentrated during the drying process. When using dried herbs, they should be lightly crumbled or ground before being added to a dish. This releases their flavor.

Spices are the bark, roots, seeds, buds, or berries of an aromatic plant. They are most often used in their dried form and can be purchased whole or ground. Whole spices should be added early during cooking to allow their flavors to carry throughout the food. Cut or ground spices should be added later in the cooking process.

Each herb or spice used in a recipe contributes its own distinct flavor to a finished dish, and several of them can be used together to create new and exciting flavor combinations. Strong, flavorful spices and herbs such as pepper, curry, cumin, basil, and oregano can often be used to reduce the amount of salt in recipes. A table of common herbs and spices is shown in Exhibit 4.18.

Storing spices and herbs properly helps to keep them fresh and flavorful. Heat, light, and air all speed the loss of flavor and color. A tight glass jar in a covered

Curry powder was originally developed in the late 1600's for the sailors of the British East India Company. The sailors had grown fond of the complexly spiced dishes they tried while working in India. The pre-mixed curry powder, which is a combination of several spices, was an easy way to take the flavor of India home with them to England.

Courtesy of Penzey's Ltd., Muskego, WI

cabinet or drawer away from any heat source is the best protection for dried herbs and spices. Everyone knows that stoves produce heat, but placing herbs and spices next to dishwashers, sinks, or air ducts should also be avoided. The best way to avoid light is to keep these flavorings in a darkened cabinet, drawer, or pantry. If you do have an open spice rack, make sure to locate it away from any direct sunlight.

As you work in the kitchen, you will hear many new words. Some culinary terms that may be unfamiliar to you are listed along with their definitions in Exhibit 4.19. Several of these terms will be explained in more detail, and

Exhibit 4.17
Fresh herbs such as these can be stored in plastic bags in the refrigerator for a short time.

Remember, even though you may not think of fresh herbs as food, they still must be kept out of the temperature danger zone and protected from cross-contamination like any other perishable ingredient.

Exhibit 4.18
Common herbs and spices.

How many of these herbs and spices have you heard of or used before?

Herbs	**Spices**
Basil	Allspice
Bay leaves	Anise
Chives	Capers
Cilantro	Caraway
Dill	Cardamom
Lavender	Chile pepper
Lemon grass	Cayenne
Marjoram	Cinnamon
Mint leaves	Cloves
Peppermint	Coriander
Oregano	Cumin
Parsley	Curry
Rosemary	Fennel
Sage	Ginger
Savory	Mace
Spearmint	Mustard seeds
Tarragon	Nutmeg
Thyme	Paprika
	Peppercorns
	Poppy seeds
	Saffron
	Sesame seeds
	Turmeric
	Vanilla bean

Exhibit 4.19
Common culinary terms.

Al dente *(all DEN-tay)*	Cook pasta or vegetables until they are tender, but still firm
Beat	Thoroughly mix foods using a vigorous over-and-over motion
Brown	Cook food briefly until the surface turns brown, sometimes in a skillet using hot fat, in the oven, or in a broiler
Butterfly	Cut of meat or seafood that is split down the middle and looks like the wings of a butterfly
Caramelize	Brown sugar using heat; the sugar may be a natural part of a food, such as onions
Chill	Refrigerate or place food in an ice bath until it is cold
Cream	Beat together ingredients, such as shortening and sugar, until soft and creamy
Drain	Remove excess liquid by pouring it off or by placing food in a strainer or colander
Dredge	Coat food with a dry ingredient such as flour or bread crumbs
Egg wash	Mixture of beaten eggs (whole eggs, yolks, or whites) and a liquid, usually milk or water, used to coat an item before baking or frying
Fold	Gentle mixing method used for delicate or whipped ingredients, using a rubber scraper or wooden spoon
Garnish	Decorate a food or dish with a small, colorful food such as parsley or a lemon slice
Grease	Spread a thin layer of unsalted shortening in a pan or use a cooking spray; prevents sticking and makes food easier to remove
Pare	Cut off a very thin layer of vegetable or fruit peel
Preheat	Turn on an appliance (oven, electric skillet, etc.) ahead of time so that it will be at the right temperature when the food is ready to be cooked
Score	Make shallow, straight cuts in the surface of food, such as a steak, to tenderize it; or shallow cuts in the skin of a vegetable, such as a cucumber, as decoration
Sift	Put dry ingredients, such as flour, through a sifter to remove lumps and give it a smoother consistency
Strain	Separate solid food pieces from a liquid using a strainer or colander
Sweat	Cook an item, usually vegetables, in a small amount of fat in a covered pan until it softens and releases moisture
Whip	Add air into a mixture by beating it vigorously, making it light and fluffy

Exhibit 4.20
Basic preparations.

Clarifying butter:

Clarified butter is butter that is pure butterfat. It can be heated to a higher temperature than whole butter without burning or breaking down because the milk solids, which scorch easily, have been removed. Clarified butter may also by used as a sauce, usually with seafood. When it's used with seafood, it is called *drawn butter.*

1. Melt the butter in a heavy saucepan over medium heat.
2. Remove the pan from the heat.
3. Skim the surface foam.
4. Pour or ladle the clarified butter into another container, being careful to leave all of the milk solids in the bottom of the pan.

Separating eggs:

Sometimes it is necessary to separate eggs when a recipe calls for either raw egg yolks or egg whites only.

1. Use two containers and a small bowl.
2. Crack open the egg over the bowl.
3. Transfer the egg back and forth between the halves of the shell, letting the white drop into the bowl.
4. Place the yolk in one of the containers.
5. Inspect the egg white. If there are any traces of yolk present, reserve it for use in other preparations. If the white is clean, transfer it to the container for egg whites.

Whipping egg whites:

1. Begin whipping the egg whites by hand or machine at a moderate speed. Tilt the bowl to make whipping by hand easier, resting the bowl on a folded towel to prevent it from slipping.
   - To add more volume and give the foam greater stability, add a small amount of lemon juice or cream of tartar.
2. When the whites are quite foamy, increase the speed of the mixer.
3. Whip to the appropriate stage.
   - Soft peak has a droopy, rounded peak.
   - Medium peak has a moist surface and forms a rounded but fairly stable peak.
   - Stiff peak has stiff, stable peaks. Stop beating while the surface is still moist and glossy.
4. Never overbeat egg whites. Overbeaten egg whites may still resemble those at the stiff peak stage, but their surface looks dry.

NOTE: The method for whipping cream is the same as that for whipping egg whites. The cream should be cold when it is whipped, and both the bowl and beaters should be chilled in advance as well to give the whipped cream more volume.

Setting up a bain marie:

A **bain marie** (bayn muh-REE) is a hot-water bath used to hold hot foods and keep them at safe temperatures.

1. Place a deep pan large enough to hold containers of food comfortably on a rack.
2. Add the food containers.
3. Pour in enough boiling water to fill one-half to two-thirds of the pan.

Making a parchment liner for a round pan:

Parchment paper is often used to line pans to prevent food from sticking to them.

1. Cut a square of parchment paper a little larger than the pan's diameter.
2. Fold the square in half to form a triangle.
3. Continue folding in half until a long, thin triangle is formed.
4. Position the triangle's narrow end above the pan's center and cut away the part that extends beyond the edge of the pan.
5. Unfold the triangle and flatten it into the pan.

practiced, in later chapters of the *Becoming a Foodservice Professional* textbooks. But for now, just take a look and see which terms you might already know.

Basic Preparations

Another part of mise en place involves certain ingredients that need to be refined before they are ready for use at the time of preparation. Basic cooking techniques in prepreparation include clarifying butter, separating eggs, whipping egg whites, setting up a bain marie (bayn muh-REE), and making parchment liners for pans. These techniques are all described in Exhibit 4.20

The basic elements of mise en place—knife cuts, flavorings, herbs and spices, and basic preparations—are the building blocks of a professional chef's training. These methods and techniques will be used throughout a professional career in food service.

Review Your Learning 4.2

1. List three examples of mise en place activities that can help you with the prepreparation of a recipe.
2. Match each knife cut on the left with the shape it creates on the right. Three letters won't be used.

_______ Julienne	a. Cube-shaped
_______ Dice	b. Shredded
_______ Brunoise	c. Long, thin rectangular pieces
_______ Batonnet	d. Cut very fine and evenly
_______ Mince	e. Round disks
	f. Football-shaped
	g. Cut slightly thicker than julienne
	h. Very small dice

3. How are herbs different from spices?
4. How is clarified butter different from whole butter?

4.3

SECTION 4.3

Cooking Methods

AFTER STUDYING SECTION 4.3, YOU SHOULD BE ABLE TO:

- Describe dry-heat cooking methods and list the foods to which they are suited.
- Describe moist-heat cooking methods and list the foods to which they are suited.
- Describe combination cooking methods and list the foods to which they are suited.

KEY TERMS

- Bake
- Barbecue
- Baste
- Blanch
- Boil
- Braise
- Broil
- Combination cooking
- Deep-fry
- Dry-heat cooking
- Grill
- Moist-heat cooking
- Pan-fry
- Poach
- Roast
- Sauté (saw-TAY)
- Shallow poach
- Simmer
- Steam
- Stew
- Stir-fry

What is your favorite way to prepare potatoes? Beef? Fish? Did you know that there are many, many ways to prepare each one? You can choose from hundreds of recipes, and you can also choose from a variety of cooking methods, each producing a different result. That's why it's important to match foods with appropriate cooking techniques to get the desired results. There are three general types of cooking methods:

1. Dry-heat cooking
2. Moist-heat cooking
3. Combination cooking

In **dry-heat cooking,** food is prepared without added liquid, with or without fat. **Moist-heat cooking** uses liquid or steam to cook foods. **Combination cooking** uses both dry and moist heat.

Dry-heat Cooking Methods without Fat

In dry-heat cooking, food is cooked either by direct heat, like on a grill, or by indirect heat in a closed environment, like in an oven. Some foods may lose moisture and become dry when cooked using dry heat. Any food prepared using dry heat must be naturally tender or prepared by barding or marinating to give it added moisture.

Dry-heat cooking methods without fat include:

- grilling
- barbecuing
- broiling
- roasting
- baking
- microwaving

Grilling is a very simple dry-heat method that is excellent for cooking smaller pieces of food. The food is cooked on a grill rack above the heat source. No liquid is added to the food during cooking. Any fats or oils used during the cooking process are intended simply to add flavor to the finished dish.

Exhibit 4.21
Grilled meats and vegetables have a hearty, smoky flavor.

The result of grilling is food with a highly-flavored outside and a moist inside. Grilled foods have a smoky, slightly charred flavor because the fats melt and help form a crust on the food as it cooks. Special woods, such as mesquite, hickory, or apple, can be used in the heat source to flavor the grilled food. Using a marinade can also give the food a unique flavor as well as make it more tender. Crosshatch marks will

Exhibit 4.22
Grilling foods.

1. Thoroughly clean and preheat the grill.
2. Season the main item; marinate or brush it with oil if necessary to prevent it from sticking to the grill.
3. Place the item on the grill.
4. Turn the item about 60 degrees to produce crosshatch marks.
5. Flip the item over to complete cooking to the desired doneness.

appear on the food's surface when it is turned and grilled properly. Crosshatch marks make the grilled food more pleasing to the eye. Steps for grilling foods are listed in Exhibit 4.22.

Barbecuing is another form of grilling. In **barbecuing,** food can be basted repeatedly with a sauce during grilling. When you **baste** a food item, you moisten it during cooking with pan drippings, sauce, or other liquid. Basting prevents food from drying out. Barbecuing can also mean grilling food over a wood or charcoal fire.

Exhibit 4.23
When food is barbequed, it is brushed with a sauce, or *basted,* while cooking.

Broiling is a rapid cooking method that uses high heat from a source located above the food. Broiled foods become browned on the top. Foods that can be broiled include only tender cuts of meat, young poultry, fish, and some fruits and vegetables.

Exhibit 4.24
Broiling foods.

1. Place the food on a cold broiler pan.
2. Do not line the pan with foil. Any fat that may be released will not be able to drain away and the food will fry; the fat could catch fire.
3. Check the recipe for the proper distance between the broiler pan and the heat. You can control how fast the food cooks by how far you place it from the heat.

As mentioned earlier, dry-heat cooking methods also include methods that use indirect heat in a closed environment. These methods include roasting and baking. **Roasting** and **baking** cook food by surrounding the items with hot, dry air in the oven. As the outer layers of the food become heated, the food's natural juices turn to steam and are absorbed into the food. These juices create a natural sauce.

Roasting generally requires longer cooking times and is most often used with large cuts of meat, whole birds (poultry), or fish. Roasted foods should have a golden-brown exterior and moist, tender interior. Foods that can be baked or roasted include fish, tender meats and poultry, and some fruits and vegetables.

Baking is simply cooking food in an oven without liquid. Depending on the recipe you follow, food may be baked covered or uncovered. Food that is baked uncovered, such as cookies and casseroles, develop a golden brown color on top. Breads, cakes, pies, cookies, and similar foods are also usually baked. Baking desserts and pastries requires specific recipes and ingredients in order to turn out perfectly. Baking will be explored in greater detail in *Chapter 5: Desserts and Baked Goods* of *Becoming a Foodservice Professional, Year 2.*

Exhibit 4.25
Roasted foods, such as turkey, ham, beef, and pork are often part of traditional American holiday meals.

Did you know?

When you bake potatoes wrapped in aluminum foil you're not really *baking*? The foil traps the potatoes' natural moisture and actually cooks them in their own steam—so really they're *steamed potatoes!*

What about microwaving? Many foods can be baked or roasted in a microwave oven. However, the microwave does not give the same results as a conventional, or convection, oven because it cooks food with waves of energy or radiation, rather than with heat. Microwaving is good for some recipes, but many foods can quickly become tough and rubbery if microwaved too long.

Dry Heat Cooking Methods with Fats

Another way to prepare food is to use dry-heat cooking methods with fats and oils. These methods include:

- sautéing
- pan-frying
- stir-frying
- deep-frying

Exhibit 4.26
Roasting.

1. Season, stuff, or marinate the main item, and sear, or quickly brown, its surface over direct heat or in a hot oven.
2. Place the food on a rack in a roasting pan so that hot air can touch it on all sides.
3. Roast the item uncovered until the desired temperature is reached. Allow for carryover cooking. *Carryover cooking* describes what happens to a piece of meat or fish after it has been removed from the oven. The roasted item holds a certain amount of heat that continues to cook the food.
4. Allow the roasted item to sit or *rest* before carving. Doing this allows the juices, which are being drawn out to the edges of the meat during roasting, to return to the center of the item and make it juicier.
5. Prepare the pan gravy in the roasting pan.
6. Carve the roasted item and serve it with the appropriate gravy or sauce.

All of these cooking methods take a brief amount of time, use high heat, and require tender, portion-sized or smaller pieces of meat, poultry, fish, and certain vegetables.

The **sautéing** (saw-TAY-ing) method cooks food rapidly in a small amount of fat over relatively high heat. The fat or oil used adds to the flavor, as well as to the moisture of the pan. The juices released during cooking form a sauce that captures the flavor of the food. The sauce is very important to sautéed foods. Sometimes the items to be sautéed are first dusted with flour. Meat strips, chicken, and fish are often prepared this way. The thinner and more delicate the piece of meat, the faster it will cook.

In **stir-frying,** as described in Exhibit 4.28 a very small amount of oil is used in a pan over high heat. The items to be stir-fried, usually meats and fresh vegetables, are cut into bite-sized pieces. Foods that are prepared by stir-frying do not have to be as naturally tender as foods that are sautéed. Stir-frying is different from sautéing because the food is stirred constantly with a spoon or spatula during cooking.

Exhibit 4.27
This bowl-shaped pan, called a *wok,* makes stir-frying a snap. A wok is usually made of rolled steel and is used for nearly all Chinese cooking methods.

Exhibit 4.28
Stir-frying.

1. Heat a small amount of oil in a wok or large sauté pan.
2. Add the main item.
3. Stir-fry, keeping the food in constant motion with a wooden paddle or spoon.
4. Add additional ingredients, including seasonings, in the proper sequence (longest-cooking ingredient in first, shortest-cooking ingredient in last).
5. Add the liquid for the sauce; add the thickener.
6. Serve the food immediately.

Exhibit 4.29
Steps for pan-frying.

1. Heat the cooking oil.
2. Add the food item (usually breaded or batter-coated) to the pan in a single layer.
3. Pan-fry the food on the first side until it is well-browned.
4. Turn the item and cook it to the desired doneness.
5. Remove the item and finish it in an oven, if necessary.
6. Drain the item on absorbent paper.
7. Season and serve it with the appropriate sauce and garnish.

Cooking techniques that use more oil include pan-frying and deep-frying. Foods prepared by **pan-frying** are often coated with batter or breading and then cooked in an oil over less intense heat. The hot oil seals the food's coated surface and locks the natural juices inside, instead of releasing them. The object of pan-frying is to produce a flavorful exterior with a crisp, brown crust, which helps retain the food's juices and flavor.

Only naturally tender foods should be pan-fried because this method of cooking brings out the food's distinct flavor and moistness. Even after cooking, the food should be tender and moist. Pan-fried foods may be held for only a short time before being served. The outside of the food should be evenly golden-brown, with a firm crust. Steps for pan-frying food are outlined in Exhibit 4.29.

Deep-frying is also called *French frying*. In this cooking method, food is breaded or batter-coated, immersed (completely covered) in hot fat, and fried until done. The result is an interesting combination of flavors and textures. The outside of the food item develops a crispy coating while the inside stays moist and tender. The coating on the food item can be a standard breading, a batter such as a tempura or a beer batter, or it may be a flour coating. Foods that can be deep-fried must be naturally tender and of a shape and size that allows them to be cooked quickly without being tough or dry.

Food Safety Tips for Breading

- Finish breading the food item one hour in advance of cooking and chill the breaded items to allow the coating to firm and dry.
- Use batter within one hour. After one hour, discard any remaining batter.
- Return batter to refrigerator to maintain product temperature at 40°F (4.4°C) or lower between batches.
- Never add old batter to new batter.

Most deep-fried foods are done when they have risen to the surface of the oil and appear golden-brown. The crust should be crisp and delicate, encasing a moist, tender piece of meat, fish, poultry, or vegetable. Steps for deep-frying foods are outlined in Exhibit 4.30. There are three slightly different methods for deep-frying foods.

1. In the *swimming method,* batter-coated foods are gently dropped in hot oil where they fall to the bottom of the fryer, then swim to the surface. Once the food items reach the surface, they need to be turned over so they brown on both sides.
2. Foods cooked in the *basket method* are breaded, placed in a basket, lowered into the hot oil, and then lifted out with the basket when they are done.
3. The *double-basket method* is used for certain foods that need to be fully submerged in hot oil for a longer period of time in order to develop a crisp crust. In this method, the food item is placed in a basket with another basket fitted on top of it. The top basket keeps the food from floating to the surface.

The amount of time it takes oil to reheat to the correct cooking temperature once food is added is called the *recovery time.* The more food items that are cooked in the oil at one time, the longer the recovery time. The *smoking point* is the temperature at which fats and oils begin to smoke, which means that the fat has begun to break down. Oils used for deep-frying should have a neutral flavor and color and a high smoking point, around 425°F (218°C).

Exhibit 4.30
Deep-frying foods.

1. Heat the fat or oil to the proper temperature, usually 325° to 375°F (162.8° to 190.6°C).
2. Add the food item (usually breaded or batter-coated) to the hot oil, using the appropriate method (swimming, basket, or double-basket).
3. Turn the item during frying, if necessary.
4. Remove the item and finish it in an oven, if necessary.
5. Blot the food with absorbent paper toweling.
6. Season and serve with the appropriate sauce and garnish.

Deep-frying Safety Tips

- Do not overheat the fat or oil. It could catch fire.
- Be sure the food to be fried is dry and does not have ice crystals on it. Moisture could cause the fat or oil to spatter and burn you.
- Wear long sleeves and heavy-duty aprons to protect yourself from hot oil.
- Be prepared to act quickly in case of a grease fire.

Moist-heat Cooking

Moist-heat cooking techniques produce foods that are delicately flavored and moist with a rich broth, which can be served as a separate course or used as a sauce base. In fact, an entire dinner, complete with meat, fish, or poultry and vegetables, can be cooked in one pot. One example of this is the classic New England boiled dinner, consisting of corned beef, cabbage, and potatoes. With moist-heat methods, you have the opportunity to create nutritious, appealing dishes with a range of flavors and textures.

Unlike dry-heat methods, there is no seal on the food to trap natural juices. That is why it's important to hold the flavor and juices in the food during the cooking process. This is done by wrapping the item in a vegetable or parchment covering, or by serving the broth as part of the finished dish.

To make sure food does not remain in the temperature danger zone, return all ingredients to refrigerated storage if you are interrupted during preparation.

Examples of moist-heat cooking include:

- boiling
- shallow poaching
- poaching
- simmering
- blanching
- steaming

To **boil** means to cook food in a liquid that has reached the boiling point (212°F/100°C). Boiling liquids bubble rapidly. Boiling is usually used to cook vegetables and starches, like carrots, pasta, and potatoes. The high temperature of the liquid would toughen the protein of meat, fish, and eggs. The rapid bubbling would break up delicate foods.

Shallow poaching cooks foods by using a combination of steam and a liquid bath. Shallow poaching is a last-minute cooking method best suited to foods that are cut into portion-sized or smaller pieces. The food is partially covered by a liquid containing an acid (usually wine or lemon juice) and herbs and spices in a covered pan. The steam cooks the items that are not directly covered by the poaching liquid. Foods that have been shallow poached should be very tender and moist, with a fragile texture. In shallow poaching, much of the flavor of the food is transferred from the food item to the liquid. To keep this lost flavor, the liquid is used as a sauce base. Exhibit 4.31 explains how to shallow poach foods.

Exhibit 4.31
Shallow poaching.

1. Heat butter in a saucepan.
2. Add the seasonings to the pan and make a level bed.
3. Add the food item and the poaching liquid.
4. Bring the liquid to a simmer.
5. Cover the saucepan.
6. Finish the food over direct heat or in an oven.
7. Remove the food item, and keep it warm and moist.
8. Reduce the poaching liquid, and prepare a sauce as desired.
9. Serve the food item with the sauce and appropriate garnish.

Did you know?

Water boils at 212°F (100°C) at sea level. No matter how high the heat is turned, the temperature of the water will go no higher.

In **poaching** and **simmering**, food is completely submerged in a liquid that is kept at a constant, moderate temperature. The liquid must be well flavored, and the food selected should be naturally tender. When poaching, the food is cooked between 160° and 180°F (71.1° and 82.2°C). The surface of the poaching liquid should show some motion, but no air bubbles should break the surface.

Less tender items can be simmered because the food is cooked at a slightly higher temperature, 185° to 200°F (85° to 93.3°C). Simmering differs from boiling in that bubbles in the liquid rise gently and just begin to break the surface. The water should not come to a full boil, because the boiling motion will cause food to become stringy and rubbery. Poached and simmered items are often served with a flavorful sauce to add zest to the dish's mild flavor. Be careful not to overcook poached and simmered foods.

Blanching is a variation of boiling. Food is placed in a pot of cold water and the liquid is then brought to a boil. The food is only boiled for a short time and is not cooked all the way. When the food is removed from the boiling water, it is rinsed in cold water to stop the cooking process. Blanching is used to preprepare fresh vegetables. Many times food that takes longer to cook thoroughly is blanched before it is deep-fried. This is a good way to prepare fried chicken.

The **steaming** method cooks food over, but not directly in, boiling liquid. Foods cooked in steam should all be naturally tender and cut into small sizes. In steaming, the food is placed on a rack above the boiling liquid within a closed cooking pot. For additional flavor, broth may be used instead of water. As the liquid comes to a boil, the steam created surrounds the food, heating it evenly and keeping it moist. Once all the ingredients are in the steamer and the cover is in place, the lid should not be removed because the steam will escape and slow down the cooking process. Steaming is described in Exhibit 4.32.

Steamed foods retain their color, shape, and flavor. Cooking time is longer with steaming than with boiling or simmering. Steamed foods should be cooked until they are just done but not overcooked. Their flavor is delicate, and their appearance is usually pale because they are not browned. Steamed foods should be moist and plump and not rubbery or chewy.

Steaming is one of the healthiest cooking methods. It does not add any fats or oils, and since food is not placed directly in the liquid, the nutrients are not rinsed or boiled away.

Exhibit 4.32
Steaming food.

1. Bring the liquid to a boil.
2. Add the food item to the pot in a single layer on a rack raised above the boiling liquid.
3. Cover the pot.
4. Steam the food to the correct doneness.
5. Serve the food immediately with the appropriate sauce and garnish.

Exhibit 4.33
This bamboo steamer is perfect for steaming salmon or other delicate food items.

Combination Cooking

Sometimes the best method for preparing certain foods is a combination of both dry-heat and moist-heat cooking methods. Such cooking is called **combination cooking.** For example, braising and stewing use both dry and moist heat to cook foods that are less tender. These are useful techniques to know because they can transform the less tender and less expensive main ingredients into delicious and tender finished products.

Combination cooking methods include:

- braising
- stewing

In **braising,** the food item is first seared in hot oil, then slowly cooked tightly covered in a small amount of liquid, and then finished in the oven or on the stovetop until it is tender. A bed of seasonings adds moisture and flavor to the food. Vegetables can be added to braised meat or poultry near the end of the cooking time. The flavor of the meat is released into the cooking liquid, which becomes the accompanying sauce.

Slow, gentle braising causes the tougher connective tissue of lean meats to become very tender. More tender foods require less cooking fluid and can be heated at lower temperatures for a shorter time. Few nutrients are lost with braising. Braised foods that are finished in the oven are less likely to be scorched than food that is finished on the stovetop. Braised foods should be extremely tender, but they should not fall into shreds.

Braising techniques include daube, estouffade, and pot roasting.

- *Daube* (dawb) is a braise usually made with red meat, often beef, and includes red wine. The main item is often marinated before braising.
- *Estouffade* (ess-too-FAHD) is the French term for both the braising method and the dish itself.
- *Pot roasting* is a common American term for braising and is also the name of a traditional dish.

Stewing techniques are similar to braising, but the main food item is first cut into bite-sized pieces that are either blanched or seared. Stewing also requires more liquid than braising, with the food being completely covered while simmering.

Various types of stews include:

- *Blanquette* (blahn-KETT) is a white stew made traditionally from veal, chicken, or lamb, garnished with mushrooms and pearl onions, and served in a white sauce.

- *Bouillabaisse* (BOO-yuh-base) is a Mediterranean fish stew combining a variety of fish and shellfish.
- *Fricassée* (frick-uh-SAY) is a white stew, often made from veal, poultry, or small game.
- *Goulash* (GOO-losh) originated in Hungary and is made from beef, veal, or poultry, seasoned with paprika, and generally served with potatoes or dumplings.
- *Navarin* is a stew usually prepared from mutton or lamb, with a garnish of root vegetables, onions, and peas.

Exhibit 4.34
This beef stew has been prepared using a combination cooking method.

Exhibit 4.35
Review of cooking methods.

Dry-heat Cooking Methods

Bake:
Cook food in a closed oven without liquid

Barbecue:
Cook food on a grill while basting with a marinade or sauce

Broil:
Cook food by placing it below a very hot heat source

Deep-fry:
Cook breaded or batter-coated food by immersing it completely in hot fat or oil

Grill:
Cook food on a rack above a heat source

Microwave:
Cook food with waves of radiation rather than with heat

Pan-fry:
Cook food in hot fat or oil over medium heat

Roast:
Cook food using indirect heat in a closed environment (requires a longer cooking time than baking)

Sauté:
Cook food quickly in a small amount of fat or oil over high heat

Stir-fry:
Cook food quickly in a small amount of fat or oil over high heat while stirring constantly

The name probably comes from the French word for turnips, *navets,* which are used as the principle garnish.

- *Ragout* (ra-GOO) is a French term for stew that means "restores the appetite."
- *Matelote* (ma-tuh-LOAT) is a special type of fish stew, usually prepared with eel.

The successful use of the combination methods of braising and stewing depends on the proper choice of main ingredients and careful attention to each step of preparation and service.

Exhibit 4.35 lists and describes the cooking methods discussed in Section 4.3.

One final note on mise en place and cooking methods: with even with the best planning, emergencies will arise in which ingredients are unavailable or scarce. Exhibit 4.36, on the next page, lists some emergency substitutions for some ingredients. Keep in mind, however, that customers should always be told truthfully what they are being served.

Exhibit 4.35 (continued)
Review of cooking methods.

Moist-heat Cooking Methods

Boil:
Cook food submerged in a liquid that has reached the boiling point

Blanch:
Cook food part-way in boiling water for a very short time

Poach:
Cook food completely submerged in liquid below the boiling point at temperatures of 180°F to 185°F (82.2°C to 85°C)

Shallow poach:
Cook food partially submerged in a liquid below the boiling point at temperatures between 160°F and 180°F (71.1°C and 82.2°C)

Simmer:
Cook food completely submerged in liquid below the boiling point at temperatures of 185°F to 205°F (85°C to 96.1°C)

Steam:
Cook food over, but not directly in, boiling liquid in a covered pot

Combination Cooking Methods

Braise:
Sear food in hot oil, then cook tightly covered in a small amount of liquid, and finish in an oven or on the stovetop

Stew:
Sear bite-sized pieces of food, then cover them in liquid and simmer in a covered pot

Exhibit 4.36
Emergency ingredient substitutions.

If you don't have:	Use this instead:
Baking chocolate (1oz)	3 Tbsp cocoa + 1 Tbsp butter or margarine
Baking powder (1 tsp)	¼ tsp baking soda plus ⅝ tsp cream of tartar
Buttermilk (1c)	1 Tbsp lemon juice or vinegar plus enough skim milk to measure 1 c, or 1 c plain yogurt
Cake flour (1 c)	⅞ c sifted all-purpose flour
Cream, heavy (1 c)	¾ c milk plus ⅓ c melted butter
Cream, sour (1 c)	⅞ c buttermilk or plain yogurt plus 3 Tbsp melted butter
Cream, whipping (1 c)	⅔ c well-chilled evaporated milk, whipped, or 1 c nonfat dry milk powder whipped with 1 c ice water
Dry mustard (1 tsp)	1 Tbsp prepared mustard
Egg (1 whole)	2 yolks
Flour, all-purpose (1 c)	1⅛ c cake flour, ⅝ c potato flour, 1¼ c whole grain flour, or 1 c cornmeal
Flour, cake (1 c)	1 c minus 2 Tbsp sifted all-purpose flour
Flour, self-rising (1 c)	1 c all-purpose flour plus 1¼ tsp baking powder plus ¼ tsp salt
Garlic (1 clove)	⅛ tsp garlic powder
Herbs (1 tsp dried, crushed)	1 Tbsp fresh, chopped
Honey (1 c)	1¼ c sugar plus 1/2 c liquid
Ketchup (1/2 c)	½ c tomato sauce plus 2 Tbsp sugar, 1 tsp vinegar, and ⅛ tsp ground cloves
Lemon juice (1 tsp)	½ tsp vinegar
Milk, skim (1 c)	1/3 c instant nonfat dry milk powder plus ¾ c water
Onion (1 small)	1 Tbsp minced dried onion or 1 tsp onion powder
Rice (1 c cooked)	1 c cooked bulgur or millet
Sugar, granulated (1 c)	1 c firmly-packed brown sugar, 1¾ c confectioner's sugar (do not substitute in baking), ½ c honey, 2 c corn syrup, or 1 c superfine sugar
Tomatoes, canned (1 c)	½ c tomato sauce plus ½ c water, or 1⅓ c chopped fresh tomatoes, simmered
Tomato juice (1 c)	½ c tomato sauce plus ½ c water plus dash each salt and sugar, or ¼ c tomato paste plus ¾ c water plus dash each salt and sugar
Worcestershire sauce (1 Tbsp)	1 Tbsp soy sauce + dash red pepper sauce
Yogurt, plain (1 c)	1 c buttermilk

Review Your Learning 4.3

1. On a separate sheet of paper, state whether each of the following cooking methods is a dry-heat (D), moist-heat (M), or combination (C) cooking method.
   a. Steaming
   b. Grilling
   c. Braising
   d. Roasting
   e. Stir-frying
   f. Sautéing
   g. Poaching
   h. Baking
   i. Simmering
   j. Broiling

2. You will be stir-frying chicken and vegetables. Which should you begin cooking first, and why?

3. What is basting?

4. Describe the texture of foods that have been deep-fried.

5. Why are braising and stewing called combination cooking methods?

Flashback

CHAPTER 4

SECTION 4.1: USING STANDARDIZED RECIPES

- A standardized recipe is made for use in a foodservice establishment.
- **Standard recipes** includes details such as a list and amounts of ingredients, yield, equipment, and cooking time and temperature, that ensure that it will be prepared in the same way each time it is made.
- Recipe skills include using customary and metric units of measure, as well as knowing how to measure liquids, dry ingredients, and fats.
- The most commonly used system of measurement in the United States is based on **customary units**, which include ounces, teaspoons, tablespoons, cups, pints, and gallons.
- **Metric units** are based on multiples of ten and include milligrams, grams, kilograms, milliliters, and liters.
- As long as you have the correct measuring equipment, it's not necessary to convert measurements from one system to the other.
- There are different procedures for measuring dry ingredients, liquids, and fats.
- Sometimes you may need to change a recipe if it is not for the amount you need. Using a simple formula, it's easy to increase or decrease many recipes.

SECTION 4.2: GETTING READY TO COOK

- **Mise en place** is French for "to put in place." It means planning ahead for efficiency and quality in the kitchen.
- The basic elements of mise en place—knife cuts, flavorings, herbs and spices, and basic preparations are the building blocks of a professional chef's training.
- Knife skills include basic cutting methods as well as more complicated cutting techniques.
- **Herbs** are the leaves, stems, or flowers of an aromatic plant. Herbs are available fresh or dried.
- **Spices** are the bark, roots, seeds, buds, or berries of an aromatic plant. They are most often used in their

dried form and can be purchased whole or ground.

- Prepreparation procedures include clarifying butter, separating and whipping eggs, preparing a **bain marie** (water bath), and cutting parchment pan liners.

SECTION 4.3: COOKING METHODS

- It's important to match foods with appropriate cooking techniques to get the desired results.
- In **dry-heat cooking,** food is prepared without added liquid, with or without fat. **Moist-heat cooking** uses liquid or steam to cook foods. **Combination cooking** uses both dry and moist heat.
- In dry-heat cooking, food is cooked either by direct heat, like on a grill, or by indirect heat in a closed environment, like in an oven.
- Dry-heat cooking methods without fat include **grilling, barbecuing, broiling, roasting, baking,** and **microwaving.**
- **Sautéing, stir-frying, pan-frying,** and **deep-frying** are examples of dry-heat cooking using a fat or oil. These methods take a brief amount of time, use high heat, and require tender, portion-sized or small pieces of meat, poultry, or fish.
- In moist-heat cooking, food is cooked in a hot liquid, steam, or a combination of both. Moist-heat cooking techniques produce foods that are delicately flavored and moist with a rich broth, which can be served as a separate course or used as a sauce base.
- Examples of moist-heat cooking include **boiling, shallow poaching, poaching, simmering, blanching,** and **steaming.**
- Combination cooking methods apply both dry heat and moist heat to the main item.
- The two common combination cooking methods are **braising** and **stewing.** These cooking methods transform less tender main ingredients into tender, delicious meals.

Richard Hynes

Northeast Regional Sales Manager
Hobart Corporation

Hobart Corporation is the oldest and largest foodservice equipment supplier in the country. I've been with Hobart for a number of years, and have seen this company grow and expand its product lines into more and more foodservice areas.

I began my career as a service technician. I was responsible for going out into the field and repairing any equipment that wasn't working correctly. Doing that introduced me to the foodservice industry and the many different facets that exist in the industry. I soon realized that the industry isn't just about restaurants, but it includes schools, hospitals, correctional facilities, and military bases.

A few years later I entered sales and spent the majority of my time traveling throughout my territory selling Hobart equipment to a variety of clients. It was great because I came in contact with all segments of the foodservice industry and really got to know my clients well. Every day was different; one day I would be on board a ship selling equipment for the kitchen galley on board, and the next I'd be at the local hospital or high school. I even worked with architects that design foodservice facilities to make sure the new building could accommodate the necessary foodservice equipment.

As a regional sales manager, I'm not out in the field as much as I used to be. I spend most of my time now working with my sales representatives, and mentoring them. I enjoy training my employees and watching them learn about the industry. It's really great to see them succeed!

Working for a foodservice supplier has allowed me to work with and meet a lot of wonderful people, both in the foodservice industry and the supplier side. I have employees that have worked as head chefs, sous chefs, and that have had front of the house experience. These people are extremely valuable because they bring firsthand knowledge to their work.

Gaining experience in any part of the industry at an early age will provide a head start to anyone interested in becoming a part of the foodservice or hospitality industry.

CHAPTER 5

Foodservice Equipment

SECTION 5.1

Receiving, Storage, and Prepreparation Equipment

AFTER STUDYING SECTION 5.1, YOU SHOULD BE ABLE TO:

- Demonstrate how to use scales and carts to receive food and supplies.
- Demonstrate measuring and portioning foods using ladles, measuring cups and spoons, scales, and scoops.
- Demonstrate how to properly sharpen and use different types of knives.
- Give examples of preparing foods using pots and pans.

KEY TERMS

- Bake pan
- Bench scraper
- Boning knife
- Brazing pan
- Butcher knife
- Can opener
- Cast iron skillet
- Chef's (French) knife
- China cap
- Chinois (chee-no-AH)
- Clam knife
- Cleaver
- Colander (CAH-len-der)
- Cook's fork
- Double boiler
- Food mill
- Grater
- Hotel pan

KEY TERMS (CONTINUED)

- Ladle
- Measuring cup
- Measuring spoon
- Offset spatula (SPACH-e-la)
- Oyster knife
- Paring knife
- Parissienne (pah-REE-see-en) scoop
- Pastry bag
- Pastry brush
- Perforated spoon
- Pie server
- Pizza cutter
- Reach-in refrigerator/freezer
- Receiving table
- Roasting pan
- Rubber spatula (SPACH-e-la)
- Sandwich spreader
- Sauce pot
- Saucepan
- Sauté (saw-TAY) pan
- Scale
- Scoop
- Serrated slicer
- Sharpening stone
- Sheet pan
- Shuck
- Sieve (siv)
- Skimmer
- Slicer (knife)
- Slotted spoon
- Solid spoon
- Steak knife
- Steel
- Stock pot
- Straight spatula (SPACH-e-la)
- Strainer
- Tongs
- Tourné (tour-NAY)
- Utility cart
- Utility knife
- Vegetable peeler
- Volume measure
- Walk-in refrigerator/freezer
- Wire whip
- Zester

Every restaurant and foodservice operation requires different pieces of equipment. Equipment needs depend on many elements, such as the size of the kitchen, number of customers served, food items offered on the menu, and style

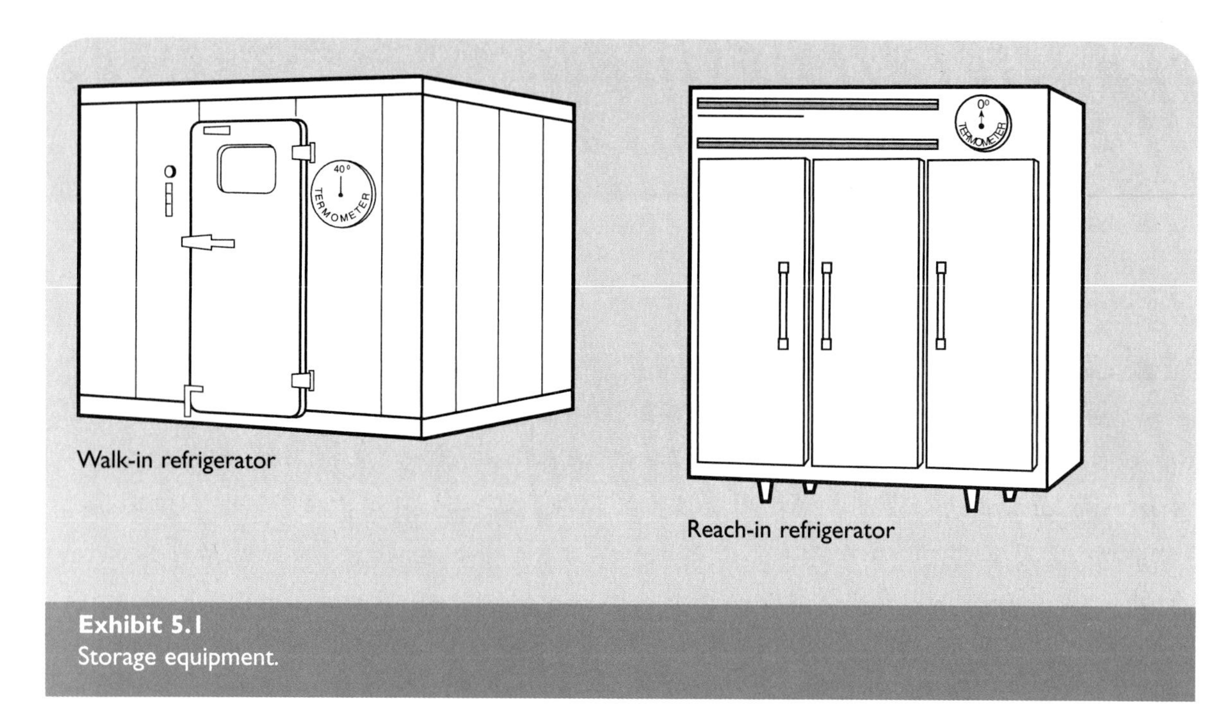

Exhibit 5.1
Storage equipment.

of service. This chapter will give you a look at the most common types of equipment used in foodservice so that no matter where you work, you will be familiar with the equipment found there.

We will discuss equipment in this chapter according to the flow of food in a foodservice operation, from the receiving area to waste disposal. As you read the following list of foodservice equipment, remember that every foodservice operation is unique and will use different kinds of equipment to suit its own special needs. In foodservice, it is important to remember that there is no *typical* kitchen.

Receiving Equipment

The receiving area is the first stop in the flow of food. It is here that all food deliveries come into a foodservice operation. Before a manager accepts the product, the quality and quantity of the food ordered must be checked against the items being delivered. This can be done using several pieces of equipment found in the receiving area.

Receiving table—Employees weigh, inspect, and check delivered items on a receiving table.

Scales—Employees weigh items using a scale. They do this to confirm that what was ordered matches what is delivered.

Utility carts—Utility carts made of heavy steel are used to carry food cases to storage areas. *Chutes, conveyors, dollies, dumbwaiters,* and *elevators* are all types of utility carts, and are used to move food and supplies from one area of the operation to another.

Storage Equipment

After food has been delivered and received into the receiving area, it must be properly stored. Dry goods such as flour, sugar, and grains must be stored off of the ground on stainless steel shelving. Perishable goods like dairy products, meat, and fresh fruits and vegetables will be stored in refrigerators and freezers. Following are just a few pieces of storage equipment that might be used in a foodservice operation.

Shelving—Shelving in storage areas should be made of stainless steel. Stainless steel should be used instead of wood because wood is difficult to keep clean and is not allowed for use by many local health departments. Stainless steel shelves are very strong and easy to clean.

Refrigerators and freezers—There are two basic types of refrigerators and freezers. A **walk-in refrigerator** and **walk-in freezer** (often called a "walk-in") are built right into the foodservice facility itself. A **reach-in refrigerator** or **reach-in freezer** can have one, two, or three internal compartments. A reach-in might have full-sized doors or half doors, windows in the doors, or doors on both sides of the freezer. Some have wheels so that they can be used in different areas of the kitchen. All refrigerators must maintain temperatures between 38°F and 42°F (3.3°C and 5.5°C). There are also *roll-in, display, on-site,* and *portable* refrigerators and freezers.

Prepreparation Equipment

Once food has passed through the receiving and storage areas, it is ready to be prepared for cooking. Following are just some of the many prepreparation utensils used in a foodservice operation. Because there are so many that can be used, we'll discuss them in the following categories:

- Measuring utensils
- Hand tools and small equipment
- Knives
- Pots and pans

Measuring Utensils

Measuring utensils come in all shapes and sizes. They are widely used in the foodservice kitchen to measure a variety of things from spices, to liquids, to dry goods like oats, grains, sugar, and flour. Below are just some of the types of measuring utensils you will recognize in the foodservice kitchen.

Balance scale—A balance scale is used in the bake shop area to weigh dry ingredients.

Ladle—Ladles come in various sizes, measured in ounces, so they can be used to portion out liquids.

Measuring cup—Measuring cups are used to measure varying quantities of both dry goods and liquids. Measuring cups with spouts are used to measure liquids, and those without spouts are used to measure dry ingredients.

Measuring spoon—Measuring spoons are usually used to measure small quantities of spices or liquids. They measure in the amounts of 1/4 teaspoon, 1/2 teaspoon, 1 teaspoon, and 1 tablespoon.

Portion scale—A scale used to measure recipe ingredients, from 1/4 oz to 1 lb.

Scoop—This short-handled measuring utensil is used to scoop out soft foods, such as ice cream, butter, and sour cream. These come in various sizes.

Volume measures—Volume measures are similar to liquid measuring cups but bigger, usually available in sizes of 1 pint, 1 quart, 1/2 gallon, and 1 gallon.

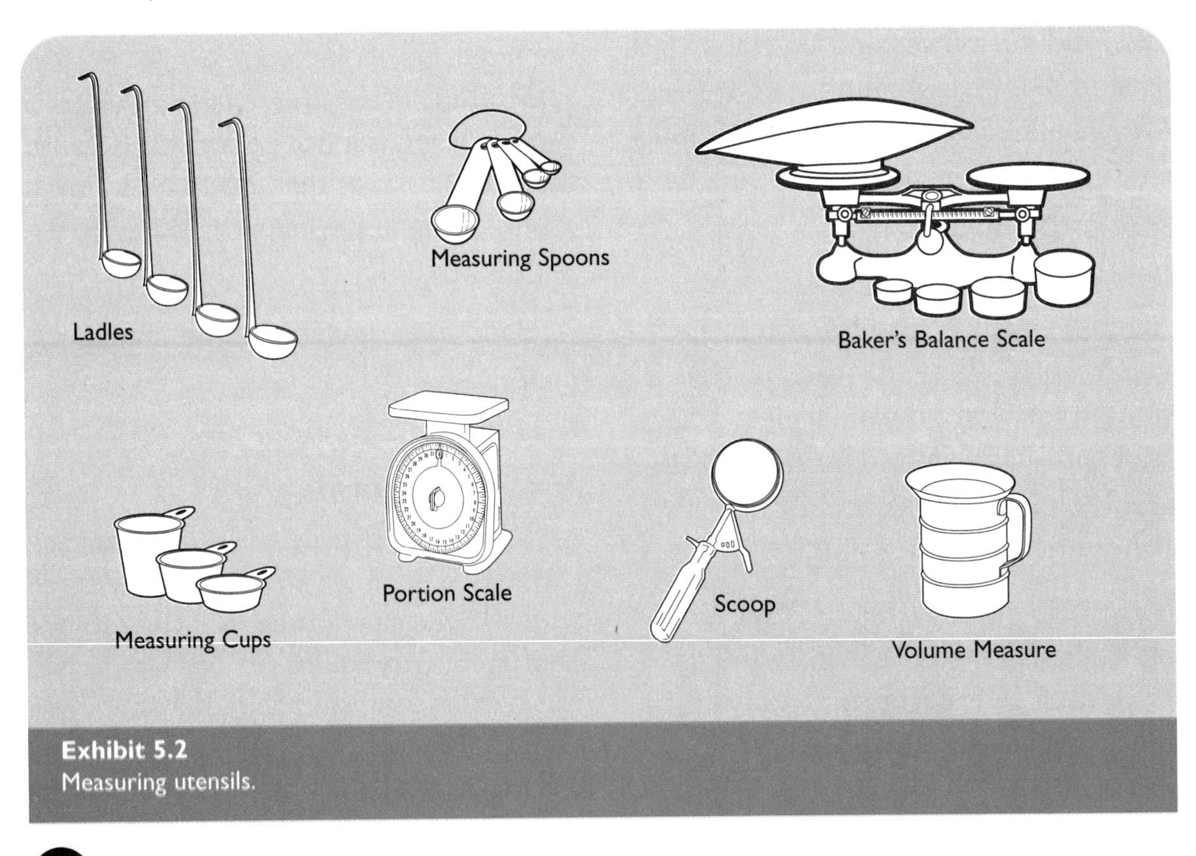

Exhibit 5.2
Measuring utensils.

Hand Tools and Small Equipment

Take a look in any foodservice kitchen and you will find many of the small hand tools and small equipment shown in Exhibit 5.3. They are easy to use, and are an essential part of food prepreparation.

Bench scraper—A flexible piece of rubber or plastic used to cut and separate dough, and scrape extra dough and flour from wooden work tables.

Can opener—In foodservice kitchens, can openers are mounted onto metal

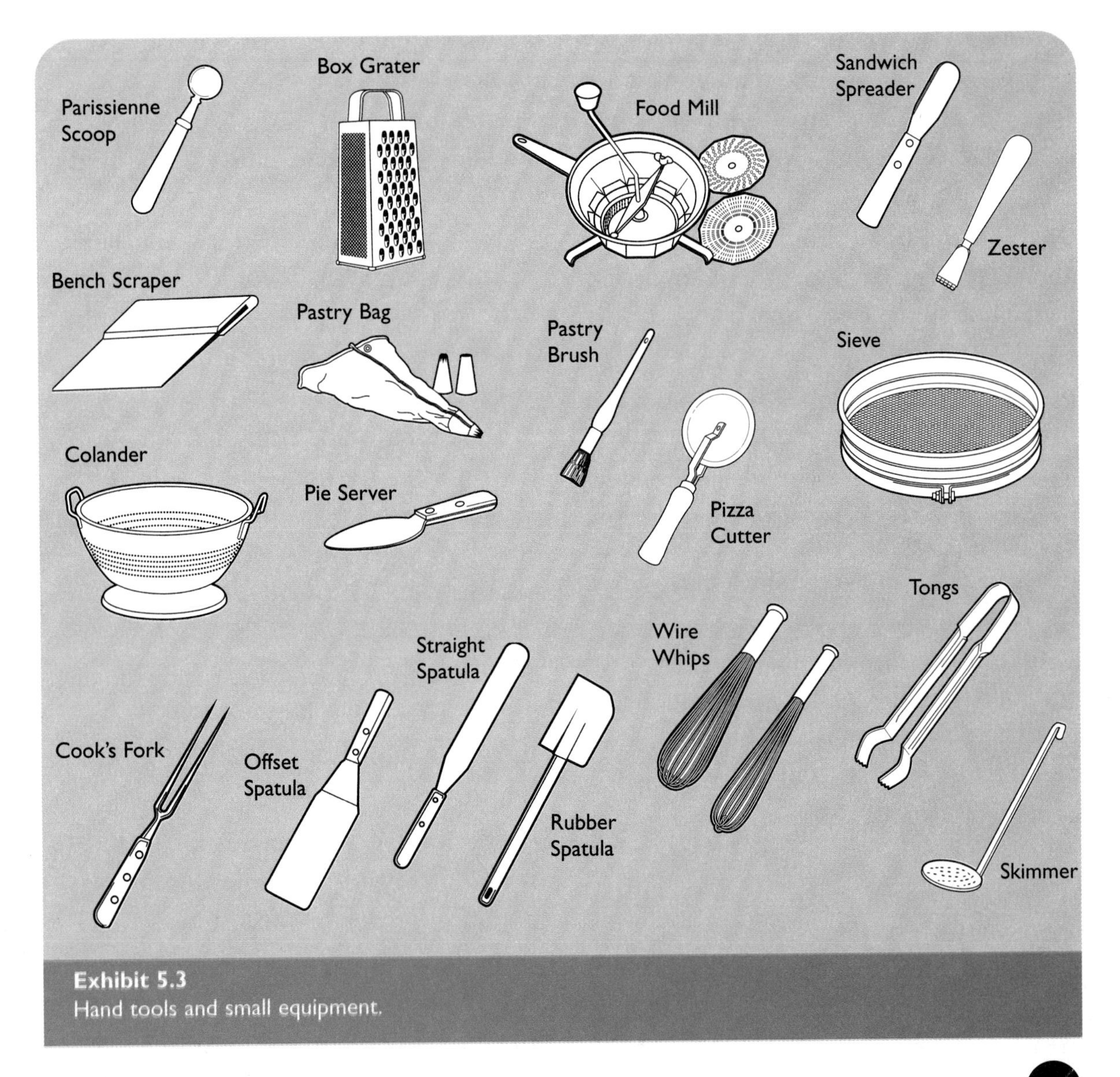

Exhibit 5.3
Hand tools and small equipment.

utility tables because they are used to open large cans. A small hand-held can opener, like those for home use, may be used in a foodservice kitchen to open small cans of food.

China cap—A cone-shaped strainer used to strain soups, stocks, and other liquids to remove all solid ingredients. A very fine China cap, called a **Chinois (chee-no-AH),** will strain out very small solid ingredients.

Colander (CAH-len-der)—A colander is used to drain liquid from cooked pasta and vegetables. Colanders stand on metal feet, while strainers are usually hand held.

Cook's fork—A fork with 2 long, pointed tines used to test the doneness of braised meats and vegetables, for lifting items to the plate, and for steadying an item being cut. A cook's fork should not be used to turn meats that are being dry-cooked because the tines may pierce the meat and release the juices.

Food mill—A machine that comes with several detachable parts used to purée foods to different consistencies.

Grater—A grater is used to grate hard cheeses, vegetables, potatoes, and other foods.

Offset spatula (SPACH-e-la)—An offset spatula is used to turn foods on a griddle or broiler. It has a wide, chisel-edged blade and a short handle.

Parissienne (pah-REE-see-en) **Scoop**—A Parissienne scoop, or melon baller, is used to cut ball shapes out of soft fruits and vegetables.

Pastry bag—A bag made of canvas, plastic, or nylon used to pipe out frostings, creams, and puréed foods. It can be used with different pastry tips to create a variety of decorations.

Pastry brush—Used to brush egg wash, melted butter, glazes, and other liquids on baked items.

Pie server—A pie server is a specially shaped spatula made for lifting out and serving pieces of pie.

Pizza cutter—Used to cut pizza and rolled-out dough.

Rubber spatula—A spatula, often called a scraper, is used to fold ingredients together and scrape the sides of bowls.

Sandwich spreader—A short, stubby spatula used to spread sandwich fillings and condiments.

Sieve (siv)—A sieve has a mesh screen and is used to sift flour and other dry baking ingredients and remove any large impurities.

Skimmer—A skimmer has a larger round, flat head with holes to remove foam from stock or soup, and to remove solid ingredients from liquids.

Spoons—Cooking spoons for quantity cooking can be either solid, perforated, or slotted. They are made of stainless steel, and hold about 3 ounces. **Solid spoons** are serving spoons without holes in them. They should be used when you want to spoon out both liquid and solid ingredients. **Perforated** and **slotted spoons** have holes that allow liquid to drain while holding the solid items on the spoon.

Straight spatula—A straight spatula is a flexible, round-tipped tool used for icing cakes, spreading fillings and glazes, leveling dry ingredients when measuring, and even turning pancakes and other foods.

Strainer—A strainer can be made of mesh-like material or metal with holes in it. Strainers come in different sizes, and often come in the shape of a bowl. Strainers are used to strain pasta, vegetables, and other larger foods cooked in liquid.

Tongs—Scissor-like utensil used to pick up and handle all kinds of solid food. To keep food safe and sanitary, food handlers should never use their hands to pick up food.

Wire whip—Wire whips of different sizes and heaviness are used to mix, beat, and stir foods.

Zester—A zester shreds small pieces of the outer peel of citrus fruits such as oranges, lemons, and limes.

Knives

Probably the most widely used piece of kitchen equipment, the knife is used in most cooking preparations, from slicing, to chopping, to shredding. Each knife is designed for a specific purpose, like paring a vegetable, or cutting meat from the bone. A good knife is made of stainless steel because it is very durable and stays sharp for a long time.

Boning knife—This six-inch knife is used in the butchering area to separate raw meat from the bone. The blade is thin and shorter than the blade of a chef's knife.

Butcher knife—The butcher knife is used to fabricate raw meat and is available with six to 14 inch blades.

Chef's (French) knife—This is an all-purpose knife used for chopping, slicing, and mincing all types of foods. Its blade is normally eight to 14 inches long and tapers to a point at the tip.

Clam knife—This short, blunt knife is used to **shuck**, or open, clams. Unlike the oyster knife, it has a very sharp edge.

Cleaver—This heavy, rectangular knife is used to chop all kinds of food, from vegetables to meat. It is also used to cut through bones.

Oyster knife—An oyster knife is a short, blunt, stubby knife used to shuck, or open, oysters.

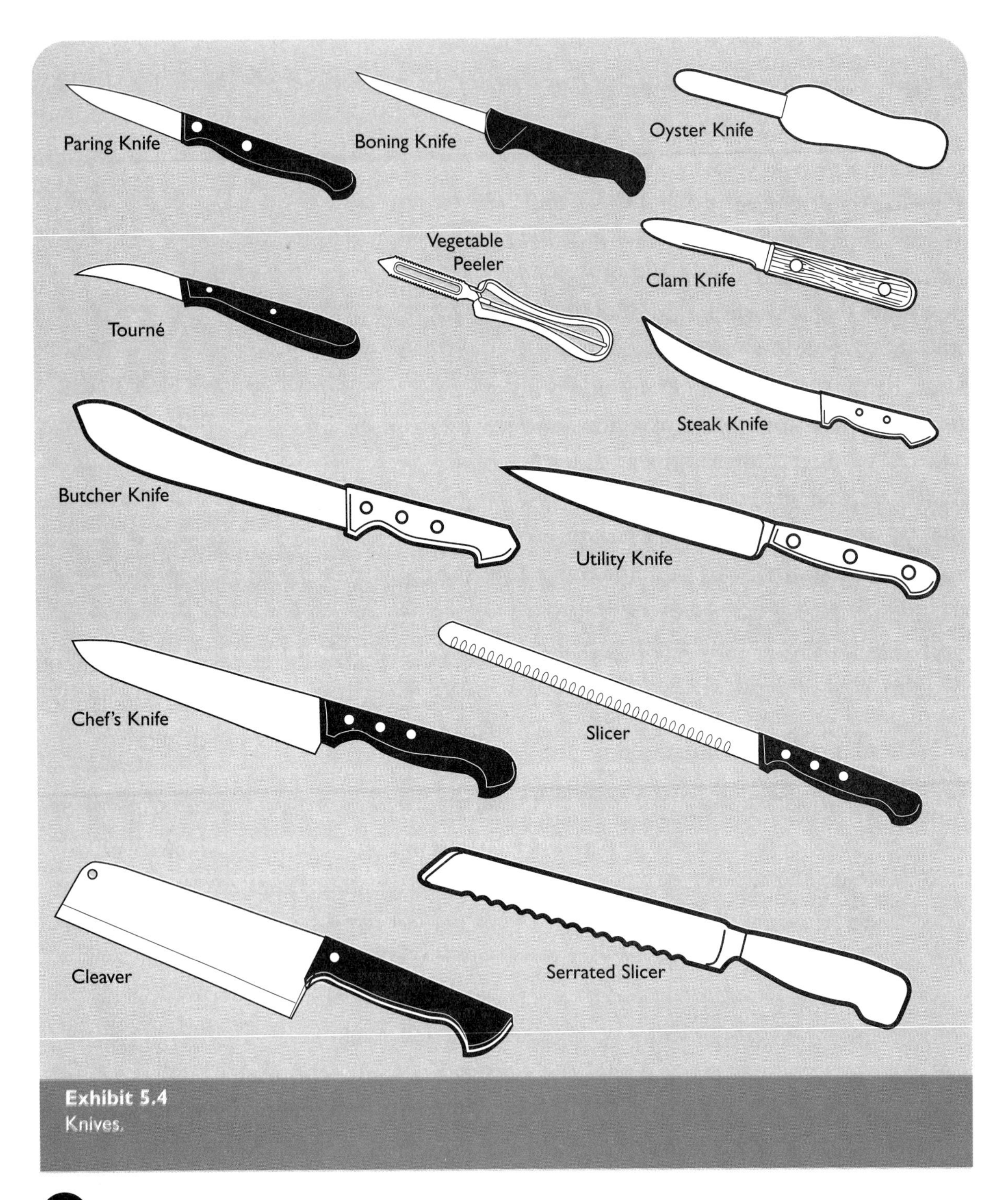

Exhibit 5.4
Knives.

Paring knife—The paring knife is used to trim and pare vegetables and fruits. It is a small knife with a rigid blade only 2 to 4 inches long.

Serrated slicer—A knife with a long, thin serrated blade used to slice breads and cakes.

Slicer—This knife is used for slicing cooked meats and its blade can be as long as 14 inches.

Steak knife—A curved knife used for cutting beef steaks from the loin.

Tourné (tour-NAY)—Similar to a paring knife, but with a curved blade for cutting the curved surfaces of vegetables.

Utility knife—An all-purpose knife used for cutting fruits, vegetables, and some meats. Its blade ranges from 6 to 8 inches long.

Vegetable peeler—This is not techncally a knife, but it has sharp edges for peeling potatoes, carrots, and other vegetables.

Working with knives is essential in cooking, so it is important to know the proper techniques for handling them. Be sure to keep your fingers away from the blade. Always face the blade away from your body, curl your fingers back, and tuck your thumb inside. Be sure to practice holding a knife before you use it.

All chefs know that knives are only useful and effective if they are kept sharp. They are also safest when they are sharp, since dull knives are more likely to slip on foods and cause you to lose your grip. Chefs keep their knives sharp by using a sharpening stone or a steel. The rough surface of the **sharpening stone** keeps knives' blades thin and sharp. A **steel** is a long metal rod used to maintain knife edges immediately after and between sharpenings.

Pots and Pans

Can you remember the last time you saw a kitchen without pots and pans? Probably not! Pots and pans are essential tools in the professional kitchen. They are available in many shapes and sizes, and are made of a variety of materials like copper, cast iron, stainless steel, aluminum, and nonstick coating.

Following are just some of the different kinds of pots and pans that are found in a professional foodservice kitchen.

Bake pan—A shallow rectangular pan used to bake all types of food.

Brazing pan—A high-sided, flat-bottomed cooking pan. It is used to braise, stew, and brown meat.

Exhibit 5.5
Pots and pans.

Cast iron skillet—A heavy, thick pan made of cast iron. It is used for pan-frying foods like meat and vegetables.

Double boiler—A pot that has an upper pot and a lower pot. The lower pot holds boiling or simmering water that gently cooks the food in the upper pot, like chocolate, milk, cream, and butter.

Hotel pan—Hotel pans are used for baking, roasting, or poaching meats and vegetables. They can also be used to hold foods for serving. Food is placed in the pan, and the pan is placed in a heating unit, such as a steam table.

Roasting pan—A shallow, rectangular pan with medium-high sides used to roast and bake foods, such as meat and poultry.

Sauce pot—These are used to prepare sauces, soups, and other liquids. Sauce pots are more shallow than stock pots, with straight sides and two loop handles for lifting.

Saucepan—A pan with flat or slightly flared sides and a single long handle. It is used for general cooking on ranges.

Sauté (saw-TAY) **pan**—This pan can be either slope-sided or straight-sided. It is used to sauté and pan-fry vegetables, meats, fish, and eggs.

Sheet pan—This very shallow pan, about 1 inch deep, is used primarily to bake cookies, rolls, and cakes.

Stock pot—A large pot used for preparing stocks. Stock pots with spigots allow the liquid to be poured out easily without losing any of the solid ingredients.

Review Your Learning 5.1

1. Match each hand utensil on the left with its use on the right. Some letters may not be used.

___ Bench scraper	a) Decorating cakes and cookies
___ Colander	b) Straining soups and sauces
___ Skimmer	c) Draining liquid from pasta, vegetables, and washed salad greens
___ China cap	d) Removing foam from the top of stock and soup
___ Pastry bag	e) Cutting and separating dough
	f) Used to turn meats
	g) Short-handled measuring utensil used to portion food

2. Match each knife on the left with its use on the right. Some letters may not be used.

___ Boning	a) Trimming vegetables
___ Cleaver	b) Separating raw meat from the bone
___ Serrated slicer	c) Cutting cakes and breads
___ Utility	d) Cutting through bones and cutting vegetables
___ Paring	e) Cutting fruits and lettuce
	f) Cutting pizza and dough
	g) Slicing breads and vegetables

For questions 3 and 4, complete the sentences using the correct equipment name from Section 5.1.

3. A(n) ___________ is used to cut ball shapes out of fruits and vegetables, while a(n)___________ is used for soft foods, such as ice cream, butter, and sour cream.

4. Similar to a strainer, a(n)_______________ stands on metal feet and is used to drain excess liquid from cooked pasta and vegetables and rinse salad greens.

5.2

SECTION 5.2

Cooking, Holding, and Service Equipment

AFTER STUDYING SECTION 5.2, YOU SHOULD BE ABLE TO:

- Explain how to store food and supplies properly on shelves and in refrigerators and freezers.
- Demonstrate how to cut and mix foods using standard kitchen equipment.
- Compare and contrast cooking foods using various types of steamers, broilers, grills, ranges, fryers, and ovens.
- Outline how to hold and serve food and beverages using kitchen equipment.
- Compare and contrast the features of dishwashing machines.

KEY TERMS

- Bain marie (bahn mah-REE)
- Charbroiler
- Circular dishwasher
- Coffee maker
- Convection oven
- Conventional (standard) oven
- Conveyor (con-VAY-er) oven
- Countertop broiler
- Deck oven
- Deep-fat fryer
- Dough arm
- Flat beater
- Flat-top burner
- Flight (rackless) dishwasher
- Food chopper
- Food warmer
- Griddle
- Hotel broiler
- Ice machine
- Microwave oven
- Mixer
- Open burner

↳

Cooking Equipment

There are many items necessary in the kitchen to prepare food for cooking. As we discussed, things like hand tools, knives, and pots and pans are important in the food preparation process. But no chef or cook would be able to do his job without being able to identify and properly use the cooking equipment in this section.

We will discuss cooking equipment in the following categories:

- Cutters and mixers
- Steamers
- Broilers
- Ranges, griddles, and fryers
- Ovens

Cutters and Mixers

In the professional foodservice kitchen, cutters and mixers are used to cut meats and vegetables and mix sauces and batters. Following are some of the cutters and mixers commonly found in a foodservice kitchen.

Food chopper—A food chopper chops vegetables, meats, and other foods using a rotating blade and bowl.

Mixer—5-quart, 20-quart, 60-quart, and 80-quart mixers are used to mix and process large amounts of food with any number of specialized attachments, including the following:

- **Flat beater**—Used to mix, mash, and cream soft foods
- **Wire whip**—Used to beat and add air

KEY TERMS (CONTINUED)

- Pastry knife
- Potwashing machine
- Pulper and extractor
- Range
- Ring-top burner
- Rotary oven
- Rotisserie (roe-TIS-er-ee)
- Salamander
- Single-tank conveyor (con-VAY-er) dishwasher
- Single-tank door dishwasher
- Slicer (machine)
- Slow-roasting oven
- Spit
- Steam table
- Steamer
- Steam-jacketed kettle
- Tilting fry pan
- Trash compactor
- Vertical cutter mixer (VCM)
- Wing whip
- Wire whip

to light foods, such as egg whites and cake frosting

- **Wing whip**—A heavier version of the wire whip used to whip, cream, and mash heavier foods
- **Pastry knife (paddle)**—Used to mix shortening into doughs
- **Dough arm (hook)**—Used to mix heavy, thick doughs

Slicer—Most slicers have a circular blade. Food is either passed through the machine automatically or by hand. Since slicer blades are very sharp, it is important to pay close attention when using them.

Vertical Cutter Mixer (VCM)—The vertical cutter mixer (VCM) cuts, mixes, and blends foods quickly with a rotating blade.

Courtesy of Hobart Corporation, Troy, Ohio

Exhibit 5.6
Vertical cutter mixer (VCM).

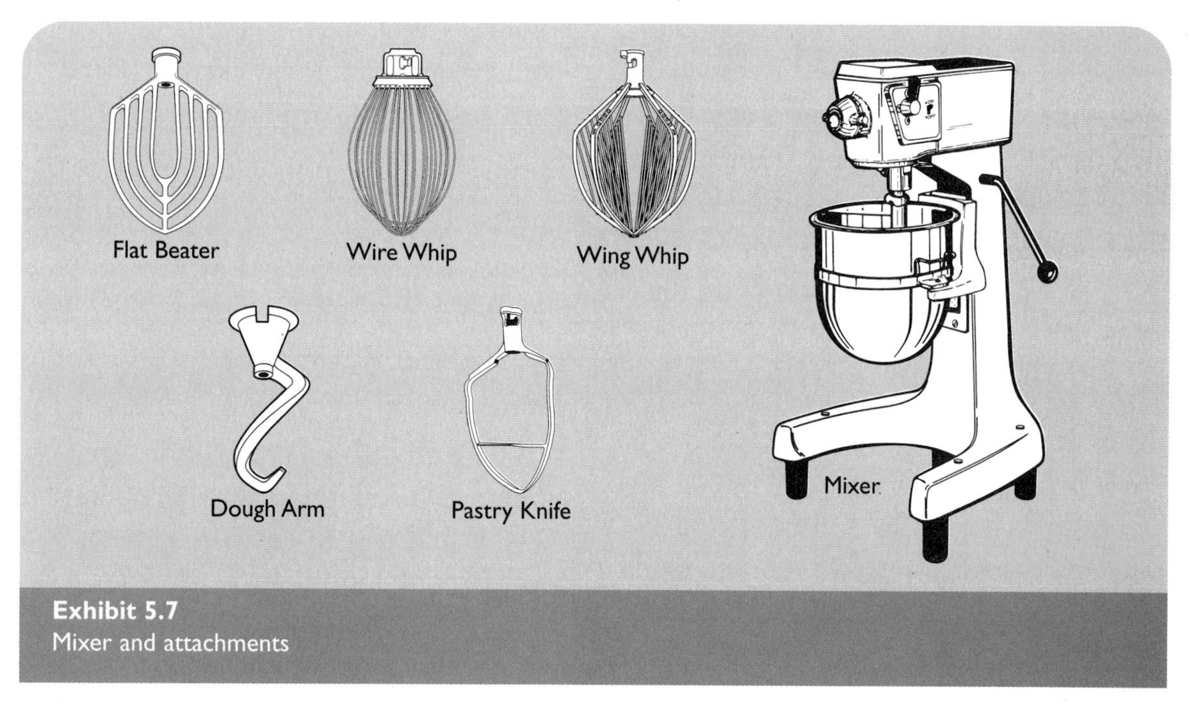

Exhibit 5.7
Mixer and attachments

All grinders, slicers, and cutting machines can be dangerous. When using these cutting machines, always use safety guards. Before using this equipment, you must be properly trained, and informed of all precautionary measures that should be taken when operating the equipment. If you aren't sure how to use the machine, always ask for help!

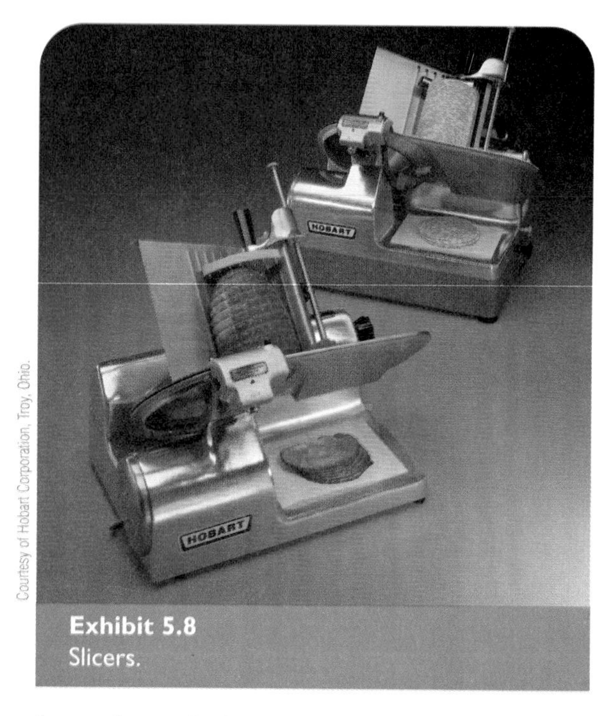

Courtesy of Hobart Corporation, Troy, Ohio.

Exhibit 5.8
Slicers.

Steamers

Steamers are used in restaurants to cook vegetables and grains. A steamer allows the food to come into direct contact with the steam, heating the food very quickly. Cooking with steam is a very efficient method of cooking. There are different types of steamers that foodservice operations use.

Steamer—A steamer is used to steam foods like vegetable and grains and uses low or high steam pressure. It often consists of a set of stacked pots. The lower pot holds boiling water. The upper pot has a perforated bottom that allows the steam to enter through and cook the food in the pot above. All types of steamers cook foods quickly in very hot (212°F or 100°C) water vapor.

Steam-jacketed kettle—A free-standing or tabletop kettle used to heat liquid foods like soups and stews, quickly and evenly. Because the entire food contact surface is heated evenly by steam instead of just the bottom by heat, the foods cook faster, more evenly, and are less likely to burn. They are available in a range of sizes.

Tilting fry pan—Although this piece of equipment is called a *fryer,* it is actually used to grill, steam, braise, sauté, and stew many different kinds of food. They are very easy to clean.

Broilers

There are several types of broilers commonly used in foodservice operations. Using very intense direct heat, broilers cook food quickly. Here are a few of the broilers most commonly found in foodservice operations.

Charbroiler—Charbroilers use gas or electricity to mimic the effects of charcoal on a grill. Food juices are allowed to drip onto the heat source to create flames and smoke, which add flavor to broiled foods. This is also dangerous, and special filters must be used to prevent fires.

Countertop broiler—This is a small broiler that sits on top of a work table. It is used primarily in quick-service restaurants.

Hotel broiler—This is used to broil large amounts of food quickly.

Rotisserie (roe-TIS-er-ee)—In a rotisserie, food is placed on a stick, or **spit,** and turned over or under a heat source. Often, chicken, turkey, and other types of poultry are cooked on a rotisserie.

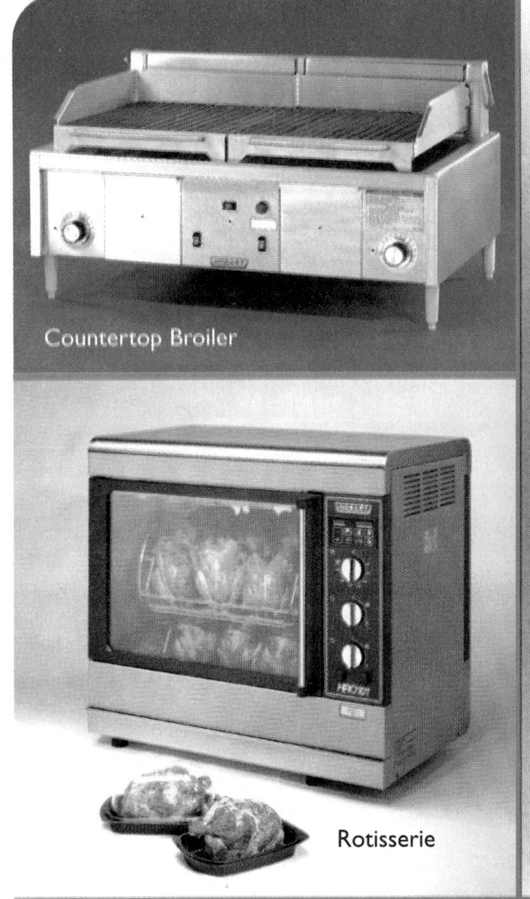

Exhibit 5.9
Broilers.

Courtesy of Hobart Corporation, Troy, Ohio.

Salamander—This is a small broiler usually attached to the back of a range. It is used mostly to brown, finish, and melt foods to order.

Ranges, Griddles, and Fryers

In most foodservice kitchens, the range is the most utilized piece of equipment. **Ranges** are cooking units with open heat sources. Like a lot of the foodservice equipment mentioned above, ranges come in a variety of sizes and variations suitable to the needs of an individual foodservice operation. We will discuss three different types of ranges: open-burner, flat-top burner, and ring-top burner.

Open burner—A grate-style burner that supplies direct heat to the item being cooked. The heat can be easily controlled.

Flat-top burner—Food is cooked on a thick slate of cast iron steel that covers the heat source. A flat-top burner provides even and consistent heat.

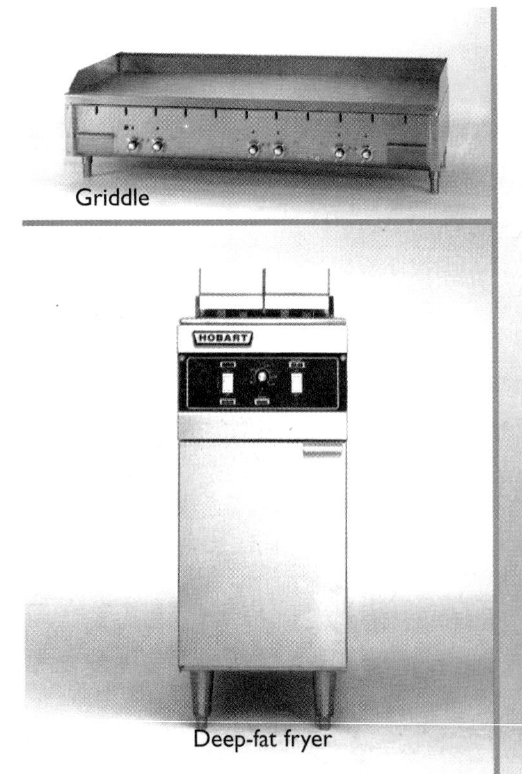

Exhibit 5.10
Ranges, griddles, and fryers.

Courtesy of Hobart Corporation, Troy, Ohio.

Ring-top burner—Different sized rings or plates can be added or removed to allow more or less heat to cook the food item. A ring-top burner provides direct, controllable heat.

Griddle—A flat heated metal surface on which foods are directly cooked. Griddles are most often found in quick-service and institutional foodservice operations.

Deep-fat fryer—Gas and electric fryers cook foods in fat at temperatures between 300°F and 450°F (149°C and 232°C). Some computerized fryers lower and raise the food baskets automatically.

Alert! Alert! Always take extra caution when cooking with deep-fat fryers. Make sure you learn how to properly use this equipment before you use it to prevent burns and fires.

Ovens

There are many types of ovens available to suit a variety of foodservice operations. They vary in size and method of operation. Following are just a few of the kinds of ovens you might find in a foodservice kitchen.

Convection oven—Convection ovens cook food with a fan that circulates heated air. This shortens cooking times and uses energy efficiently.

Conventional (standard) oven—In a conventional oven, the heat source is located on the floor of the oven. Heat is conducted to the cavity, or open space in the oven. Food is cooked on racks. These ovens are usually found below a range top burner. This type of oven is

Exhibit 5.11
Ovens.

Courtesy of Hobart Corporation, Troy, Ohio.

inexpensive and easy to integrate with other pieces of cooking equipment.

Conveyor (con-VAY-er) **oven**—In this type of oven, a conveyor belt moves the food back and forth in the oven. It cooks from both top and bottom heat sources.

Deck oven—A deck oven is a type of conventional oven in which 2 to 4 shelves are stacked on top of each other. Food is cooked directly on these shelves, or decks.

Microwave oven—Microwave ovens heat foods not with heat but with microwaves of energy that cause a food's molecules to move rapidly and create heat inside the food. They are used in restaurant kitchens mainly to thaw and reheat foods.

Rotary oven—A rotary oven has 3–5 circular shelves on which food cooks as the shelves move around a central rod.

Slow-roasting oven—This oven is used to roast meats at low temperatures. This helps preserve the meat's moisture, reduce shrinkage, and brown its surfaces.

Holding and Service Equipment

Once the food arrives in holding and service area, it is usually ready to be presented to the guest. All care and precautions have been taken to ensure that the meals being served to guests have been prepared accurately and with care.

Though most of the hard work in preparing a meal has already been done, the final touches that are made in the holding and service areas are important to delivering the most quality meal.

Bain marie (bahn mah-REE)—
A bain marie is any type of hot-water bath meant to keep foods warm. Food is placed in stainless steel inserts, and the inserts are placed in a container holding hot water. Inserts come in many sizes, ranging from 1 to 36 quarts.

Coffee maker—Coffee makers come in a variety of sizes, from coffee makers that make only a few cups, to machines that make several gallons.

Food warmer or **steam table**—A food warmer holds foods between 100°F and 300°F (37.8°C and 149°C). It should never be used to cook or reheat foods, and food should not be held longer than 4 hours.

Ice machine—Ice machines make ice in cubes, flakes, chips, and crushed ice. Ice should be scooped only with a proper ice scoop.

Never scoop ice with glass or any other breakable utensil. Pieces of glass may break off into the ice and be served to customers.

When holding hot foods for service:

- Keep food out of the temperature danger zone.
- Stir foods regularly to keep them evenly heated.
- Do not add newly cooked food to food already in hot holding.

Dishwashing and Disposal Equipment

Dishwashing machines come in a wide variety of sizes and styles. Because a dishwashing machine is a large investment, it is important to know the specific needs of your kitchen.

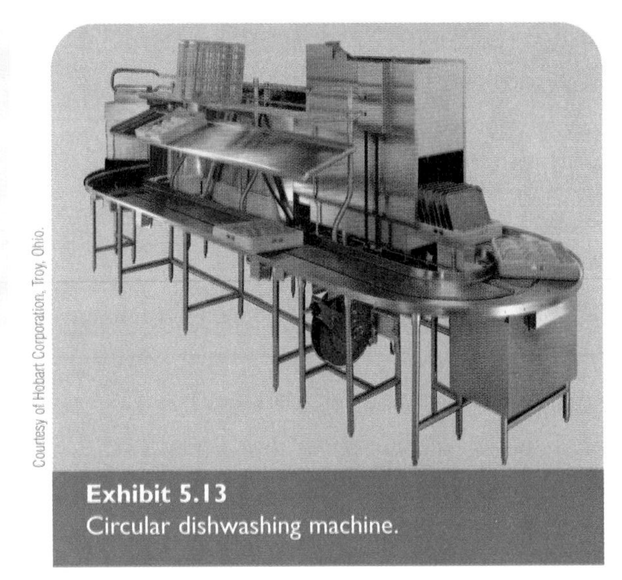

Courtesy of Hobart Corporation, Troy, Ohio.

Exhibit 5.13
Circular dishwashing machine.

Courtesy of Hobart Corporation, Troy, Ohio.

Exhibit 5.12
Potwashing machine.

Circular dishwasher—A circular dishwashing machine circulates dishes through two or three tanks. These machines are very labor efficient because very little is done by hand.

Flight (rackless) dishwasher—A flight dishwashing machine contains tanks that prewash, wash, and rinse dishes. They are used mostly in operations with very large volume.

Potwashing machine—Potwashing machines pump water harder than dishwashing machines, and are big enough to hold large pots and pans.

Single-tank conveyor (con-VAY-er) **dishwasher**—With a single-tank conveyor dishwasher, dishes are scraped manually and loaded into the single-tank conveyor machine, then sent through wash and rinse cycles.

Single-tank door dishwasher—This machine washes the dishes with hot sprayed water, after the dishes have been scraped, loaded, and unloaded by hand.

Pulper and extractor—The pulper and extractor waste disposal system removes all the moisture from waste and reduces it to a paper-like substance. This takes up less space in a sewer system than untreated waste.

Trash compactor—Trash compactors reduce the volume of trash and garbage by smashing it down, making it more compact.

Courtesy of Hobart Corporation, Troy, Ohio.

Exhibit 5.14
Pulper and extractor.

Courtesy of Hobart Corporation, Troy, Ohio.

Exhibit 5.15
Single-tank door dishwashing machine.

Review Your Learning 5.2

1. Complete the following sentences using the correct key terms from Section 5.2.
   a. A freestanding or tabletop kettle, the ______________________________ kettle circulates heat evenly through the sides.
   b. The ________________________________ is an attachment to a mixer that mixes heavy, thick bread dough.
   c. A small broiler, the ________________________________, is usually attached to the back of a range.
   d. A(n)__________________________ is used to grill, steam, braise, sauté, and stew many different types of food.

2. Match the utensil on the left with its use on the right.

   ___flat-top burner
   ___conventional oven
   ___food warmer
   ___dishwasher
   ___pulper and extractor

   a. Holds foods between 100°F and 300°F (37.8°C to 149°C)
   b. Thick slate of cast iron steel that covers the heat source and provides even and consistent heat to cook food
   c. Waste disposal system that reduces waste to a paper-like substance
   d. Heat is conducted to the cavity, or open space, from the heat source on the floor of the oven
   e. Labor efficient tank that circulates dishes through three tanks

3. What pieces of equipment might be used if you were preparing a grilled chicken breast dinner for a guest in your foodservice operation? List items from the cooking, holding, and service areas.

5.3

SECTION 5.3

Cleaning and Caring for Equipment

AFTER STUDYING SECTION 5.3, YOU SHOULD BE ABLE TO:

- Outline the order in which food and supplies flow through a food service.
- Demonstrate proper cleaning and sanitizing of foodservice equipment and utensils.

KEY TERM

- **Fixed equipment**

Flow of Food

If you take a look at different foodservice operations, you'll most likely find the kitchen and preparation areas set up in one of a few kinds of layout. In general, the way equipment is set up and arranged should be done in the order the equipment is used. Kitchen equipment is used in the order that food goes through the operation.

First, food is received, then it is put into storage, usually refrigerators, freezers, or dry storage rooms. Storage areas and equipment should be next to prepreparation equipment. For example, cutters, mixers, and choppers should be next to produce-rinsing sinks. Cooking equipment, like ranges, steamers, ovens, broilers, and griddles, are most often located near holding and service equipment. Holding and service equipment, like the bain marie, are also near the dining room, so food can be taken quickly to customers. There should be a smooth flow between the dining room and the dishwashing area, and dishwashers must have access to waste disposal equipment. Exhibit 5.16 shows how food should flow in an operation.

Exhibit 5.16
Knowing how food flows through an operation helps you plan equipment needs.

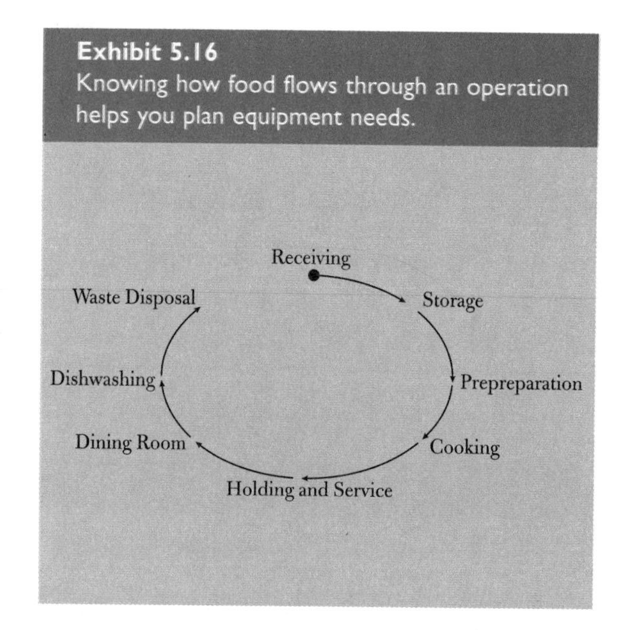

Equipment Standards

Commercial foodservice equipment is more durable than equipment found in homes. It is also designed for sanitation. Sanitation is an important factor when choosing kitchen equipment. This is because equipment that comes into contact with food (either directly or through splashing) can often serve as a home for bacteria and pests.

Organizations such as NSF International (formerly the National Sanitation Foundation) and Underwriters Laboratories, Inc., have guidelines for choosing proper equipment to see whether it meets specific sanitation standards. To pass inspection, foodservice equipment must:

- Be easy to clean.
- Be made from non-toxic and non-absorbent materials.
- Have rounded edges or corners.
- Have smooth surfaces.
- Be resistant to cracking and chipping.

If a piece of equipment meets these standards, one of the symbols shown in Exhibit 5.17 will be stamped on its side.

Exhibit 5.17
Equipment safety symbols are given to equipment that meets specific sanitation standards.

Reprinted with permission of NSF INternational, Ann Arbor, Michigan, and Underwriters Laboratories, Inc., Northbrook, IL.

It is very important that refrigerators and freezers be easy to clean. Food is often held in refrigerators for long periods of time, and unclean refrigerators and freezers increase the risk of cross-contamination. Refrigerators and freezers should also be equipped with fans that force the air to circulate and keep temperatures at the proper levels. Upright, reach-in units should be raised six inches off the floor to allow for easy cleaning underneath.

When choosing refrigerator and freezer units, check to see that they meet the sanitation requirements of NSF International and UL symbols.

Cleaning and Sanitizing Equipment

All dishes, glasses, flatware, pots, pans, utensils, and equipment must be cleaned and sanitized after every use to avoid possible cross-contamination.

Remember that being clean is not the same as being sanitary. Clean means being free of visible soil, such as dirt, dust, or food waste. Clean refers to outward appearance, while sanitary refers to the sanitary condition of an item. Sanitary means free of harmful levels of disease-causing micro-organisms and other harmful contaminants. Because such contaminants may be invisible, all surfaces that come into contact with food must be washed, rinsed, and sanitized.Clean and sanitize food-contact surfaces:

- After each use.
- After an interruption of service.
- At least every four hours for equipment in constant use.
- Once a day for grill surfaces.

General Safety Guidelines for Cleaning Equipment:

- Always turn off the machine. Make sure the plug is pulled from the electrical power source before removing guards or any other parts.
- Clean the blades and moving parts following the same cleaning and handling procedures as for knives. Wear safety gloves when handling blades. Turn the points and blade edges away from the body, and wipe away from sharp edges.
- Reassemble the machine while it is still off and unplugged. Tighten all blades and moving parts that have been cleaned. Replace all guards. Settings should be at zero or off.
- After putting the machine back together, plug it in, and turn it on for several seconds to be sure that the equipment is running properly.

Remember!

Cleaning and rinsing must be done before sanitizing.

Tableware, equipment (including cutting boards), and utensils can be cleaned and sanitized by hand in a three compartment sink. Many high-volume kitchens prefer to use a dishwashing machine. Here are the proper steps for both the manual and machine methods of cleaning and sanitizing.

Cleaning and Sanitizing Manually

1. Scrape and presoak items, then sort.
2. In the first sink, wash in clean, hot detergent solution.
3. In the second sink, rinse in clear, hot, drinkable water.
4. In the third sink, sanitize items using either a chemical sanitizing solution or hot water (170°F or 76.7°C) for 30 seconds. Use a dip basket to hold items.
5. Air dry all items. Do not towel dry.

Cleaning and Sanitizing by Machine

1. Flush, scrape, or soak items.
2. Load the machine so all sides of an item are sprayed by wash and rinse water.
3. Run machine following the manufacturer's instructions.
4. Air dry all items. Do not towel dry.

Fixed equipment is permanently placed, and cannot be moved for cleaning. Some examples of fixed equipment are slicers, grinders, and cutting machines. Fixed equipment comes with manufacturers' instructions for disassembling and cleaning. You should always follow these instructions.

Cleaning and Sanitizing Fixed Equipment

1. Make sure equipment is turned off.
2. Unplug electrical equipment.
3. Unfasten removable parts.
4. Wash and sanitize each part, turning blades and points away from your body.
5. Rinse and sanitize other surfaces with chemical sanitizer, following the manufacturer's directions.
6. Air dry all parts before putting back together.

Some equipment, such as automatic ice making machines and soft-serve ice cream and frozen yogurt dispensers, are designed to be cleaned by having a detergent solution, hot water rinse, and sanitizing solution pass through them. These are called clean-in-place equipment.

When using chemicals and detergents to clean and sanitize, always follow manufacturer's directions to avoid injury or poisoning! Store chemicals in clearly labeled containers away from food preparation and storage areas.

Working with Clean-in-Place Equipment

- Read and follow manufacturers' instructions carefully. Keep them nearby for easy reference.
- Cleaning and sanitizing solutions must remain in the tubes and pipes for a specific predetermined time.
- Make sure no cleaning solution is left in the machine, as it could come into contact with food and beverages being dispensed.
- Clean-in-place machines must be self-draining. Inside parts must be easily accessible for inspection.

Review Your Learning 5.3

1. On a separate sheet of paper, using the words below, diagram how food flows through an operation.

HOLDING AND SERVING	RECEIVING
DISHWASHING	WASTE DISPOSAL
COOKING	FOOD PREPREPARATION
STORAGE	DINING ROOM

2. What are some standards that must be met by foodservice equipment in order to pass inspection?
3. Explain the difference between *clean* and *sanitary*.
4. How often should food-contact services be cleaned and sanitized?
5. You have 1 gallon of a chemical cleaner left in a 5 gallon bucket. If you want to transfer it to a smaller container what is the proper way to do it? What kind of container should you not use to store the chemical?

Flashback

CHAPTER 5

SECTION 5.1: RECEIVING, STORAGE, AND PREPREPARATION EQUIPMENT

- Foodservice managers need to be familiar with all types of equipment—from the time food is received through preparation, service, and waste disposal.
- **Receiving table, scales,** and **utility carts** are kept in the receiving area.
- Food must be properly stored using the appropriate stainless steel **shelving** and **walk-in** or **reach-in refrigerators** and **freezers.**
- Measuring utensils, like **ladles, measuring cups, measuring spoons, volume measures, balance** and **portion scales,** and **scoops** are used to prepare food for cooking.
- Hand tools and small equipment are easy to use and are an essential part of food prepreparation. Some of these tools include **spatulas, sandwich spreaders, pizza cutters, colanders,** and **graters.**
- All knives are made for a specific cutting purpose and must be handled with care. Using a **steel** to maintain knife edges and a **sharpening stone** to sharpen knives are part of proper knife maintenance.
- Pots and pans are an essential part of a foodservice kitchen. They are available in many shapes and sizes and are made of a variety of materials, like copper, cast iron, stainless steel, aluminum, and nonstick coating.
- Some pots and pans include the **bake pan, brazing pan, cast iron skillet, double boiler, hotel pan, roasting pan, sauce pan, sauce pot, sauté pan, sheet pan,** and **stock pot.**

SECTION 5.2: COOKING, HOLDING, AND SERVICE EQUIPMENT

- Cooking equipment can be grouped as cutters and mixers; steamers; broilers; ranges, griddles, and fryers; and ovens.

- Cutters and mixers are used to cut meats and vegetables, mix sauces and batters, and include **mixers, vertical cutter mixers (VCM), food choppers,** and **slicers.**
- Steamers allow food to come in direct contact with the steam, heating food very quickly. **Steamers, steam-jacketed kettles,** and **tilting fry pans** are steamers commonly found in the foodservice kitchen.
- Broilers use very intense direct heat to cook food. Some broilers include the **charbroiler, countertop broiler, hotel broiler, rotisserie,** and **salamander.**
- **Open-burner, flat-top burner,** and **ring-top burner** are just three types of ranges mentioned in this chapter.
- A **griddle** is a flat heated metal surface on which foods are directly cooked.
- The most common type of fryer, the **deep-fat fryer,** cooks food in fat at temperatures between 300°F and 450°F (149°C and 232°C).
- Ovens you may find in a foodservice operation are the **convection oven, conventional (standard) oven, conveyor oven, deck oven, microwave oven, rotary oven** and **slow roasting oven.**
- Holding and service equipment are necessary to make the appropriate final touches to a meal.
- A **bain marie, coffee maker, food warmer (steam table),** and **ice machine** are common holding and service equipment used in foodservice operations.
- Selection of dishwashing equipment depends on the size of the foodservice operation. They are the **circular dishwasher, flight (rackless) dishwasher, potwashing machine, single-tank conveyor,** and **single-tank door dishwasher.**
- Waste disposal equipment includes the **pulper and extractor,** hood (exhaust system), and **trash compactor.**

SECTION 5.3: CLEANING AND CARING FOR EQUIPMENT

- Regardless of the type of operation, equipment is arranged according to how food flows in the operation: receiving; storage; food prepreparation; cooking; holding and service; dining room; dishwashing; and waste disposal.

- Organizations such as NSF International and Underwriters Laboratories, Inc., inspect foodservice equipment to see whether it meets specific sanitation standards.
- When choosing equipment, make sure they have the NSF International and UL symbols for passing inspection.
- All dishes, glassware, flatware, pots, pans, utensils, and equipment must be cleaned and sanitized after every use to avoid cross-contamination.
- *Clean* means being free of visible soil, such as dirt, dust, or food waste.
- *Sanitary* means free of harmful levels of disease-causing micro-organisms and other harmful contaminants.
- The appropriate steps must be followed for cleaning and sanitizing food-contact surfaces and fixed equipment; cleaning and sanitizing manually and by machine; and working with clean-in-place equipment.

Lisa Haselhorst, R.D., L.D.

Quality Nutrition, Inc.
Trenton, Illinois

I decided to enter the field of nutrition when I was a freshman in college. I went to Illinois State University in Normal, and planned to go into Business Education. One of the classes I took as a freshman was basic nutrition. Much to my surprise, I really enjoyed it! From that point on, I was hooked. I decided to get a Bachelor of Science degree in Home Economics/Dietetics. I took a variety of classes to complete my degree. These classes included chemistry, communications, educational psychology, and diet therapy. I even took a cooking class, where I learned how to cook, set tables, and plan well-balanced meals.

After college, I began consulting in a hospital. I've been consulting ever since! I worked in the area of wellness in both a health club and a hospital. After that, I continued to work as a consultant, and started my own company, Quality Nutrition, Inc. Working as a dietetic consultant is really challenging. As a consultant, I visit clients that include nursing homes, hospitals, home health care, and state facilities. I work closely with dietary managers there to ensure the patients are receiving the best nutritional care possible. Working with home health care companies is great, because I go to patients' homes and can see exactly what and how they eat. It's fun to meet with patients on an individual basis, and they really enjoy the company!

Right now in the field of dietetics, consulting is extremely popular. There are now more opportunities than ever in the area of nutrition. My company is even becoming involved in giving supermarket tours for the general public in which small groups of people visit the supermarket to learn how to select the best and most nutritious foods to suit their needs. We also publish a health newsletter that discusses all sorts of topics in the field of dietetics and nutrition.

It is extremely rewarding to help people make better food choices, and even help prevent disease. I really enjoy helping my clients feel better. If you're interested in the field of dietetics, I suggest starting out by working in a nursing home or a hospital with a dietitian. Hopefully, you'll enjoy it as much as I do!

CHAPTER 6

Nutrition

SECTION 6.1

The ABCs of Nutrition

AFTER STUDYING SECTION 6.1, YOU SHOULD BE ABLE TO:

- Characterize the roles of carbohydrates, hormones, fiber, starch, and fats in people's diets and identify foods that contain these nutrients.
- Describe cholesterol and foods in which it is found.

A major goal of foodservice managers is to offer a variety of healthful, appealing, and high-quality foods to their customers. Most people typically think of food as a way to satisfy their hunger or give them pleasure. But eating food goes beyond simply satisfying hunger pangs. Food provides the body with essential nutrients. The energy the body needs to function only comes from the nutrients in food. Without good nutrition, it is difficult to perform well. To provide customers with food that is good and good for them, foodservice managers need a basic knowledge of proper nutrition.

KEY TERMS

- **Calorie**
- **Carbohydrate**
- **Cholesterol**
- **Essential fatty acid**
- **Fat**
- **Fiber**
- **Glucose**
- **Hormone**
- **Insulin**
- **Macronutrient**
- **Micronutrient**
- **Nutrient**
- **Oxidation**
- **Starch**

NUTRIENTS

Nutrients are chemicals in food that the body needs to work properly. The three main reasons the body needs nutrients are:

- To provide energy.
- To build and repair cells.
- To keep the different systems in the body working smoothly, such as breathing, digesting food, and building red blood cells.

There are six groups of nutrients: carbohydrates, fats, proteins, vitamins, minerals, and water. All six groups of nutrients are necessary for good health and all must work as a team, each one playing an essential role. Think of yourself as the coach. It is your job to choose the foods that will provide all the nutrients you need. If just one nutrient is missing, the rest of the team cannot work properly. Some nutrients, however, are needed in greater amounts than others—these are carbohydrates, fats, proteins, and water.

Exhibit 6.1
Many consumers are concerned about proper nutrition and staying healthy.

Carbohydrates, fats, and proteins are called **macronutrients.** *Macro* means large. The body needs these nutrients in a relatively large quantity. Macronutrients are important because they provide fuel for energy. Vitamins, and minerals are called **micronutrients.** *Micro* means small. The body needs only small amounts of vitamins and minerals. Vitamins and minerals are necessary because they tell the carbohydrates, fats, and proteins when to release their energy. The energy released by some nutrients is measured in **calories.** We need food energy to live. How much energy do carbohydrates, proteins, and fats supply? Here is the breakdown:

- *1 gram of carbohydrate = 4 calories*
- *1 gram of protein = 4 calories*
- *1 gram of fat = 9 calories*

Energy generated from calories allows us to walk, run, talk, think, breathe, and of course, eat!

Carbohydrates and Fiber

Carbohydrates are the body's main energy source. They help the body use protein and fat efficiently. Sugar, starch, and fiber are the main forms of carbohydrates in the food we eat. There are two types of carbohydrates: simple carbohydrates and complex carbohydrates. Why are some called simple and others complex? It all depends on their chemical structure.

Sugars are called *simple carbohydrates* because their chemical structure is relatively simple compared to starch and fiber (which are called complex carbohydrates). Sugars are found naturally in small amounts in some foods, such as fruits, vegetables, and milk. **Glucose** is a very important simple sugar. It is our primary source of energy and is the only source of energy for the brain and nervous system. Good sources of glucose are fruits, vegetables, and honey.

Hormones are special messengers that regulate many different body functions. The digestion process is not possible without a hormone called **insulin,** which is produced in the pancreas. It allows glucose, or blood sugar, to travel throughout the body for energy use. Problems with insulin production and blood sugar levels can be symptoms of diabetes or other diseases that stress the body, causing weakness and fatigue.

The two major *complex carbohydrates* are **starch** and **fiber.** Some foods that are good sources of complex carbohydrates include dry beans and peas; starchy vegetables, such as potatoes and corn; rice, grits, pasta, oatmeal, and cornmeal; and breads and cereals. Starch is also found in some fruits, such as bananas. To maintain good health, it is important to eat lots of complex carbohydrates every day.

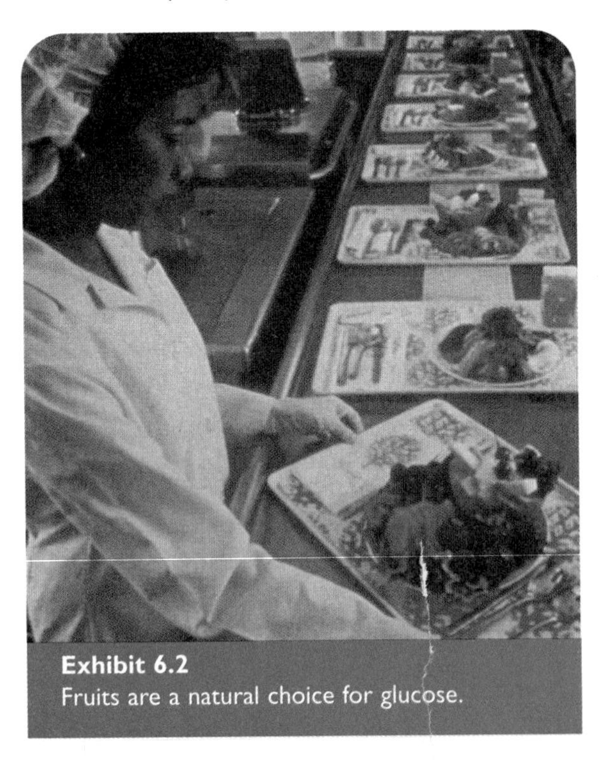

Exhibit 6.2
Fruits are a natural choice for glucose.

Fiber is found only in plant foods. It is the part of the plant that cannot be digested by humans. Since it cannot be broken down, fiber is not absorbed in the intestines and is eliminated. High-fiber foods include bran, legumes, fruits, vegetables, and whole grains. Like nutrients, dietary fiber is essential for good health.

Fat and Cholesterol

Many people wish to reduce the amount of fat in their diets, although a certain amount of fat is necessary for proper nutrition. **Fat** usually refers to both fats and oils. There are some basic differences between fats and oils. Fats are solid at room temperature and oils are liquid at room temperature; fats usually come from animals, while oils come from plants. Fat is an essential nutrient that supplies chemicals called **essential fatty acids** that are needed for healthy skin, healthy cells, and other bodily functions. Fat also carries vitamins A, D, E and K through the body. In addition, the body stores fat to provide a reserve supply of energy.

Exhibit 6.3
These foods provide us with starch and fiber.

Essential fatty acids are important to good nutrition. They are used to make substances that regulate vital body functions, such as blood pressure, contraction of certain types of muscles, blood clotting, and immune responses. They are necessary for normal growth.

There are three types of fatty acids.

1. Saturated
2. Monounsaturated
3. Polyunsaturated

All fat in foods is made up of different combinations of the three types of fatty acids. If a food contains mostly saturated fatty acids, it is considered a saturated fat; if it contains mostly polyunsaturated fatty acids, it is a polyunsaturated fat. Animal fats generally are more saturated than liquid vegetable oils. Foods such as fish,

poultry, and meat contain saturated fats. Polyunsaturated and monounsaturated fats are found in vegetable oils and foods such as peanuts, olives, and avocados.

Oxidation is a chemical process that causes unsaturated fats to spoil. Because heat, light, salt, and moisture help speed up oxidation, it is best to store fats and oils in tightly closed containers kept in a refrigerator or a cool dark place.

Cholesterol is a white, waxy substance that helps the body carry out its many processes. Cholesterol is made in the liver; it is an important part of all cell membranes, is the starting material for the production of several hormones, and is found in large amounts throughout the nervous system. Cholesterol is also a part of the bile acids which break down fat globules in the small intestine, a necessary part of the body's digestive system. Cholesterol is found only in animal foods, specifically in liver, egg yolks, dairy products, meat, poultry, fish, and shellfish. While cholesterol is essential in many ways for body functions, high levels of cholesterol in the blood are linked with heart disease. Exhibit 6.4 shows the foods that provide fats and cholesterol.

Exhibit 6.4
Food sources of fats and cholesterol.

Type of Fat	Food Sources
Saturated fat	Meat, poultry, fish, dairy products, butter, lard, palm oil, palm kernel oil, coconut oil
Monounsaturated fat	Olive, canola, peanut, avocado, and nut oils
Polyunsaturated fat	Safflower, sunflower, soybean, corn, cottonseed, and sesame oils, fish oils
Cholesterol	Egg yolk, liver and other organ meats such as brains, kidneys and tongue, whole milk and whole milk cheeses, cream, ice cream, butter, meat, poultry, fish, some shellfish

Review Your Learning 6.1

1. Explain why carbohydrates are so important in a daily diet. Then, name some examples of carbohydrates you have eaten today.

2. Which of the following foods would be the best choice if you are trying to increase your dietary fiber?
   a. Yogurt.
   b. Stir fried vegetables on noodles.
   c. Cheeseburger.
   d. Turkey and gravy.

3. List two reasons you should be concerned about good nutrition in your diet.

For questions 4–8, use the words below to complete the following correct statements on a separate sheet of paper.

Glucose	Essential fatty acids	Nutrients
Cholesterol	Insulin	

4. ________________ is a white, waxy substance that helps the body carry out its many processes but can be unhealthy in large amounts.
5. The hormone that is very important in digestion is ______________.
6. Chemicals in food that the body needs in order to work properly are called ____________.
7. ______________________ are needed for healthy skin and healthy cells.
8. ___________________ is the only source of energy for the brain and nervous system.

6.2

SECTION 6.2

The Role of Proteins, Vitamins, Minerals, and Water

AFTER STUDYING SECTION 6.2, YOU SHOULD BE ABLE TO:

- Characterize the roles of proteins, water, vitamins, and minerals in people's diets and identify foods that contain these nutrients.
- Differentiate between complete and incomplete proteins.

PROTEINS

Proteins are needed to build new cells and repair injured ones. They also help the body to grow. Proteins are made up of 22 building blocks called **amino** (uh-MEAN-oh) **acids.** The body can make 13 of these amino acids; the other 9, which the body cannot make, are called **essential amino acids** because they must be provided by the food you eat.

About one-fifth of your body's total weight is protein. Skin, hair, nails, muscles, and tendons are all made of protein. When tissues are destroyed—as when someone gets burned, has surgery, or has an infec-

KEY TERMS

- Amino (uh-MEAN-oh) acid
- Complete protein
- Essential amino acid
- Fat-soluble vitamin
- Incomplete protein
- Mineral
- Protein
- Vitamin
- Water-soluble vitamin

tion—more protein than usual is needed. Extra protein is also required during pregnancy and times of physical growth.

Complete proteins are called complete because they contain all the essential amino acids in the right amount. Good sources of complete proteins are meat, poultry, fish, eggs, and dairy products.

Incomplete proteins lack one or more of the essential amino acids. Foods from plant sources are incomplete proteins. Dried beans, dried peas, grains, and nuts have more protein than other vegetables and fruits. To get complete proteins from plant foods, combine them with other foods. For example, combine cooked dry beans or peas with a grain product (such as lentils and rice) or combine a plant food with an animal protein (such as macaroni and cheese).

Exhibit 6.5
Protein is found in these foods.

Vitamins and Minerals

Vitamins are chemical mixtures found in foods. They help carbohydrates, proteins, fats, and minerals work properly. There are two types of vitamins: water-soluble vitamins that mix only with water; and fat-soluble vitamins that mix only with fat. **Water-soluble vitamins** (vitamins C and B) are found in foods such as oranges and grapefruit. The body needs these vitamin sources every day. These vitamins are vulnerable to cooking because some may be destroyed by heat or washed away by steam or water. **Fat-soluble vitamins** (vitamins A, D, E, and K) are found in foods containing fat and are stored in the liver and body fat. The body draws on these stored vitamins when needed.

Minerals are classified as major or trace, according to how much is needed in the diet. Some examples of *major minerals* are calcium, phosphorus, potassium, sodium, and magnesium. Calcium and phosphorus help build strong bones and teeth. Potassium and sodium are needed for maintaining the body's water balance. Iron, copper, zinc, and iodine are examples of *trace minerals.* While they are as important as major minerals, only a tiny amount of trace minerals is required. Iron is essential for replenishing red blood cells. Even though some minerals are needed in very tiny amounts, getting the right amount is important to good health.

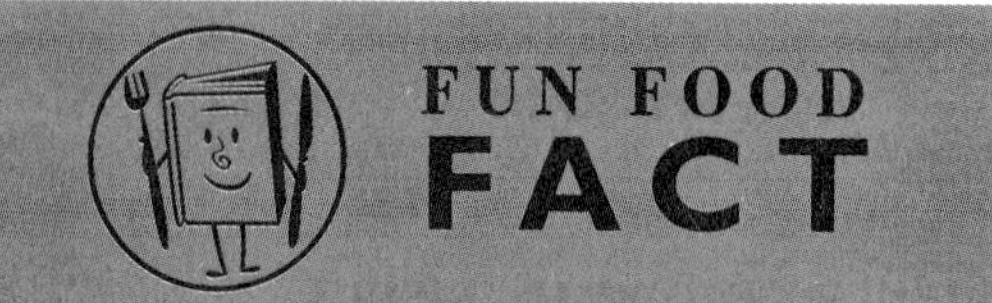

Early British sailors were called "limeys" because they ate limes on board their ships. Eating limes, which are high in vitamin C, helped prevent scurvy, a disease caused by lack of vitamin C. It causes spongy, bleeding gums, bleeding under the skin, and weakness and fatigue. Fresh fruit was not plentiful on ships, so sailors were very susceptible to this disease.

Water

Water is essential for human life. More than half of the body (including bones and blood) consists of water. Water is necessary for the digestion, absorption and transportation of nutrients, and for the

Exhibit 6.6
Water is an extremely important nutrient.

elimination of wastes through the kidneys, colon, and lungs. It helps distribute heat throughout the body and allows heat to be released through the skin by evaporation. Water also lubricates the joints and cushions body tissues. Besides water itself, other beverages provide some water, as do many foods, particularly fruits and vegetables. The human body can live a long time without many other nutrients, but only a few days without water.

Review Your Learning 6.2

1. Besides drinking water, what are some other sources of water that you have consumed today? Why is water so important to the body?

2. On a separate sheet of paper, write the name of the main nutrients found in the food items listed.

   a. Grapefruit   c. Bread   e. Spinach   g. Carrots
   b. Chicken   d. Dairy   f. Beans

3. On a separate sheet of paper, complete the following statements with the words or phrases listed below. *Hint:* some may be used more than once.

   amino acids   fat-soluble vitamin   complete protein
   potassium   sodium   water-soluble vitamin

   a. Vitamin C is an example of a ______________________.
   b. Proteins are made up of 22 building blocks called ______________________.
   c. Vitamin E is an example of a ______________________.
   d. Red beans and rice combined is an example of a ______________.
   e. The type of vitamin contained in grapefruits and oranges is a ______________.
   f. __________ and __________ are needed for maintaining the body's water balance.

SECTION 6.3

Nutritional Guidelines

AFTER STUDYING SECTION 6.3, YOU SHOULD BE ABLE TO:

- Use Recommended Dietary Allowances (RDAs) and the Food Guide Pyramid to plan meals.
- Describe a healthy diet.
- Interpret information on a nutrition label.

Eating a variety of foods is a good way to get all the nutrients the body needs. Nutrition experts have developed food guides to help people make healthy food choices. There are many different types of food guides.

KEY TERMS

- **Dietary Guidelines for Americans**
- **Food Guide Pyramid**
- **Osteoporosis (AHS-tee-oh-purr-OH-sis)**
- **Recommended Dietary Allowances (RDA)**

RECOMMENDED DIETARY ALLOWANCES

The **Recommended Dietary Allowances,** or **RDAs,** are daily nutrient standards established by the U.S. government. RDAs suggest the average nutritional needs of various population groups. Different RDAs are offered for men and women, and for different age, height, and weight groups. The nutrients recommended are protein, eleven vitamins, and seven minerals.

DIETARY GUIDELINES FOR AMERICANS

The **Dietary Guidelines for Americans** are more general than RDA standards. The Dietary Guidelines are intended as good advice for all people rather than nutritional calculations for specific groups. These guidelines are for healthy Americans aged 2 years and older. Here is a summary:

- *Eat a variety of foods.* The human body requires more than 40 different nutrients for good health. These nutrients should come from a variety of foods. One way to ensure variety is to choose foods each day from the five major food groups. Any food that supplies calories or nutrients can be part of a nutritious diet.
- *Maintain healthy weight.* People who are either overweight or underweight have increased chances of developing health problems. Being overweight is linked with high blood pressure, heart disease, stroke, the most common type of diabetes, certain cancers, and other types of illness. Being underweight is sometimes accompanied by malnutrition, eating disorders, dehydration, and is linked with osteoporosis in women and greater risk of early death in both women and men.

Osteoporosis (AHS-tee-oh-purr-OH-sis) is a condition in which the bones gradually lose their minerals, becoming weak and fragile. As a result, posture may become stooped and bones can break easily. The following guidelines will help.

Choose a diet low in fat, saturated fat, and cholesterol. High levels of saturated fat and cholesterol in diets are linked to increased risk for heart disease. A diet low in fat makes it easier to include the variety of foods needed for nutrients without exceeding calorie needs, because fat contains more than twice the calories of an equal amount of carbohydrate or protein.

Here are some suggested limits for fats:

- Total fat: an amount that provides less than 30% of total calories
- Saturated fat: an amount that provides less than 10% of total calories
- Cholesterol: eating less fat from animal sources will help lower cholesterol (as well as total fat and saturated fat) in your diet.

These limits apply to the diet over several days, and not to a single meal or food. Some foods that contain fat, saturated fat, and cholesterol, such as meats, milk, cheese, and eggs, also contain high quality-protein and are our best sources of certain vitamins and minerals.

Choose a diet with plenty of vegetables, fruits, and grain products. Adults should eat at least three servings of vegetables and two servings of fruits daily; and at least six servings of grain products, such as breads, cereals, pasta, and rice, with an emphasis on whole grains. Children should also be encouraged to eat plenty of these foods. Eating suggested amounts of these foods will help increase carbohydrates and dietary fiber, and decrease fats in your diet.

Use sugars in moderation. High-sugar foods supply calories and energy but are limited in nutrients. They should be used in moderation by most healthy people and sparingly by people with low calorie needs. For very active people with high calorie needs, sugars can be an additional source of calories.

Use salt and sodium in moderation. Most people consume much more salt and sodium than they need, especially from packaged, canned, snack, and fast foods. Eating less salt and sodium is good for everyone, especially for people with high blood pressure.

THE FOOD GUIDE PYRAMID

The new **Food Guide Pyramid** makes it easy to see how many servings of each group should be eaten daily. The tip of the Food Guide Pyramid—fats, oils, and sweets—presents the biggest dietary challenge to Americans of all ages. Fats, in particular, are the key target of the pyramid. No more than 30 percent of total calories should come from fat. With a

What's a Serving?

Bread, Cereal, Rice, Pasta

- 1 slice of bread
- 1 oz of ready-to-eat or cooked cereal
- 1/2 cup rice or pasta

Vegetable

- 1 cup of raw leafy vegetables
- 1/2 cup other vegetables, cooked or chopped raw
- 3/4 cup of vegetable juice

Fruit

- 1 medium apple, orange, or banana
- 1/2 cup of chopped, cooked, or canned-fruit
- 3/4 cup fruit juice

Milk, Yogurt, and Cheese

- 1 cup of milk or yogurt
- 1.5 oz of natural cheese
- 2 oz of processed cheese

Meat, Poultry, Fish, Dry Beans, Eggs, and Nuts

- 2-3 oz of cooked lean meat, poultry, or fish
- 1/2 cup of cooked dry beans, 1 egg, or 2 tablespoons of peanut butter each count as 1 oz of lean meat

Source: USDA

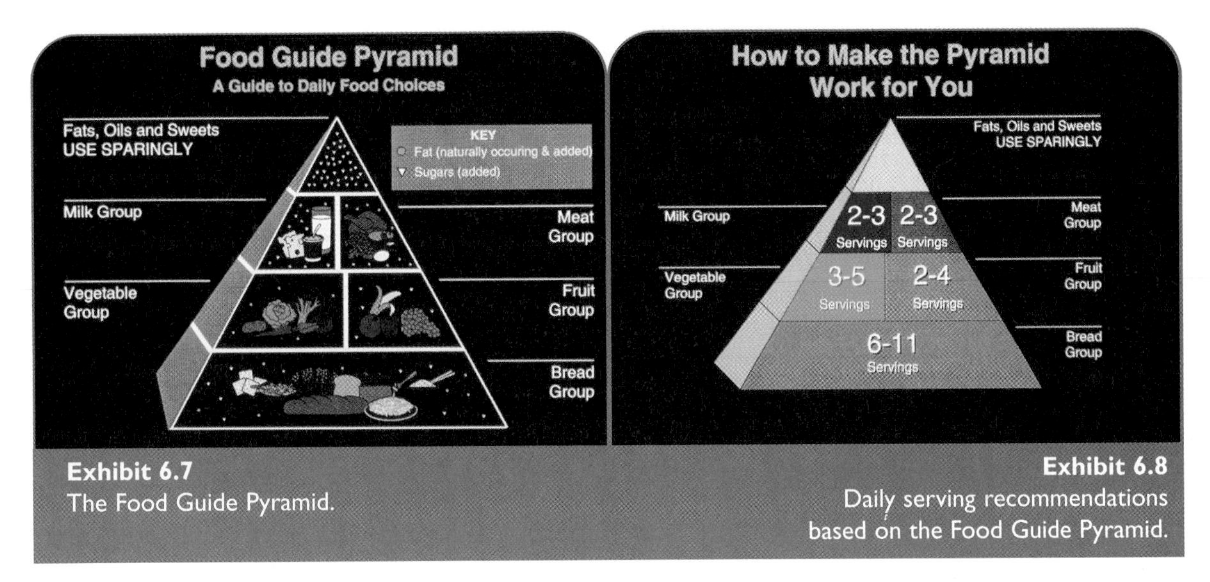

Exhibit 6.7
The Food Guide Pyramid.

Exhibit 6.8
Daily serving recommendations based on the Food Guide Pyramid.

knowledge of nutrition, foodservice managers can meet dietary guidelines without making customers feel they are being put on a low-fat diet.

Reading a Nutrition Label

In January 1993, the U.S. government created a new food label. Using this label can help you make healthful food choices and plan healthful meals. It also gives information to help make wise food choices that may reduce the risk for certain health problems, such as high blood pressure, stroke, heart disease, and others.

All food labels have five main features, as shown in Exhibit 6.10 on the next page.

Number ❶ refers to nutrition facts.

Number ❷ refers to the serving size. This information gives the standard serving size and tells how many servings are in the package. It also lists how many calories are in each serving.

Number ❸ refers to the percent (%) daily value, which is based on a diet of 2000 calories per day. This shows how a food fits into an overall daily diet, and lists total fat, cholesterol, sodium, total carbohydrates, and protein. The percent daily value acts as a yardstick to measure the nutrients in a specific food against recommended daily food needs. For example, let's say a food has 13 grams of fat and the percent daily value is 20%. This means that the 13 grams of fat contained in this particular food supply one fifth of the total daily fat recommended for a person who eats 2000 calories each day.

Exhibit 6.9
How do you use the Food Guide Pyramid?

- Build a base with grains. For example, start with breakfast and include cereal or toast; use bread to begin building lunch; pretzels as a snack; and pasta as the foundation for dinner.
- Add three to five servings of vegetables and fruit. For example, fruit juice at breakfast; celery or carrot sticks at lunch; an apple in the afternoon; and salad at dinner.
- Complete the pyramid with two to three servings each from the meat and dairy group. For example, low-fat milk at breakfast; hamburger at lunch; lowfat frozen yogurt as a snack; and turkey at dinner.
- Eat fats, oils, and sweets in moderation.

Number ❹ lists the amounts of vitamins A and C, calcium, and iron contained in the food.

Number ❺ lists the daily values. These values are based on current nutrition information. Some of these values are recommended maximum amounts of certain nutrients a person should have each day, and other values are recommended minimum amounts a person should have each day. Personal nutrient needs may vary, so these are general guidelines only. On the sample label in Exhibit 6.10, the total fat contained in the food item is 13 grams. The recommended maximum daily amount of fat is between 65 and 80 grams.

Food labels also list all ingredients by weight, beginning with the ingredient that weighs the most. For example, a canned soup that lists potatoes first means that it contains more potatoes by weight than any other ingredient.

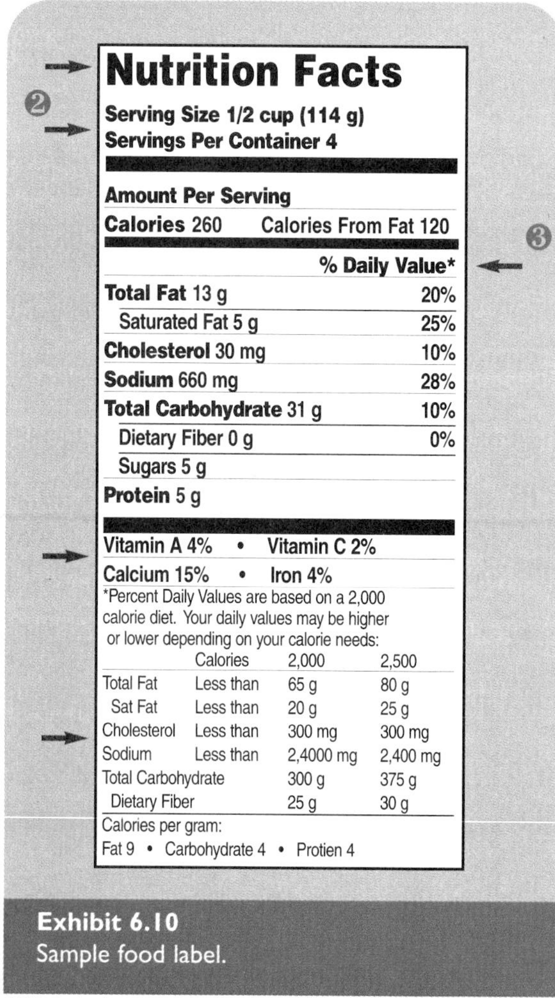

Exhibit 6.10
Sample food label.

Review Your Learning 6.3

Based on what you have learned about nutrition labels, use the food label shown to answer questions 1–5.

1. How many servings are in this box?
2. How many crackers equal one serving?
3. What is the percent (%) daily value of total carbohydrates in each serving?
4. What is the percent (%) of iron contained in each serving?
5. What is the main ingredient (by weight) in this package?

Nutrition Facts

Serving Size 16 crackers (29 g)
Servings Per Container About 10

Amount Per Serving	
Calories 140	Calories From Fat 50
	% Daily Value*
Total Fat 6 g	9%
Saturated Fat 1 g	5%
Cholesterol 30 mg	10%
Sodium 0 mg	0%
Total Carbohydrate 19 g	6%
Dietary Fiber 2 g	6%
Sugars 2 g	
Protein 2 g	

Vitamin 0% • Vitamin C 0%
Calcium 2% • Iron 4%

*Percent Daily Values are based on a 2,000 calorie diet. Your daily values may be higher or lower depending on your calorie needs:

	Calories	2,000	2,500
Total Fat	Less than	65 g	80 g
Sat Fat	Less than	20 g	25 g
Cholesterol	Less than	300 mg	300 mg
Sodium	Less than	2,4000 mg	2,400 mg
Total Carbohydrate		300 g	375 g
Dietary Fiber		25 g	30 g

Calories per gram:
Fat 9 • Carbohydrate 4 • Protien 4

Nabisco Wheat Thins

6. Based on what you have learned about the Food Guide Pyramid and what you have eaten today, what types of food should you have for dinner tonight? What can you do to improve or change your diet tomorrow?

7. Which of the following counts as one serving of fruit?

   a. 1/2 cup fruit juice.
   b. 1 medium apple.
   c. 2 large oranges.
   d. 2-3 ounces of fruit juice.

8. According to the Food Guide Pyramid, how many servings of bread, cereal, rice, or pasta should a person eat daily?

   a. 1-2 servings.
   b. 3-4 servings.
   c. 4-5 servings.
   d. 6-11 servings.

9. Dieters should eat a variety of foods low in ________and high in _________.

   a. fat; nutrition
   b. size; liquid
   c. dessert; canned foods
   d. bread; lettuce

6.4

SECTION 6.4

Making Menus More Nutritious

AFTER STUDYING SECTION 6.4, YOU SHOULD BE ABLE TO:

- Identify recipes that preserve nutrients in quantity cooking.
- Suggest ways to make recipes more healthful.
- Suggest healthful substitutes for high-fat ingredients.

KEY TERMS

- **Caramelize**
- **Legume (lay-GOOM)**
- **Liaison**
- **Reduce**
- **Tahini (tuh-HEE-nee)**

Prepping Foods

Purchasing fresh, high-quality products is the first step toward providing nutritious meals. Because some nutrients will be lost during preparation and cooking, it is best to begin with the freshest food available. Storage procedures affect nutrient content of both fresh and processed foods. In general, nutrients are destroyed by heat and light (oxidation) and humidity (causes ripening and decay).

When preparing vegetables, wash them quickly and thoroughly. Letting produce soak causes some vitamins to wash off or leach out. Excessive trimming can also waste a lot of nutrients. Skin and leaves, for example, are rich in many vitamins and minerals. Using vegetable trimmings in stock or soup base is one way to recover some of this nutrient loss.

In addition, cutting produce exposes surface areas to air and heat that destroy

Exhibit 6.11
Restaurants should provide several healthy menu selections.

vitamin C. It is best to prepare vegetables and fruit close to serving time and to keep them intact as much as possible until you are ready to use them. When cooking, try to use whole vegetables or cut larger pieces. Using sharp knives prevents bruising produce, which can quicken the loss of vitamins A and C.

Cooking Foods

When cooking any food, remember that the lower the temperature and the shorter the cooking period, the less nutrient loss there will be. With vegetables, the size of the vegetable and the amount of water used are also important. If less water is used, more vitamin B and C are retained. Stir-frying and brief steaming are good methods to use. Also, baking root vegetables in their skins retains nutrients better than peeling, cutting, and boiling.

Be careful not to overwash grains. Some imported or bulk grains may contain dirt and impurities and will need to be rinsed. Washing can greatly affect vitamin content. White rice, for example, can lose 25 percent of its thiamin; brown rice can lose 10 percent. In general, the amount of nutrients in a cereal product depends on what is left after milling and washing, what nutrients are added, and how the product is cooked. The best way to preserve vitamins in grains is by not overbaking them and keeping grains covered.

Grilling, dry sautéing, and sautéing in a pan brushed with oil are good ways to eliminate excess fat. Also, "wet" sautéing with a small amount of water, vegetable juice, or stock reduction can reduce unnecessary fat. Fats can easily be removed from stocks and soups by chilling them and skimming the solidified layer of fat off the top.

Lean cuts of red meat are usually lower in fat, and smaller portions of high-fat cuts can be served to concerned guests. Lean cuts of meat come from the round, loin, and sirloin, and include tenderloin, strip loin, top (inside) round, and top sirloin butt. Leaner cuts must be carefully prepared to avoid becoming tough. Marinating, pounding, and moist cooking on low heat are all ways to tenderize meat. In addition, recipes that use beef as an ingredient, such as stir-fried beef or shish kabobs, provide other ways to serve smaller portions of meat.

During cooking, nutrients in meats primarily are lost through water, which evaporates or goes into the drippings. Protein losses are minimal. However, the longer the meat is cooked, the more thiamin and vitamin B_6 are lost. Additional ideas for cooking meats healthfully can be found in *Chapter 8: Meat, Poultry, and Seafood* of *Becoming a Foodservice Professional, Year 2.*

Exhibit 6.12
Cooking fresh vegetables quickly reduces nutrient loss.

Exhibit 6.13
Tips for making food more healthful.

- Use less fat in cooking.
- Use the freshest, highest quality food available.
- Modify portion sizes.
- Know the nutritional content of foods.
- Reduce the amount of salt and sodium used.
- Avoid excessive trimming and cooking time of produce.
- Do not overwash produce or grains, or use too much water during the cooking process.

Vegetables can be grilled, steamed, and stir-fried, or cooked in other ways to avoid adding fat. Both fruits and vegetables can be caramelized to intensify their color and flavor. **Caramelizing** means to brown them with a small amount of sugar in the presence of heat. Additional ideas for cooking fruits and vegetables healthfully can be found in *Chapter 11: Fruits and Vegetables.*

Changing Ingredients

Recipes can also be made more healthful by deleting ingredients or substituting ingredients. Use unusual grains, legumes and bean products, and common vegetables as substitutes for other high-calorie or high-fat ingredients. The key is to be flexible and creative!

The **legume** (lay-GOOM) family includes a large assortment of protein-rich beans, peas, and other pod-growing plants. Some examples of legumes are black beans, black-eyed peas, garbanzo beans, kidney beans, and lentils. These are commonly used in dishes such as chili, salads, soups, and dips. Foods in this group provide fiber, as well as complex carbohydrates for energy. Legumes complement grains and are rich in several minerals.

Dairy products are naturally high in fat, but low-fat alternatives can be used. Yogurt is often used in place of sour cream. Tofu (soybean curd) is sometimes used in custard pies, lasagnas, dips, spreads, and many other dishes instead of cheese. Soy milk and soy cheese have less fat, no saturated fat, and no cholesterol, and can be used in place of regular milk or cheese in many recipes. Nondairy creamers, whipped toppings, and other such products are high in fat, so read nutrition labels carefully.

Exhibit 6.14
Many dairy products that are made from whole milk are naturally high in fat.

It is difficult to eliminate fat from sauces because a **liaison,** a mixture of egg yolks and cream, is often used to thicken and enrich sauces, as well as for taste and glossy appearance. To make sauces low in fat, thicken them with arrowroot, potato starch, or cornstarch—but use it sparingly. A sauce may also be thickened by reducing it. **Reduce** means to decrease the volume of a liquid by simmering or boiling. A little butter, oil, cream, or egg yolk can be added to finish a sauce because the amount one person will receive is small. Other ingredients that can help fill out a sauce include vegetable purées, whipped soft tofu, gelatin, and low-fat creams consisting of yogurt and ricotta or cottage cheese blends.

Heavy, fat-based dressings do not have to be used. Cream and egg-based dressings can be diluted with broth or skim milk. Broth alone is a good base for salad dressings, along with puréed vegetables, puréed soft tofu, honey, mustard, and tahini.

Tahini (tuh-HEE-nee) is a paste made from sesame seeds. There are many mono- or polyunsaturated vegetable and nut oils that can be used lightly to enhance flavor.

Cereal grains contain many healthful nutrients in just the right amounts: vitamins, minerals, complex carbohydrates, and protein. Whole grains are inexpensive and versatile. Some examples of popular grains include durum wheat, used for pastas; hard wheat, used for baking bread; and couscous, used in salads and main dishes. Each kind of grain has a different taste, texture, and appearance.

Exhibit 6.16
Desserts are often loaded with saturated fat, cholesterol, sugar, and calories.

Most whole grains are good alone or with steamed greens or other vegetables, herbs, and a little high-quality flax or olive oil. Although basic cooking instructions call for water, grains can be prepared with stock, juice, or any liquid.

Exhibit 6.15
Fresh bread is made with wheat grain.

Grains are the basis of international dishes such as Spanish paella, Creole jambalaya, and Middle Eastern tabouleh. Grains can be made into croquets and fritters; added to breads and batters; used to thicken soups and stews; and combined with meat, shellfish, or vegetables to make pilaf. Whole grain products need to be kept cool and should be used as soon as possible after milling. Additional ideas for cooking cereals and grains healthfully can be found in *Chapter 2: Potatoes and Grains* of

Becoming a Foodservice Professional, Year 2.

Seasonings such as garlic salt, onion salt, monosodium glutamate (MSG), and soy sauce are all high in sodium. Seasonings and flavorings used in place of salt can enhance a dish and make it more flavorful. There are many ways to reduce sodium without sacrificing good taste. Try substituting fresh garlic and onions for garlic and onion powders. Common salt substitutes include herbs and spices, lemon juice, peppers and chilies, concentrated stocks, pan juices, wine, vinegar, bitters, and liquor.

Dessert tends to be the least nutritious part of a meal when loaded with saturated fat, cholesterol, sugar, and calories. However, creative uses of fruit, sherbet, ice milk, compotes, crustless tarts, cakes, and sugarless jams can make simple desserts look elegant. Evaporated skim milk and thickeners such as cornstarch can be used in sauces. Sugar often can be reduced by as much as half or more, without affecting a dessert's sweetness. Honey, brown sugar, and molasses sometimes are offered as alternatives to white sugar. Additional ideas for cooking desserts healthfully can be found in *Chapter 5: Desserts and Baked Goods* of *Becoming a Foodservice Professional, Year 2.*

Exhibit 6.17
Common ingredient substitutes.

Instead of:	Use:
Bacon	Canadian bacon
Butter	Powdered butter granules plus liquid (either skim milk or water)
Chocolate	Cocoa (vegetable oil may be added as needed)
Cream cheese	Reduced-fat or nonfat cream cheese
Emulsified salad dressing	Start with a base of reduced-fat or nonfat yogurt, sour cream or mayonnaise, then thin with skim milk
Light cream	Equal portions of 1% milk and evaporated skim milk
Mayonnaise	Reduced-fat mayonnaise (can be mixed with reduced-fat or nonfat sour cream)
Sour cream	Reduced-fat or nonfat sour cream; drained, reduced-fat or nonfat plain yogurt
Whipped cream	Whipped, chilled evaporated skim milk

Review Your Learning 6.4

1. Look at the two versions of the brownie recipe below. Which one, A or B, is lower in fat, calories, and sugar if the serving size is equal? How are the ingredients in the two recipes different from each other?

Fudge Brownies (Recipe A)

	U.S. measure	*Metric measure*
Unsweetened chocolate	4 oz	120 g
Cake flour	1 lb	450 g
Cocoa powder	9 oz	270 g
Salt substitute	2 tsp	10 ml
Egg whites	12	12
Whole eggs	8	8
Granulated Sugar	2 lbs 2 oz	1 kg
Corn syrup	2 lbs	900 g
Unsweetened applesauce	1 1/2 pts	670 ml
Canola oil	7 oz	210 g
Vanilla extract	2 Tbsp	30 ml

Yield: one sheet pan

Fudge Brownies (Recipe B)

	U.S. measure	*Metric measure*
Unsweetened chocolate	2 lbs	1 kg
Butter	2 lbs	1 kg
Eggs	20	20
Sugar	5 lbs 12 oz	2.9 kg
Vanilla extract	2 oz	60 ml
All-purpose flour	1 lb 10 oz	750 g
Pecan pieces	1 lb	500 g

Yield: one sheet pan

2. Look at one of your favorite recipes for cookies, brownies, or cake. How could you change the recipe to make it more nutritious?

For questions 3–10, use the words below to complete the following correct statements on a separate sheet of paper.

Caramelized	Cereal grains	Marinating
Overwashing	Seasonings	Soy milk
Spices	Steaming	Tofu

3. One cooking method that helps to retain nutrients is ____________.
4. ________________________ contain nearly everything we need for health in just the right amounts of vitamins, minerals, complex carbohydrates, and protein.
5. Fruits and vegetables can be _____________ to intensify their color and flavor.
6. __________________ grains can greatly affect their vitamin content.
7. _____________ is sometimes used in many dishes, such as lasagnas, in place of cheese.
8. _________________ leaner cuts of meat can tenderize them.
9. _________________ can be used in place of regular milk in recipes.
10. __________ and ___________ can be used in place of salt to make dishes more flavorful.

Flashback

CHAPTER 6

SECTION 6.1: THE ABCs OF NUTRITION

- **Nutrients** are chemicals in food that the body needs in order to work properly.
- Nutrients serve three main functions: to provide energy, to build and repair cells, and to regulate body processes.
- There are six groups of nutrients: carbohydrates, fats, proteins, vitamins, minerals, and water.
- While all six are necessary for good health, some nutrients are needed in greater quantities than others—these are carbohydrates, fats, proteins, and water. The body needs only relatively small amounts of vitamins and mineals.
- Vitamins and minerals regulate the release of energy from carbohydrates, fats, and proteins.
- **Fat** usually refers to both fats and oils.
- Fats have many different purposes in the body. The **essential fatty acids** are vital for normal growth.
- While fats and oils have much in common, fats are solid at room temperature and oils are liquid; and fats usually come from animals, while oils come from plants.
- There are three types of fatty acids: saturated, monounsaturated, and polyunsaturated.
- **Cholesterol** is a white, waxy substance that helps the body carry out its many processes.
- While cholesterol is essential in many ways for body functions, high levels of cholesterol in the blood are linked with heart disease.

SECTION 6.2: THE ROLE OF PROTEINS, VITAMINS, MINERALS, AND WATER

- **Proteins** are a major part of the body and are the substances that are needed to build new cells and repair injured ones.
- Proteins are made up of 22 building blocks called **amino acids.**

- The body can make 13 of these amino acids; the other 9, which the body cannot make, are called **essential amino acids** because they must be present in the diet.
- Vitamins and minerals are activators and regulators in various body functions.
- There are two types of vitamins: **water-soluble vitamins** that mix only with water; and **fat-soluble vitamins** that mix only with fat.
- Water-soluble vitamins (vitamins C and B) are found in foods such as oranges and grapefruit. Fat-soluble vitamins (vitamins A, D, E, and K) are found in foods containing fat and can be stored in the liver and body fat.
- **Minerals** are substances classified as major or trace, according to how much is needed in the diet.
- Water is essential for human life. Besides water itself, other beverages provide some water, as do many foods, particularly fruits and vegetables.

SECTION 6.3: NUTRITIONAL GUIDELINES

- The **Recommended Dietary Allowances,** or **RDAs,** are daily nutrient standards established by the U.S. government.
- The **Dietary Guidelines for Americans** are more general than RDA standards and are embodied in the **Food Guide Pyramid.** There are seven key points:
  1. Eat a variety of foods.
  2. Maintain a healthy weight.
  3. Choose a diet that is low in fat, saturated fat, and cholesterol.
  4. Choose a diet with plenty of vegetables, fruits, and grain products.
  5. Use sugars only in moderation.
  6. Use salt and sodium only in moderation.
  7. Drink alcohol only in moderation.
- Valuable information is listed on a food's nutrition label. Using this label can assist foodservice managers in making healthful food choices and planning healthful meals for customers.
- Five key features of the nutrition label include: nutrition facts, serving size, % daily value, vitamin and mineral content, and daily values of certain nutrients.
- The nutrition label also lists all ingredients in the food item.

SECTION 6.4: MAKING MENUS MORE NUTRITIOUS

- Purchasing fresh, high-quality products is the first step toward creating nutritious meals.
- Storage procedures affect nutrient content of both fresh and processed foods.
- The second important step in serving nutritious foods is to properly prepare them. When preparing vegetables, wash them quickly and thoroughly.
- Letting produce soak can cause some vitamins to wash off or leach out. Excessive trimming can also waste a lot of nutrients. It is best to wait to prepare vegetables and fruit until close to serving time and keep them intact as much as possible until you are ready to use them.
- When cooking produce, the lower the temperature and the shorter the cooking period, the less nutrient loss there will be. Stir-frying and brief steaming are good methods to use for cooking vegetables.
- When working with grains, do not wash them if they are clean. Some imported or bulk grains may contain dirt and impurities and will need to be rinsed. However, washing can greatly affect vitamin content.
- Vitamin content can be preserved by not over-baking grains.
- During cooking, nutrients in meats primarily are lost through water, which evaporates or goes into the drippings. The longer the meat is cooked, the more thiamin and vitamin B_6 are lost.
- Deleting ingredients, substituting ingredients, or changing cooking techniques are standard ways of making recipes more healthful.
- There are many ways to reduce sodium without sacrificing good taste. Seasonings and flavorings used in place of salt can enhance a dish when used with care. Common salt substitutes include herbs and spices, lemon juice, peppers and chilies, concentrated stocks, pan juices, wine, vinegar, bitters, and liquor.
- Reduce fat by trimming excess fat from meats.
- Leaner cuts can be used or smaller portions can be served. Leaner cuts must be prepared carefully to avoid becoming tough. Marinating or pounding can tenderize meats. Also, moist cooking on low heat will prevent the meat from becoming tough.

- Several different cooking methods can minimize fat in meats, poultry, and fish: broiling, grilling, roasting, baking, poaching, or steaming over water, en papillote, lettuce, or other vegetable leaves or husks.
- Dairy products are also high in fat, but low-fat alternatives are available. Since nondairy creamers, whipped toppings, and other such products are high in fat, it is important to read nutrition labels carefully.
- Vegetables can be grilled, steamed, and stir-fried, or cooked in many other ways to avoid extra fat.
- Grains and legumes are inexpensive, versatile, and each kind has a different taste, texture, and appearance. Most whole grains are good alone or with steamed greens or other vegetables, herbs, and a small amount of high-quality flax or olive oil.
- The **legume** family includes a large assortment of protein-rich beans, peas, and other pod-growing plants. Legumes complement grains and are rich in several minerals.
- Creative uses of fruit, sherbet, ice milk, compotes, crustless tarts, cakes, and sugarless jams can make simple desserts look elegant.
- Sugar often can be reduced by as much as half or more, without affecting a dessert's sweetness. Honey, brown sugar, and molasses sometimes are offered as alternatives to white sugar.

Now that you're working in a professional establishment, you will start applying your understanding of basic kitchen skills and foodservice preparations and learn the fundamentals of professional on-the-job interactions.

UNIT 3

Mark Segobiano

Chef Instructor,
Purdue University

I've worked in the foodservice industry for as long as I can remember. I've enjoyed almost every aspect of the industry. I started out working in a restaurant in my home town when I was in high school. I really liked the fast pace the restaurant provided, and I liked the extra money too!

I decided to make restaurants my career and enrolled in the Restaurant, Hotel, and Institutional Foods program (RHI) at Purdue University. After completing my Bachelor of Science degree, I decided to increase my knowledge of culinary arts by taking continuing education courses at The Culinary Institute of America.

From The Culinary Institute of America, I went on to work as Executive Chef in quite a few operations. As Executive Chef for Campus Catering at The University of Missouri at Columbia, I was responsible for meal planning, among other things. Of course, serving college students food isn't always easy. Everyone knows that breakfast is the most important meal of the day. We had to make sure that we were providing a variety of breakfast food choices to please all of those hungry kids! Usually, we'd arrive in the kitchen around 5:00 am or so and begin mixing batters for waffles and pancakes, and cooking the oatmeal. The kitchen opened up for breakfast at 7:00 am, and we had to be ready to go!

At 10:00 am we'd begin to prepare for lunch. After the mise en place was set, we'd get started making the hot entrées, set up the salad bar, and situate the sandwich fixings. I really liked preparing both breakfast and lunch, especially in a large college setting. Doing so helped me move on to other things, like catering and managing a restaurant. In both situations, my knowledge of breakfast and lunch preparation was extremely helpful. I've used those skills in lots of different jobs.

Even now, as a Chef Instructor at Purdue, I deal with breakfast and lunch preparation. I teach my students how to calculate and prepare large quantities of food, for everything from a cafeteria school setting, like the one I worked in at The University of Missouri, to a more fancy, white-linen operation.

Working in the foodservice industry is an incredible opportunity, not only to prepare lots of great food, but to experience many different aspects of a growing industry.

CHAPTER 7

Breakfast Foods and Sandwiches

SECTION 7.1

Dairy Products

AFTER STUDYING SECTION 7.1, YOU SHOULD BE ABLE TO:

- Explain and demonstrate how to keep milk products safe and sanitary.
- Differentiate between butter and margarine by listing the characteristics of each.
- List the characteristics of ice cream.
- Distinguish among several different types of cheeses and give examples of each.

KEY TERMS

- **Clarified butter**
- **Cream**
- **Homogenization (huh-MAH-juh-ni-ZAY-shun)**
- **Margarine**
- **Pasteurization (PASS-cher-i-ZAY-shun)**

Milk, cheese, and butter must be selected and stored carefully. Dairy products are potentially hazardous foods. Because of their high protein content, they have a great potential for carrying microorganisms that could cause a foodborne illness.

Milk, cheese, and butter hold a prominent place on any operation's menu. While most Asian cuisines use few or no dairy products, most Western cooking relies heavily on them. Milk and milk products are essential as beverages and as key ingredients in many dishes. Cheese is an important food served by itself and also as a component in sandwiches and many recipes.

Fresh dairy items should be stored in a refrigerator at 40°F (4.4°C) or lower in a tightly sealed container. They should be stored separately from other foods, especially those with strong odors. Dairy products tend to absorb other flavors quickly and easily.

Milk Products

Milk can be purchased as a whole liquid, dry, evaporated, or condensed. All of these forms are **pasteurized** (PASS-cher-ized), heated to destroy harmful bacteria, and may also be **homogenized** (huh-MAH-juh-nized), treated so that milkfat appears uniformly throughout the product. Milk is classified according to its percentage of fat and milk solids. **Cream** is the fatty component of milk. There are two kinds of cream—heavy or whipping cream and light cream.

Courtesy of the Wisconsin Milk Marketing Board, Madison, Wisconsin.

Exhibit 7.1
Wisconsin, also known as the Dairy State, has over 30,000 dairy farms that produce almost 2 billion pounds of cheese each year.

Milk or cream from separate containers should never be combined. The freshness periods are different and contamination could occur.

Ice Cream

To be accurately labeled "ice cream," ice cream must contain a certain amount of milkfat. Vanilla ice cream must contain no less than 10% milkfat; other flavors must contain at least 8% milkfat. Quality ice cream has a custard base (cream and/or milk and eggs), melts readily in the mouth, and does not weep, or separate, when it softens at room temperature.

Butter and Margarine

Butter is made by mixing cream that contains between 30% and 45% milkfat at a high speed. Sweet butter is butter made only from sweet cream. Most commercially sold butter is lightly salted. Unsalted butter, which is slightly sweeter, is also available.

Butter is often **clarified**, which means it has been heated to remove milk solids and water. Clarified butter is better for many cooking processes because the milk solids in whole butter burn easily, and because the water in butter can thin a food's consistency.

While **margarine** looks, cooks, and tastes like butter, it is a manufactured food

product that contains no milk products. Margarine is made of various vegetable and animal fats and oils with added flavoring ingredients, emulsifiers, colors, preservatives, and added vitamins. Contrary to what many people believe, margarine is not much lower in fat than butter; 80% of its calories come from fat.

Both butter and margarine must be stored in tightly sealed containers to prevent the flavors of other foods from transferring to them.

Cheese

Cheeses can be unripened or ripened. Unripened or fresh cheeses include cream cheese, cottage cheese, and mozzarella.

Some cheeses are ripened by external molds (Brie, Bleu, Roquefort, Camembert), and some by internal bacteria (Swiss, Havarti).

Processed cheese is pasteurized to prevent it from aging. Its taste is usually mild compared to aged cheeses. The variety of cheeses ranges from mild to sharp to pungent (very sharp). The type of milk used determines the cheese's flavor and texture.

Following are a number of categories of cheese and examples of each.

- Fresh cheese—Cottage, Ricotta, Cream, Neufchâtel, Mozzarella, Feta
- Semi-soft cheese—Edam, Bel Paese, Fontina, Port Salut, Muenster, Brick
- Soft cheese—Brie, Camembert, Liederkranz, Limburger, Brillat Savarin, Boursin
- Grating cheese—Parmesan, Romano
- Goat cheese—Chèvre, Pyramide
- Hard cheese—Cheddar, Colby, Monterey Jack, Swiss, Gouda, Provolone, Jarlsberg, Appenzeller, Raclette, Gruyere
- Blue-veined cheese—Roquefort, Gorgonzola, Saga, Bleu, Stilton

Exhibit 7.2
Cheeses add flavor and texture to many favorite recipes.

Courtesy of the Wisconsin Milk Marketing Board, Madison, Wisconsin.

Receiving and Storing Milk and Dairy Products

- Store at 40°F (4.4°C) or below. Never accept them without measuring their temperatures with a thermometer.
- All milk products should be pasteurized and delivered before their expiration date.
- Store all milk and milk products in the refrigerator.
- Special things to look for in cheese:
  - Clean, unbroken rind (outer skin)
  - Usual flavor and texture
- Special things to look for in butter:
  - No bad odor
  - No signs of mold or dirt

Review Your Learning 7.1

1. Why should milk from different containers never be combined?

2. Why is milk homogenized?

3. Why is milk pasteurized?

4. Give an example of an unripened cheese.

5. Why would you clarify butter?

Use the following words to complete the statements below on a separate sheet of paper.

Grating cheese Processed cheese Homogenized
Sweet butter Margarine Pasteurized

6. ____________ is made with sweet cream.

7. ____________ is a manufactured product that looks like butter but contains no milk products.

8. Milk is both ____________ and ____________.

9. Parmesan cheese is an example of a ____________.

10. ____________ does not age and usually has a mild taste.

7.2

SECTION 7.2

The Versatile Egg

AFTER STUDYING SECTION 7.2, YOU SHOULD BE ABLE TO:

- List the characteristics of eggs and include size and grade.
- Prepare and serve eggs using a variety of cooking methods.
- Describe the ways to keep eggs and egg products safe and sanitary.

KEY TERMS

- **Baste**
- **Omelet**
- **Poach**
- **Quiche (keesh)**
- **Ramekin (RAM-uh-kin)**
- **Shirr**
- **Soufflé (soo-FLAY)**

The egg is one of the most versatile and essential foods. In fact, the egg has been called the chef's magic ingredient. Eggs are useful in many ways—thickening, coloring, adding moisture, and enriching other foods. These highly perishable foods must be purchased and stored carefully. Eggs appear on menus throughout the day, from breakfast dishes to dessert soufflés.

Characteristics of Eggs

An egg is composed of the outer shell, the white (albumen), and the yolk. The white consists of protein and water; the yolk contains protein, fat, and lecithin, a natural emulsifier (thickener). The membranes that hold the egg yolk in place are called chalazae.

How do you select and store these delicate foods? There are federal grades for shell eggs—Grade AA, A, and B. Buyers purchase the top two grades (Grade AA

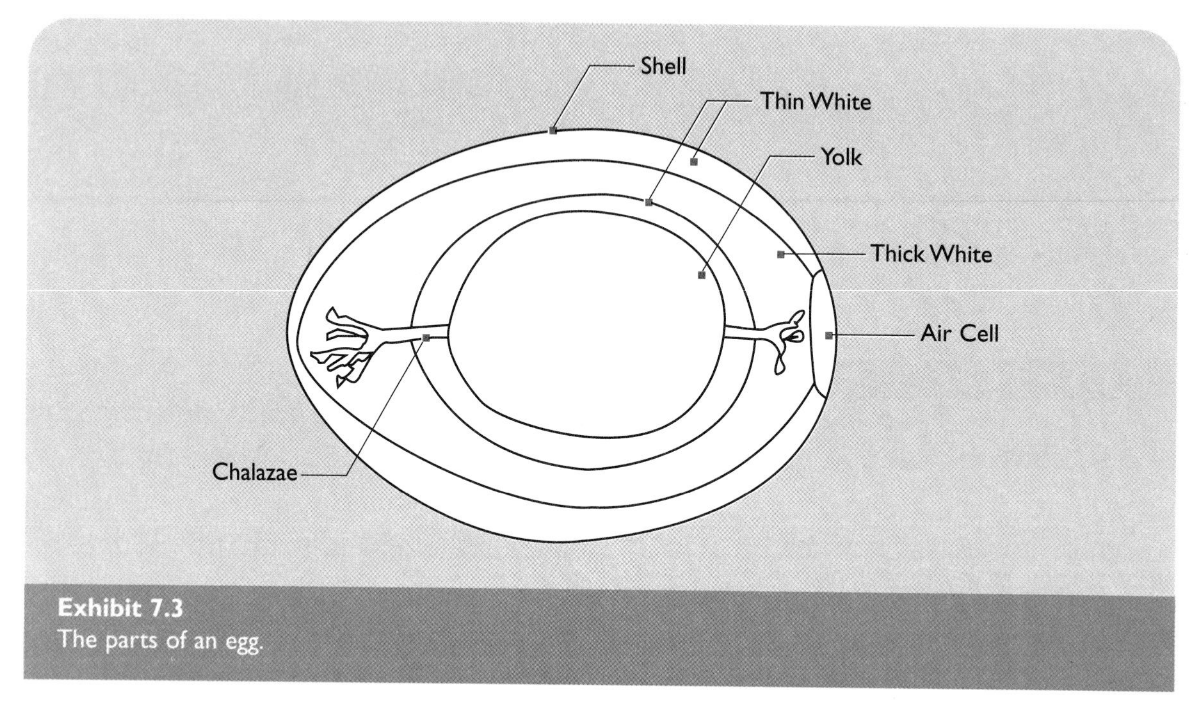

Exhibit 7.3
The parts of an egg.

and Grade A) for menu items in which the egg's appearance is important. A USDA Grade AA egg means that the yolk is high and the white will not spread too much when the shell is broken. Grade B eggs are appropriate for use in menu items that will hide their appearance, such as baked items. As eggs age, they lose density. This means the thick part of the white becomes larger, and the egg spreads over a larger area when it is broken.

In addition, buyers must choose eggs by size—ranging from peewee (15 oz per dozen) to jumbo (30 oz per dozen). Many operations use large eggs (24 oz per dozen) for all purposes. Most recipes are based on this size. Size and grade together determine the cost of eggs. What if the recipe you're preparing calls for jumbo eggs and you only have medium eggs in stock? Most recipes call for a

Exhibit 7.4
Egg sizes.

	Minimum Weight per Dozen	
Size	**U.S.**	**Metric**
Jumbo	30 oz	840 g
Extra large	27 oz	756 g
Large	24 oz	672 g
Medium	21 oz	588 g
Small	18 oz	504 g
Peewee	15 oz	420 g

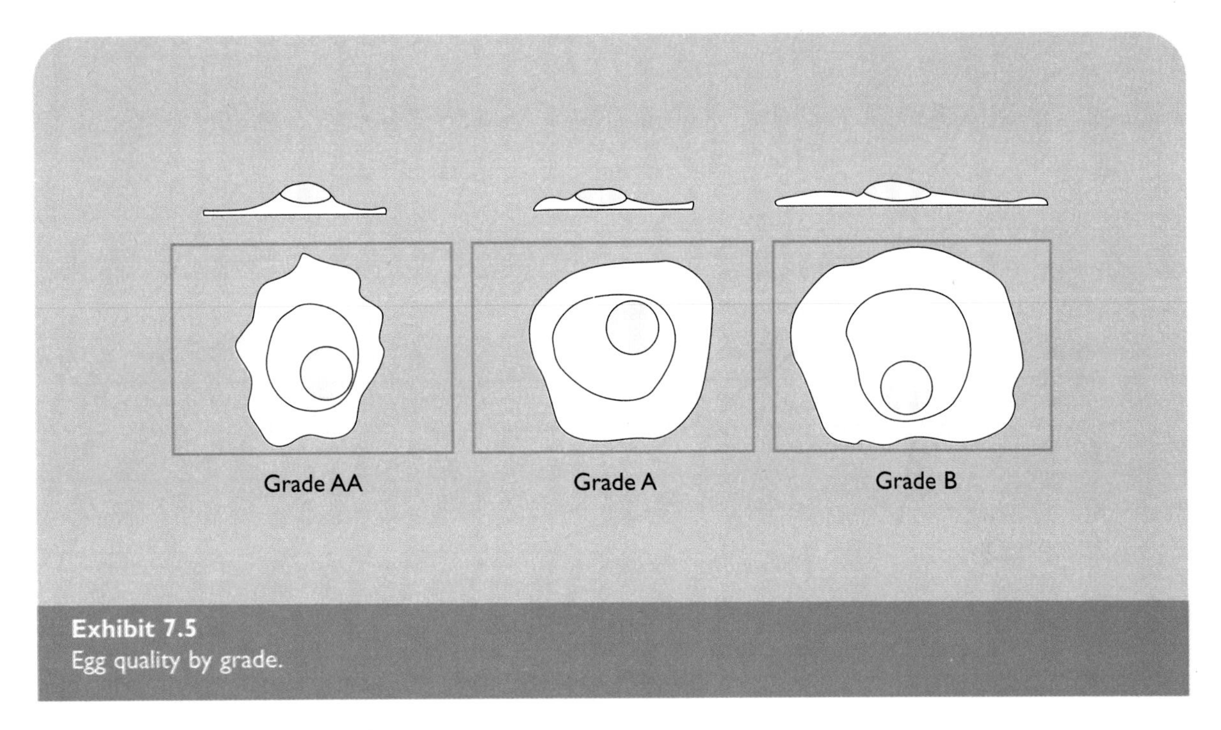

Exhibit 7.5
Egg quality by grade.

certain number of ounces of egg yolks. For example, if you know how many ounces are in a jumbo egg and a medium egg, you can calculate how many medium eggs you will need to use to equal the amount called for in the recipe.

Young hens produce smaller eggs, which are generally of a better quality than larger eggs. Medium eggs are best for breakfast cooking because the appearance of the cooked eggs is important.

Like all purchased items, shell eggs should be evaluated and ordered based on such characteristics as their color, form, packaging, intended use, and preservation method. Eggs should be received and stored according to proper sanitation procedures: refrigerated, covered, and protected from temperature fluctuations. Eggs must be inspected carefully upon delivery. Always discard

Tips for Handling Eggs

- Never pool eggs (hold large amounts of raw eggs) for any length of time to hold for cooking.
- For menu items calling for eggs that will not be cooked to 140°F (60°C), such as meringues and Caesar salads, use pasteurized eggs instead of shell eggs.
- When cooked eggs are held for service, they must be held at 140°F (60°C) or higher.

Exhibit 7.6
Market forms of eggs.

Fresh (shell) eggs	These are most often used for breakfast cooking.
Frozen eggs	■ Whole eggs ■ Whites ■ Yolks ■ Whole eggs with extra yolks Frozen eggs are usually made from high-quality fresh eggs and are excellent for use in scrambled eggs, omelets, French toast, and in baking. They are pasteurized and are usually purchased in 30 lb cans. Frozen eggs take at least 2 days to thaw at refrigerated temperatures.
Dried eggs	■ Whole eggs ■ Yolks ■ Whites Dried eggs are used primarily for baking. They are not good for breakfast cooking. Dried eggs do not store well and must be kept refrigerated or frozen and tightly sealed.
Egg substitutes	May be entirely egg-free or made from egg whites, with dairy or vegetable products substituted for the yolks. These substitutes are important for people with cholesterol-free diet requirements.

Safety Steps for Cooking Eggs

- Eggs are potentially hazardous foods. They are highly susceptible to contamination by Salmonella micro-organisms, which can cause foodborne illness. Cooking to 140°F (60°C) or higher kills these micro-organisms.
- For recipes calling for uncooked or undercooked eggs, use frozen, liquid, or dried pasteurized eggs rather than fresh shell eggs. These menu items include meringues, mousses, Caesar salad dressings, hollandaise and Bernaise sauces, eggnog, and mayonnaise.
- Hold egg dishes for no more than one-half hour, then replace with new product.

any eggs that have cracked or dirty shells because they might be contaminated.

Eggs can be purchased many different ways. Exhibit 7.6 identifies the various market forms of eggs and their uses in cooking.

It is important to remember that fresh eggs should always be refrigerated. To prevent risk of foodborne illness, use Exhibit 7.7 to learn the recommended temperatures and time periods for egg storage.

Exhibit 7.7
Guidelines for storing eggs.

Type of Egg	Recommended Product Temperature	Maximum StoragePeriods	Comments
Eggs in shell	40°F/4.4°C	1 week	Do not wash or remove from container
Leftover yolks/whites	40° to 45°F/4.4° to 7.2°C	2 days	Cover yolks with water
Dried eggs	40° to 45°F/4.4° to 7.2°C	1 year	Cover tightly
Reconstituted eggs	40° to 45°F/4.4° to 7.2°C	1 week	Store in refrigerator

Cooking Eggs

There are many ways to prepare eggs. In fact, the 100 pleats on a toque (a chef's white hat) are said to represent the 100 ways a chef can prepare eggs! Eggs are cooked in several ways—hard-cooked, baked, poached, fried, scrambled, omelets, quiches, and soufflés. No matter how they are prepared, safety steps must always be followed to ensure properly cooked eggs.

Hard-cooked eggs are simmered, then put into cold water immediately after cooking to stop the cooking and make them easier to peel. Boiling can cause fragile eggshells to crack, and the egg to become tough. In addition to breakfast dishes, hard-cooked eggs are an important ingredient in a number of other popular preparations, such as cold hors d'oeuvres, canapés, salads, and garnishes.

Exhibit 7.8
How to simmer or hard cook eggs.

How to simmer eggs:

- Place the eggs in enough water to completely cover them.
- Bring the water to a slow boil; then, reduce the water to a simmer.
- Start timing the cooking once the water has reached a simmer.

Tips for perfect hard-cooked eggs:

- Use enough water to completely cover the eggs.
- Lower the eggs into the water prior to simmering, instead of dropping them.
- Reduce the heat under the pot once a simmer is reached.
- Cool and peel hard-cooked eggs immediately after they have finished cooking. This prevents a green ring from forming around the yolk.

Exhibit 7.9
Cooking times for shell eggs.

Cooking Style	Time	Comments
Coddled	30 seconds	Lower cold eggs into already simmering water
Soft-cooked	1 to 2 minutes	
Medium-cooked	3 to 5 minutes	
Hard-cooked	10 minutes	Variation on technique calls for eggs to be removed from heat when water reaches a boil, covered, and allowed to remain for 20 to 30 minutes.

Different egg preparations, from hard-cooking to coddling, require different cooking times. When preparing eggs, it is important to time the cooking. Exhibit 7.9 lists the cooking times for various types of cooked eggs.

Another way to prepare eggs is to bake them. Baked eggs can be easily combined with a number of additional ingredients to create a fun, satisfying breakfast. Exhibit 7.10 describes how to bake eggs.

Exhibit 7.10
How to bake eggs.

- Prepare the baking dish by buttering it generously.
- Add any additional ingredients in an even layer to the baking dish.
- Bake the eggs (in a bain-marie if desired) until the whites are set and milky in appearance.
- Unmold the eggs, if desired, garnish, and serve hot.

Like baked eggs, shirred eggs can be cooked with other ingredients, such as cheese, vegetables, meats, and sauces. **Shirred** eggs are cooked in butter, and sometimes cream, in a **ramekin** (RAM-uh-kin) a small, ceramic oven-proof dish.

Changing the size, shape, and material of the baking dish can affect the texture of the finished item. The egg must be fresh because its appearance is very important in the service of this dish. Most importantly, it will prevent the yolk from breaking.

Poached eggs are shelled (taken out of the shell) and simmered in water. Poached eggs are popular in classic dishes such as Eggs Benedict and Eggs Florentine, and as toppings for hash and baked potatoes. A properly poached egg should be tender and well shaped. The yolk should be centered and the white should not be rough or ragged.

Exhibit 7.11
How to poach eggs.

- Combine water, salt, and vinegar in a shallow skillet or pan and bring it to a simmer.
- Break the eggs into a clean cup and slide the egg carefully into the poaching water. Cook until the whites are set and opaque.
- Remove the eggs from the water and blot them on an absorbent towel.
- Trim, if desired, and serve hot.

Scrambled eggs should have a light texture, creamy consistency, and delicate flavor. They are best when served very hot. The eggs should be blended just until the yolks and whites are combined, and then add any seasonings. Scrambled eggs must be cooked over gentle heat and constantly stirred and scraped from the bottom and sides of the pan to be creamy and to prevent them from burning.

Fried eggs are quick and easy to prepare. To make sure that eggs are fried with the yolks high and centered, use the correct heat level, fresh eggs, and an appropriate amount of cooking fat. The yolk should be cooked to the required doneness. Eggs fried up, sometimes called sunnyside up, are fried only on the bottom. Eggs fried over easy are turned over and fried very lightly on their top sides. **Basted** eggs are fried and then steamed in a covered pan.

Omelets and Soufflés

Omelets are made from eggs that are slightly beaten. They are cooked in a skillet usually with a filling such as cheese, mushrooms, onions, or ham. Omelets are either rolled, flat, or souffléed. A rolled omelet should be golden-yellow with a creamy, moist interior and must be made to order. Flat omelets may be made in individual portions or in larger quantities. Souffléed omelets have a light, fluffy texture because the egg whites are whipped before cooking. Exhibit 7.12 describes the three different methods of preparing omelets.

In the year 1945, Americans ate an average of 403 eggs per person. By 1995, the number had dropped to 237 per person. What do you think are the reasons for this drop?

Another favorite egg dish that can be carried over to lunch or dinner is **quiche** (keesh), an egg custard baked in a crust. Eggs are blended with milk or cream until smooth. Seasonings and garnish are added.

Exhibit 7.12
Making omelets.

Rolled omelet

- Blend the eggs, liquid (milk, cream, and/or water), and seasonings.
- Pour the egg mixture into a heated and oiled pan.
- Swirl the pan over the heat, stirring and scraping the eggs simultaneously, until curds begin to form.
- Add a filling, if desired.
- Cook the omelet until it is set.
- Roll the omelet—completely encasing the filling—out of the pan directly onto a heated plate. Shape it, using a clean towel, if necessary.
- Rub the surface with butter, if desired.

Flat omelet

- Blend the eggs, liquid (milk, cream, and/or water), and seasoning.
- Sauté any garnish ingredients.
- Pour the egg mixture into a hot, oiled pan over the garnish, swirling the pan so the egg mixture covers the entire bottom of the pan.
- Cook, without stirring, until the edges are set.
- Finish the omelet in a hot oven, adding other garnish ingredients, such as grated cheese.
- Brown under a broiler, if desired.

Souffléed Omelet

- Whip the eggs until they are frothy. Add any seasonings and garnish ingredients.
- Pour the egg mixture into a heated and oiled pan.
- Cook the omelet until the edges and bottom are set.
- Finish in a hot oven.

The mixture is poured into a prepared crust, baked in a moderately heated oven, and served hot. Quiches are easily reheated in a microwave oven just before serving.

Soufflés (soo-FLAYS) are made of eggs but are rarely served for breakfast because they take time to bake and must be made to order. A soufflé is a preparation made with a sauce base, whipped egg whites, and flavorings. The egg whites cause the soufflé to puff during cooking. Soufflés are not difficult to prepare, but timing is everything. The

HINTS FOR PERFECT OMELETS

- *Always use high heat.*
- *Use the right size omelet pan.*

kitchen staff and the serving staff must work together very closely to assure that the customer receives the soufflé while it is still hot and puffy. Cheese soufflés are very popular. The following exhibit describes how to prepare soufflés.

Exhibit 7.13
Making soufflés.

- Prepare a base and add the flavoring.
- Whip egg whites and fold the whites into the base.
- Fill the molds.
- Place them in a hot oven.
- Once they are done, serve the soufflés immediately.

Review Your Learning 7.2

1. Using the numbers (1) smallest to (6) largest, rank the following egg sizes.

_____Medium	_____Peewee	_____Small
_____Jumbo	_____Extra large	_____Large

2. Which of the following eggs has the shortest cooking time?
   a. Medium-cooked eggs.
   b. Soft-cooked eggs.
   c. Hard-cooked eggs.
   d. Coddled eggs.

3. Which of the following recipes is finished by baking?
   a. Eggs Benedict.
   b. Shirred eggs.
   c. Scrambled eggs.
   d. Omelet.

4. What size eggs are used in most recipes?

On a separate sheet of paper unscramble the following popular ways to cook eggs. Then, briefly describe how to prepare two of them.

5. RHAD-OKOEDC	7. IEFRD	9. MEEOLT
6. AKBED	8. RASCLEMBD	10. HICQUE

7.3

SECTION 7.3

Breakfast Foods

AFTER STUDYING SECTION 7.3, YOU SHOULD BE ABLE TO:

- Prepare pancakes, crêpes, waffles, and French toast.
- Prepare ham, hash, grits, cold cereals, oatmeal, and sausage.
- Prepare coffee, tea, and cocoa.

KEY TERMS

- **Chemical leaveners**
- **Crêpe (crape or crepp)**
- **French toast**
- **Hash**
- **Hash browns**
- **Home fries**
- **Pancake**
- **Quick bread**
- **Waffle**

Breakfast Breads

Breads (including muffins, quick breads, English muffins, and bagels) are a tradition at breakfast, served hot or cold. **Quick breads** are made with **chemical leaveners** (baking soda or baking powder) that allow dough to rise more quickly than yeast. Muffins, scones, and biscuits are examples of popular quick breads served at breakfast. For more information on quick breads, see *Chapter 5: Desserts and Baked Goods* of *Becoming Foodservice Professional, Year 2*.

Exhibit 7.14
How to mix quick breads with the muffin method.

- Thoroughly combine the dry ingredients. Sift if necessary.
- Combine all liquid ingredients, including melted fat or oil.
- Add the liquids to the dry ingredients and mix together just until the flour is moistened. The batter will look lumpy, but don't overmix it.
- Pour the batter into pans and bake immediately. Don't stir the mix or the batter will be tough.

Pancakes, Crêpes, Waffles, and French Toast

Other popular breakfast foods include pancakes, crêpes, waffles, and French toast. The batters for these items are simple to make and many can be cooked in a few minutes. **Pancakes** are made with a medium-weight pour batter, pan-fried on an open, greased griddle. **Crêpes** (crapes or crepps), sometimes called Swedish pancakes, are made from a thin pour batter and cooked on a slightly greased griddle.

Exhibit 7.15
Making pancakes, crêpes, waffles, and French toast.

- Prepare the batter according to the particular recipe.
- While letting the batter rest, heat the pan, griddle, or waffle iron.
- Add oil or butter to the pan, and pour in the batter.
- Turn the item and completely cook on the other side.

Waffles are made from a medium-weight pour batter similar to that used for pancakes, and are formed in a specially designed waffle maker, or iron, that creates grid-like holes. **French toast** is sliced bread dipped in an egg-and-milk mixture, lightly fried on a lightly greased griddle or pan.

Lumberjacks in the northern frontier depended on "sweat pads," or pancakes spread with molasses or bacon grease and topped with sausages, to give them energy until lunch. Today, pancakes range from hearty buckwheat or multi-grain to delicate, thin, dessert crêpes. Pancake houses became popular in the 1950s and 1960s—but many restaurants serve pancakes and breakfast items all day long.

Pancakes, crêpes, waffles, and French toast can be served with butter and syrup, powdered sugar, fresh fruit, or whipped cream. For additional variety, ingredients such as chocolate chips or blueberries can be added to pancake or waffle batters. Exhibit 7.15 shows how to make pancakes, crêpes, waffles, and French toast.

Breakfast Meats

Breakfast meats, such as bacon, sausage, ham, Canadian bacon, and hash, are often included to complete the breakfast meal. Bacon and sausage are cooked at low temperatures. Bacon is about 70% fat and shrinks a great deal. You can control some of this shrinkage by cooking bacon at low temperatures. Bacon should be cooked until crisp, and should be properly drained of fat. Sausage should be cooked completely through, also at low temperatures. Precooked link sausages cook quickly and are easier to hold for quantity service. Ham for breakfast service is almost always precooked and only needs to be heated and browned slightly on a griddle or under the broiler. Canadian bacon is boneless pork loin that is cured and smoked. It should be cooked like ham, heated and browned. Fish, such as smoked salmon or trout, is often offered on breakfast and brunch menus.

Hash is a mixture of chopped meats, potatoes, and onions. The ratio of meat to vegetable is not an exact one, and the chef can include a wide variety of vegetables to give the dish color and flavor.

Exhibit 7.16
Different breakfast foods can be combined to make healthy breakfasts.

Breakfast Potatoes

Potatoes are prepared in a variety of ways for breakfast and brunch. Most often they are made into hashed brown potatoes or home fries. Hashed brown potatoes, or **hash browns,** are grated or chopped potatoes pan-fried to a crispy brown. **Home fries** are thickly sliced or large-diced potatoes lightly pan-fried.

Cereals

Hot and cold cereals are becoming more popular as breakfast entrées. A wide variety of cold cereals featuring oat bran and granola are common breakfast requests. Cold, prepackaged cereals need no formal preparation. Serve cold cereals with accompanying milk or cream, sugar (brown sugar is attractive), and fruit, such as bananas or strawberries.

There are two types of hot cereals: whole, cracked, or flaked cereals (oatmeal and cracked wheat) and granular cereals (farina and cornmeal). When you prepare hot cereals, be sure to measure the correct amount of water, salt, and cereal according to package directions. Adding milk makes the cereal creamier—and more expensive. If you do use milk, take care not to boil or scorch it. Always add the cereal slowly, stirring constantly to prevent lumps. To prevent dryness, keep the cereal covered until it is served. Oatmeal, cream of wheat or rice, grits, and cornmeal mush are all typical hot cereals.

Breakfast Drinks

Traditional breakfast beverages include coffee, tea, and hot chocolate. However, juice and milk- or juice-based blender drinks are also popular. Always serve hot beverages very hot and steaming. Both coffee and tea contain caffeine, which is a stimulant. People who are sensitive to the effects of caffeine will often ask for decaffeinated options.

Many times a sip of coffee is the first and last impression a customer has of a restaurant. Since these impressions are very important, always purchase, brew, and pour good-quality coffee.

Coffee should be held at 185°F to 190°F (85°C to 87.8°C). Avoid holding brewed coffee for over an hour. After one hour, the loss of flavor is considerable. Serve coffee hot and steaming. Plan coffee production so that coffee is always fresh.

Coffee urns should be cleaned regularly to avoid calcium build-up and to ensure good-tasting coffee. Run a solution of 1 part white vinegar and 4 parts water through the brewing cycle. Follow this by running plain cold water through the brewing cycle three more times.

Tea is generally less expensive than coffee, although some rare teas can be

Exhibit 7.17
Tips for great-tasting coffee.

- Use the right proportions.
- Always measure carefully and accurately.
- Use only fresh, cold water.
- Use water at the right brewing temperature (195°F to 200°F, or 90.6°C to 93.3°C).
- Use the right brewing procedure.
- Use clean equipment.
- Use the right filters.
- Use proper holding procedures. *Don't hold coffee too long.*

About Coffee

- *Coffee beans are really the berries of a tropical shrub. The beans are roasted to develop their flavor. The degree of roasting, which can be light, medium, or dark, affects the flavor of the coffee.*
- *Americans generally prefer medium roast, while dark roast coffees are popular in Europe. Coffee is often served as an after-dinner beverage in French and Italian restaurants.*
- *The use of flavored coffees is also becoming popular—at breakfast, lunch, and dinner. Flavors range from the most popular such as hazelnut, almond, mint, and chocolate, to the most exotic such as blueberry and strawberry.*

quite expensive. One cup of tea has about half the caffeine contained in a cup of coffee. It is served either very hot or iced. There are black teas (tea leaves that have been fermented) and green teas (tea leaves that are not fermented). Oolong tea is partially fermented. Herbal teas are made from many different fruits and herbs and are naturally caffeine-free. After tea is graded, teas are blended to ensure consistency and uniformity. Some tea blends may contain as many as 30 individual teas. To make hot tea, follow the steps in Exhibit 7.18.

Exhibit 7.18
How to make hot tea.

- Put tea leaves into a preheated, empty pot. (Use 1 tsp loose tea or one single service tea bag for each 6 oz of water.)
- Pour boiling water into the pot.
- Let the tea steep (soak) for 3 to 5 minutes.
- Serve immediately after steeping. Tea will become bitter if left to steep too long.

To many soldiers in the American Civil War, coffee was the most important ration. One weary soldier wrote in his diary that after a long night's march, he felt refreshed and invigorated after drinking a pint of steaming hot coffee. After the Civil War, coffee became a national drink.

Review Your Learning 7.3

1. Which of the following is a mixture of chopped meats, potatoes, and onions?
   a. Omelet.
   b. Hash.
   c. Hash Browns.
   d. Grits.

2. Which of the following is an example of a quick bread?
   a. Soufflé.
   b. Scone.
   c. Grits.
   d. Crêpe.

3. Which of the following will minimize shrinkage of bacon?
   a. Frying it quickly with high heat.
   b. Baking in a microwave oven.
   c. Frying it in deep fat.
   d. Cooking it at low temperatures.

4. What is included in quick breads that allows the dough to rise more quickly than yeast?

5. What are some breakfast foods made from pour batters?

6. What are some common breakfast meats?

7. What is the longest amount of time coffee should be held in order to ensure its quality?

8. Which has more caffeine per cup, coffee or tea?

7.4

SECTION 7.4

Sandwiches

AFTER STUDYING SECTION 7.4, YOU SHOULD BE ABLE TO:

- Give examples of different types of sandwiches, including simple hot, open-faced, hors d'oeuvres, grilled, deep-fried, and simple cold.
- Explain the roles of the three components of a sandwich: bread, spread, and filling.
- Develop a list of sanitation procedures for preparing sandwiches.
- List the necessary tools and equipment to make sandwiches at a sandwich station.
- Prepare common sandwich spreads and fillings.
- Demonstrate preparation of several types of sandwiches.

KEY TERMS

- **Canapé (CAN-uh-pay)**
- **Club sandwich**
- **Hors d'oeuvres (or DERVS)**
- **Multidecker sandwich**
- **Open-faced sandwich**
- **Pullman loaf**
- **Tea sandwich**

Sandwiches are the most popular lunch food in the United States. They're fast, fresh, satisfying, and have many variations. Foodservice operators and chefs have much freedom of creativity when they develop sandwiches for their menus. A great variety of ingredients, including sliced meats, salads, vegetables, and fish, can be served hot or cold, on or between slices of bread. Almost any filling and spread can be combined with bread to create a fun, filling, and satisfying meal.

All sandwiches fall into one of two general categories: either hot or cold.

Hot Sandwiches

A simple hot sandwich consists of hot fillings, such as hot roast beef or grilled vegetables, between two slices of bread or two halves of a roll. Additional items such as fresh tomatoes, lettuce, or onions may be added for flavor. In the United States, hamburgers and hot dogs are among the most popular hot sandwiches.

Open-faced sandwiches are made by placing one slice of buttered or unbuttered bread or roll on a serving plate with hot meat or other filling, and covering it with a hot topping such as gravy, sauce, or cheese. The sandwich can then be broiled quickly to give it a golden color. Some open-faced hot sandwiches can be made in smaller versions as hors d'oeuvres. **Hors d'oeuvres** (or DERVS) are hot or cold bite-sized finger foods that are served before a meal.

Grilled sandwiches (or toasted sandwiches) are another type of hot sandwich. They are buttered on the outside of the bread and browned on the griddle or in a hot oven. Grilled cheese, grilled ham and cheese, and tuna melts (grilled tuna salad and cheese) are popular varieties.

Deep-fried sandwiches are dipped in beaten egg (sometimes with bread crumbs) and then deep-fried. The sandwich can be cooked on the griddle or in the oven—to reduce fat and make it less greasy. One example is a Monte Cristo sandwich featuring turkey or chicken breast, ham, and Swiss cheese.

To avoid burning yourself and others with hot oil, follow proper safety precautions when using a deep fryer.

Cold Sandwiches

A simple cold sandwich consists of two slices of bread or two halves of a roll, a spread, and a filling. As with hot sandwiches, the choices for filling are many. The most common fillings are meats and cheeses, or a salad, such as egg salad or tuna salad. A submarine sandwich is a cold sandwich usually served on a long sliced roll with several types of cheese, meats, lettuce, tomatoes, onions, and more.

A **multidecker sandwich** is made with more than two slices of bread (or roll) with several ingredients in the filling. The **club sandwich** is one example of a multidecker sandwich. A traditional club sandwich is made from three slices of

The Midwest is the regional home of the hamburger and hot dog. These American staples were introduced in St. Louis in 1904. Their names come from the cities in Germany where they originated: hamburgers from Hamburg and frankfurters from Frankfurt.

toasted bread spread with mayonnaise and filled with an assortment of sliced chicken and/or turkey, ham, bacon, cheese, lettuce, and tomato, and is cut into four triangles. Exhibit 7.19 shows the easiest, and most common way, of cutting a club sandwich.

Open-faced sandwiches can also be cold sandwiches, made with a single bread, with the filling or topping attractively arranged and garnished. A smaller version of the open-faced cold sandwich is a **canapé** (CAN-uh-pay) a tiny open-faced sandwich served as an hors d'oeuvre.

Canapés can be made from bread or toast cutouts, English muffins, crackers, melba toasts, and tiny unsweetened pastry

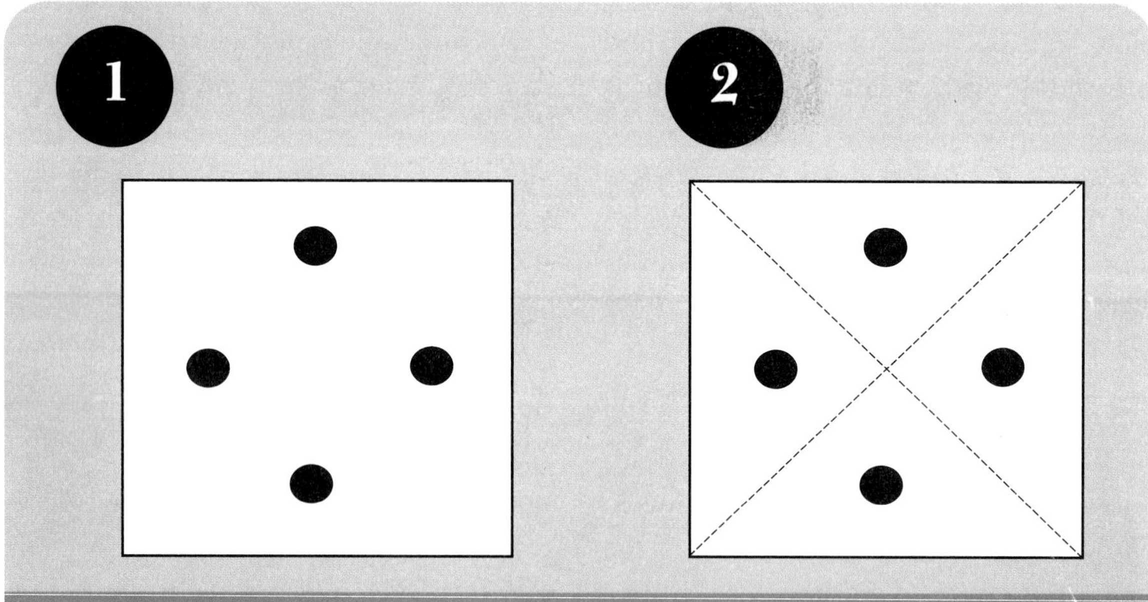

Exhibit 7.19
How to cut a club sandwich.

1. Place four long, frilled toothpicks in the middle of each side of the sandwich.
2. Cut the sandwich into quarters from corner to corner. Plate the sandwich with with points facing upward.

Exhibit 7.20
An open-faced cold sandwich.

Tips for Protein Salads and Sandwiches

- Make sure protein-rich foods such as tuna, eggs, ham, and chicken are properly cooked before mixing in salads or salad sandwiches. This should also be done for potato and pasta salads made with mayonnaise (which contains eggs).
- Always refrigerate meat and protein salad sandwiches. Harmful bacterial may multiply if they are not held under refrigeration. Even when sandwiches are refrigerated, the insulating properties of the bread may prevent sandwich fillings from cooling quickly enough.

shells. Spreads can be as simple as flavored butter or softened cream cheese. Meat or fish spreads can be used to give a more zesty flavor. An attractive garnish is the finishing touch to a canapé. Follow the guidelines in Exhibit 7.21 for creating canapés.

Tea sandwiches are small cold sandwiches usually served on bread or toast, trimmed of crusts, and cut into shapes. The fillings and spreads may be the same as those for canapés.

Setting Up the Sandwich Station

Sandwich preparation involves a great deal of handwork. It's important to reduce your hand motions whether you're preparing sandwiches in quantity or to order. The set-up for a sandwich station depends on the operation's menu and on available equipment and space. Every sandwich station needs two basic things.

1. Ingredients
2. Equipment

Ingredients

Sandwich ingredients must be prepared ahead of time. This is called mise en place—getting ready for the job to be done. Depending on the sandwich, you might need to separate lettuce leaves, slice tomatoes, prepare garnishes, slice meats and cheeses, mix fillings, or prepare spreads.

Arrange and store the ingredients to reduce your hand movement. All the

Exhibit 7.21
Guidelines for great canapés.

- Prepreparation is essential. All bases, spreads, and garnishes must be ready ahead of time.
- Use quality ingredients.
- Assemble canapés as close as possible to serving time. Bases quickly become soggy, and spreads and garnishes dry out easily. As trays are completed, they can be covered lightly with plastic and refrigerated for a short time. Always follow rules for safe food handling.
- Keep spreads and garnishes simple and neat. Spreads and garnishes that are too fancy can fall apart—on the tray or in the guest's hands.
- Use flavor combinations in spreads and garnishes that are appealing both in taste and in appearance. The ingredients must blend well together and look attractive.
- Use spicy or flavorful ingredients.
- Arrange the canapés carefully and attractively on trays.

items should be within your reach so you can work quickly and safely.

In a busy sandwich station, every second counts. Sliced items are portioned by count and by weight. Fillings are also portioned by weight. To keep recipes accurate, each ingredient must be either counted or weighed properly.

Equipment

The type of equipment needed in a sandwich station depends on the size of the menu and the operation. An efficient sandwich station makes it easier to prepare sandwiches in large quantities. Most stations have the following.

- *Work table*—Big enough to spread out ingredients and do work
- *Storage facilities*—Refrigeration equipment for cold ingredients and a steam table for hot ingredients
- *Hand tools*—Spreader, spatula, serrated knife, chef's knife, cutting board, and power slicer (power slicer may be needed for any slicing not done ahead of time)
- *Portion control equipment*—Scoops for fillings, portion scale for measuring ingredients
- *Cooking equipment for hot sandwiches*—Griddles, grills, broilers, deep-fryers, microwave ovens

Preparing Sandwiches

Preparing hot and cold sandwiches to order is an important skill for anyone who works in food service. Many operations prepare sandwiches to order to ensure their freshness. Sandwiches prepared ahead of time should be covered with plastic wrap and stored in a refrigerator for service within three hours, or individually wrapped and refrigerated for two to three days.

Bread is the basic ingredient of any sandwich. While it serves as an edible container for the food inside, it also provides bulk and nutrients. **Pullman loaves,** sandwich loaves of sliced white bread, are still the most frequently used sandwich bread, but a variety of hard rolls, pita bread, French bread, tortillas, multi-grain, and cinnamon and raisin bread are also very popular.

Always follow safe knife handling procedures when cutting sandwiches.

Any bread or roll must be served fresh. Exhibit 7.22 lists some helpful tips for keeping bread fresh.

There are many different types of spreads that can be used when preparing a sandwich. Spreads serve three main purposes: to prevent the bread from soaking up the filling; to add flavor; and to add moisture. Butter and mayonnaise are the most common spreads used. Butter must be soft enough to spread easily without tearing the bread. Butter can be softened by whipping it in a mixer or letting it stand at room temperature for about 30 minutes. Butters flavored with lemon, chive, mustard, honey, and other ingredients are often used to add a unique flavor to a sandwich.

Submarines, heroes, hoagies, and _grinders_ are regional names for the same sandwich: lots of ingredients on a long loaf of bread. In New Orleans it's called a _poor boy._ The Creoles called it _la Médiatrice,_ or _peacemaker,_ because husbands in trouble used them to appease their angry wives.

While mayonnaise is often used instead of butter because it has more flavor, it actually adds moisture to the bread and can make it soggy. Commercially-prepared mayonnaise has been made with pasteurized eggs and is therefore less hazardous than homemade mayonnaise.

Exhibit 7.22
Tips for keeping bread fresh.

- Bread should be delivered daily, if possible.
- Keep bread wrapped in moisture-proof wrapping until it is used.
- Store bread between 75°F and 85°F (23.9°C and 29.4°C) rather than in a refrigerator.
- Use French bread and other hard-crusted breads the day they are delivered or baked.
- If bread must be kept more than one day, store it in the freezer. Thaw frozen bread inside its wrapping.
- Day-old bread can be used for toasting without loss of quality.

Safety Steps for Meat and Cheese Fillings

- Avoid slicing meats and cheeses farther ahead of time than necessary.
- Keep sliced meats and cheeses covered to prevent them from drying out.

- Store meats, cheeses, and spreads between 32°F and 36°F (0°C and 2.2°C) to prevent foodbome illness.

Safety Step for Mayonnaise-based Salads

- Seafood fillings and mayonnaise-based fillings are potentially hazardous foods. They should always be kept tightly covered and refrigerated below 40°F.

Raw eggs that have not been pasteurized should never be used to make mayonnaise.

Condiments

Several additional ingredients that add texture and flavor to a sandwich are called *condiments.* Condiments include sauces such as ketchup, mustard, and horseradish. Flavorful vegetables like olives and pickles are considered condiments also.

Many sandwiches are prepared with potentially hazardous foods and must be handled following proper time and temperature guidelines.

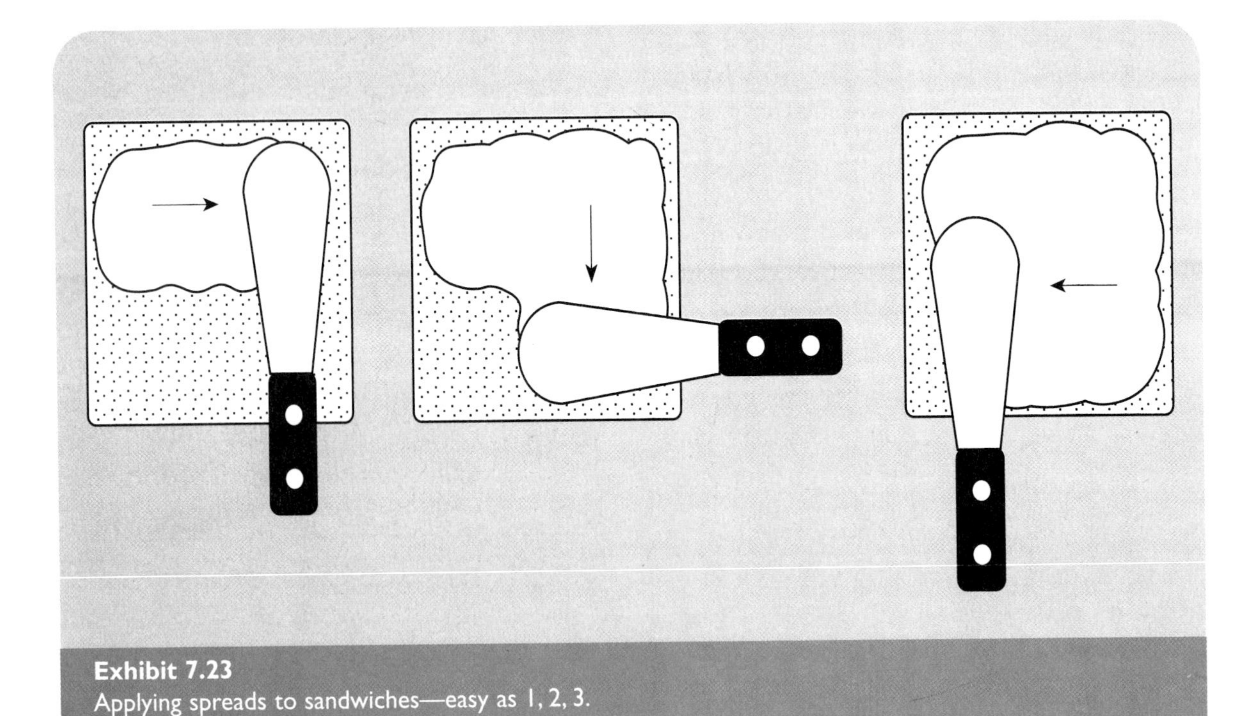

Exhibit 7.23
Applying spreads to sandwiches—easy as 1, 2, 3.

Exhibit 7.24
Popular sandwich fillings.

Beef
- Roast beef slices, cold or hot
- Hamburger patties
- Small steaks
- Corned beef
- Pastrami

Pork products
- Roast pork
- Ham
- Bacon
- Canadian bacon

Cheese
- Cheddar
- Swiss
- Provolone
- Cream and Neufchâtel
- Processed
- Spreads
- Goat

Mayonnaise-based salads
- Egg salad
- Tuna salad
- Chicken salad
- Turkey salad
- Crabmeat salad
- Ham salad

Poultry
- Turkey breast
- Chicken breast

Vegetables
- Lettuce
- Tomatoes
- Onions, raw or grilled
- Sprouts (alfalfa, bean, etc.)
- Spinach and other greens

Fish and shellfish
- Tuna
- Sardines
- Smoked salmon and lox
- Shrimp
- Anchovies
- Fried fish

Condiments
- Mustard
- Horseradish
- Ketchup
- Pickles
- Relish
- Olives

Other fillings
- Peanut butter
- Jelly
- Hard-cooked eggs
- Fruits, fresh or dried
- Nuts (such as almond slices)

The choice of filling is limited only by the chef's imagination. Whenever you use meat, poultry, or cheese, remember that thin slices are more tender and make the sandwich easier to eat. Exhibit 7.24 provides a list of some popular sandwich fillings.

Just for Fun!

What are some of your favorite sandwich fillings? Can you think of some other foods that could be considered sandwiches? How about gyros—pita bread with lamb, onions, tomatoes, and yogurt sauce, and tacos—corn shells filled with beef, chicken, avocado or other ingredients?

Serving Sandwiches

Except for hamburgers and hot dogs, sandwiches should be cut before serving.

Cutting a sandwich in half makes it easier to hold and eat, and it makes a more attractive presentation. A large, multidecker sandwich or a very thick sandwich should be cut into thirds or quarters, with each section held in place with a toothpick. To make an attractive presentation, display the cut edges, rather than the crust edges, to the outside. This way the ingredients are easily seen, and the sandwich looks appealing and appetizing. Hamburgers and other uncut sandwiches can be served open-faced to show their ingredients.

While the sandwich is probably as old as meat and bread, the name was adopted in the 18th century for John Montague, the 4th Earl of Sandwich. The earl was such an avid gambler that he would spend up to 24 hours at a stretch at the gambling tables. Rather that interrupt his play for meals, he insisted on having sliced cold meat and bread brought to him regularly. And so the "sandwich" was born.

Review Your Learning 7.4

1. What are the main parts of a sandwich?
2. List some common sandwich fillings.
3. List some vegetables commonly used in sandwiches.
4. What are some tools and equipment commonly used by a chef in a sandwich station?
5. Draw a diagram showing how you would set up the following ingredients for a basic sandwich station: bread, lettuce, tomatoes, cheese, ham, tuna salad, mayonnaise, mustard, ketchup, pickles, potato chips.

On a separate sheet of paper, list an example of each of the sandwich types listed below.

6. Open-faced hot
7. Canapé
8. Simple cold
9. Deep-fried
10. Grilled
11. Open-faced cold
12. Simple hot

Flashback

CHAPTER 7

SECTION 7.1: DAIRY PRODUCTS

- Dairy products include milk,yogurt, cheese, and butter. Most Western cooking relies heavily on the use of them.
- All dairy products are highly perishable and must be stored carefully.
- Milk comes in whole liquid, evaporated, and condensed forms. All forms of milk are **pasteurized** and **homogenized.**
- Cheeses are ripened or unripened. Processed cheeses are pasteurized to prevent aging.
- The variety of cheeses ranges from mild to sharp to pungent (very sharp).

SECTION 7.2: THE VERSATILE EGG

- The egg is one of the most versatile and essential foods. Eggs are useful in many ways—thickening, coloring, adding moisture, forming emulsions, foaming, and enriching other foods.
- Eggs appear on menus throughout the day, from breakfast dishes to dessert soufflés.
- Eggs are graded according to USDA Grade AA, A, and B and range in size from 15 ounces per dozen (peewee) to 30 ounces per dozen (jumbo). Most recipes use large eggs (24 ounces per dozen).
- Like all purchased items, shell eggs should be evaluated and ordered based on such characteristics as their color, form, packaging, and preservation method.
- Eggs should be received and stored according to proper sanitation procedures and must be inspected carefully upon delivery.
- Egg cookery includes several techniques: boiled eggs, baked eggs, **poached** eggs, fried eggs, scrambled eggs, **omelets,** and **soufflés.**
- Another favorite egg dish that can be carried over to lunch or dinner at very little cost is **quiche,** which is basically an egg custard baked in a crust.

SECTION 7.3: BREAKFAST FOODS

- Other breakfast foods include **pancakes, crêpes, waffles,** and **French toast.** The batters for these items are simple to make and many recipes can be prepared a day in advance.
- Hot and cold cereals, served with milk, cream, and fruits, are popular, easy-to-make breakfast dishes. Typical cold cereals include those made with oat bran and granola, while oatmeal, cream of wheat or rice, grits, and cornmeal mush are all typical hot cereals.
- Breakfast meats, such as bacon, sausage, ham, Canadian bacon, and hash, complete the breakfast meal.
- **Hash** is a mixture of chopped meats, potatoes, and onions that is filling and cost effective. Fish, such as smoked salmon or trout, is a popular breakfast and brunch item.
- Potatoes are prepared in a variety of ways for breakfast and brunch. Most often they are made into hashed brown potatoes or **hash browns,** and home fried potatoes.
- Breakfast beverages include coffee, tea, juice, hot chocolate, and milk. Milk- or juice-based drinks are also very popular.
- Hot beverages should always be served very hot and steaming.

SECTION 7.4: SANDWICHES

- Foodservice operators and chefs are limited only by their own creativity when they develop sandwiches for their menus.
- A great variety of ingredients, including sliced meats, salads, vegetables, and fish, can be served hot or cold on or between slices of bread.
- In the United States, sandwiches are the number one choice for lunchtime food.
- It's important to know the basic methods of sandwich making and how to set up a sandwich station.
- Preparing sandwiches in large quantities is not difficult once the sandwich station is in place. Always practice safe and sanitary measures in preparing and storing sandwiches.
- Almost any filling or spread can be used between two slices of bread to create a fun and satisfying meal. All sandwiches fall into one of two categories: hot sandwiches or cold sandwiches.
- Hot sandwiches include simple hot sandwiches (hamburgers, hot dogs), grilled sandwiches (grilled cheese and

grilled ham and cheese), and deep-fried sandwiches (Monte Cristo).

- Cold sandwiches include simple cold sandwiches (from a cheese sandwich to a submarine sandwich), **multidecker sandwiches (club sandwich)**, and **open-faced sandwiches (tea sandwiches, hors d'oeuvres, and canapés).**
- Sandwich preparation involves a great deal of handwork and mise en place.
- It's important to reduce your hand motions whether you're preparing sandwiches in quantity or to order. Ingredients and equipment items should be within easy reach.

James Moran

Food and Beverage Director
Arlington Race Track, Arlington, Illinois

For the five months we operate, we hire 23 managers and about 325 employees to make our season successful. We have two weeks to train the managers—one week for the other associates—prior to opening. We don't have the luxury of fine-tuning things over time; everyone must be ready right out of the gate, and our systems must be in order so that guests are served in the excellent manner they've come to expect.

We train people fast and often. After initial training, we hold daily 15-minute pre-shift meetings of all employees, so that we can make sure everyone is there, and everyone is fully uniformed and prepared for the day's work. We brief each other on special events, promotions, and even things like weather conditions.

The number-one responsibility of my job is to support and coach my employees. It's my job to make sure everyone has what they need to get their job done right, and share the organization's customer focus with everyone. I must lead by example by staying organized and always put my customers first, both internal and external. If I do this, then everyone can focus their energy on guest satisfaction.

Our guests probably don't realize the effort that's necessary to keep things running smoothly, but they do appreciate the outstanding service they get and how hard everyone here works to make sure they enjoy their visit. It takes all of us working together to provide that much fun.

CHAPTER 8

Working with People

8.1

SECTION 8.1

Learning to Work Together

AFTER STUDYING SECTION 8.1, YOU SHOULD BE ABLE TO:

- Explain how stereotypes and prejudices can negatively affect how people work together.

KEY TERMS

- **Dialect**
- **Diversity**
- **Prejudice**
- **Stereotype**

We live in a world of instant communication, global markets, and international corporations, where many people and products cross boundaries and borders each year. The result is often a clash of cultural values in the workplace.

Diversity refers to the great variety of people and their backgrounds, experiences, opinions, religions, ages, talents, and abilities. In a diverse environment, people must learn to value and respect others, no matter how different they are.

Think about the kinds of people that live in your neighborhood, go to your school, or are on your sports team; chances are that there are people from many different backgrounds and cultures represented. That's because you live in a culturally diverse world, and will continue to meet people that are different from you in many ways. You will be a part of the workforce in the 21st century—a century that will be characterized by greater diversity than ever before. No matter where you work, cultural diversity will be increasingly prevalent—at school, at work, and beyond.

Exhibit 8.1
Diversity refers to the great variety of people and their backgrounds, experiences, opinions, religions, ages, talents, and abilities.

Diversity is both an asset and an opportunity. Since the U.S. customer base is also becoming more diverse, guests can be drawn in and often feel more comfortable if they see employees that have a similar heritage, culture, or background as they do. Internally, employees of various backgrounds provide a wide variety of ideas about marketing approaches, menu items, service behaviors, and other aspects that can help organizations attract and keep customers. For example, an employee may suggest to his manager that they include some Asian entrées on the menu to attract and keep those customers that really enjoy Asian food, while exposing others to a unique type of cuisine.

Today's diverse workforce requires everyone to work hard to work through prejudices. **Prejudices** are usually negative biases, or feelings, towards people of a particular ethnicity or culture and are not based on fact. Every operation's success—as well as your personal success—depends on developing positive attitudes towards different people.

Part of developing a positive attitude towards others is to become aware of your own stereotypes. A **stereotype** is an assumption that all members of a group fit the same pattern. Learning about the different cultures that exist in our world and being knowledgeable about their differences will help you avoid stereotypical thinking.

How to Communicate across Cultural Differences

Differences in accent, fluency, and dialect often interfere when people communicate with each other. A **dialect** is the variation of a language spoken by a particular group of people, such as Easterners, Southerners, or Bostonians. Even if everyone is speaking the same language, members of different groups must often work hard to understand what is being said.

> **Try This...**
>
> **What other dialects of English can you think of?**

For many people, especially those working in the foodservice industry, English is a second language. It takes a lot of concentration and energy to master something new when you're not completely familiar with the language. Be patient with people who are still learning. Don't let the way a person speaks prejudice you.

Conflict and tension can result when people misunderstand each other. If someone says something that is unclear to you, politely ask him or her to explain. On the other hand, if you mistakenly offend someone, don't insist that you're right. Apologize and try again. Situations can usually be smoothed over when the people involved say they are sorry.

In addition to speaking, we also communicate through body language. The way we walk, stand, or sit is affected by the practices and traditions of our culture.

Whenever you communicate with bosses, coworkers, classmates, or customers whose backgrounds are different from yours, be aware of their reactions—reactions that might show they have misunderstood something you've said or done. Here are some guidelines that will help you accept and understand people from all walks of life.

- Be aware that not everyone has the same behaviors you do.
- If you suspect that your misinterpreted behavior has offended someone, clarify and apologize. If you are the offended one, let the other person know.
- See and treat people as individuals, rather than members of a particular group.

Exhibit 8.2
Misunderstandings can usually be resolved through effective communication.

Working as a Team

As a student, you know what it's like to be a member of a team. Whether in sports, student government, or in class working together, you spend much of your day interacting with others. In food service, teamwork is also an important part of the job. People who work together can usually accomplish more than those who work alone.

Do you remember a time when you tried to accomplish a task by yourself, only to realize you needed the help of a friend, classmate, or coworker? Chances are the two of you finished the task more efficiently than by doing it alone. Being an active member of a team is valuable for many reasons; it's a good way to share knowledge and information with other coworkers and pitch in and help each other when necessary.

Teamwork also encourages effective communication between coworkers and management. The more you work with other people, whether it be at school or at work, the easier it will be to express yourself and share your ideas and thoughts with your coworkers and supervisors.

Review Your Learning 8.1

On a separate sheet of paper, list the letter of the description on the right that matches the term on the left.

1. Stereotype
2. Diversity
3. Dialect
4. Prejudice
5. Culture

a. People with different backgrounds, experiences, opinions, and abilities.
b. Variation of a language spoken by a particular group.
c. Assumption that all members of a group fit the same pattern.
d. Biased judgment or opinion not based on facts.
e. Social structure, habits, and traditions of a group of people.

6. Being knowledgeable about your own stereotypes will help you:
   a. get a raise.
   b. learn effective listening.
   c. eliminate stereotypical thinking.
   d. clarify misinterpreted behavior.

7. Indicate whether each of the following statements is true (T) or false (F):
   a. Problems often occur between people because they don't communicate well with each other.
   b. The first step in eliminating prejudice is to become aware of your own stereotypes.
   c. Diversity is not evident in the foodservice industry.
   d. It is impossible to communicate with a person who has a dialect different from yours.
   e. We use nonverbal communication even when we do not intend to.
   f. You should always deal with people as individuals.
   g. It is okay to expect everyone to behave in the same manner as you do.
   h. The way we walk or stand is affected by our culture.

8. Teamwork is valuable because:
   a. it's a good way to share knowledge and information with coworkers.
   b. it prevents new employees from having to do all of the work.
   c. managers can closely monitor their employees' performances.
   d. it allows employees to talk and get to know each other.

9. Give three examples of situations or activities in which teamwork is essential.

8.2

SECTION 8.2

Interviewing and Orientation

AFTER STUDYING SECTION 8.2, YOU SHOULD BE ABLE TO:

- List and demonstrate effective legal interviewing skills.
- State the importance of having new-employee orientation.
- Describe common elements of orientation programs.

KEY TERMS

- **Closed question**
- **Discrimination**
- **Open-ended question**
- **Orientation**

No matter what career you choose, interviewing or being interviewed will be a part of it. Whether the position is in food service, law, health care, finance, or another industry, you will have to go through a formal interviewing process. The information in this section gives you an idea of what you can expect when you are being interviewed, as well as what you should do when you are the one interviewing and hiring employees.

Exhibit 8.3
No matter what career you choose, you will have to go through a formal interviewing process.

Applying for a Job

As we discussed in *Introduction: Preparing for a Successful Career,* the key to interviewing well is being prepared. One way to prepare is to practice talking about the kinds of things that will be asked during an interview. Although it's impossible to know exactly what a potential employer will ask, questions often fall into distinct categories like past work experience, education, attitude about work, character traits, and how well you interact with others.

> **Give it a Try...**
>
> **Think of at least one question that an employer might ask during an interview in each of the following: past work experience, education, attitude about work, character traits, and teamwork.**

Interviewing Job Applicants

At some point in your career, you will probably be expected to interview and hire prospective employees. Unlike being interviewed, your job will be to ask questions and think about how well that person will fit in to the operation.

Sometimes it is difficult to know the right questions to ask an applicant during a job interview. Asking the wrong type of questions can make it hard to find the most qualified people. The wrong questions may also be illegal. Selecting and interviewing applicants are strictly regulated by laws that protect the civil rights of job applicants. An employer must have hiring and employment practices that will protect these civil rights. In addition, employers must keep good records to prove they have observed the laws.

All hiring and interviewing practices must be fair and directly related to the job. To avoid charges of **discrimination** or making a decision based on a prejudice, employers should use identical application forms and tests for everyone who applies for the same job. Job applicants should be asked the same kinds of questions in interviews, and each one should receive the same information about the job and the organization. Employers *cannot* ask about the following.

- Race
- Ethnic background
- Country of origin
- Former or maiden name
- Parents' names
- Languages other than English (unless a second language is a requirement of the job)

- Prior arrests (arrests are not convictions; there is no proof that the applicant is guilty of a crime)
- Marital status
- Children, plans to have children, or childcare arrangements
- Any information about a spouse
- Religion
- Credit history or personal financial information
- Disabilities an applicant might have unless they have a direct bearing on job performance
- Height, weight, hair color, or other questions about an applicant's appearance

Interviewers need to keep all job requirements and interview questions directly related to the job. Exhibit 8.4 provides guidelines for asking appropriate and legal questions during an interview.

In planning to conduct interviews, employers should remember to:

- Prepare a list of legal and appropriate interview questions.
- Schedule interviews when there will be no distractions.
- Inform other employees and coworkers that they cannot be disturbed during interviews.
- Interview applicants in private areas.
- Make sure that all paperwork has been read and reviewed before the interview.
- Have any information about the operation available for applicants.
- Try to involve other appropriate supervisors, such as managers, chefs, and kitchen managers, in the interviewing process. This provides several opinions of job applicants.
- Check job applicants' references. The standard question to ask references is: "Would you hire this person again?" If references are willing to talk to you, ask about candidates' punctuality, dependability, and attitude toward work.

Two Kinds of Questions

While there are many different kinds of questions that might be asked during a job interview, they all can be categorized as closed questions or open-ended questions. **Closed questions** can be answered with a simple *yes* or *no* or with a brief, factual statement. **Open-ended questions** encourage job applicants to talk about themselves, making them feel more

Exhibit 8.4
Guidelines for appropriate and legal job requirements.

Illegal question/job requirement	Legal question/job requirement
1. Must be single/no children.	1. Position requires some overtime/weekend work.
2. Do you need to be with your children at night? Have you made arrangements for child care while you work?	2. Position requires a two-year commitment to our manager training program. Position requires frequent travel. Position might require relocation. Are you willing to work at night? Are you willing to work weekends?
3. Are you married? Do you plan to have children?	3. Are you willing to travel? We'd like to hire someone who is committed to staying with our company for a substantial amount of time. Can we count on your employment with us for more than one year?
4. How old are you?	4. Are you at least 21 years old? (Ask this only if there is a legal reason for doing so, such as for serving alcohol.)
5. Should be over/under _______ years old (unless the job requires driving, serving liquor, or another task directly related to an age-based law).	5. No mention.
6. Must own a car. Do you own a car?	6. Must have reliable transportation to work. Must be punctual. Do you have reliable transportation to work?
7. Must be male/any type of gender inquiry.	7. Must be able to lift and carry _______ pounds.
8. Must be physically able/healthy. Do you have any disabilities? Are you disabled?	8. Do you have any physical conditions that would prevent you from performing the vital functions required of this position?
9. Must be thin/attractive/blonde, etc.	9. Employees must maintain a neat, well-groomed appearance.
10. How tall are you? How much do you weigh?	10. No mention.
11. What groups or organizations do you belong to?	11. Please list any honors you've received.
12. Have you ever been arrested?	12. Have you ever been convicted of a felony? (This type of question should be accompanied by a statement that a conviction does not bar the applicant from employment.)

comfortable and giving the interviewer important information and valuable insight about the applicant.

While closed questions often provide interviewers with the information they need, they don't lead anywhere. Open-ended questions, on the other hand, are usually thought-provoking, requiring applicants to develop in-depth responses and become actively involved in the interviewing process.

See the Difference?

Closed Question:
Do you like working in food service?

Open-ended Question:
What do you like about working in food service?

A closed question can be turned into an open-ended question by simply adding one or two key words, such as *what* or *how*. For example, instead of asking an applicant "Can you work on weekends?" a better, open-ended question might be "What hours can you work?" Rather than asking "Do you like to travel?" an interviewer can ask, "How do you feel about traveling?"

Creating and answering interview questions are skills that must be developed. Just like any other skills, interviewing techniques improve with practice.

Orientation

As we discussed in *Introduction: Preparing for a Successful Career,* the process of orientation is an important part of starting a job. Though every organization has a different orientation program, all orientation programs have a common purpose—to help new employees feel more comfortable in their new jobs and to give them a positive impression about their coworkers, the operation, and its management. **Orientation** is the process of helping new employees learn about the establishment, introducing them to other employees, and explaining various procedures and policies.

Orientation programs may vary depending on the size of the operation. Larger operations may provide videos, lectures, and printed employee manuals as part of the orientation process. Smaller operations may provide a typed employee manual, a tour of the operation, and a personal introduction to coworkers.

During orientation, new employees will also learn about the history of the

Exhibit 8.5
Orientation might include a manager's explanation of important policies or duties.

foodservice operation, key company goals that are important to the new employee's job, and how the company is organized.

Managers must ensure that new people feel welcome and know that they are valuable members of the foodservice team. Providing orientation to new employees is a good way to familiarize new employees with their surroundings. Managers should also let current workers know that new employees are coming on board. Current employees should know the names of new employees, when they will be starting, what they will be doing, and with whom they will be working. Everyone should be as helpful as possible to all new employees.

No matter how big or small the operation, you can expect to go through orientation. It is an important part of starting a new job, and will help make you feel like a true member of the foodservice team.

Exhibit 8.6
New employees often learn about key company goals and how the operation is organized.

Review Your Learning 8.2

1. You are going on a job interview for the position of server in a quick-service restaurant. What are five questions you should be prepared to answer?

2. Turn each of the following closed questions into an open-ended question:
   - Do you like working with people?
   - Do you plan to stay in the area for at least two years?
   - Would you be satisfied with $300 a week?

3. You need to hire a babysitter for your younger sister or brother. What are five questions you will ask?

4. Rewrite each of the following incorrect statements about the orientation process, making them correct.
   a. Every operation has the same type of orientation.
   b. Only the person who is introducing a new employee needs to make the new employee feel welcome.

5. "Are you available to work Wednesday evenings?" is an example of what type of question?
   a. Past work experience
   b. Internal
   c. Closed
   d. Complex

8.3

SECTION 8.3

Training and Evaluation

AFTER STUDYING SECTION 8.3, YOU SHOULD BE ABLE TO:

- Summarize and discuss effective group and on-the-job training.
- List and apply effective techniques used in performance evaluations.

KEY TERMS

- **Feedback**
- **Group training**
- **On-the-job training**
- **Performance appraisal form**
- **Role-play**

Job training begins after an employee has gone through the orientation process. Why is training so important? Well-trained employees have the skills, knowledge, and confidence to perform their jobs well. They are also motivated to stay on the job longer and have fewer safety-related, on-the-job accidents. Training encourages employees to work together as a team and allows managers to objectively evaluate employee progress through a training program.

In the end, good training encourages employees to have a positive attitude toward the operation, its management, other employees, and guests.

On-the-Job Training

On-the-job training is appropriate for teaching skills that are easily demonstrated and practiced, such as preparing menu items, operating cash registers, and sanitizing utensils. Employees receive this type of training as they work in the foodservice industry. On-the-job train-ing allows employees to demonstrate skills

Exhibit 8.7
Training encourages employees to work together as a team.

and reinforce what they have been taught. It also allows the trainer to monitor employee progress, give **feedback,** comments about or corrections to an action or process, and correct tasks that are not being done properly.

Before on-the-job training can actually begin, the new employee's duties should be broken down into separate work steps. For example, if you were learning how to take payment from a customer while working the cash register, you would practice two steps:

1. Repeat aloud the amount of money the customer gives you.
2. Lay the payment on top of the cash drawer until the entire transaction is complete.

The trainer should make sure to explain to new employees why it is important to learn the skills being covered in training. In the example above, the cashier must take correct payments from customers in order for the operation to stay in business and employees to get paid.

Before trainers can demonstrate a task, they themselves must be able to perform the task very well. Imagine how frustrated you would feel if your math teacher weren't able to explain a difficult math

Exhibit 8.8
Five key points of effective employee training.

1. Both the employee and trainer must be motivated.
2. Training should be designed for the new employee and the task to be learned. All new employees do not learn at the same rate.
3. The new employee should be continually involved in the training by using hands-on practice and demonstration.
4. Realistic goals must be set so that the trainer and new employee know what is to be accomplished.
5. Feedback is essential to help the new employee remember each task. Positive results should always be emphasized, even when correcting the way an employee performs a task.

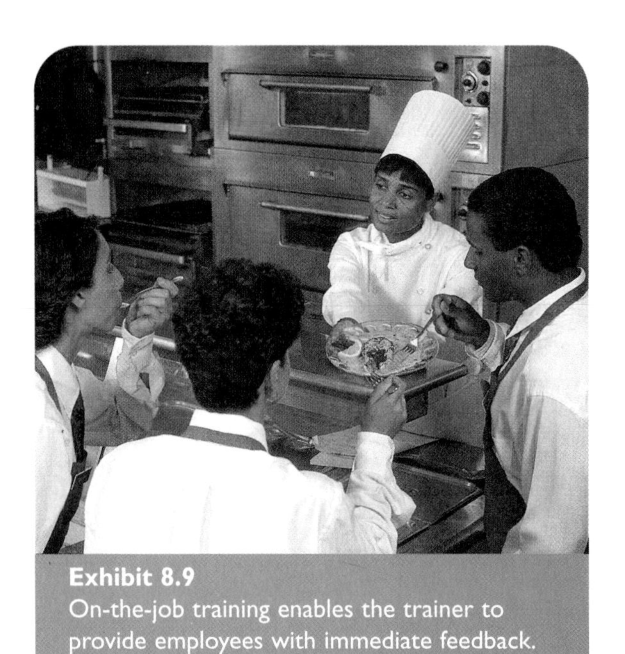

Exhibit 8.9
On-the-job training enables the trainer to provide employees with immediate feedback.

concept to you. Would you go back to the teacher for help later on? Probably not! A good trainer will understand what needs to be learned and be comfortable with his or her own knowledge and ability to communicate that knowledge to new employees.

Group Training

Group training is the best method to use when there are large numbers of employees who need to learn a task. It is also ideal for orienting and training a group of new employees or many temporary employees who must begin working right away.

Group training is used when demonstration and practice at a work station or with equipment is not necessary. This type of training encourages group discussion, allowing new employees to offer input, get information, and work together to solve problems. Much of your learning in high school is accomplished through group training—the class you are in now is an example of group training.

Another type of training can happen by doing a **role-play** exercise, which means to act out parts of the job function being discussed and learned. If you're learning how to be a server, for example, you might play the part of the server, while two classmates take the roles of customers waiting to be served. This type of practice helps students build confidence and allows them to make mistakes in front of a friendly audience before interacting with real customers.

Let's try it!

Write three questions to start a group discussion in your class about careers available in the foodservice industry.

Exhibit 8.10
Group training is effective for training large groups of people.

The Employee Performance Evaluation Process

Employee performance evaluation is similar to school grades or report cards. Just as a report card lets you know how well you are doing in school, a performance evaluation shows employees' progress on the job. All employees want to receive good evaluations because in many workplaces, promotions and salary increases (raises) are determined based on these evaluations.

Formal evaluations give the manager and employee an opportunity to communicate, discuss how well the employee is doing, and set performance goals. The evaluations become part of the employee's permanent record at the particular company, just as your grades are part of your permanent academic record.

A good evaluation program begins on the employee's first day on the job, with employee progress reviewed regularly throughout his or her employment with the operation. Managers and employers should keep files on each employee and record any important information, including pay raises, special projects completed, achievements, problems with coworkers, excessive lateness, or absenteeism.

When meeting with an employee about workplace performance, it's important to focus on the employee's responsibilities, not on his or her mistakes. If an employee is not performing well, the manager and employee must set goals in order to improve the situation. If employee performance does not change, the manager must document problems, counsel the employee, and give verbal and written warnings. If problems continue, the employee might be fired. All conversations about performance should be private between the employee and the manager.

Exhibit 8.12
Sample performance appraisal form.

Employee____________________ Position ____________________
Department____________________ Supervisor ____________________
Period covered in appraisal ____________________
Rating scale:

5 = excellent (far exceeds expectations and standards)
4 = good (meets or exceeds expectations and standards)
3 = satisfactory (meets expectations and standards)
2 = marginal (fails to meet expectations and standards consistently)
1 = unsatisfactory (fails to meet expectations and standards)

ADHERENCE TO POLICIES

Dependability:
Maintains good attendance, is punctual, and reports and requests leave in a timely manner. 1 2 3 4 5

Manner and appearance:
Reflects—in dress, grooming, behavior, language, and maintenance of work area—the professional image of the operation. 1 2 3 4 5

OPERATIONAL SKILLS

Job knowledge:
Possesses knowledge necessary to perform in position according to standards in job description. 1 2 3 4 5

Job skills:
Demonstrates the skills necessary to perform in position according to standards in job description. 1 2 3 4 5

Quality of work:
Work is accurate, consistent, thorough, and at the level defined in standards for the position. 1 2 3 4 5

Quantity of work:
Work is completed in acceptable amounts and in a timely manner. 1 2 3 4 5

Organizational skills:
Uses resources to minimize cost and maximize productivity. 1 2 3 4 5

TEAMWORK

Maintains cooperative relations with coworkers, supervisors, and subordinates. 1 2 3 4 5

Supportiveness:
Promotes operation's best interest through willingness to respond when needed to exert special effort beyond requirements of the position. 1 2 3 4 5

Loyalty:
Words and actions reflect willingness to promote the policies and objectives of the organization. 1 2 3 4 5

Communication:
Conveys information to others and retrieves information from appropriate people in order to achieve intended results. 1 2 3 4 5

INITIATIVE

Independence:
Is willing to take independent action when appropriate and necessary. 1 2 3 4 5

Incentive:
Works toward achieving goals beyond what is expected. 1 2 3 4 5

Leadership:
Directs, guides, and sets a positive example for others. 1 2 3 4 5

Judgment:
Arrives at sound decisions that results in the intended consequences. 1 2 3 4 5

The most effective way to rate employee performance is through the use of a performance appraisal form, as shown in Exhibit 8.11. A **performance appraisal form** is used by a manager to help evaluate an employee's performance. After discussing each area on the form, the manager and employee must agree on measurable goals for the future.

Before ending a performance evaluation meeting, employees are often asked to sign and date the written appraisal form indicating that they have seen it and agree with the evaluation. Employees are also given the chance to ask questions or make final comments about their progress.

No matter how employees are rated, managers should always end evaluation meetings on a positive note. Both manager and employee should walk out of these meetings looking forward to achieving future goals and accomplishments.

Review Your Learning 8.3

1. For each of the following situations, indicate which training method (on-the-job, group, or role-play) is best and why.
   a. You have been asked to train five of your classmates on how to change a flat tire on a car.
   b. You need to train employees on how to sanitize cutting boards.
   c. You are going to train 20 classmates on how to serve customers for a large student banquet.
2. Indicate whether each of the following statements is true (T) or false (F).
   a. Training discourages teamwork.
   b. Before group training can begin, a new employee's duties must be broken down into separate work steps.
   c. During a training session, only the employee must be motivated.
   d. Feedback is essential to help the trainee learn each task.
   e. Group training is best for demonstrating one-on-one tasks, such as how to operate a cash register.

3. Write a role-play exercise to help train servers on how to handle a customer complaint.

4. Which of the following uses a rating system to help managers evaluate employee performances?
   a. Group evaluation meetings
   b. Feedback
   c. Important information kept in employee files
   d. Performance appraisal forms

5. What should a manager do during workplace performance reviews:
   a. If an employee has not been performing well?
   b. If employee performance has still not improved?
   c. If problems continue?

Flashback

CHAPTER 8

SECTION 8.1: LEARNING TO WORK TOGETHER

- **Diversity** refers to the great variety of people and their backgrounds, experiences, opinions, religions, ages, talents, and abilities. In a diverse environment, people must learn to value and respect others, no matter how different they are.
- Nowhere is diversity more evident than in the foodservice industry. Employee diversity is both an asset and an opportunity.
- Today's diverse workforce requires everyone to work hard to work through **prejudices.** Every operation's success depends on developing positive attitudes toward people.
- It is important to become aware of your own stereotypes. A **stereotype** is an assumption that all members of a group fit the same pattern.
- Differences in accent, fluency, and dialect often interfere when people communicate with each other. A **dialect** is the variation of a language spoken by a particular group of people.
- Conflict and tension can result when people misunderstand each other. Situations can usually be smoothed over when the people involved say they are sorry.
- In addition to talking, we communicate through body language. The way we walk, stand, or sit are affected by the practices and traditions of our culture.
- Whenever you communicate with people whose backgrounds are different from yours, be aware that not everyone has the same behaviors you do; if you suspect that your misinterpreted behavior has offended someone, clarify and apologize; if you are the offended one, let the other person know; and see and treat people as individuals.
- People who work together can usually accomplish more than those who work alone.

- Being an active member of a team is valuable for many reasons; it's a good way to share knowledge and information with coworkers and help each other when necessary.
- Teamwork encourages effective communication between coworkers and management.

SECTION 8.2: INTERVIEWING AND ORIENTATION

- No matter what career you choose, interviewing or being interviewed will be a part of it.
- When job applicants get ready for an interview, the key is to be prepared. One way to prepare is to practice talking about the kinds of things that will be asked during an interview.
- All hiring and interviewing practices must be fair and directly related to the job. To avoid charges of **discrimination,** employers should use identical application forms and tests for everyone who applies for the same job.
- Job applicants should be asked the same kinds of questions in interviews, and each one should receive the same information about the job and the organization.
- Employers cannot ask about race, ethnic background, country of origin, former or maiden name, parents' names, languages spoken other than English, prior arrests, marital status, children, spouses, religion, personal financial information, disabilities (except those that have a direct bearing on job performance), or anything about an applicant's appearance.
- In planning to conduct interviews, employers should prepare a list of legal and appropriate interview questions; schedule interviews when there will be no distractions; inform other employees and coworkers not to disturb them during interviews; interview applicants in private areas; make sure that all paperwork has been read and reviewed before the interview; have information about the operation available for applicants; involve other appropriate supervisors in the interviewing process; and check job applicants' references.

- **Closed questions** can be answered with a simple *yes* or *no* or with a brief, factual statement. **Open-ended questions** encourage job applicants to talk about themselves, making them feel more comfortable and giving the interviewer important information about and valuable insight into the applicant.
- The most important thing that a manager can do when orienting new employees is to give them a positive impression about their coworkers, the operation, and its management.
- **Orientation** is the process of helping new employees learn about the establishment, introducing them to other employees, and explaining various procedures and policies. Orientation programs help new employees feel comfortable in their new jobs and know what their responsibilities will be.
- Orientation may vary depending on the size of the operation.
- During orientation, new employees can expect to learn about the history of the foodservice operation, key company goals that are important to the new employee's job, and how the company is organized.
- Managers should let current workers know that new employees are coming on board. Current employees should know the names of new employees, when they will be starting, what they will be doing, and with whom they will be working.

SECTION 8.3: TRAINING AND EVALUATION

- Well-trained employees have the skills, knowledge, and confidence to perform their jobs well. They are also motivated to stay on the job longer and have fewer safety-related on-the-job accidents.
- Training encourages employees to work together as a team and allows managers to objectively evaluate employee progress through a training program.
- **On-the-job training** is appropriate for teaching skills that are easily demonstrated and practiced. It allows employees to demonstrate skills and reinforce what they have been taught. It also allows the trainer to monitor employee progress, give **feedback,** and correct tasks that are not being done properly.

- Before on-the-job training can actually begin, the new employee's duties should be broken down into separate work steps.
- The trainer should make sure to explain to employees why it is important to learn the skills being covered.
- Before trainers can demonstrate a task, they themselves must be able to perform the task very well.
- **Group training** is the best method to use when there are large numbers of employees who need to learn a task. It is also ideal for orienting and training a group of new employees or many temporary employees who must begin working right away.
- Group training is used when demonstration and practice at a work station or with equipment are not necessary.
- **Role-play** exercises help students build confidence and allow them to make mistakes in front of a friendly audience before interacting with real customers.
- Employee performance evaluation charts employees' progress on the job. Formal evaluations give the manager and employee an opportunity to communicate, discuss how well the employee is doing, and set performance goals.
- When meeting with an employee about workplace performance, it's important to focus on the employee's responsibilities, not on his or her mistakes.
- The most effective way to rate employee performance is through the use of a **performance appraisal form,** which is also used to set future performance goals.

Edwin Rios

Food and Beverage Director
Palmer House Hilton, Chicago, Illinois

I've been a part of the restaurant and hospitality industry for many years. If there is one thing I've learned it is the importance of presentation! First impressions truly count—from the penthouse suite to the main course in the formal dining room, everything the customer comes in contact with must look (and taste) its best.

Before working at The Palmer House Hilton, I worked for Hyatt as a Penthouse Captain, where I was responsible for taking care of our VIP customers. I had to be prepared to exceed customers' expectations on a daily basis—and I was up for the challenge!

It is in my nature to continuously seek additional challenges. Soon, I was working my way up the corporate ladder, and in 1985 I joined the Hilton Corporation as an Opener. In this position I traveled to various Hilton locations to assist each management team in opening new hotels. I even formed my own team called the Imperial Crew that included experts from all areas of the hotel. Together with each individual management team, we helped new Hilton hotels get off on the right foot.

Now I am employed at The Palmer House Hilton. My goal as a Food and Beverage Director is to give all customers more than they expect from us. I make sure this attitude can be felt by presenting beautifully and carefully prepared meals to our customers. The presentation of food can make a wonderful first impression and gives us our first chance to exceed the customers expectations. One way to make a plate visually appealing is to add a creative garnish. The garnish should not overshadow the meal, but should be an enhancement to the dish. Its color, texture, and size should complement the food and the size/design of the plate.

As Food and Beverage Director of The Palmer House Hilton, I am constantly being asked to improve service to please our customers. Simply the easiest and oftentimes most effective way to do this is to make sure we present the food we serve as attractively as we can. If we do that, then we've done our job—and the customer walks away happier than when he came in!

CHAPTER 9

Salads and Garnishes

SECTION 9.1

Salads

AFTER STUDYING SECTION 9.1, YOU SHOULD BE ABLE TO:

- Identify and describe the various ingredients used to make salads.
- Demonstrate designing attractive salads.
- Classify and compare types of salads served at different points in the meal.
- Demonstrate appropriate methods to clean salad greens.
- Design a procedure to prepare and store salads properly.

The salad section on most menus goes beyond the simple dinner salad, and the salad has developed from a first course

KEY TERMS

- Accompaniment salad
- Appetizer salad
- Arugula (ah-ROO-guh-luh)
- Base
- Body
- Bound salad
- Chef's salad
- Combination salad
- Complement
- Cooked salad
- Dessert salad
- Escarole (ESS-kuh-role)
- Fruit salad
- Garnish
- Gelatin
- Main course salad
- Radicchio (rah-DEE-key-oh)
- Salad
- Salad dressing
- Separate course salad
- Vegetable salad

into a main entrée at both lunch and dinner. Special salads incorporate fancy or unusual meats or cheeses, pastas, potatoes, or fresh fruit. Each of these dishes fits the definition of a **salad:** a single food or a mix of different foods accompanied or held together with a dressing.

Types of Salads

There are five types of salads: appetizer salads; accompaniment salads; main course salads; separate course salads; and dessert salads. **Appetizer salads** should stimulate the appetite and have fresh, crisp ingredients (cheese, ham, salami, shrimp, crabmeat, vegetables) lightly coated with a tangy, flavorful dressing. Shrimp cocktail is one example of an appetizer salad. Appetizer salads should be light enough for a first course—substantial enough, but not so large as to be filling. Appearance is important, so garnishes should be attractive. A satisfying, attractive salad can set the tone for the rest of the meal.

Need something healthy and delicious to eat? How about a salad? Salads can be served in a variety of forms from main course to appetizer salads. Salad greens have virtually no fat and have very few calories. They are high in vitamin A and C, iron, and fiber.

Exhibit 9.1
A salad can include a wide variety of ingredients.

Accompaniment salads should be light and flavorful, but not too rich. They should balance and complement the rest of the meal. To **complement** means to enhance or go well with. For example, never serve a starchy salad, such as potato salad, when the main entrée also contains a starch (potatoes, rice, or pasta). Sweet fruit salads can accompany ham and pork. Vegetable salads are good choices for hearty meals. Heavier salads, such as macaroni or pasta, should only be served if the main entrée is light. For example, a small scoop of potato salad is a good complement to a sandwich.

Main course salads should be large enough to serve as a full meal and also contain protein ingredients, such as meat, poultry, seafood, egg salad, beans, or cheese. Main course salads should be a well-balanced meal, both visually and nutritionally. In addition, the salad should contain a variety of vegetables, greens, and/or fruits. One popular main course salad is a **chef's salad,** containing mixed greens, raw vegetables, strips of meat, and cheese. Another example is shrimp or crabmeat salad with tomato and lemon wedges and avocados served on a bed of lettuce, accompanied by cottage cheese and fresh fruit.

Exhibit 9.2
Beef is featured in this main course salad.

Exhibit 9.3
Separate course salads are served between courses to refresh the appetite.

Separate course salads cleanse the palate after a rich dinner and before dessert. This means they refresh or stimulate a person's appetite for the dessert or next course. They are often served in classic French meals. Separate course salads must be very light—such as bibb lettuce or Belgian endive lightly dressed with vinaigrette, or a fruit salad. Heavy dressings made with mayonnaise or sour cream should be avoided for separate course salads.

Dessert salads are usually sweet and often contain fruits, sweetened gelatin, nuts, cream, and whipped cream. These salads are often too sweet to be served as appetizers or accompaniments, and are best served as dessert or as part of a buffet or party menu.

Preparing Salads

The four basic parts of any salad are the :

1. base or underliner.
2. body.
3. garnish.
4. dressing.

The **base** of a salad is usually a layer of salad greens that line the plate or bowl in which the salad will be served. Leafy greens usually form the base of a salad, while cup-shaped Boston lettuce or iceberg lettuce leaves give height to salads and form edible containers. Romaine, chicory, and loose leaf lettuce can also be used as a salad base.

The **body** of the salad is the main ingredient. A salad's main ingredient can be a mixture of vegetables, such as lettuce, tomatoes, carrots, etc.; meats, such as turkey breast or ham; or cheeses and various fruits, such as mandarin oranges. Mayonnaise-based salads such as tuna salad or crabmeat salad can be used as a salad body placed on a base of lettuce. Salad ingredients can vary by season or occasion, but freshness is always important.

Garnish adds color and appeal to the salad, and sometimes flavor. Simple garnishes are the best. Garnishes can be mixed with the other salad ingredients or added at the very end to enhance presentation. For instance, a dash of parsley may be tossed into a salad to add flecks of green. Or it may be sprinkled on the top after the salad is prepared. Sometimes the salad ingredients are attractive in themselves and don't require a garnish. Often the garnish is very simple—a light dash of paprika sprinkled over a scoop of potato salad, or a fresh cherry tomato next to a plate of coleslaw. Garnishes are discussed in more detail in Section 9.3.

When buying salad dressing, check the expiration date and make sure the container is sealed tightly. Always refrigerate salad dressings after they have been opened.

Salad dressings are liquids or semi-liquids used to flavor salads. Sometimes they are called *cold sauces* because their purpose is to flavor, moisten, and enrich foods. Tart or sour dressings should be used for green salads and vegetable salads. Slightly sweetened dressings are used for fruit salads. Depending on the salad, the dressings might be added at service time or served separately for the customer to add. Some dressings are mixed with the ingredients ahead of time, as with egg salad or

Exhibit 9.4
Arranging salads.

- Look at the plate or bowl as a picture frame. Select the right dish for the portion size. Keep the salad off the rim of the dish.
- Maintain a good balance of colors. Spark up plain iceberg lettuce with shredded carrots, red cabbage, another colored vegetable, or darker greens. Remember, three colors are usually enough. Too many colors are unappetizing.
- Height makes a salad more attractive. Ingredients that are mounded on a plate are more interesting and appealing than if they are spread flat over it. Place tomato or fruit wedges so that they overlap or lean on each other.
- Always cut the ingredients neatly and uniformly.
- Be sure every ingredient can be easily identified. Cut every ingredient into large enough pieces so that the customer can recognize them immediately. Bite-sized pieces are preferred, unless the food item can be cut with a fork, such as tomato slices or cucumber. Items used as seasoning, such as onions, can be finely chopped.
- Keep the arrangement of ingredients simple. Remember, you want the customer to want to eat the salad, not just look at it.

potato salad. A salad mixed with a heavy dressing, such as mayonnaise, is called a **bound salad** because the mayonnaise holds, or binds, the ingredients together. Salad dressings are discussed in more detail in Section 9.2. Exhibit 9.4 lists some guidelines for arranging salads.

For all salads, greens should be selected and prepared carefully. It's important to keep in mind the range of individual flavors, textures, and colors of lettuces and other greens to produce a well-balanced, attractive salad. For example, the flavor of tender delicate lettuces, such as Boston or bibb, can be overwhelmed by more robust greens, such as **escarole** (ESS-kuh-role), **radicchio** (rah-DEE-key-oh), and **arugula** (ah-ROO-guh-luh). The green salad deserves the same attention to detail, preparation, and quality as any other dish. Edible flowers, such as nasturtium, are also considered acceptable salad greens.

Exhibit 9.5 describes various salad greens, their qualities, and their most common uses.

Exhibit 9.5
Salad greens.

Arugula
Pungent, distinctive flavor; tender, perishable; dark green; must be washed thoroughly

Belgian endive (witloof chicory)
Narrow, pointed heads, 4-6 inches long; pale yellow-green to white; crisp leaves, waxy texture; pleasant bitter taste; can be served alone with mustard vinaigrette

Bibb (limestone) lettuce
Smaller and more delicate than Boston lettuce; dark green outside and creamy yellow inside; tender, delicate flavor; small, whole leaves are perfect for an after-dinner salad when tossed with a light vinaigrette

Boston lettuce
Small round heads with soft, fragile leaves; deep green outside, white inside; buttery texture; does not keep well; cup-shaped leaves are excellent for salad bases; mild yet flavorful leaves

Chicory (curly endive)
Narrow, curly leaves; firm texture; bitter flavor; outside dark green, inside yellow or white; best used with other greens or as a base or garnish; not served alone

Chinese cabbage (celery cabbage)
Long, light green heads with broad, white center ribs; tender and crisp; mild cabbage taste; adds flavor to green salads; used with Chinese cooking

Dandelion greens
Young, tender leaves; rich green color; best in spring

Escarole (broad-leaf endive)
Broad, thick leaves, also in bunches; coarse texture, slightly bitter flavor; needs to be mixed with other greens, not served alone; often served as a vegetable in Italian cooking, braised with olive oil and garlic

Iceberg (head) lettuce
Most popular American salad green; firm, compact head with crisp, mild-tasting pale green leaves; can be served alone, but best when mixed with other greens, such as romaine, to add flavor

Loose-leaf lettuce
Grows in bunches; soft, delicate leaves with curly edges; green or shades of red; wilts easily; gives mild flavor, variety, and color to salads

Radicchio
Attractive red-leafed Italian variety of chicory; white ribs and small, round heads; crunchy texture; slightly bitter flavor; use only a leaf or two to add color and flavor to a salad

Romaine lettuce
Elongated head with dark green, coarse leaves, crisp texture and full, sweet, mild flavor; keeps well; easy to handle; essential ingredient in Caesar Salad

Sorrel, French
Small to medium-sized, semi-curly, spade-shaped leaves; white to green stems; contains oxalic acid and can be toxic in large amounts; fairly mild flavor

Spinach
Dark, leafy green leaves are good alone or mixed with other greens; must be washed very thoroughly; remove coarse stems before service; fairly mild flavor

Sprouts
Small, round leaves on tender stalks; delicate texture; peppery, pungent flavor

Watercress
Small, dark green, oval leaves; pungent, peppery flavor; used as garnish and in salads; remove thick stems

The first step in preparing good-tasting, interesting, attractive salads is to start with clean, fresh ingredients. Always wash greens thoroughly because dirt can be lodged between leaves. Exhibit 9.6 outlines important steps for cleaning greens and preparing salads.

Precleaned, precut salad greens are sold in large, sealed plastic bags. They are more perishable than unprocessed greens and need to be refrigerated. When preparing salads, be careful not to handle ingredients too much. Do not open the bags until you are ready to use them. Unopened bags can be stored for two to three days. Always test the quality of the product before serving it to customers.

Besides the commonly used green salad, there are vegetable salads, cooked salads, fruit salads, combination salads, and gelatin salads. **Vegetable salads** contain vegetables as the main ingredient, resting on a bed of lettuce or other greens. Some vegetables are used raw, such as celery, cucumbers, green peppers, cauliflower, and broccoli. Other vegetables, such as asparagus, green beans, beets, or artichokes, must be cooked first, chilled, and then used. Sometimes meat, poultry, fish, or cheese are added to these vegetable salads. With the addition of protein, any vegetable salad can be served as a main course salad. Exhibit 9.7 lists guidelines for preparing vegetable salads.

Cooked salads contain cooked foods as their main ingredient—meat, poultry, fish, eggs, starches, and vegetables. Typical ingredients include chicken, ham, turkey, tuna, crab, shrimp, lobster, eggs, potatoes, pasta, rice, and mixed vegetables. The cooked food can be mixed with a dressing,

According to the *Virginia Housewife*, a cookbook written in 1860 by Mary Randolph, a relative of Thomas Jefferson, colonial Virginians wanted their salad greens extremely fresh. To make a perfect green salad, she recommended that the greens be picked early in the morning, washed and stored in cold water, and just before dinner, assembled attractively on the plate, with scallions arranged around the edge of the salad.

Before eating salad greens, be sure to wash them thoroughly in water to remove all excess dirt that may be on the salad greens. It is even recommended to wash greens with soap, as well. Just make sure to rinse them really well!

Exhibit 9.6
Cleaning greens and preparing salads.

- **Keep greens refrigerated** until they are to be prepared and served.
- **Clean greens thoroughly** to remove all traces of sand, grit, and insects. Repeatedly dip the entire head of lettuce in and out of water. Avoid soaking greens because they tend to absorb water. Instead, plunge the leaves into cold water, then lift them out to make sure that the grit stays in the water, not on the leaves. It may be necessary to repeat this step several times to properly remove all impurities.
- **Carefully remove the core** from head lettuce by striking the core gently against the side of the sink and twisting it out. Cut through the core of all other greens or separate the leaves so that all traces of sand and grit can be removed.
- **Dry the greens** as thoroughly as possible after rinsing.
- **Remove any tough stems or wilted spots.** Tearing is preferred for delicate greens, but be careful not to bruise the leaves.
- **To store clean greens,** place them on plastic sheet trays that have been covered with plastic wrap. Cover them loosely, first with lightly dampened paper towels, and then with plastic wrap. When the greens have been rinsed and dried, they can be stored under refrigeration for a few hours. Sturdy greens, such as iceberg lettuce or romaine lettuce, can be held for as long as 24 hours.
- **Tear or cut the greens** into bite-size pieces. Customers should not have to cut the greens. The preferred serving size for a piece of lettuce is about the size of half of a dollar bill. If you cut greens instead of tearing them (to save time), always use sharp, stainless steel knives.
- **Toss the greens** gently until they are uniformly mixed. It's okay to add a non-juicy raw vegetable garnish, such as green pepper strips or carrot shreds. Cut the garnish into broad, thin slices or shreds.
- **Place the salad on cold plates,** using a base if necessary. Avoid putting salad ingredients on plates more than an hour or two before service because they will wilt or dry.
- **Garnish** with tomato wedges, cherry tomatoes, cucumber slices, radishes, pepper rings, as desired. Garnish that will become soggy or discolored, such as croutons or avocados, should be added just before service.
- **Refrigerate.**
- **Dress the greens appropriately,** with only enough dressing to lightly coat the greens, as close to service time as possible. The normal ratio is one-third ounce of dressing per ounce of greens.

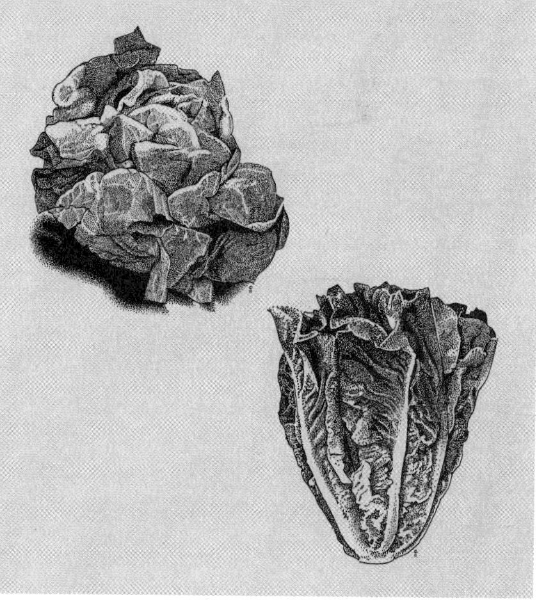

- All ingredients must be cut neatly. The shapes of the vegetables are important to the appearance of the salad.
- Cut the vegetables as close to service time as possible.
- Cooked vegetables should be firm, with a crisp texture and good color.
- After they are cooked, thoroughly drain and chill vegetables before mixing them with the salad.
- Vegetables that are marinated before being made into salads (such as three-bean or pasta salad) should not be put on plates too far ahead of time. Use sturdy, crisp greens for the base like iceberg, romaine, or chicory because these greens will not wilt easily.

Exhibit 9.7
Preparing vegetable salads.

Always follow sanitation procedures when preparing cooked salads to ensure food safety:

- Keep all ingredients below 40°F or above 140°F.
- If ingredients, both before and after combining in the salad, are kept between 40°F and 140°F, they should be held for no more than 4 hours *total.*
- Chill all ingredients, including mayonnaise, fresh vegetables and fruits, cooked foods, and canned foods, before combining.
- Wash your hands when you're finished cutting and preparing *each ingredient.*
- Clean and sanitize your knives, cutting board, and other utensils after you're finished cutting and preparing *each ingredient.*
- Keep the salad chilled once it's prepared.

such as vinaigrette or mayonnaise. Exhibit 9.8 provides guidelines for preparing cooked salads.

Fruit salads are very popular as desserts or as part of combination lunch plates. As the name indicates, fruits are the main ingredients, often accompanied by cheese or nuts. Follow the steps in Exhibit 9.9 when preparing fruit salads.

Combination salads are combinations of different kinds of ingredients or even two different kinds of salads. The chef's salad is a good example of a popular combination salad because it contains a green salad, vegetables, and cooked ingredients.

Exhibit 9.8
Preparing cooked salads.

- Cooked ingredients must be well chilled before being mixed with mayonnaise or mayonnaise-based dressing. The complete salad must be kept chilled at all times to avoid any danger of food-borne illness.
- While cooked salads are a good way to use left-overs, the leftover foods must have been cooled and stored under proper sanitation procedures.
- Potatoes used in cooked salads should be cooked whole and then peeled and cut.
- Cut the salad pieces no smaller than bite-size, or the final product will look like a pasty mound.
- Crisp foods are added for flavor and interest: celery, carrots, green peppers, chopped pickles, onions, water chestnuts, and apples. Be sure that the flavors complement each other.
- Potatoes and seafood may be marinated in a light vinaigrette before being mixed with other salad ingredients. Be sure to drain excess liquid first.
- Fold in thick dressings gently to avoid crushing or mashing the main ingredient, as with potato or egg salad.
- Cooked salads are usually portioned with a scoop to provide portion control and give height and shape to the salad.
- Serve on chilled, lettuce-lined plates and use colorful garnishes.

Practice food safety procedures when handling combination salads.

Because combination salads are usually made up of two different kinds of salads:

- Observe the guidelines for preparing the different components, such as green salads, vegetable salads, cooked salads, and fruit salads.
- Observe the guidelines for attractive salad arrangement.

Unflavored gelatin is often added to vegetable or fruit salads, such as shredded cabbage and carrots. Unflavored

Exhibit 9.9
Preparing fruit salads.

- Most fruit salads, with the exception of Waldorf Salad, are arranged on the plate—not mixed together—because fruit breaks easily.
- Place broken or less attractive pieces of fruit on the bottom of the salad. Save the best pieces of fruit for the top.
- Some fruits discolor after they are peeled and cut, such as bananas. Sprinkle these fruits with an acid, such as tart fruit juice or lemon to keep their appetizing appearance.
- Fruits do not hold well after they have been cut and peeled. Prepare fruit salads to order.
- Drain canned fruits well before mixing them in a salad. Some of the liquid can be saved and used in fruit salad dressings or in other preparations.
- Dressings for fruit salads are usually sweet, but a little tartness gives additional flavor. Fruit juices are often used in the dressings.

Exhibit 9.10
Preparing gelatin salads.

- Use the right amount of gelatin for the volume of liquid in the recipe. Too much gelatin makes a rubbery product; too little gelatin makes a watery salad. Basic proportions for unflavored gelatin are 2 1/2 oz dry gelatin per gallon of liquid (19 g per liter), but sometimes you will need more gelatin depending on the ingredients in the salad. Basic proportions for sweetened, flavored gelatin are 24 oz of gelatin per gallon of liquid (180 g per liter).
- Since acids (fruit juices and vinegar) weaken the setting properties of gelatin, a higher proportion of gelatin to liquid is needed. Sometimes as much as 4 oz of gelatin or more per gallon of liquid is needed. Whipping the product into a foam or adding a large quantity of chopped foods weakens the setting properties of gelatin. Test each recipe before using it on the menu.
- Gelatin dissolves at about 100°F (37.8°C), but higher temperatures will dissolve it faster. To dissolve unflavored gelatin, stir it into cold liquid to avoid lumping. Let it stand for 5 minutes to absorb water. Heat it until dissolved, or add hot liquid and stir until dissolved. To dissolve sweetened, flavored gelatin, stir it into boiling water.
- To make the gelatin set more quickly, dissolve it in up to half of the liquid and add the remaining cold liquid to lower the temperature. For even faster results, add crushed ice in place of an equal weight of cold water. Stir until the ice is melted.
- Raw pineapple or papaya should never be added to gelatin salads. They contain enzymes that dissolve the gelatin, and the gelatin will not set. Cooked or canned pineapple or papaya should be used instead of raw.
- Add solid ingredients when the gelatin is partially set. At this stage, the gelatin should be very syrupy and thick—this will keep solid ingredients evenly mixed, not settling to the bottom.
- Always drain canned fruits well or the liquid will dilute the gelatin.
- Pour into pans or individual molds and allow to set. Then cut into equal portions and garnish.
- To unmold gelatin:
  - Run a thin knife blade around the top edges of the mold to loosen the salad
  - Dip the mold three-quarters into hot water (120°F to 140°F, or 48.9°C to 60°C) for one or two seconds
  - Quickly wipe the bottom of the mold and turn it over onto the salad plate. Or you can invert the salad plate over the mold and carefully flip the plate and mold over together.
  - Avoid holding the gelatin mold in hot water for more than a few seconds or the gelatin will melt.
- Always refrigerate gelatin salads until just before serving to keep them firm. This is especially important in extremely hot weather.

gelatin is used so it does not compete with the natural flavor of the vegetable or fruit. Originally, **gelatin** was prepared in the professional kitchen by extracting it from bones that had been boiled to release all moisture. To save time, most gelatin products today are made from prepared mixes with sugar and color added. Exhibit 9.10 provides guidelines for preparing gelatin salads.

Colonial cooks made unflavored gelatin by boiling calves' and pigs' feet. Granular, unflavored gelatin became available in 1890. By 1900, flavored gelatin was popular for use in molded fruit salads and desserts. The tasty combination of carrots and pineapple in orange-flavored gelatin is a distinctly American recipe.

Exhibit 9.11
Combination salads can be made by combining different ingredients together such as green salad, pasta, cheese, and tomatoes.

Review Your Learning 9.1

Use the following words and phrases to complete the statements below on a separate sheet of paper.

Clean	Refrigerator	Base
Plastic wrap	Drain	Body
Dressing	Garnish	Damp towels

1. The four basic parts of any salad are the ______________, ________________, ______________, and ______________.
2. Always ______________ canned fruits.
3. To make sure that salad greens will be crisp, ____________________ them and store them in a ____________ wrapped loosely in ____________ ______________ and ____________ ______________.

Match the salad types on the left with the correct example or description on the right.

4. Dessert
5. Appetizer
6. Accompaniment
7. Main-course
8. Separate-course
9. Combination
10. Fruit

e) Waldorf salad

f) Chef's salad

g) Classic coleslaw

h) Light salad with bibb lettuce lightly dressed with vinaigrette (served before dessert)

i) Supreme Hawaiian salad with pineapple, marshmallows, and macadamia nuts, garnished with whipped cream and an almond cookie

j) Petite shrimp cocktail

k) Fresh crabmeat salad with tomato and lemon wedges and avocados

9.2

SECTION 9.2

Dressings, Dips, and Condiments

AFTER STUDYING SECTION 9.2, YOU SHOULD BE ABLE TO:

- Differentiate among various oils and vinegars.
- Demonstrate the preparation of a vinaigrette.
- List the ingredients of and prepare an emulsified salad dressing.
- Select ingredients to prepare mayonnaise.
- Match dressings to salad greens and other ingredients.
- Give examples of ingredients used to make dips.
- Choose the ingredients and prepare several dips.

KEY TERMS

- Condiment
- Dip
- Emulsified (uh-MUL-si-fide) vinaigrette dressing
- Guacamole (gwah-kuh-MOE-lee)
- Hummus
- Mayonnaise (MAY-uh-naze)
- Salsa
- Vinaigrette (vin-uh-GRETT)
- Virgin olive oil

Salad Dressings

The flavor of a salad dressing should enhance and complement the salad ingredients. Delicate dressings should be used with delicately flavored greens. More robust dressings should be used with more robust greens.

The basic dressings are **vinaigrette** (vin-uh-GRETT), which is made of oil and vinegar, emulsified vinaigrette, and mayonnaise. There are also dressings that contain sour cream, yogurt, and fruit juices as the main ingredients. Many of these are designed specifically for fruit salads or for low-calorie diets.

One important note about dressing ingredients: since most salad dressings are served fresh, without cooking, dressing quality depends directly on the quality of the ingredients used to prepare it.

Looking for a low-calorie or a fat-free salad dressing that still tastes great? Try a dressing with a fruit or vegetable base, or top salads with fresh lemon juice or red wine vinegar.

Refer to Exhibit 9.12 for various types of oils and vinegars.

The recipe for basic vinaigrette includes approximately three parts oil to one part vinegar. The ingredients should be remixed just before serving. Salad dressing should be prepared in quantities that will last no more than three days.

Exhibit 9.12
Oils and vinegars.

Types of oil:

- *Corn oil:* Light golden color, nearly tasteless
- *Cottonseed oil, soybean oil, canola oil, safflower oil:* Bland, nearly tasteless
- *Peanut oil:* Mild, but distinctive flavor; somewhat expensive
- *Olive oil:* Distinctive, fruity flavor; greenish color; not an all-purpose oil, but good for specialty salads, such as Caesar salad
- *Walnut oil:* Distinctive flavor; expensive; used mostly in elegant restaurants with specialty salads
- *Winterized oil:* Oil that has been treated so it will remain a clear liquid when chilled. Winterized oil should be used with dressings that will be refrigerated.

Types of vinegar:

- *Cider vinegar:* Made from apples; brown color; slightly sweet taste
- *White/distilled vinegar:* Distilled and purified to give it a neutral flavor
- *Wine vinegar:* White or red color; has a wine flavor
- *Flavored vinegars:* Have flavor of other products added to them, such as tarragon, garlic, or raspberries
- *Sherry vinegar:* Made from sherry wine; has sherry flavor
- *Balsamic vinegar:* Special wine vinegar aged in wooden barrels; dark brown color and sweet taste
- *Specialty vinegars:* Malt vinegar, rice vinegar, and vinegars flavored with fruits, such as raspberry
- Sometimes lemon juice is used in place of or in addition to vinegar in some salad dressings.

Exhibit 9.13
Oil and vinegar are commonly used for salad dressing.

Certain vinegars with sharp flavors should be used sparingly—tarragon and balsamic vinegars, for example. Strongly flavored oils, such as extra virgin or **virgin olive oils,** which are made from the first pressing of the olives, and nut oils contribute a flavor of their own and can overpower the other flavors in the dressing and the salad.

Exhibit 9.14 discusses how to make vinaigrette dressing. Some other examples of vinaigrette dressing include basic French dressing, Italian dressing, oriental vinaigrette, Dijon vinaigrette, and herbed vinaigrette.

Emulsified (uh-MUL-si-fide) **vinaigrette dressings** and light mayonnaise dressings are thick and coat the ingredients more heavily. They are especially flavorful for salads that include ingredients such as grains, pastas, meat, or fish. Exhibit 9.15 discusses how to make emulsified vinaigrette dressing. It has the same ratio of major ingredients as basic vinaigrette, with the addition, traditionally, of egg yolks.

Exhibit 9.14
How to make vinaigrette dressing.

- Combine the vinegar and seasonings.
- Slowly whip in the oil until a homogeneous mixture is formed.
- Serve the dressing immediately or refrigerate it.
- Before dressing the salad, thoroughly recombine all of the ingredients by stirring or shaking vigorously.

Exhibit 9.15
How to make emulsified vinaigrette dressing.

- Beat the egg yolks until they are frothy. Add a little water if the yolks are very thick.
- Add a small amount of the vinegar or lemon juice.
- Gradually mix in two-thirds of the oil, whipping the mixture constantly.
- Add the remainder of the vinegar or lemon juice and blend well.
- Gradually mix in the remainder of the oil and any additional seasonings or flavoring ingredients.
- Serve the dressing at once or store it under refrigeration.

Mayonnaise (MAY-uh-naze) is the most stable emulsified dressing. It contains a higher ratio of oil to vinegar and a greater quantity of egg yolks than is required for an emulsified vinaigrette. Perfect mayonnaise is creamy, pale ivory, but not too thick. Sometimes mustard or garlic is added to mayonnaise for flavor. Mayonnaise and mayonnaise-based dressings coat salad ingredients and bind them together.

Exhibit 9.16 discusses the basics of making mayonnaise. Examples of mayonnaise-based dressings include Thousand Island dressing, Louis dressing, Russian dressing, Roquefort dressing, and blue cheese dressing.

While homemade mayonnaise is fresh-tasting, it is usually best to use commercially-prepared mayonnaise in a foodservice operation because the acidity in commercially-prepared versions has been raised to make them less prone to becoming a home and breeding ground for harmful micro-organisms.

Dips and Condiments

Condiments are cooked or prepared flavorings, such as horseradish, ketchup, relishes, prepared sauces, and dips. **Dips** can be served hot or cold and as an accompaniment to other foods. Cold dips often use mayonnaise, sour cream, or cream cheese as a base. Cold dips are made the same way as mayonnaise-based salad dressings, although dips are normally thicker than salad dressings.

It's important for dips to have the proper consistency. Any dip you prepare should be soft enough to scoop up with a cracker or chip, but it must also be thick enough to stay on them. Dips must be served at the proper consistency and serving temperature. Most dips become thicker as they are held in the refrigerator. Some dips are heated in the oven or microwave before serving. Exhibit 9.18 discusses how to make a simple cold dip.

Exhibit 9.16
How to make mayonnaise.

- Add water to pasteurized egg yolks and beat until they are frothy.
- Add a small amount of the vinegar or lemon juice.
- Gradually mix in two-thirds of the oil, whipping the mixture constantly.
- Add the remainder of the vinegar or lemon juice and blend well.
- Gradually mix in the remainder of the oil and any additional seasonings or flavoring ingredients.
- Serve the dressing at once or refrigerate it.

Exhibit 9.17
Matching dressings and salad greens.

Dressing	Greens
Vinaigrette dressing made with vegetable oil and red wine vinegar	Any greens: iceberg, romaine, leaf lettuce, butter-head lettuce, escarole, curly endive, Belgian endive, radicchio, baby lettuces, sorrel, arugula, dandelion
Vinaigrette dressing made with a nut oil and balsamic vinegar	Delicate greens: butterhead lettuce, bibb lettuce, Belgian endive, radicchio, baby lettuces, arugula, watercress
Emulsified vinaigrette dressing	Any greens: romaine, leaf lettuce, butterhead lettuce, escarole, curly endive, Belgian endive, radicchio, baby lettuces, sorrell, arugula, watercress
Mayonnaise-based dressing	Hardy greens: iceberg, romaine, leaf lettuce, escarole, curly endive, sorrel, dandelion greens

Ethnic variations of special salads and accompaniments are very popular as dips. **Guacamole** (gwah-kuh-MOE-lee) (avocado dip) and **salsa** (peppers, such as jalapeño or serrano, onions, and tomatoes) from Mexico, and **hummus** (chick pea dip with garlic and tahini) from the Middle East are just three examples. Their texture and flavors are exciting, as well as nutritious.

- Select your base. If you use cream cheese as a base, first soften it by mixing in an electric mixer.
- Add the selection of flavoring ingredients (chopped cooked vegetables, chopped cold vegetables, chopped cold cooked fish, seafood, herbs, spices, etc.).
- Blend all ingredients well.
- Adjust the consistency by adding milk, butter-milk, cream, sour cream, or another liquid that is suitable for the dip.

Exhibit 9.18
How to make a simple cold dip.

Review Your Learning 9.2

Use the following terms to correctly complete the statements below on a separate sheet of paper. Each term will be used only once.

Egg yolks
Oil, vinegar
Three days
Mayonnaise
Emulsified vinaigrette

1. Emulsified vinaigrette contains ____________, but regular vinaigrette does not.
2. The normal ratio of dressing to greens in a salad is three parts ____________ to one part ____________.
3. Freshly-made salad dressings should be stored for only ____________.
4. The most stable emulsified dressing is ____________.
5. ____________ dressings are thick and coat salad ingredients more heavily.

Indicate whether each dressing below is an oil and vinegar dressing or a mayonnaise-based dressing.

6. Louis dressing
7. Basic French dressing
8. Thousand island dressing
9. Dijon vinaigrette
10. Russian dressing
11. Oriental vinaigrette
12. Roquefort dressing
13. Blue cheese dressing
14. Italian dressing

9.3

SECTION 9.3

The Art of Garnishing

AFTER STUDYING SECTION 9.3, YOU SHOULD BE ABLE TO:

- Give an example of a garnish.
- Describe and prepare ingredients commonly used as garnishes.
- Demonstrate garnishing plates.
- Demonstrate the preparation of toppings for soups.

KEY TERMS

- Accompaniment
- Classical French garnish
- Consommé (CON-suh-may)
- Dollop (DOLL-up)
- Plating
- Profiterole (pro-FEET-uh-roll)

The way to a person's stomach is through the eyes, and attractive food whets the appetite. As we discussed in Section 9.1, *garnish* means to decorate or embellish the appearance of a food item by adding other food items. Garnishing is essential when plating food. **Plating** means arranging the presentation of food items on the serving plate or dish. The garnish itself should complement the dish in color, flavor, and texture.

Exhibit 9.19
Garnishes like tomato, asparagus, and parsley are used to complement a dish.

Exhibit 9.20
French garnish terms.

Bouquetière	Bouquet of vegetables
Clamart	Peas
Crécy	Carrots
Doria	Cucumbers cooked in butter
Dubarry	Cauliflower
Fermière	Carrots, turnips, onions, and celery cut into uniform slices
Florentine	Spinach
Forestière	Mushrooms
Jardinière	Garden vegetables
Judic	Braised lettuce
Lyonnaise	Onions
Niçoise	Tomatoes concassée cooked with garlic
Parmentier	Potatoes
Primeurs	First spring vegetables (carrots, turnips, peas, pearl onions, green beans, cauliflower, asparagus, artichokes)
Princesse	Asparagus
Printanière	Spring vegetables
Provençale	Tomatoes, garlic, and parsley; sometimes mushrooms and olives
Vichy	Carrots

Classical French garnish is what many modern chefs call **accompaniments** to a main entrée. Accompaniments include side dishes—potatoes, rice, or even vegetables, to name just a few.

During the 18th and 19th centuries, there were so many types of classical garnish that one French handbook listed over 209 items. Some of these classic terms have carried over to the modern professional kitchen. Exhibit 9.20 describes the most commonly used classical French garnish terms.

Platter garnish doesn't have to be elaborate to be effective. A simple assortment of colorful fresh vegetables, cooked to perfection, is an elegant garnish to the most sophisticated platter presentation. A succulent roast of beef adorned with a colorful variety of fresh garden vegetables is always appealing for banquet crowds.

Exhibit 9.21
Plating and garnishing hot platters.

- Vegetables should be arranged in ways that are simple and practical. A mound of peas on a platter is unattractive and difficult to serve. Instead, choose vegetables that are available in easy-to-handle pieces, such as cauliflower, broccoli, whole green beans, etc. Small vegetables, such as peas, can be served easily if they are contained in artichoke bottoms or tomato halves.
- Arrange the garnishes around the platter for the best effect, emphasizing different sizes and colors.
- Be careful that the platter garnish isn't too elaborate. The attractiveness of the main food item should not be overshadowed by garnish.
- Any extra sauce or gravy should be served in a sauce boat. Only use a small amount of gravy or sauce when preparing a platter of meat, fish, or poultry.
- Serve hot foods on a hot platter.

The arrangement of the main food item, complete with accompaniments of colorful vegetables and starches, may not require additional garnish. Always avoid cluttering a plate.

A simple garnish may be necessary when the accompaniments consist of something bland like a baked potato or rice. For example, when serving fried chicken with french fries, or a steak sandwich accompanied by a baked potato, a sprig of parsley would be a good garnish. Simple garnishes should be edible, suitable to the main food item, and carefully arranged on the plate.

Exhibit 9.22
Lemon peel can be used to garnish vegetables.

FUN FOOD FACT

***Le Repertoire de la Cuisine*, a French cookbook written a few hundred years ago, listed 209 different garnishes, each with its own name, along with 7,000 other recipes! Here is one especially elaborate garnish.**

***Tortue*: Quenelles, mushroom heads, gherkins, garlic, collops of tongue and calves' brains, small fried eggs, heart-shaped croutons, crayfish, slices of truffles.**

One important rule of garnish: *Keep it simple and appropriate to the food item.*

Exhibit 9.23 lists popular simple garnishes and the foods they go with. The numbered techniques are explained in the table. Most of the garnishes are uncooked; cooked garnishes are considered accompaniments or side dishes.

Garnishes for soups are classified into three groups: garnishes in the soup, toppings, and accompaniments. Garnishes in soup are ingredients in clear soups that serve as the garnish. For example, the vegetables in a clear vegetable soup are considered garnish. Some added garnishes may be a dash of chopped parsley or chives.

Exhibit 9.23
Common garnishes.

Fried Parsley

1. Separate sprigs and remove coarse stems.
2. Wash and dry thoroughly.
3. Deep fry at about 375°F (192.1°C) for just a few seconds, until crisp but still green.
4. Drain on absorbent paper. Serve immediately.

Cucumbers

1. For slices, score unpeeled cucumber with a fork, or flute with a channel knife, then slice.
2. For twists, cut slices three-fourths of the way across, twist open, and stand on plate.
3. For cups, cut fluted cucumber in one-inch sections, hollow out slightly with a melon ball cutter or spoon, and fill with an appropriate condiment sauce.

Mushroom Caps

1. Cut the stem out and scoop out any remaining stem without breaking the cap.
2. To keep mushrooms white, simmer 2 to 3 minutes in salted water with a little butter and lemon juice.

Radishes

1. Radishes can be cut in many ways to make decorative garnishes.
2. After cutting, soak the radishes in ice water until they open up.

Scallion Brushes

1. Cut off the root ends of the scallions, including the little hard core. Cut the white part into 2-inch sections.
2. With a thin-bladed knife, split both ends of the scallion pieces with cuts 1/2 inch deep. Make enough cuts to separate the ends into fine shreds.
3. Soak in cold water until the ends curl.

Pickles

1. To make fans, with the stem end of the pickle away from you, make a series of thin vertical slices the length of the pickle, but do not cut through the stem end.
2. Spread the pickle into a fan shape.

Frosted Grapes

1. Separate grapes into small bunches.
2. Brush with water.
3. Sprinkle with granulated sugar.
4. Let dry before serving.

Lemons

1. Fluted lemon slices and twisted slices are cut the same way as for cucumbers. Slices placed directly on fish or meat are cut from peeled lemons.
2. Dip half the lemon slice in paprika or finely chopped parsley for a colorful effect. For just a line of paprika down the center, bend the lemon slice between the fingers and dip lightly in paprika.
3. Wedges are often more attractive if the ends of the lemons are cut off first. For added color, dip the edge of the lemon wedge in paprika.
4. For lemon halves, first cut a thin slice from each end of the lemon so the halves will stand straight. Then cut the lemon in half. Cut a long strip of rind from the outer edge of the lemon half but do not detach it. Tie a decorative knot in the strip, being careful not to break it, or you may cut two strips, one from either side, and make two knots. Decorate with parsley.
5. For a sawtooth edge, cut a sawtooth pattern, piercing all the way to the center of the lemon with the knife. Separate the two halves. Decorate with parsley, or dip the points of the teeth in paprika.

Toast Points

1. Cut slices of sandwich bread in half diagonally. Trim the crusts off and cut each piece into a heart shape. Save the trimmings for bread crumbs.
2. Sauté the pieces in butter or oil until golden on both sides.
3. Dip the tips into the sauce that is being served with the dish to be garnished, and then dip into chopped parsley.

Consommés (CON-suh-mays), rich, clarified stocks or broths, are named after their garnishes. For example, *consommé julienne* is made of onion or leek, carrot, and celery, cut into julienne shapes. Vegetable cream soups are traditionally garnished with carefully cut pieces of the vegetable that is the main ingredient. Garnishes in vegetable cream soups are part of the recipe, not an add-on.

Toppings are added to soups as a garnish as well. Toppings for thick soups (such as cream of potato, cream of mushroom, and cream of leek) may include:

- Chopped parsley or chives
- Toasted, sliced almonds
- Grated cheese
- Sieved egg yolks
- Chopped hard-cooked eggs
- Croutons
- Crumbled bacon
- Paprika
- **Dollop** (DOLL-up), a small scoop or spoonful, of sour cream or whipped cream

Any topping should be placed on the soup just before service because it will either melt or sink to the bottom. Be sure the flavor of the topping is appropriate to the flavor of the soup.

Accompaniments with soups include crackers, melba toast, corn chips, breadsticks, cheese straws, whole-grain wafers, and **profiteroles** (pro-FEET-uh-rolls), which are tiny, unsweetened cream puff shells.

Garnishes for sandwiches include pickle slices, lettuce leaves, tomato and onion slices; potato chips surrounded by wedges of a club sandwich, parsley, and whole or sliced olives. Sometimes a few raw vegetables, attractively cut on a small bed of sprouts and accompanied with a dip, or a fresh piece of melon or orange, are served for variety.

Review Your Learning 9.3

If you went with several friends to a formal French restaurant and your friends asked you to describe the following items on the menu, what could you tell them? (*Hint*: look at the French garnish terms listed in Exhibit 9.20 for clues.)

1. Beef Filet Crécy
2. Eggs Florentine
3. Filet of Sole Provençale
4. Chicken Vichy
5. Beef Tips Lyonnaise

For each garnish listed below, list one word that describes its color.

6. Tomato wedges
7. Parsley
8. Fluted lemon slices
9. Radish roses
10. Pickle fans

For each of the following entrées, choose an appropriate garnish based on color, texture, and flavor. Be creative. Explain why you chose the garnish you did.

11. Veal with marinara sauce
12. Scrambled eggs
13. Green bean casserole
14. Black bean soup
15. Broiled catfish

Flashback

CHAPTER 9

SECTION 9.1: SALADS

- The salad section on the contemporary menu goes far beyond the simple tossed salad. **Salads** are served as a first course, entrée, even as a dessert.
- There are five types of salads: appetizer salads, accompaniment salads, main course salads, separate course salads, and dessert salads.
- **Appetizer salads** should stimulate the appetite and have fresh, crisp ingredients.
- **Accompaniment salads** should balance and **complement** the rest of the meal and be light and flavorful, but not too rich.
- **Main course salads** should be large enough to serve as a full meal and also contain protein ingredients, such as meat, poultry, seafood, egg salad, or cheese.
- **Separate course salads** should cleanse the palate after a rich dinner and before dessert.
- **Dessert salads** are usually sweet and contain fruits, sweetened gelatin, nuts, cream, or whipped cream.
- The four basic parts of any salad are the **base** or underliner, the **body**, the **garnish**, and the **dressing**.
- The body of the salad is the main ingredient.
- Garnish adds color and appeal to the salad, and sometimes flavor.
- Garnishes can be mixed with the other salad ingredients or added at the very end.
- **Salad dressings** are liquids or semi-liquids used to flavor salads. Tart dressings should be used for green salads and vegetable salads; slightly sweetened dressings are used for fruit salads.
- A salad mixed with a heavy dressing, such as mayonnaise, is called a **bound salad** because the mayonnaise holds the ingredients together. Salad arrangements should be attractive and very appetizing.

- Greens should be selected and prepared carefully for all types of salads. It's important to keep in mind the range of individual flavors, textures, and colors of lettuces and other greens to produce a well-balanced, attractive salad.
- Salad greens include **escarole, radicchio,** chicory, endive, spinach, and **arugula,** as well as lettuce.
- All salad greens need to be cleaned, prepared carefully, and refrigerated until they are to be prepared and served.
- Dress greens appropriately, with only enough dressing to lightly coat the greens, as close to service time as possible.
- Besides the commonly used **green salad,** there are **vegetable salads, cooked salads, fruit salads, combination salads,** and **gelatin salads.**

SECTION 9.2: DRESSINGS, DIPS, AND CONDIMENTS

- The flavor of a salad dressing should enhance and complement the salad ingredients. Delicate dressings should be used with delicately flavored greens; more robust dressings should be used with more robust greens.
- The basic dressings are **vinaigrette, emulsified vinaigrette,** and **mayonnaise.** Mayonnaise is the most stable emulsified dressing.
- Mayonnaise and mayonnaise-based dressings coat salad ingredients and bind them together.
- **Condiments** range from horseradish and ketchup to special relishes and prepared sauces and dips.
- **Dips** can be served hot or cold and as an accompaniment to other foods.
- Ethnic dips and **accompaniments** have become very popular. **Guacamole, hummus,** and **salsa** are just some examples. Their texture and flavors are exciting, as well as nutritious.

SECTION 9.3: THE ART OF GARNISHING

- **Garnish** means to decorate or embellish the appearance of a food item by adding other food items. Garnish is an essential component of the final presentation of the food.
- Platter garnish doesn't have to be elaborate to be effective. A simple assortment of colorful fresh vegetables is an elegant garnish to the most sophisticated platter presentation.

- Garnish is not an afterthought; it is an important element of the entire food or entrée presentation.
- Some plates need no additional garnish.
- Garnishes for soups are classified into three groups: garnishes in the soup, toppings, and accompaniments.
- Sandwiches are also garnished with condiments, lettuce, tomato, onion, or potato chips.
- Always be certain that the garnish is appropriate to the food item being served. The flavor and texture of the garnish should always complement, never overpower, the flavor of the main food item.

After your first professional work experience, you now know that business involves the mastery of a number of different skills for success. Plus, you're really seeing your kitchen skills improving by leaps and bounds.

UNIT 4

Margaret Thompson

Food Service Manager
Marriott Food Service
Argo Community High School
Summit, Illinois

I work in contract food service in a high school setting. It is my job to provide students with a variety of good meals within a specific, controlled price range.

Controlling portion sizes is important in running any foodservice operation, but especially in the business of contract foodservice. By controlling costs and guaranteeing quality, the overall profitability of the operation will be positively affected. For example, a sandwich recipe lists the needed ingredients as 4 oz of sliced beef per serving. The price for each sandwich would be determined using 4 oz per serving. Making the sandwich with 5 oz would increase the cost of the product, but the final price of the sandwich would remain the same.

Portion controls also affect inventory. If 100 sandwiches need to be made using 4 oz of beef per sandwich, 400 oz (25 lb) of finished cooked beef should be purchased. If an extra ounce is added to each sandwich by accident, only 80 sandwiches will be made, and 20 unhappy customers will not be fed!

My days are long, but full of activity. In general I supervise my staff, do paperwork, and help in the kitchen when needed. Some of the paperwork that is done every day is determining how much product was used compared with how much was prepared. By doing this, I know how much food was consumed.

I also discuss the upcoming menus with the cooks, and make changes if necessary. There is a certain amount of each product that is prepared for the students. The school always lets me know if there will be significantly more or fewer students in attendance so I can prepare the right amount of food.

CHAPTER 10

Business Math

SECTION 10.1

The Basics

AFTER STUDYING SECTION 10.1, YOU SHOULD BE ABLE TO:

- Given a list of numbers, add, subtract, multiply, and divide using basic math operations.
- Given a list of fractions, decimals, whole numbers, and percents—add, subtract, multiply and divide.

KEY TERMS

- **Borrow**
- **Denominator**
- **Divisor**
- **Dividend**
- **Lowest common denominator**
- **Numerator**
- **Percent**

Math skills are extremely important in foodservice settings. Foodservice managers are expected to have a basic understanding of math and know how to apply mathematical principles to business situations. Math skills are also essential in the professional kitchen. Chefs and managers need to know how to determine recipe yields, convert recipes from customary to metric measure, and change the yields of recipes.

Before we discuss food cost control, let's review some basic math concepts.

Mathematical Operations

As you have learned in previous math classes, there are several operations performed on numbers, and each corresponds to a familiar symbol. Numbers can be added ($10 + 2 = 12$), subtracted ($10 - 2 = 8$), multiplied ($10 \times 2 = 20$), and divided ($10 \div 2 = 5$). They can also be expressed as fractions, which is the same as dividing them ($\frac{10}{2} = 10 \div 2 = 5$).

These basic four math functions are the basis upon which all other mathematical functions are performed. Knowing these four functions well will help you as you continue to learn in this chapter about business math.

Numbers are added by lining them up in columns and then assigning each column of digits a value of 1, 10, 100, 1,000, and so on, beginning with the right-most column. In the number 372, for example, 2 is in the *ones* column, 7 is in the *tens* column, and 3 is in the *hundreds* column.

When adding a column, if the sum of a column contains two digits, then the right digit is written below the sum line, and the left digit is added to the next column as you move from right to left.

```
 1
 24
+17
 41
```

When subtracting large numbers, a technique known as **borrowing** is often used. If a digit in one column is too large to be subtracted from the digit above it, then 10 is borrowed from the column immediately to the left.

```
 71
 82
-17
 65
```

To check your work on a subtraction problem, simply add the answer to the subtracted number. The result should be the first number.

```
 1
 65   (answer)
+17   (subtracted number)
 82
```

To multiply large numbers, the digit in the ones column of the second number is first multiplied by the digits above it, going from right to left.

For example, to solve 32 × 4:

Step 1: multiply 4 by 2
result is 8

```
 32
 ×4
  8
```

Step 2: multiply 4 by 3
result is 12

```
 32
 ×4
128
```

The final result is 128.

Exhibit 10.1 will help you review multiplication for the numbers 1 through 12.

Larger numbers are divided using a combination of division and subtraction. The **dividend** is placed inside the long division sign, and the **divisor** is placed

Exhibit 10.1
Multiplication table.

	1	2	3	4	5	6	7	8	9	10	11	12
1	1	2	3	4	5	6	7	8	9	10	11	12
2	2	4	6	8	10	12	14	16	18	20	22	24
3	3	6	9	12	15	18	21	24	27	30	33	36
4	4	8	12	16	20	24	28	32	36	40	44	48
5	5	10	15	20	25	30	35	40	45	50	55	60
6	6	12	18	24	30	36	42	48	54	60	66	72
7	7	14	21	28	35	42	49	56	63	70	77	84
8	8	16	24	32	40	48	56	64	72	80	88	96
9	9	18	27	36	45	54	63	72	81	90	99	108
10	10	20	30	40	50	60	70	80	90	100	110	120
11	11	22	33	44	55	66	77	88	99	110	121	132
12	12	24	36	48	60	72	84	96	108	120	132	144

outside. For example, in the problem 728 ÷ 14, 728 is the dividend, and 14 is the divisor.

To solve 728 ÷ 14:

Step 1: divide 14 into 72
result is 5
14 × 5 = 70
subtract from 72

```
     5
14 |728
   - 70
      2
```

Step 2: bring down 8
divide 14 into 28
result is 2
14 × 2 = 28
subtract from 28

```
     52
14 |728
   - 70
      28
    - 28
       0
```

The final result is 52.

Fractions, Decimals, and Percents

In adding and subtracting fractions, **numerators,** the upper portion of a fraction, are added and subtracted the same way as whole numbers (for example $\frac{1}{3} + \frac{1}{3} = \frac{2}{3}$). **Denominators,** the lower portion of a fraction, are not. If the denominators to be added or subtracted are the same, as in the example above, the denominators remain unchanged.

If the denominators to be added or subtracted are different from each other, then we must first determine the **lowest common denominator,** which is the smallest number that both denominators can be divided into evenly. The next step is to multiply each numerator by the number that its corresponding denominator was multiplied by in order to arrive at the lowest common denominator. For example, in the next problem, both the numerator and the denominator in $\frac{2}{3}$ are multiplied by 4, giving us the new, equivalent fraction $\frac{8}{12}$.

$$\frac{2}{3} + \frac{3}{4} =$$
$$\frac{8}{12} + \frac{9}{12} = \frac{17}{12}$$
$$\frac{17}{12} = 1\frac{5}{12}$$

Fractions are often expressed as decimals. All decimals are based on one-tenth, one-hundredth, one-thousandth, etc. For example, 1.4 is 1 and 4-tenths, and 6.21 is 6 and 21-hundredths.

Decimals are added, subtracted, multiplied, and divided just like non decimal numbers. When adding or subtracting decimals, the key is to line up the decimal points.

$$\begin{array}{r} 8.46 \\ \underline{+4.23} \\ 12.69 \end{array} \qquad \begin{array}{r} 8.46 \\ \underline{-4.23} \\ 4.23 \end{array}$$

Exhibit 10.2
Common fractions and their decimal equivalents.

$\frac{1}{8}$ = 0.125	$\frac{5}{8}$ = 0.625
$\frac{1}{6}$ = 0.1667	$\frac{2}{3}$ = 0.6667
$\frac{1}{4}$ = 0.25	$\frac{3}{4}$ = 0.75
$\frac{3}{8}$ = 0.375	$\frac{5}{6}$ = 0.8333
$\frac{1}{2}$ = 0.50	

When multiplying decimals, you must determine where to place the decimal point once you've calculated your final total answer. To do this, count the total number of digits to the right of all decimal points in the numbers that you are multiplying together and then place the decimal point in your final answer by counting that many places from the right. For example, there are a total of four digits to the right of the decimal points in 8.46 and 4.23. Therefore, the decimal point goes four places from the right in the answer, 35.7858.

$$\begin{array}{r} 8.46 \\ \underline{\times 4.23} \\ 2538 \\ 16920 \\ \underline{338400} \\ 35.7858 \end{array}$$

When dividing decimals, simply bring the decimal point up directly above the long division sign.

$$4.23\overline{)8.46} = 2.00$$

When a calculator or computer is used, numbers will often have more digits to the right of the decimal point than are practical or useful. In these cases, numbers are rounded to the nearest tenth, hundredth, or thousandth. Numbers are sometimes rounded to the nearest whole number in order to eliminate the decimal point.

In rounding, if the next digit to the right is less than 5, then the number is usually rounded down (5.12 is rounded to 5.1). If the number to the right is 5 or above, then the number is rounded up (5.19 is rounded to 5.2). The number 5.192635 can be rounded to the nearest thousandth (5.193), hundredth (5.19), tenth (5.2), or whole number (5).

One of the first mathematical operations you'll come in contact with is percentages. Foodservice managers and employees often express numbers as **percents,** or parts per 100. If you're working with a fraction that you want to express as a percent, the first step is to convert the fraction into a decimal. For example, to express $\frac{1}{2}$ as a decimal, the numerator (1) is divided by the denominator (2) for an answer of 0.5. We then add a zero (0) in the hundreds place (0.50), and the two digits to the right of the decimal point are expressed as 50 percent, or 50%.

To determine a certain percent of a given number, the percent is first expressed as a decimal and then multiplied. For instance, to find 20% of 60, multiply 60 by 0.20.

$$\begin{array}{r} 60 \\ \times 0.20 \\ \hline 00 \\ 1200 \\ \hline 12.00 \end{array}$$

Thus, 20% of 60 is 12.

Give it a try:

The sports store at the mall is having a 25% discount sale on name-brand T-shirts. If the T-shirts usually sell for $15, what will the price be during the sale?

We can also determine that one number is a percent of another number. For instance, if 60 customers out of a total of 300 are ordering the house special, the percentage of customers ordering the special is found by dividing the portion (60) by the total (300).

$$\frac{60}{300} = 0.20 = 20\%$$

Therefore, 60 is 20% of 300. 20% of the customers are ordering the special.

Review Your Learning 10.1

1. A foodservice operator budgets 4% of her total $856,000 budget for marketing. What is her marketing budget?

2. In the number 3,897, the 9 occupies which of the following columns?
   a. Ones b. Tens c. Hundreds d. Thousands

3. Of 4,500 customers last month, 710 ordered items from the lighter menu selections. What percent is this?

4. A vendor's invoice for purchases is shown below. On a separate sheet of paper, calculate the amounts for each item on the invoice, the delivery charge, and the invoice total.

10 cases lettuce	@ $35.76/case	$
12 cases tomatoes	@ $25.00/case	$
6 cases radishes	@ $14.28/case	$
4 cases strawberries	@ $47.84/case	$
next-day delivery charge 7% of order sub-total		$
	invoice total	$

5. After tabulating the results of a survey sent to frequent customers, an operation determines the following information about how customers rate the establishment's service:

Number of customers	Rating
200	Excellent
250	Very good
330	Good
200	Fair
20	Poor

What percent of customers rated the operation's service as very good or better?

10.2

SECTION 10.2

Weights and Measures

AFTER STUDYING SECTION 10.2, YOU SHOULD BE ABLE TO:

- Convert recipes from original yield to desired yield using conversion factors.
- Given a problem, approximate recipe yields.
- Given a set of numbers, convert between customary and metric units of measure.
- Given a problem, calculate as purchased (AP) and edible portion (EP) amounts.
- Given an example, calculate standard recipe cost and cost per serving.

Cooking and baking require exact weighing and measuring of ingredients to ensure consistent quality and minimal waste. Exhibit 10.3 shows the customary units of measure commonly used in the United States, as well as their equivalence to each other.

KEY TERMS

- **As purchased (AP) amount**
- **Centi-**
- **Conversion factor**
- **Cross multiply**
- **Deci-**
- **Degree Celsius (SELL-see-us)**
- **Desired yield**
- **Edible portion (EP) amount**
- **Gram**
- **Kilo-**
- **Liter**
- **Meter**
- **Metric system**
- **Milli-**

Exhibit 10.3
Units of measure: U.S. system.

Weight

1 pound	=	16 ounces									

Volume

16 cups	=	1 gallon	=	128 fluid ounces	=	4 quarts	=	256 tablespoons	=	768 teaspoons
1 quart	=	32 fluid ounces	=	2 pints	=	4 cups	=	64 tablespoons	=	192 teaspoons
1 pint	=	16 fluid ounces	=	2 cups	=	32 tablespoons			=	96 teaspoons
1 cup	=	8 fluid ounces	=	16 tablespoons	=	48 teaspoons				
1 fluid ounce	=	2 tablespoons								
1 tablespoon	=	3 teaspoons								

Length

1 foot	=	12 inches

Knowing the equivalents for the basic units of measure can be very helpful. If, for example, you were to double a recipe that originally called for 2 cups of milk, you would know that the new amount required would be 1 quart (4 cups = 1 quart). If a recipe calling for 1 pint of cream were halved, the new recipe would require 1 cup.

Converting Recipes

Sometimes you have to change a recipe if the yield is not the amount you need. Using basic math skills, it's easy to increase or decrease the ingredient amounts in recipes.

Most recipes can be successfully doubled. Keep in mind, however, that larger equipment may be necessary, and cooking times often need adjustment. For many baked goods, it is best to use two baking pans of the original size rather than one larger pan. Also, when converting recipes, some ingredient amounts might need to be altered a bit because straight conversion can affect the flavor of the final product.

To increase or decrease recipe yields, follow these steps.

1. Decide how many servings you need, or the **desired yield.**
2. If necessary, determine the **conversion factor,** or the number that each ingredient amount is multiplied by in order to adjust the yield of the recipe.

Exhibit 10.4
Converting the yield from 96 brownies to 250 brownies.

Figuring the Conversion Factor: $\frac{\text{Desired Yield}}{\text{Original Yield}} = \frac{250}{96} = 2.6$

Ingredients	Amount for 96 pieces		Conversion Factor		Amount for 250 pieces
Unsweetened chocolate	1 lb = 16 oz	×	2.6	=	41.6 oz = 2 lb 10 oz
Butter	1 lb 8 oz = 24 oz	×	2.6	=	62.4 oz = 3 lb 14 oz
Eggs	1 lb 8 oz = 24 oz	×	2.6	=	62.4 oz = 3 lb 14 oz
Sugar	3 lb = 48 oz	×	2.6	=	124.8 oz = 7 lb 13 oz
Vanilla	2 Tbsp	×	2.6	=	5.2 Tbsp
Cake flour	1 lb = 16 oz	×	2.6	=	41.6 oz = 2 lb 10 oz
Baking soda	1.5 tsp	×	2.6	=	4 tsp
Chopped walnuts/pecans	1 lb = 16 oz	×	2.6	=	41.6 oz = 2 lb 10 oz

The conversion factor can be calculated using the following formula:

$$\frac{\text{Desired yield}}{\text{Original yield}} = \text{Conversion factor}$$

For example, if a recipe serves eight and you need to serve only four, the conversion factor is 0.5 (4 ÷ 8).

3. Multiply each ingredient amount by the conversion factor. This keeps all the ingredients in the same proportion as in the original recipe.
4. Convert ingredient amounts into logical, measurable quantities, if necessary, according to the equipment you will be using for measuring. For example, $\frac{6}{4}$ cups flour = $1\frac{1}{2}$ cups, or 12 tablespoons brown sugar = $\frac{3}{4}$ cup.
5. Make any necessary adjustments to equipment, temperature, and time. The depth of food in a pan, for example, affects how fast that food will cook. Use pans that are the right size for the amount of food you're working with.

Exhibit 10.4 shows a recipe for brownies that we'll convert from the original yield of 96 to 250.

To convert a decimal representing ounces into figures representing pounds and ounces, the first step is to divide the number of ounces by 16 because there are 16 ounces in a pound. In the example above for unsweetened chocolate, 41.6 oz ÷ 16 oz = 2.6 lb. We now know that we need 2 full pounds plus .6, or $\frac{6}{10}$, of a pound. Since there are 16 ounces in a pound, the next step is to convert $\frac{6}{10}$ into a fraction with a denominator of 16:

$$\frac{6}{10} = \frac{?}{16}$$

The easiest way to solve this problem is to **cross multiply,** or multiply the numerator of the first fraction by the denominator of the second and set the result equal to the product of the denominator of the first fraction and the numerator of the second.

$$\frac{6}{10} = \frac{X}{16}$$

$$6 \times 16 = 10x$$

Solving, we get 10x = 96, or x = 9.6. Thus, 2.6 pounds is 2 lb 9.6 oz, or, rounding, 2 lb 10 oz.

If your original recipe doesn't indicate the yield, you can determine the recipe's approximate yield based on ingredient amounts and the weight or size of one portion. If the total weight isn't given, convert all weights to a common unit, add them together, and then divide the total by the estimated weight or size of one portion. In the brownie recipe, for example, the total weight is 9 lb 1 oz, or 145 oz. If we estimate that the weight of one portion is 1.5 ounces, then dividing the weight of one portion into the total results in the approximate yield:

$$\frac{145}{1.5} = 96$$

Thus, the recipe yields approximately 96 brownies.

The Metric System

While the United States uses the measurement system you're probably familiar with, most of the rest of the world uses the **metric system,** in which each measurement is based on multiples of 10. The four basic units of measure in the metric system are:

- **Gram** (weight)
- **Liter** (volume)
- **Degree Celsius** (SELL-see-us) (temperature)
- **Meter** (length)

Larger and smaller units are made by dividing and multiplying the units above by 10, 100, 1,000, and so on. The following Latin prefixes representing these multiples of 10 are used to identify the larger or smaller units:

kilo- 1,000 (1 kilogram equals 1,000 grams)
deci- 1/10 (1 deciliter equals one-tenth of 1 liter)
centi- 1/100 (1 centiliter equals one-one hundredth of 1 liter)
milli 1/1,000 (1 millimeter equals one-one thousandth of 1 meter)

For a refresher on metric and customary equivalents, take another look at Exhibit 4.4 on page 184.

Exhibit 10.6
Percentage yields of various produce items.

Product	Percentage Yield
Artichoke, globe	80% (whole, trimmed) 30% (bottoms only)
Artichoke, Jerusalem	80%
Asparagus	55%
Bean, green or wax	88%
Bean, lima	40%
Beet	40-45% (75% purchased without tops)
Broccoli	65-75%
Brussels sprout	80%
Cabbage (white, green, or red)	80%
Carrot	75-80%
Cauliflower	55%
Celery	75%
Celery root (knob celery or celeriac)	75%
Corn (on the cob)	28% (after husking and cutting from cob)
Cucumber (slicing type)	75-95% (depending on peeling)
Eggplant	90% (75% if peeled)
Garlic	88%
Kohlrabi	55%
Leek	50%
Lettuce	75%
Mushroom	90%
Okra	82%
Onion, dry	90%
Onion, green (scallion)	60-70%
Parsley	85%
Parsnip	70-75%
Peas (green and black-eyed)	40%
Peas, edible pod	90%
Pepper, sweet (green or red)	82%
Potatoes, white	80%
Potatoes, sweet (including yams)	80%
Radish	90%
Spinach and other greens	50-70%
Squash, summer (including zucchini)	90%
Squash, winter	65-85%
Tomato	90% (peeled)
Watercress	90%

Product Yields

Most vegetables have to be trimmed and cut before being used in recipes. As a result, the untrimmed **as purchased (AP) amount** needed to yield the correct trimmed, **edible portion (EP) amount** called for must be calculated.

Exhibit 10.6 indicates the percentage yields for a variety of produce items.

To determine how much of an item is needed to yield an AP amount, simply divide the edible portion amount needed by the yield percentage. For example, a recipe for seafood salad calls for 4 pounds of cauliflower. Checking Exhibit 10.6, we see that cauliflower has a 55% yield percentage. To calculate how much will be needed to prepare 4 pounds of trimmed cauliflower, we divide the desired EP amount by the yield percentage:

$$\frac{\text{4 lb trimmed cauliflower}}{0.55} = \text{7.27 lb untrimmed}$$

Thus, the chef needs to purchase 7.27 pounds of untrimmed cauliflower. The formula can also be used in reverse. For example, the chef has 10 pounds of untrimmed cauliflower, which has a 55% yield percentage.

$$\text{10 lb untrimmed cauliflower} \times 0.55 = \text{5.5 lb trimmed cauliflower}$$

Exhibit 10.7
Chefs trim raw ingredients needed for recipes with yield percentages in mind.

After trimming, there will be 5.5 pounds of cauliflower.

Costing Recipes

Other factors that are essential in quantity food production are standard recipe cost and cost per serving. To find the total cost of a standard recipe, you must know both the ingredient amounts needed and the market price of each one. Then, multiply or divide the ingredient amounts by the prices. To further explore how to calculate standard recipe cost, let's revisit the ingredients for the brownie recipe in Exhibit 10.8.

If you recall, the recipe yields 96 servings. To find the cost per serving, divide the total cost by the yield:

$$\frac{\$36.45}{96} = 0.3797$$

When rounded, the cost per serving is $0.38.

Ingredient costs are usually rounded to the nearest cent. Portion costs are ordinarily carried out to $\frac{1}{10}$ of a cent.

Many operations price out all recipes and then check them every six months to see whether they are still accurate. Some establishments compare standard recipe costs to the national price index twice a year. If the index rises or drops a specific percentage, the total recipe cost is raised or lowered by this percentage, and the portion or yield cost is recalculated. While this method simplifies the recalculation process, foodservice operations should really do a complete revision every year.

Exhibit 10.8
Standard recipe cost calculation for the brownie recipe in Exhibit 10.4.

Ingredient	Amount	Unit Cost
Unsweetened chocolate	1 lb	$5.50/lb
Butter	1 lb 8 oz	2.50/lb
Eggs	1 lb 8 oz	5.50/lb
Sugar	3 lb	2.50/lb
Vanilla	2 Tbsp	6.50/pt
Cake flour	1 lb	3.50/lb
Baking soda	1 1/2 tsp	2.75/lb
Chopped walnuts/pecans	1 lb	1.49/lb

Ingredient	Amount × Unit Cost		Ingredient Cost
Unsweetened chocolate	1 lb × $5.50 =		$5.50
Butter	1.5 lb × $2.50 =		$3.75
Eggs	1.5 lb × $5.50 =		$8.25
Sugar	3 lb × $2.50 =		$7.50
Vanilla	$6.50 ÷ 32	= 0.203 × 2 =	$0.41
Cake flour	1 lb × $3.50 =		$3.50
Baking soda	$2.75 ÷ 96	= 0.029 × 1.5 =	$0.04
Chopped walnuts/pecans	1 lb × $1.49 =		$1.49
		Total cost of recipe:	**$36.45**

Sometimes it's necessary to combine portion costs. A steak, for example, may cost $6.50 served by itself, but the cost increases to $10.99 when the steak is served with a salad, french fries, a roll, and butter. Some operators calculate the exact cost of each food item and then add the figures together to determine the total cost. Others simply calculate the average cost of all such extras and add this figure to appropriate items.

Exhibit 10.9
The portion cost for grilled fish increases when served with extras, like vegetables.

When patrons help themselves at a salad bar, there may be some question as to how to cost out a meal. The usual procedure is to both keep an account of the cost of foods in the salad bar and track the number of salad bar patrons served from it. Dividing the number of patrons into the total cost of the salad bar will result in the average cost per serving. This figure is then added to the basic entrée cost. For example, if an operation spends $95.68 per day to keep its salad bar stocked and an average of 84 guests eat from the salad bar per day, the average cost per serving is:

$$\frac{\$95.68}{84} = \$1.14 \text{ per serving}$$

Review Your Learning 10.2

1. If a recipe calling for 3 pints of cream is tripled, how many *quarts* of cream are needed?
   a. 4.5 b. 6.0 c. 7.5 d. 9.0

2. On a separate sheet of paper, convert the following recipe for 12 portions so that it yields 80 portions.
   Stir-Fried Chicken
   3 lb chicken 6 oz soy sauce 1 lb green peppers
   $1^1/_2$ lb scallions 2 oz ginger 2 cups water

3. A recipe requires 5 pounds of trimmed broccoli, which has a 75% yield. How much untrimmed broccoli is needed?
   a. 3.8 lb b. 4.8 lb c. 5.2 lb d. 6.7 lb

4. For each of the following, provide the equation for calculating it and include a numerical example related to the foodservice industry.
   a. Cost per serving c. Conversion factor
   b. Degrees Fahrenheit d. As purchased amount

5. Determine the total cost and the cost per serving for the following recipe. (The yield is 26 servings.)
   Chili

Ingredient	Unit Cost
4 lb ground beef	$2.09/lb
3 lb tomatoes	1.59/lb
2 lb onions	0.99/lb
1 lb green pepper	1.39/lb
4 oz garlic	2.49/lb
8 oz tomato paste	1.69/pint

10.3

SECTION 10.3

Controlling Food Costs

AFTER STUDYING SECTION 10.3, YOU SHOULD BE ABLE TO:

- Describe and give examples of controllable costs, fixed costs, and variable costs related to food and labor.
- Given a set of numbers, calculate depreciation.
- Differentiate between the two categories of food purchase: perishable and nonperishable.
- Outline and follow basic receiving procedures.
- State the appropriate storage guidelines and temperatures for different perishable foods.

KEY TERMS

- **Cost**
- **Cost control**
- **Depreciation (deh-PREE-she-AY-shun)**
- **Directly variable cost**
- **Directs**
- **FIFO method**
- **Fixed cost**
- **Invoice**
- **Issue**
- **Nonperisable**
- **Overhead costs**
- **Perishable**
- **Perpetual inventory**
- **Physical inventory**
- **Prime cost**
- **Purchase specification**
- **Requisition**
- **Semivariable cost**
- **Stores**
- **Variable cost**

Tasteful decor, excellent food, and satisfied customers don't guarantee a profitable foodservice operation. **Cost control** is necessary in every area of the foodservice establishment, including those discussed below.

Purchasing. The proper kind of food and its cost, quantity, and quality must be determined. Then an appropriate supplier should be found. If the wrong kind, quantity, or quality of food is bought at the wrong cost, the operation will lose money.

Receiving. When receiving food items, an operation must check to see that exactly what was ordered has been delivered. This inspection process is the initial step in a series of accounting and inventory practices important to cost control.

Storage. Storage procedures must be carefully controlled in order to reduce or eliminate loss as a result of spoilage, contamination, or employee theft.

Issuing. To control the cost of food moving into preparation and production, product issuing from inventory must be exact. **Issuing** is the process of distributing food items from inventory storage.

Preparation and production. Preparation and production are usually controlled by the use of standardized recipes and by following proper kitchen procedures. Being careless by leaving potatoes too long in a peeler or overcooking a roast, for example, results in loss of product quality, as well as waste.

The successful foodservice manager closely monitors operating costs and, based on these costs, adjusts the way the establishment operates. Understanding the relationship between cost and sales, along with realistic planning and forecasting, is vital to the profitability of any foodservice operation.

Understanding Foodservice Costs

In the foodservice industry, **cost** is the price to an operation of goods or services when the goods are received or the services are rendered. There are various categories of costs—fixed and variable; controllable and noncontrollable; unit and total; and historical and planned. Exhibit 10.10 highlights those costs often relevant to the foodservice industry, along with a brief definition of each.

Fixed costs do not change significantly when sales increase or decrease. For example, real estate taxes and rent are unaffected by changes in business volume.

Exhibit 10.10
Types of foodservice cost.

Cost	Definition
Controllable cost	Can be changed in the short term
Directly variable cost	Changes in sales volume automatically bring a corresponding change in these costs
Discretionary cost	Nonessential; at management's discretion
Fixed cost	Not affected by changes in sales revenue
Historical cost	Documented through records, such as invoices, wage rates, and contractual agreements
Joint cost	Shared by two or more departments
Noncontrollable cost	Cannot be changed in the short term
Opportunity cost	Incurred when pursuing a change
Planned cost	Anticipated or expected; usually based on historical costs; used in budgeting and forecasting
Relevant cost	Directly affects a particular decision
Semivariable cost	Has both a fixed and variable element
Standard cost	Projected for a given level of sales
Sunk cost	Must be paid regardless of the outcome of a decision-making process
Total cost	Complete cost of food or labor for one period (one week, one month, etc.)
Unit cost	Single food portion or hourly employee rate
Variable cost	Affected by sales revenue

Depreciation (deh-PREE-she-AY-shun), another fixed cost, is the decline in value of an asset over time. The simplest formula used to determine depreciation is:

$$\frac{\text{Cost of asset - Trade-in value}}{\text{Life of asset}} = \text{Depreciation value}$$

For example, if you purchase a stove for $5,000 and you plan to trade it in in five years for $500, the depreciation is $900 for each of the five years.

$$\frac{\$5,000 - \$500}{5 \text{ years}} = \$900 \text{ per year}$$

Variable costs are directly related to business volume. Food and payroll costs, for example, are variable, since they increase or decrease depending on sales. To be more precise, food costs are **directly variable** because every increase or decrease in sales volume automatically brings a corresponding increase or decrease in their cost. Payroll costs, on the other hand, are considered **semi-variable** because they have both a fixed and a variable component: fixed-cost, salaried employees, such as managers and bookkeepers, have hours that do not change with business volume, while variable-cost, wage employees, such as servers and kitchen workers, have hours that do vary with business volume.

Prime cost refers to the total of all costs directly related to doing business and includes the cost of food sold, as well as payroll, payroll taxes, and employee benefits. **Overhead costs** include all costs other than the prime cost.

Purchasing

Depending on an organization's structure and management policies, responsibility for food purchasing might be given to a number of different people: managers, owners, chefs, or stewards. It is important to note that, for control purposes, purchasing responsibility should be given to only one person.

The primary purpose of establishing control over purchasing is to ensure a continuing supply of sufficient quantities of necessary foods, each of the quality appropriate to its intended use, purchased at the most favorable price. Purchasing is covered in greater detail in *Chapter 7: Purchasing and Inventory Control* of *Becoming a Foodservice Professional, Year 2.*

One of the first steps in controlling food purchasing is to set quality and quantity standards. Quality standards are set by developing standard **purchase specifications.** These specifications list the food items that are to be purchased, along with the desired characteristics of each, and are subject to continual revision. The purchase specifications for canned peaches at one establishment appear in Exhibit 10.11.

Exhibit 10.11
Specifications for canned peaches.

- Yellow, cling halves—canned
- U.S. grade A (Fancy), heavy syrup
- 19-24 Brix, minimum drained weight
- Federal Inspector's certification of grade required
- 66 ounces per #10 can
- Count per can: 30 to 35
- Quote by dozen #10 can

Foods for purchase fall into two categories: perishables and nonperishables. **Perishables** have a relatively short shelf life. They should be purchased for immediate use in order to retain quality and must be kept refrigerated or frozen. A daily inventory of perishables should be taken, with anticipated demands being noted.

Nonperishables have a longer shelf life than perishables and can be stored in the containers in which they are packaged, often on shelves and at room temperature, for weeks or even months. Having a lot of extra nonperishables on hand should be avoided, and shelves should be labeled so it is easy to see which supply levels are low.

Receiving

The second area of food cost control is receiving. The primary purpose of receiving is to make sure that the items received match the orders placed. In many foodservice operations, a clerk performs the receiving job, and, as in purchasing, it is essential that only one person be held responsible. Ultimately, the quantity, quality, and price of every item delivered should match both the purchase order and the supplier's **invoice,** or bill.

If possible, delivered items should be weighed or counted and carefully checked to see whether their quality is acceptable. Once the receiving clerk has verified the quantity, quality, and price of each item, the invoice is stamped or initialed with approval. All invoices for food items delivered on a given day are listed on the receiving clerk's daily report.

Completed paperwork must then be forwarded to the proper people and all delivered food moved to the appropriate storage areas as soon as possible. This can decrease the likelihood of spoilage and theft that frequently occur between the receiving and storage functions.

In many operations, food items are divided into two categories: those purchased for immediate use and those purchased and kept in inventory for future use. In food control, all foods

Exhibit 10.12
The receiving clerk's daily report.

Invoice No.	Vendor	Unit	Amt.	Article	Unit Price	Total Amount	Directs	Stores
1234	Happy Times Food Service	Cs.	5	Tomato Sauce	$10.00	$ 50.00		
7654	McCarthy Meats	Cs.	25	10#, 3-1 burgers	$15.00	$375.00	$150.00	$50.00
5697	PePe's Produce	Cs.	3	Head Lettuce	$35.76	$107.28	$107.28	$225.00

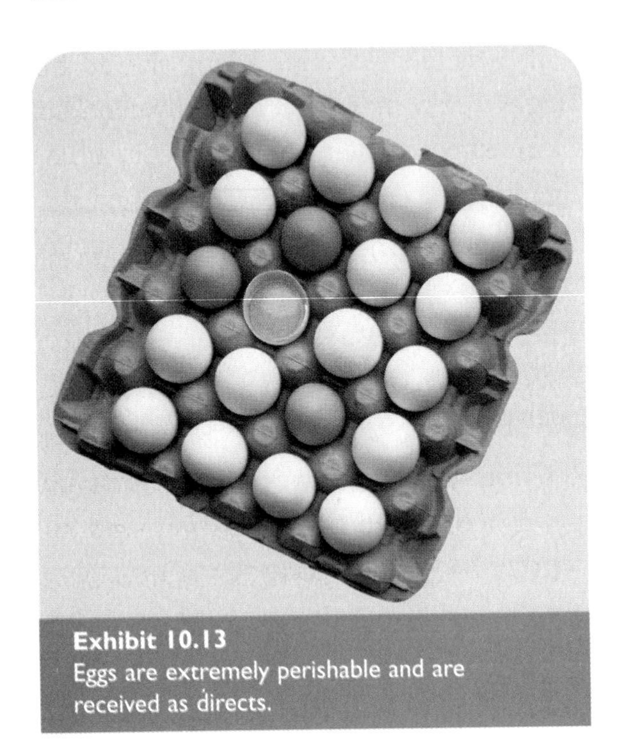

Exhibit 10.13
Eggs are extremely perishable and are received as directs.

charged immediately to cost are called **directs;** all foods charged to cost when they are issued from inventory are called **stores.**

Because of their extremely perishable nature, directs are generally purchased daily. Foods in this category include fresh fruits, vegetables, fresh baked goods, and most dairy products. Directs are purchased for immediate use and are, therefore, issued to food preparers as soon as they are received. Directs are included in food cost figures on the day of their delivery.

Stores are those food items that will not significantly diminish in quality if they are not used immediately. Foods in this category include properly stored meats, as well as canned, bottled, and boxed items. Stores are issued to the kitchen as they are needed and are charged to food cost at that time.

Employees in the receiving area must be trained to recognize established purchase specifications. When examining meats, they should be able to determine grade, degree of freshness, and extent of trimming. For produce items, employees must be able to check for ripeness. Managers should occasionally be present when food deliveries arrive in order to keep an eye on receiving procedures.

Storage

Food storage standards are important to ensure the proper arrangement of food items, security of storage areas, and dating and pricing of stored foods.

One of the key elements in storage control is temperature, especially for perishables. Food life is maximized when items are stored at proper temperatures. If temperatures rise above specific levels, shelf life is shortened, and waste and spoilage are increased.

Temperature gauges on refrigerated storage areas should be checked regularly. The temperatures that follow are generally accepted for storing the foods indicated, but certain items, such as bananas and potatoes, may need to be kept at higher temperatures. Consult USDA publications for specific storage guidelines.

Fresh meats	32°F to 36°F (0°C to 2.2°C)
Fresh produce	40°F to 45°F (4.4°C to 7.2°C)
Fresh dairy products	38°F to 40°F (3.3°C to 4.4°C)
Fresh fish	30°F to 34°F (-1.1°C to 1.1°C)
Frozen foods	10°F to 0°F (-23.3°C to -17.8°C)
Dry goods	room temperature: 50°F to 70°F (10°C to 21.1°C)

Food should also be stored in appropriate containers. Most staple items—such as sugar, salt, flour, and baking soda—are purchased in airtight containers. Items purchased in unsealed containers should be transferred to airtight containers to protect them from insects and rodents. Many raw foods, such as apples and potatoes, may be stored as purchased, while fresh fish should be packed in shaved ice. Finally, cooked foods and opened canned goods must be stored either wrapped or appropriately covered in stainless steel containers.

There are several other important things to remember when storing foods.

Shelving. Proper shelving is essential. Perishable foods should be kept on slatted refrigerated shelving, made of several thin strips with space in between to permit maximum air circulation. Steel shelving is recommended for nonperishables. No food item should ever be stored on the floor. Shelving raised a few inches above floor level must be provided for large or heavy containers.

Cleanliness. Cleanliness is vital at all times. Storage areas must be cleaned and swept daily to eliminate spoiled foods and to discourage insect and rodent infestation. Professional pest extermination should be performed regularly.

Food item location. Appropriate locations for all food items must be selected. Each item should always be kept in the same place, with new deliveries of the item also stored in the same location. Certain foods, such as eggs and fish, absorb flavors and odors from other foods more quickly than others and should be stored separately whenever possible.

Stock rotation. Stock must be properly rotated by using the **first-in, first-out (FIFO) method.** The first food items to be received must be the first issued from inventory. New deliveries should be stored behind older quantities on hand in order to reduce the possibility of spoilage.

Storage facility location. Ideally, storage facilities for both perishable and non-perishable foods should be located between the receiving and preparation areas in order to speed the process of storage and issuing, maximize security, and reduce labor requirements.

Establishment of control standards. Control standards should be established for issuing food from storage. One system requires a member of the kitchen staff to prepare a written requisition for items needed from the storeroom. A **requisition** is a form used to record items that are being requested from inventory. The requisition is reviewed, approved, signed by the chef or kitchen manager, and then given to the storekeeper who fills the order.

Exhibit 10.14
Fresh foods should always be properly stored.

For record keeping purposes, directs are charged to food cost as they are received, while stores are considered part of inventory and are not included in cost figures until they are issued. Since meat items can be very costly, special attention is often given when issuing them from storage. Some establishments attach a tag to each piece of meat, removing it as the meat is issued and then recording the corresponding dollar value on the requisition. The unit cost of staple items must also be entered and then multiplied by the number of units issued in each case.

Since the goals of food control include determining food cost as accurately as possible and matching food cost with food sales, it is also necessary to maintain records of the cost of food transferred. A transfer of food items between two areas of the same establishment is called an *intraunit* transfer. An *interunit* transfer might occur between two locations of one food chain.

Issuing and Inventory Tracking

In order to control food costs, an establishment must keep careful track of its inventory. Some operations take a **perpetual inventory** through the use of continuous records of requisitions. Others take a **physical inventory** at the end of each month by actually counting items on hand. With either method, the closing inventory value is used to calculate the cost of goods sold for the month:

Opening inventory
\+ Monthly purchases
\- Employee meals
\- Interunit transfers
\- Closing inventory

Cost of goods sold

For example, if an operation had $4,160 in inventory on May 1 and $3,940 on May 31, purchased $7,120 in food, provided $880 in employee meals, and transferred $1,760, the cost of goods sold is:

	$ 4,160
+	7,120
-	880
-	1,760
-	3,940
	$ 4,700

Review Your Learning 10.3

1. Which of the following are fixed costs?
   - Insurance premiums
   - Food costs
   - Advertising costs
   - Depreciation
   - Rent
   - Payroll costs for hourly employees
   - Real estate taxes

2. All invoices for foods delivered on a given day are listed on the:
   a. purchase specification.
   b. receiving clerk's daily report.
   c. pricing standard form.
   d. standing order.

3. Explain the difference between the following terms:
   a. unit cost and total cost
   b. perishable and nonperishable
   c. directs and stores
   d. perpetual inventory and physical inventory
   e. interunit transfer and intraunit transfer

4. What are the proper storage temperatures for the following food items?
   - Fresh halibut
   - Frozen pizza
   - Fresh Swiss cheese
   - Flour
   - Fresh lettuce
   - Fresh turkey

5. An operation had an opening inventory worth $11,208 on June 1 and a closing inventory on June 30 of $10,776. Its June food purchases totaled $7,628. What was the operation's cost of goods sold for June?

10.4

SECTION 10.4

Food Production

AFTER STUDYING SECTION 10.4, YOU SHOULD BE ABLE TO:

- Outline proper techniques for portion control, including standard portion size, standardized recipe, and standard portion cost.
- Forecast sales by analyzing and evaluating sales histories, popularity indices, and production sheets.

KEY TERMS

- **Cooking loss test**
- **Forecasting**
- **Par stock control**
- **Popularity index**
- **Portion inventory and reconciliation**
- **Production sheet**
- **Sales history**
- **Standard portion cost**
- **Standard portion size**
- **Void sheet**
- **Yield percentage**

THE NEED FOR STANDARDIZATION

Establishing food production standards helps reduce customer discontent, eliminate excessive costs, and ensure that all kitchen employees have needed production information readily available. In addition to direct monitoring techniques, customers' reactions are a good way to determine whether employees are using portion standards. All customer complaints should be investigated immediately. Portion control includes the standardization of portion sizes, recipes, and portion costs.

Standard portion size, the fixed quantity served to a customer for a fixed selling price, is one of the most important standards that a foodservice establishment sets. To determine standard portion size, menu items must first be quantified by weight, volume, or count. Among the many kitchen tools available to help an operator standardize portions are *scoops, slotted spoons, ladles, portion scales,* and *measuring cups.* Since the cost of food items varies with the quantity served, the cost of any particular item will be proportional to the quantity served to the customer.

As you learned in *Chapter 4: Kitchen Basics,* a standardized recipe lists ingredients and quantities to be used and a procedure to be followed each time an item is prepared. This standardization ensures that the quality and quantity of an item is the same each time the item is prepared. Standardized recipes must be available for those employees who prepare food and should be either recorded on recipe cards or maintained in computer files.

Once standard portion sizes and recipes have been established, standard portion costs can be calculated. **Standard portion cost** is the dollar amount that a standard portion should cost, given the standards and standard procedures for its production. These planned portion costs can be computed for each menu item. One way to determine standard portion cost is to divide the cost of an item by the number of portions it contains:

$$\frac{\text{Purchase price per unit}}{\text{Number of portions per unit}} = \text{Standard portion cost}$$

For example, if potatoes cost $35 per case and there are 175 portions in each case, the standard portion cost is $0.20 *($35 ÷ 175 = 0.20).*

Another method for calculating standard portion cost is the use of a standard recipe card, which indicates a predetermined number of standard portions. To determine the cost of preparing one portion, simply divide the number of portions produced (the yield) into the total cost of preparing the recipe. As you may recall, total cost is determined by listing each item and quantity from a recipe and then multiplying each by its unit cost.

Portion Control of Meat, Poultry, and Fish

For some food items, such as meat, poultry, and fish, processing must take place and inedible parts removed before the yield, or the number of usable portions produced, can be determined. To calculate the cost per usable pound and cost per usable ounce, the following formulas are used.

$$\frac{\text{Total value of usable item}}{\text{Weight of usable item}} = \text{Cost per usable pound}$$

$$\frac{\text{Cost per usable pound}}{\text{16 ounces per pound}} = \text{Cost per usable ounce}$$

For example, if the total value of 4.5 pounds of processed sirloin veal chops is $48.25, the cost per usable pound will be $10.72 *($48.25 ÷ 4.5 pounds)*, and the cost per usable ounce will be $0.67 *($10.72 ÷ 16 ounces per pound)*.

Exhibit 10.15
Meats must be processed to determine the number of usable portions.

Once management sets portion size, portion cost can then be determined with the following formula:

$$\text{Portion size} \times \text{Cost per usable ounce} = \text{Portion cost}$$

If the portion size for the veal chops in the same example is 8 ounces, the portion cost will be $5.36 *(8 ounces × $0.67 per usable ounce)*.

Food items like beef roasts, pork, lamb, and other meats cannot be portioned until after they have been cooked because of the weight loss that occurs in the cooking process. To determine the standard portion cost of these kinds of items, the **cooking loss test** is used. This control method requires the foodservice operator to record cooking time, temperature, and a series of weights.

- The trimmed weight is subtracted from the original weight of the meat.
- The cooked weight is subtracted from the trimmed weight to determine the loss in cooking.
- Usable meat must be removed from any bone and weighed to determine the quantity available for portioning. This weight is subtracted from the cooked weight in order to determine the amount of waste.

Once the weight and value of the usable meat have been recorded, the remaining calculations are the same as those for the yield test.

Another important figure used in a number of calculations involving meat, poultry, and fish is the **yield percentage,** the percent of an entire purchase that is available for portioning after all in-house processing (trimming, cooking, etc.) has been done. If a foodservice operator knows the portion size, yield percentage, and number of portions needed, for example, the quantity that should be purchased can be determined with the following formula:

$$\frac{\text{Number of portions} \times \text{Portion size (expressed as a decimal)}}{\text{Yield percentage}} = \text{Quantity to purchase}$$

Suppose you want to buy enough lamb to provide six-ounce portions of lamb roast to 30 people. After having performed a cooking loss test, you know that the yield factor is 52.3%. The quantity to purchase can then be calculated.

$$\frac{30 \text{ portions} \times .375 \text{ (6 ounces)}}{.523} = 21.51 \text{ lbs}$$

When rounded, the amount of lamb to purchase is 21.5 lbs.

Controlling Production Volume

In order to estimate production needs and reduce waste, the aim is to produce the number of portions likely to be sold in a day. In controlling production volume, three standard procedures are needed: maintaining sales history, forecasting portion sales, and determining production quantities.

Maintaining sales history. A **sales history** is a written record of the number of portions of each item sold every time the item appeared on the menu. This data should be recorded either by hand or electronically by servers. One of the most common pieces of information included in sales histories is a description of weather conditions, since they have a direct impact on sales volume. Special events, such as conventions and holidays, are also included because they are helpful in forecasting sales volume.

Another useful figure is the **popularity index,** the percentage of total portion sales represented by each item. The popularity index is calculated by dividing the number of portions of a given item sold by the total number of portions of all menu items sold on the same day or in the same time period.

$$\frac{\text{Portions of menu item sold}}{\text{Total number of portions of all menu items sold}} \times 100 = \text{Popularity Index}$$

For example, if a foodservice operation sells a total of 306 entrées in one day and 44 of these are lasagna, the popularity index for lasagna is 14.4 *(44 ÷ 306 × 100).*

Forecasting portion sales. **Forecasting** is a procedure in which data are used to predict what is likely to occur in the future. This educated guesswork is highly valuable in the foodservice industry and can be a major factor in profitable operations and cost control. When sales volume has been accurately predicted, necessary adjustments in purchasing and production can be made, reducing waste, spoilage, and overproduction. There are four steps to forecasting.

1. Refer to the sales history.
2. Evaluate the effects of external conditions.
3. Predict the total anticipated volume, or the anticipated numbers of customers for particular days or particular meals.
4. Predict the anticipated number of sales of each item on the menu.

The completed forecast represents management's best estimate of anticipated sales volume. With accurate predictions, labor and purchasing costs can be controlled more effectively.

Determining production quantities. Production quantities can be determined using a production sheet. A **production sheet** lists all menu items that are going to be prepared for a given date. The sheets will vary according to an operation's individual needs and forecasts.

Managers should train employees to record accurate, complete information about the daily number of menu items sold. One way to check how well employees meet production standards is with a void sheet. Used to keep records of portions rejected by customers, the **void sheet** lists the server, the reason the item was returned, and the sales value of the menu item. Evaluating the void sheet can alert managers to problems among kitchen and serving staff.

Another control method requires the use of a **portion inventory and reconciliation** form. The form lists each menu item, inventory of any leftover portions that can be used again, number of portions prepared, additional quantities prepared,

Exhibit 10.16
The void sheet keeps records of portions rejected by customers.

DATE: 5/23

Check #	Waiter #	Menu Item	Reason for Return	Authorization	Menu Price
11031	6	O	Too well done	SJC	$7.95
11034	6	M	Dropped on floor	SJC	$5.95
11206	4	O	Too well done	SJC	$7.95
11227	3	O	Too well done		$7.95

inventory of portions on hand, and the number of portions consumed. At the close of the day, any differences between kitchen records and portion sales records are determined. The portion inventory and reconciliation form is most practical for entrées, since they are usually the most expensive items on the menu.

Par stock control of preportioned entrées is another useful technique. Expensive cuts of meat are either purchased already portioned or portioned in-house before being cooked. These items are ordinarily cooked to order and held in a refrigerator close to the broiler or range. The par stock control sheet lists the item, portions issued, any additional issues, total issues, amount returned to the kitchen, and portions consumed. The par stock technique indicates discrepancies between the forecast and production. Managers can then take steps to determine the cause of major discrepancies.

Review Your Learning 10.4

1. How does a standardized recipe help control food costs?

2. If a leg of lamb costs $21.97 and yields 8 portions, what is the standard portion cost?
   a. $1.75 b. $2.25 c. $2.75 d. $3.25

3. On a separate sheet of paper, match the term on the left with its equation on the right.
   1) Portion cost for meat, poultry, and fish
   2) Popularity index
   3) Cost per usable pound
   4) Standard portion cost
   5) Quantity needed

   a. $\frac{\text{Total value of usable item}}{\text{Weight of usable item}}$
   b. Portion size × Cost per usable ounce
   c. $\frac{\text{Number of portions} \times \text{Portion size (expressed as a decimal)}}{\text{Yield percentage}}$
   d. $\frac{\text{Purchase price per unit}}{\text{Number of portions per unit}}$
   e. $\frac{\text{Portions of menu item sold}}{\text{Total number of portions of all menu items sold}}$

4. On a separate sheet of paper, complete the popularity index table shown below.

Item	Portion Sold	Percent of Total Sales (Popularity Index)
Spaghetti	36	_______
Lasagna	_______	_______
Baked Chicken	41	_______
Pizza	_______	35.4
TOTAL	178	100.0%

5. One way to check how well employees meet production standards is through the use of:
   a. forecasting. b. a void sheet. c. a standard recipe card. d. the cooking loss test.

10.5

SECTION 10.5

Labor Cost Control

AFTER STUDYING SECTION 10.5, YOU SHOULD BE ABLE TO:

- List factors contributing to labor costs, such as employee turnover, business volume, and quality and quantity standards.

KEY TERMS

- **Average cover formula**
- **Cover**
- **Dupe (doop)**
- **Employee turnover**
- **Operational plan**
- **Organization chart**
- **Peak hours**
- **Standard employee hours**

The cost of labor, or employees, in the hospitality industry is usually high. It can range anywhere from 15 to 45 percent of sales. In some nonprofit operations, labor cost percentages are as high as 60 percent. With these figures in mind, it is obvious that maintaining control over labor costs is essential. Labor cost control is the process by which managers try to obtain a desired level of performance at an appropriate level of cost. Labor cost control is more than the mere reduction of payroll costs; management must also hire and keep well-qualified employees at a fair wage.

Planning, Organizing, and Staffing

Planning and organizing help to divide the workload evenly and lead to positive communication among employees and managers. There are several questions that should be asked during operation and managerial planning.

- What do I want to accomplish?
- How will I accomplish it?
- When will I accomplish it?
- Why does it need to be accomplished?
- Who will accomplish it?

Once the planning stage has been completed, there are several additional questions that can be used to get organized.

- How many labor hours are needed?
- How many employees do I need?
- What type of equipment do I need?
- What supplies do I need?
- What is the cost of supplies?
- What is the cost of labor?

Staffing involves determining how many employees will be needed to get a job done. This process includes forecasting the labor hours and the skill levels that will be necessary to perform various tasks.

In staffing, managers must consider both the operation's peak and slow hours. **Peak hours** are those times when the establishment is very busy—during breakfast, lunch, dinner, and weekends, as well as holidays that the operation is open. As far as slow periods are concerned, most establishments have slow hours (between meals, for example), and some foodservice operations also experience seasonal slow times. A university cafeteria, for instance, may be busy only during the nine months of the school year.

Directly related to the staffing function is **employee turnover,** the ratio of employees who leave to total employees. If an operation has a total of 63 employees and 24 have left in the past year, its turnover rate is 38% ($\frac{24}{64} \times 100$). High turnover results in tremendous labor costs since managers must constantly fill vacant positions and train new employees. Various hidden costs, such as fees for placing help-wanted ads and using employment agency services, are incurred as well. One way to prevent high turnover is to ensure that employees receive ongoing training. When appropriately trained, employees perform more effectively and experience greater job satisfaction, an important factor in reducing turnover.

At the most basic level, training may involve showing an experienced employee the location of a new dishwasher or explaining the operation of equipment. New employees should be trained in proper kitchen and serving procedures for safety, sanitation, and quality control. Sales training may include explaining new menu items and promotional strategies or teaching inexperienced employees the basics of serving and selling. In the long run, effective training pays off: it produces a more efficient, effective, and knowledgeable staff. As a result, customers are more satisfied and revenues increase.

Maximizing Labor Force Efficiency

The primary purpose of labor cost control is to maximize the efficiency of employees as they meet their operation's established standards of quality and service. The first step is to identify variable-cost employees and fixed-cost employees. Variable-cost employees, such as servers and kitchen workers, relate in number to business volume: as volume increases or decreases, the number of variable-cost employees changes accordingly. Fixed-cost employees, such as managers and cashiers, don't relate in number to business volume: as volume increases or decreases, the number of fixed-cost employees remains fairly constant.

Once variable-cost and fixed-cost employees have been identified, managers must organize the work of all employees. There are three steps in the work organization process: 1) establish an operational plan; 2) prepare job descriptions; and 3) prepare an analysis of business volume.

Establishing an operational plan—An **operational plan** gives an organization a clear vision of the operation's goals. Both the product and service offered should be evaluated, as well as various relationships among employees. An **organization chart** showing job positions according to function within the operation can be created to examine these relationships.

Exhibit 10.17
A server is a variable-cost employee.

Exhibit 10.18
Sample organization chart.

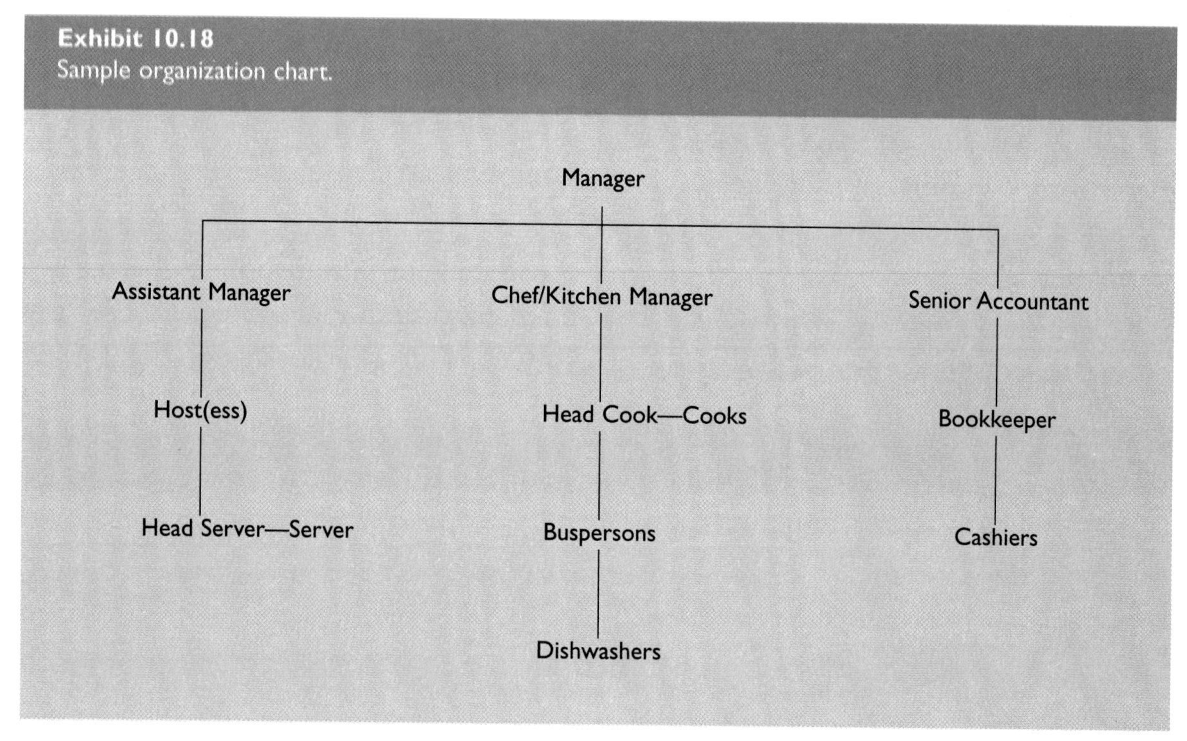

Such a chart lists positions according to their functions within the operation, with lines indicating authority, responsibilities, and relationships between positions.

Preparing job descriptions—Man agers should answer the following questions when preparing job descriptions.

- What is to be done?
- When is it to be done?
- Where is it to be done?

Effective job descriptions include the job title and department in which the job is located, a summary of the duties of the job, and an actual list of duties assigned to the job. A sample job description is shown in Exhibit 10.19.

Analysis of business volume—This involves keeping hourly and daily tallies of the numbers of **covers,** or customers, served. These figures can assist management in forecasting the number of employees needed to meet business volume. One way to calculate the number of customers is to use the **average cover formula.** Here, the total dollar sales for a period of time is divided by the number of customers served in the period. For example, $24,000 in sales divided by 3,000 customers results in an $8.00 average cover.

There are three ways to determine hourly average cover.

1. The host or hostess can count and record the number of customers seated in the dining room every hour, on the hour.
2. Guest checks or **dupes** (doops), duplicates of these guest checks, can be time-stamped as orders are given to the cooks.
3. The cashier can record the number of covers served as customers pay their checks.

After all the information has been gathered, managers should tabulate the hourly volume of business for a given day, as well

Exhibit 10.19
Sample job description.

JOB TITLE: Server

WORKING HOURS: Schedule for week posted each Friday. Hours and days vary each week.

JOB SUMMARY: Servers greet seated guests, take orders, serve food and drinks, present checks with last service, and clear/reset tables.

DUTIES:

1. Report to supervisor one hour before meal period to assist in preparing dining room for opening.
2. Pour water; take food and drink orders; place orders in kitchen and bar; pick-up and serve food and drink; present checks to guests; clear and reset tables.
3. Follow standard service procedures: serve food from guest's left; beverages from right. Remove all china, glassware, and silver from guest's right.
4. Attend daily briefing 15 minutes before the scheduled opening of the dining room to learn about daily specials, service techniques, and other matters of importance.
5. Pool all tips: 10% of the tip pool goes to bartenders; remainder is divided equally among servers. Tips are distributed the following day.
6. Provide own uniform, as follows. Black pants or skirt; white dress shirt with long sleeves and buttoned cuffs; black bow tie; polished black shoes with flat heels. No high heels. Servers will be given an allowance of $5.00 per week to care for their uniforms.
7. Standards for personal appearance:
   - Showered or bathed prior to work
   - Underarm deodorant required
   - Clean fingernails
   - Hair clean and neat
   - No excessive jewelry

MALES:

A. Clean shaven preferred. Moustache permitted if neat and trimmed.
B. No facial or ear jewelry.
C. Hair cannot extend beyond shirt collar.

FEMALES:

A. No excessive jewelry, make-up, or perfume.
B. Long hair must be in hair net.
C. No long false nails.

as for a series of days, such as Fridays. Then the numbers can be translated into a graph that shows the hourly volume of business over a specific period of time.

Once the three steps for work organization have been completed, managers can schedule both variable-cost and fixed-cost employees. To schedule variable-cost employees, managers must forecast total business volume on a daily basis, assigning employees to meet the anticipated demands.

Labor Cost Control Standards

Standards for controlling labor costs fall into two categories: quality standards and quantity standards. *Quality standards* are maintained through effective hiring, training, and employee development practices. *Quantity standards* are established by determining the number of times a task must be performed within a certain time period. One method, often conducted in operations where sales levels remain relatively the same, is to routinely look at staffing needs. Managers must use their memory to determine whether staffing has been adequate or if adjustments must be made.

A second, more accurate method requires information to be collected during a test period. Sales volume records, the number of covers served each day, and the number of people on duty in both the fixed-cost and variable-cost categories are analyzed. Charts can be prepared for the test period, and a table of employee requirements formulated. This table might show staff needs at various levels of business volume. **Standard employee hours,** or the number of employee work hours required in each job category to perform forecasted work, can be determined. Forecasted hours and actual hours worked can then be compared, allowing managers to evaluate the overall efficiency of labor.

Cost Control in the 21st Century

Computers will continue to play an important role in cost control into the 21st century—and beyond. Through the use of computerized cash registers, guest checks, and various software programs, today's foodservice manager has access to invaluable control tools. Two of the computer's most valuable control applications are monitoring operations in a timely manner and increasing control over employees' actions by requiring them to follow standard procedures.

According to studies by the National Restaurant Association, the use of online, computer-based financial systems for foodservice establishments will be widespread by the turn of the century. Managers will need to be computer proficient and able to use financial and accounting software. In return, computer-based financial systems will enable them to run their operations more efficiently and profitably.

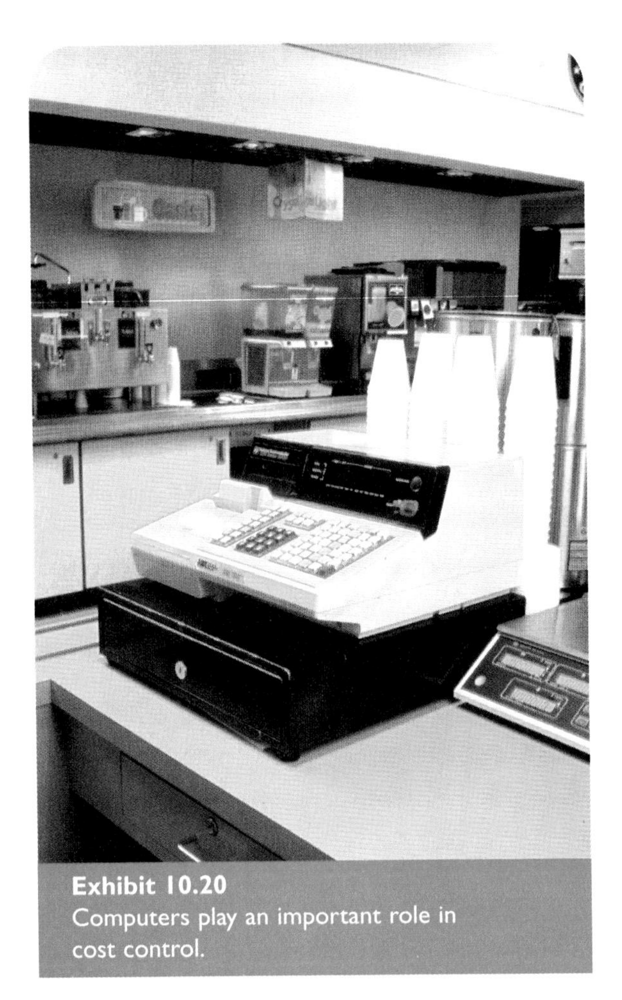

Exhibit 10.20
Computers play an important role in cost control.

It is predicted that, in the 21st century, what a manager gets paid will be directly linked to performance through bonus and incentive systems. This means that managers will have to take a greater responsibility for the bottom line results of their operations. Successful foodservice managers will be those who come armed with at least two essential tools: cost control techniques and business math skills.

Review Your Learning 10.5

1. How do managers determine their staffing needs?

2. One way that foodservice managers can prevent high turnover is to provide employees with:
   a. parking spaces.
   b. ongoing training.
   c. name badges.
   d. late-night hours.

3. A restaurant employs 75 people. In the past year, 21 have left. What is the establishment's employee turnover rate?

4. Give three examples of:
   a. fixed-cost employees.
   b. variable-cost employees.

5. Time-stamping dupes as orders are given to cooks is one way to determine:
   a. par stock.
   b. standard employee hours.
   c. hourly average cover.
   d. quantity standards.

Flashback

CHAPTER 10

SECTION 10.1: THE BASICS

- Successful foodservice managers need to have a basic understanding of math and know how to apply math principles to business operations.
- Math skills are also essential in the professional kitchen to determine recipe yields and convert recipes from U.S. standard to metric measures.
- Accurate budgeting, forecasting, and other cost control measures depend on the manager's ability to apply basic mathematical formulas.

SECTION 10.2: WEIGHTS AND MEASURES

- Cooking and baking require exact weighing and measuring of ingredients to ensure consistent quality and minimal waste.
- Most recipes can be successfully doubled, but larger equipment may be required and cooking times often need adjustment.
- In the **metric system,** each measurement is based on multiples of 10.
- Since most vegetables must be trimmed and cut before being used in recipes, the **edible portion (EP)** amount must be calculated, given the **as purchased (AP)** amount.
- Other factors that are essential in quantity food production are standard recipe costs and cost per serving. To find the total cost of a standard recipe, you must know both the ingredient amounts needed and the market price of each one. Then multiply or divide the ingredient amounts by the prices.
- Ingredient costs are usually rounded off to the nearest cent. Portion costs are ordinarily carried out to 1/10 of a cent. Many operations price out all recipes and then check them every six months to see whether they are still accurate.

SECTION 10.3: CONTROLLING FOOD COSTS

- **Cost control** is necessary in every area of the foodservice operation: purchasing, receiving, storage, issuing, and preparation/production.
- In the *purchasing* function, the proper kind of food and its cost, quantity, and quality must be determined. The right supplier should be found. If the wrong kind, quantity, or quality of food is bought at the wrong cost, the operation will lose money.
- The primary purpose of *receiving* control is to verify that the items received match the orders placed.
- *Storage* procedures must be carefully controlled so that there will be no loss as a result of spoilage, contamination, or employee theft. Key elements in storage control include temperature, storage containers, shelving, cleanliness, food item location, storage facility location, and stock rotation.
- To control the cost of food moving into preparation/production, product **issuing** must be exact.
- *Preparation and production* are usually controlled by the use of standardized recipes and by following proper kitchen procedures.
- The successful foodservice manager is able to closely monitor operating costs and, based on these costs, to adjust the manner in which the establishment operates. An understanding of the relationship between cost and sales, along with realistic planning and forecasting, is vital to the profitability of any foodservice operation.
- In the foodservice industry, **cost** is the price to an operation of goods or services when the goods are received or the services are rendered. There are various categories of costs—fixed and variable, controllable and noncontrollable, unit and total, and historical and planned.
- **Fixed costs** do not change when sales increase or decrease. **Variable costs** are directly related to business volume.
- Foods for purchase can be categorized as **perishables** or **nonperishables.**
- Since the goals of food control include determining food cost as accurately as possible and matching food cost with food sales, it is also necessary to keep records of the cost of the food transferred. A transfer of food items between two areas of the same stablishment is called an *intraunit* transfer. An *interunit* transfer might

occur between two locations of one food chain.

- There are two methods used to control food inventory. **Perpetual inventory** is taken through the use of continuous records of requisitions. **Physical inventory** requires actually counting items on hand at the end of each month. With either method, the closing inventory value is used to calculate the cost of goods sold for the month.

SECTION 10.4: FOOD PRODUCTION

- Establishing food production standards helps reduce customer discontent, eliminate excessive costs, and ensure that all kitchen employees have needed production information readily available.
- In addition to direct monitoring techniques, customers' reactions are a good way to determine whether employees are using portion standards. All customer complaints should be investigated immediately.
- Portion control includes the standardization of portion sizes, recipes, and portion costs. Among the many kitchen tools available to help foodservice operators standardize portions are *scoops, slotted spoons, ladles, portion scales,* and *measuring cups.* Since the cost of food items varies with the quantity served, the cost of any item will be proportional to the quantity served to the customer.
- **Forecasting** is a procedure in which data are used to predict what is likely to occur in the future. This educated guesswork is highly valuable in the foodservice industry and can be a major factor in profitable operations and cost control. When sales volume has been accurately predicted, necessary adjustments in purchasing and production can be made, reducing waste, spoilage, and overproduction.
- The completed forecast represents management's best estimate of anticipated sales volume. With accurate predications, labor and purchasing costs can be controlled more effectively.

SECTION 10.5: LABOR COST CONTROL

- The cost of labor in the hospitality industry can range from 15 to 45 percent. In some nonprofit operations, labor cost percentages are as high as 60 percent. Maintaining control over these costs is essential.

- Labor cost control is the process by which managers try to obtain a desired level of performance at an appropriate level of cost. Labor cost control is more than the mere reduction of payroll costs; it requires hiring and keeping well-qualified employees at a fair wage.
- Planning and organizing help to divide the workload evenly and lead to positive communication among employees and managers.
- Staffing involves determining how many employees will be needed to get a job done. **Employee turnover** is the ratio of employees who leave to total employees.
- There are three steps in the work organization process: 1) establish an operational plan; 2) prepare job descriptions; and 3) prepare an analysis of business volume.
- Computers play an important role in cost control. Computerized cash registers, guest checks, and different software programs are easy-to-use control tools for foodservice managers. Two of the computer's most valuable control applications are monitoring operations in a timely manner and increasing control over employees' actions by requiring adherence to established standard procedures.

Joseph Stubbs

Director of Foodservice Sales
Sunkist Growers
Sherman Oaks, California

Sunkist began more than 100 years ago as a cooperative of orange, lemon, and grapefruit farmers. It's grown to be such a large company that it now has its own Foodservice Sales department to oversee how products are sold, shipped, and packaged for restaurants and other foodservice operations.

I began my career in hospitality as a bell hop at a Marriott hotel. I got into the food business as a butcher, later finding my way to Sunkist as a sales director.

This is a very old, consumer-friendly company. It's my job to see that my customers—foodservice managers—get what they want and need in fresh fruits. Knowledgeable managers are in a position to share with Sunkist new ideas for packaging, uses for their products, and ways to ensure high quality. There are so many creative people in the restaurant business. It's an industry full of entrepreneurs. To succeed, you just have to have a feel for what people want, and give it to them.

Our department caters to a very choosy group of customers. Restaurant managers and owners know what they need, when they need it, and how it must be handled both before and after it arrives at their operation. If Sunkist, and I, don't meet those customer needs, we'll be out of business.

The food business is always changing. We provide the best-quality products we can for the best price we can offer. My job's not always easy, but it's always fun because I'm part of an exciting industry. Eating out is a great pleasure to people, and I love being a part of it.

CHAPTER 11

Fruits and Vegetables

SECTION 11.1

Identifying Fruits

AFTER STUDYING SECTION 11.1, YOU SHOULD BE ABLE TO:

- Identify, describe, and demonstrate the preparation of different types of fruits.

Scientifically speaking, a **fruit** is an organ that develops from the ovary of a flowering plant and contains one or more seeds. From a culinary point of view, a fruit is the perfect snack food, the basis of a dessert, colorful sauce, or soup, or an accompaniment to meat, fish, shellfish, or poultry. In fact, no food group offers a greater variety of colors, flavors, and textures than fruit.

KEY TERMS

- **Clingstone**
- **Drupe (droop)**
- **Freestone**
- **Fructose (FROOK-tose)**
- **Fruit**
- **Summer fruit**
- **Tropical fruit**
- **Winter fruit**

Fruits are both delicious and nutritious—they are refreshing and are an excellent source of dietary fiber. The sweetness of fruits comes from **fructose** (FROOK-tose), a natural form of sugar. Fruit is often used in sweet dishes, such as puddings, pies, and jellies. Fruits can be found in salads, appetizers, eaten as snacks, and served in soups. They are even used to cut the richness of meats like pork and duck, and to brighten the delicate flavor of fish and veal.

Fruits are classified by growing season and location. The three main groups of fruit are *summer, winter,* and *tropical.*

SUMMER FRUITS

Summer fruits include berries, cherries, grapes, melons, peaches, nectarines, plums, and pears. Most summer fruits are delicious raw, and they are also popular baked or cooked in different foods.

Of the summer fruits, *berries* are the most highly perishable, tender, and fragile. Varieties include blueberries, raspberries and blackberries, boysenberries, and strawberries. The best way to work with berries is to handle them very little and serve them as soon as possible.

Cherries, available in numerous varieties, come in many shades of red, from the light crimson of the Queen Anne cherry to the very dark, almost black Bing cherry. They vary in texture from hard and crisp, to soft and juicy. Cherry flavors run from very tart to very sweet. The most popular varieties are sweet dark cherries; tart light-red cherries (Montmorence) are also popular and are best used as maraschino cherries, candied, or canned for baking. Cherries, along with *plums, peaches, nectarines,* and *apricots,* are called **drupes** (droops) because they have a central pit enclosing a single seed.

Cherries are native to the upper Midwest, along the eastern shores of Lake Michigan. Traverse City, Michigan, is the cherry capital, and celebrates the harvest with a cherry festival every July.

Exhibit 11.1
The tender, sweet strawberry is a popular summer fruit.

Grapes, another summer fruit, grow in clusters on vines. They are available with or without seeds. Technically, grapes are berries, but because they come in so many varieties and have so many uses (including eating, cooking, and wine making), grapes are grouped separately. Two of the most popular varieties are

California Seedless, which are suitable for both cooking and eating raw, and Napoleon Red, a good table variety. Like all fresh fruit, grapes must be washed thoroughly to remove all traces of industrial insecticides.

Besides being sweet, tender, and colorful, melons of all kinds are nutritionally packed with many essential vitamins and minerals. For example, cantaloupe is a terrific source of vitamin A and ascorbic acid. Ascorbic acid is a form of vitamin C, and is necessary to absorb iron into the body. It also helps lower blood cholesterol levels. So, treat yourself to some fresh melon for breakfast, as a snack, or for dessert with some ice cream!

Unlike berries and drupes, melons are a fruit related to vegetables: squash and cucumbers. *Melons* are succulent, fragrant fruits and come in many varieties and sizes. Melons are easily categorized into two groups: sweet melons and watermelons. Popular sweet melons are *cantaloupe (muskmelon), crenshaw,* and *honeydew.* Sweet melons are characterized by their tan, green, or yellow skin. The rind is very tough and the flesh is rich and flavorful. These melons have a network of seeds in the center that are taken out before eating.

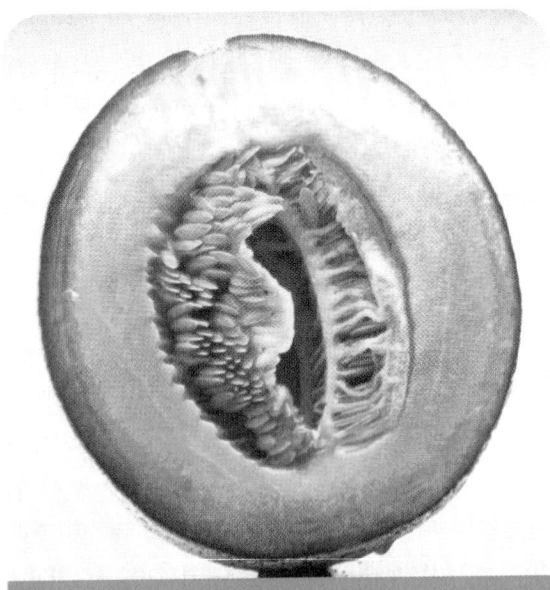

Exhibit 11.2
The bright orange color and network of seeds identify this melon as a cantaloupe.

Unlike sweet melons, *watermelons* have a smooth, thick green skin, and are much larger in size. The flesh of watermelons is deep pink with a light crisp texture and seeds are found scattered throughout the melon. Melons can be served as appetizers, salads, or desserts. They are very attractive when cut into decorative shapes for use in fruit trays, salads, and garnishes.

Peaches, also a drupe, are sweet and juicy, with a distinctive fuzzy skin. There are two categories of peaches: freestone and clingstone. The flesh of **freestone** peaches separates easily from the pit, while **clingstone** peaches have flesh that clings to the pit. Peach flesh varies in color, from white, to creamy yellow, to yellow-orange, to red.

Apricots resemble peaches with their fuzzy skin, but they are smaller and slightly drier. *Nectarines* are similar to peaches in color, shape, and flavor, but they have smooth skin, with flesh that resembles the texture of plums. These fruits are all delicious, low in calories, and high in fiber. Peaches, nectarines, and apricots are available fresh, frozen, canned, dried, preserved, and as juice.

Plums, a very popular fruit, range in size from as small as an apricot to as large as a peach. They come in many shades of green, red, and purple. There are two categories of plums: *dessert* and *cooking*. Cooking plums are generally drier and more acidic than dessert plums, but both types can be eaten raw.

Pears are well liked because of their sweet taste and smooth, juicy flesh. Pears are available in many varieties, but the most common are *Bartlett, Bosc, d'Anjou,* and *Seckel.* Pears do not ripen entirely on the tree. They are usually picked and left to continue ripening. A properly ripened pear will have a good fragrance and be tender on the stem end.

Exhibit 11.3
Peaches have a distinctive fuzzy skin and sweet juicy flavor.

The state that grows the most peaches is not Georgia, but California. California also produces the most grapes in the nation.

Winter Fruits

Though summer fruits are abundant, winter also offers a good selection of fruits that provide plenty of nutrition and great taste. **Winter fruits** include citrus fruits and apples. *Citrus fruits* are characterized by thick skins, aromatic oils, and segmented flesh. They are also abundant in vitamin C. The most common citrus fruits are oranges, grapefruits, lemons, limes, tangelos, and tangerines.

The flavor of citrus fruits ranges from a very sweet orange to a very tart, sour lemon.

All citrus fruits can be served fresh, candied, and as juice; as appetizers, garnishes, and desserts; or as part of salads or main dishes.

Apples, also a winter fruit, are among the most commonly used and available fruits. *Red Delicious, Golden Delicious, Rome, McIntosh,* and *Granny Smith* are the most popular varieties. The flavor of apples ranges from very tart, like the Granny Smith, to very sweet, like the Golden Delicious. Tart apples are used for cooking and baking. Sweet apples are best when eaten raw. Exhibit 11.5 shows selected apple varieties and their uses.

Exhibit 11.4
Pink grapefruit is usually sweeter than white grapefruit.

Who doesn't love a banana split? Or how about bananas on cereal, or peanut butter and banana sandwiches? Bananas are everywhere, and are one of the most popular fruits eaten in America today, and for good reason. They are packed with vitamins, and are a great source of carbohydrate. Carbohydrate is what gives us energy, and allows us to do all of the things we enjoy.

Tropical Fruits

Tropical fruits are named for the climatic conditions under which they are grown, and include figs, dates, kiwis, mangos, bananas, papayas, pomegranates, and passion fruit.

Bananas are the most common of the tropical fruits. Unlike most fruits, bananas are picked almost green and allowed to ripen as they travel from the farm to the buyer. Bananas are rich in carbohydrates, fiber, vitamins, minerals, and potassium. Fully ripe bananas are excellent for eating and baking. Green bananas can be used for cooking.

Figs, a very versatile fruit, are green or black and are best when they are eaten raw. Often they are used in baking pies,

Exhibit 11.5
Selected apple varieties.

Variety	Color	Flavor and Texture	Peak Season	Uses
Red Delicious, Golden Delicious	Red or golden-yellow with blush	Sweet, semi-firm	September to May	All-purpose
Granny Smith	Green	Crisp, tart	April to July	All-purpose
Greening, Rhode Island, North West	Green	Firm, mild, tart-sweet	October to March	Pie, sauce, bake, freeze
Jonathan	Bright red with some yellow-green	Tender, tart, flavorful	September to January	Fresh, pie, sauce, freeze
McIntosh	Red with some yellow-green	Tender, semi-tart	September to June	Fresh, pie, sauce, bake, freeze
Rome Beauty	Bright red	Firm, mild, tart-sweet	October to June	All-purpose
Winesap	Bright red with some yellow-green	Firm, tart-sweet, flavorful	October to June	Fresh, freeze, pie, sauce, bake

cookies, and cakes. Figs can be purchased fresh, candied, or dried.

Kiwis have a fuzzy skin and bright green-colored flesh that make them a very unique fruit. The inside has tiny edible seeds, and the flavor can be similar to that of strawberries. Kiwis are excellent as garnish or for adding color and texture to fruit salads.

Mangos are medium-sized, thick-skinned fruits. They have a light yellow flesh, and a spicy-sweet flavor. They are an excellent addition to fruit salads, and go well with spices, such as curry.

Papayas have a soft, juicy, pink-orange flesh with a central mass of black seeds. Papayas are an excellent source of vitamins A and C, and their content of vitamin C increases as they ripen. Ripe papayas can be eaten raw, and unripened papayas can be cooked and served like vegetables. Freezing papayas destroys their flavor and texture.

A very popular tropical fruit is the *pineapple.* It can be purchased fresh or canned in its own juices or in a heavy syrup. This fruit is often used in baking, and can be puréed to make fresh pineapple juice.

Exhibit 11.6
Fresh kiwis make an excellent addition to fruit salads.

While *coconuts* are native to Malaysia, they now grow in South America, India, Hawaii, and throughout the islands of the Pacific Ocean. The coconut has several layers. Its outermost layer is a smooth, light brown covering that is usually removed before shipping. Next is the familiar dark brown, hairy shell. Beneath that is a thin brown skin covering the bright white meat. Coconut meat is eaten raw, cooked in many dessert recipes, and pressed to make coconut oil. In the center is the juice. Coconut milk is not the juice from the center, but is a simmered mixture of water and coconut meat.

A ripe coconut should be heavy and sound full of liquid when shaken. Whole, unopened coconuts can be stored at room temperature for up to six months.

Exhibit 11.7 on the next page lists several fresh fruits and their signs of quality.

FUN FOOD FACT

The food we most associate with Hawaii—the pineapple—is not native to Hawaii at all. It was brought to Hawaii from Central and South America by Portuguese sailors and pirates.

Exhibit 11.7
Characteristics of fresh fruit.

Fruit	Signs of Good Quality	Signs of Poor Quality, Spoilage
Apples	Firmness; crispness; bright color	Softness; bruises. (Irregularly shaped brown or tan areas do not usually affect quality)
Apricots	Bright, uniform color; plumpness	Dull color; shriveled appearance
Bananas	Firmness; brightness of color	Grayish or dull appearance (indicates exposure to cold and inability to ripen properly)
Blueberries	Dark blue color with silvery bloom	Moist berries
Cantaloupes	Stem should be gone; netting or veining should be coarse; skin should be yellow-gray or pale yellow	Bright yellow color; mold; large bruises
Cherries	Very dark color; plumpness	Dry stems; soft flesh; gray mold
Coconuts	Liquid inside when shaken; hard shell	Cracks; wet "eyes"
Figs	Plumpness	Soft areas; dull color
Grapefruit	Should be heavy for its size	Soft areas; dull color
Grapes	Should be firmly attached to stems. Bright color and plumpness are good signs	Drying stems; leaking berries
Honeydew	Soft skin; faint aroma; yellowish white to creamy rind color	White or greenish color; bruises or watersoaked areas; cuts or punctures in rind
Lemons	Firmness; heaviness; rich yellow color	Dull color; shriveled skin
Limes	Glossy skin; heavy weight	Dry skin; molds
Mangos	Plumpness; firmness	Clear color; blemishes
Nectarines	Plumpness; firmness	Green skin; very hard or soft skin
Oranges	Firmness; heaviness; bright color	Dry skin; spongy texture; blue mold
Papayas	Firmness; symmetry	Dark green skin; bruises
Peaches	Slightly soft flesh	A pale tan spot (indicates beginning of decay); very hard or very soft flesh
Pears	Firmness	Dull skin; shriveling; spots on the sides
Pineapples	"Spike" at top should separate easily from flesh	Mold; large bruises; unpleasant odor; brown leaves
Plums	Fairly firm to slightly soft flesh	Leaking; brownish discoloration
Raspberries	Stem caps should be absent; flesh should be plump and tender	Mushiness; wet spots on containers (signs of possible decay of berries)
Strawberries	Stem cap should be attached; berries should have a rich red color	Gray mold; large uncolored areas
Tangerines	Bright orange or deep yellow color; loose skin	Punctured skin; mold
Watermelon	Smooth surface; creamy underside; bright red flesh	Stringy or mealy flesh (spoilage difficult to see on outside)

Source: Applied Foodservice Sanitation, Fourth Edition. Copyright© 1992 by The Educational Foundation of the National Restaurant Association, Chicago, IL.

Review Your Learning 11.1

1. Match the fruit on the left with the appropriate category to which it belongs on the right. Letters may be used more than once.

Peach	a. Tropical
Grapefruit	b. Summer
Fig	c. Winter
Cherry	
Kiwi	
Apple	
Coconut	
Papaya	
Grape	
Tangerine	

2. Find the correct words from Section 11.1 to complete the following sentences.
   a. Fruit contains a natural from of sugar, called ________________ that gives it its natural sweetness and flavor.
   b. Cherries, plums, peaches, and nectarines, are known as ________________ because they contain a single seed enclosed by a pit in the center of the fruit.
   c. Two categories of peaches are ________________ and ________________.

3. Using your cafeteria as an example, how are some of the fruits in this section most commonly presented and served?

11.2

SECTION 11.2

Identifying Vegetables

AFTER STUDYING SECTION 11.2, YOU SHOULD BE ABLE TO:

- Identify, describe, and demonstrate the preparation of different types of vegetables.

A **vegetable** is an edible herb-like plant. The parts of vegetables that we eat include the leaves, fruit, stems, roots, tubers, seeds, and flowers. Unlike fruits, vegetables are most often eaten cooked. Vegetables are often categorized by their botanical origins. In this chapter, however, we will categorize vegetables by their edible parts. The categories of vegetables we will discuss in this chapter are flower, fruit, green leafy, seed, roots and tubers, and stem vegetables.

Flower Vegetables

Flower vegetables include broccoli, cauliflower, Brussels sprouts, and cabbage. They are called flower vegetables because the flower of the plant (floret) and the attached stems are eaten.

KEY TERMS

- Babaganoush (bah-bah-gahn-OOSH)
- Crudité (croo-dee-TAY)
- Flower vegetable
- Fruit vegetable
- Fungi (FUN-ghee)
- Green leafy vegetable
- Root vegetable
- Seed vegetable
- Stem vegetable
- Tempura (tem-POO-rah)
- Tuber
- Vegetable

Exhibit 11.8
Broccoli is a popular and nutritious flower vegetable.

To prepare *broccoli,* cut the stems lengthwise and cook them with the heads attached. This ensures that the cooking times for both the stems and the florets are the same.

Cauliflower is often cooked by steaming, stir-frying, or as an ingredient in stews and **tempura** (tem-POO-rah), which are Japanese-style breaded and deep-fried vegetables. It can also be served with cheese sauce, lemon juice, or tartar sauce. Broccoli and cauliflower can be served either raw or cooked, and are often used as salad ingredients and as **crudités** (croo-dee-TAY), or raw vegetables.

Cabbage is used often in coleslaw or stir-fried. Its thick, waxy leaves lay tight together and form a large, round head. *Brussels sprouts* resemble miniature cabbage, and grow on a thick stalk. Brussels sprouts are best roasted or steamed.

Fruit Vegetables

Fruit vegetables include avocados, cucumbers, eggplants, peppers, squash, and tomatoes. With the exception of eggplant, these vegetables are usually served raw.

Exhibit 11.9
The thick, waxy green leaves of cabbage stand up well in stir-frying and in soups.

Flower vegetables such as broccoli, cauliflower, and Brussels sprouts are a great source of vitamin C. Each cup serving contains at least 70 milligrams of vitamin C. What does vitamin C do for you? It helps the body heal wounds, promotes absorption of iron into the body, and protects against injury and infection.

Avocados have green or black leathery skin. Their flavor is rich and buttery. Avocados are usually served with lime or lemon juice to prevent the flesh from turning brown. Guacamole (gwak-ah-MOE-lee), a favorite traditional Mexican dip, uses mashed avocados as the main ingredient.

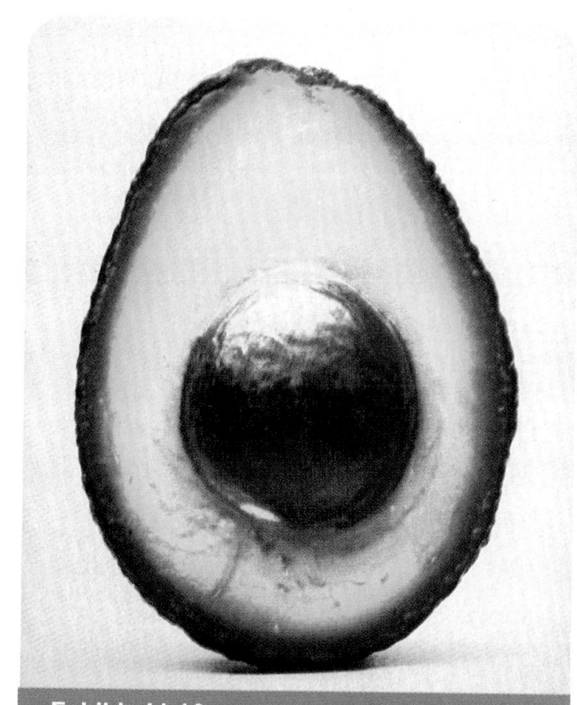

Exhibit 11.10
The avocado has a rich, buttery flavor and is often used in salads, and mixed with spices to make Guacamole.

Eggplants are purple-black, glossy, firm vegetables that usually range from 10 to 12 inches long. Eggplant is always served cooked, never raw. **Babaganoush** (BAH-bah-gahn-OOSH), a Middle Eastern dip, uses eggplant as the main ingredient. Eggplant is also used in Greek cooking.

Bell or *sweet peppers* are named for their shape. All varieties start out green, but as they ripen, their color changes to red, green, yellow, cream, or purple. Bell peppers can be served raw, as a seasoning in other dishes, or as a main entrée. *Chili peppers* are in the same family as bell peppers, but they are smaller and much hotter. Most of the hot, spicy flavor is in the seeds, so seeded chili peppers are not quite as hot as whole chili peppers. These can be purchased fresh, canned, and dried. Both bell and chili peppers are also an excellent source of vitamin C.

Squash is classified as either winter squash or summer squash. Some popular varieties of winter squash include butternut, acorn, spaghetti, banana,

Exhibit 11.11
Winter squash have hard shells and large seeds.

hubbard, and pumpkin. Winter squash generally have hard shells and large seeds. These vegetables are often baked, steamed, or sautéed.

Summer squash include yellow crookneck, pattypan, and zucchini. Unlike winter squash, summer squash is much smaller with soft skin and small seeds that are eaten. Though summer squash is good raw, it can also be grilled, sautéed, steamed, or baked. Most types of squash are available fresh, frozen, or canned.

Cucumbers range from 10 to 12 inches long, but some varieties can be as long as three feet! Cucumbers are made mostly of water; this makes them crisp, low in calories, and high in taste. Cucumbers are excellent in salads or when served with a dip. Cucumbers are an especially popular vegetable used in Middle Eastern cooking.

The *tomato* is really a type of berry and is grown in hundreds of varieties, ranging in colors from green, to yellow, to bright red. Tomatoes are at their best when they are vine-ripened. The versatile tomato is a colorful and nutritious addition to many dishes, and a popular ingredient in salads. Sliced tomatoes are also commonly served alone, seasoned with a dash of salt or pepper. Tomatoes may be stewed, fried, grilled, baked, pickled, boiled, or made into sauce or juice. The size of a tomato determines how it is used.

- Large green tomatoes are best for frying.
- Jumbo red tomatoes are good plain, stuffed, or baked.
- Medium-sized tomatoes are good for slicing.
- Overripe tomatoes are excellent in stews, sauces, and casseroles.

Green Leafy Vegetables

Green leafy vegetables include various types of lettuce, mustard greens,

Exhibit 11.12
When they are ripe, fresh tomatoes should be plump and have a bright, smooth, shiny skin.

Although the tomato was grown in North and South America for centuries, it did not gain popularity in the United States until President Thomas Jefferson began promoting it to his colleagues in the late 1700s. In fact many Americans believed the tomato was poisionous.

spinach, and swiss chard. Green leafy vegetables are very high in vitamins A and C, iron, and magnesium. With the exception of lettuce, most green leafy vegetables can be purchased fresh, frozen, or canned.

Lettuce has been a part of the human diet for over 2,000 years. It is grown all over the world. The most common types of lettuce are iceberg, romaine, and leaf.

The light-green leaves of *iceberg lettuce* are tightly packed together. Its mild flavor makes it good to use in salads and as a garnish for sandwiches. Unlike iceberg lettuce, both *romaine* and *leaf lettuce* are loosely packed. Their leaves grow upward in bunches, and their edges are slightly ruffled. Leaf lettuce has a milder flavor than romaine lettuce, and is also good in salads. The crisp, more flavorful romaine lettuce is often used in Caesar salad.

Mustard greens have a bitter, strong flavor. The leaves are usually dark green and are served raw, in salads, or lightly sautéed with vinegar and herbs. *Spinach* is one of the most versatile greens used in cooking. From soups, to salad, to casseroles, its high nutrient content and tart flavor make it a great addition to any meal.

Popeye knew it and so do we! Spinach is one of the most nutritious green leafy vegetables around. It is low in calories and packed with many vitamins and minerals, mainly vitamin A and vitamin K. Vitamin A is a water-soluble vitamin that helps strengthen eyes and prevent eye diseases. Vitamin K is essential to blood clotting. Make it a part of your diet!

Exhibit 11.13
Spinach is one of the most versatile greens used in cooking.

Swiss chard is actually a type of beet that does not have a root. It produces dark green wide leaves that are often steamed, sautéed, and used in soups. Like spinach, it has a rich, tart flavor.

Seed Vegetables

Seed vegetables include corn, peas, and beans. They are most flavorful and sweet when they are eaten young and fresh. Once these vegetables are picked, they begin to convert their natural sugars into starch. They can lose their sweetness as soon as one day after being harvested; after a few days, they become mealy. Most seed vegetables are available fresh, frozen, or canned.

Sweet corn, served on the cob, can be grilled or boiled. It should be served very soon after it is picked; otherwise its natural sugars will begin to turn to starch, making the corn less sweet and much chewier. Flavors vary among the white, yellow, and bicolored varieties. Corn is available fresh on the cob, frozen, and canned. *Popcorn* is a variety of corn grown especially for its small ears and pointed kernels that explode when heated.

The most common *peas* are green garden peas. They have a sweet, delicate flavor, and are best when steamed. They are also a colorful addition to salads, soups, and as a garnish.

Beans are another seed vegetable. Fresh beans include green beans, yellow wax beans, and French haricot verts (HAIR-ee-ko VAIR). These beans are small, and are most often eaten while still

How did Bibb lettuce get its name? Major John Bibb was born in Virginia in 1789. After moving to Kentucky, he spent his life experimenting with plants. The lettuce variety he cultivated, and that bears his name, has a delicate buttery flavor, and is very sweet and tender.

Though small and delicate, green peas definitely provide their fair share of nutritional value. Like spinach and many other vegetables, peas are a good source of vitamin A. They also contain calcium, phosphorus, and potassium. The role that potassium plays in the diet is important. It helps the heart and other major muscle groups to contract, which keeps us going strong!

in the pod, or long, outer shell. *Lima* beans and *fava* beans are examples of beans that are shelled, or removed from the pod. They are larger and more firm than green beans, and stand up well to cooking. Beans of all kinds are very good sautéed, steamed, or microwaved. They add flavor and color to soups, salads, and as nutritious side dishes.

Root and Tuber Vegetables

Root vegetables and tubers are grouped together because part, or all, of the plant is grown underground. **Root vegetables** are rich in sugars, starches, vitamins, and minerals, and exist both above and below ground. A single root extends into the ground and provides nutrients to the part of the vegetable that is above the ground. Some common root vegetables are carrots, beets, radishes, turnips, and onion.

Carrots contain a large amount of carotene, a pigment easily convertible to vitamin A. Carrots can be served raw, as crudités, and as a garnish or ingredient in salads, soups, and desserts. Cooked carrots make excellent side dishes. Carrots are available fresh, frozen, or canned.

Beets were originally grown for their tops, not their roots; today, however, the roots are by far more commonly used. Smaller beets are preferred to larger ones for two reasons: their appearance is better, and they cook faster than larger beets. Beets are available fresh, frozen, or canned. Canned beets can be purchased

Exhibit 11.14
Sweet corn, or corn on the cob, is a common seed vegetable.

sliced, diced, quartered, julienned (cut into small thin strips), and whole. Beets are a popular, colorful item in salads. Pickled beets add spice and zest to salads or to a side dish.

Radishes are small, round roots that are available in many colors, from deep red to pale cream. Their crisp texture and peppery flavor make them a flavorful and colorful addition to salads, or they can be decoratively cut as a garnish or an appetizer with vegetable dip.

Like radishes, *turnips* have a hot, peppery flavor that is best when baked. They are larger than radishes, and usually have a rose-colored skin and bright white flesh.

Onions are worldwide favorites. All varieties of onions have a pungent flavor and aroma, and can be used as seasonings. Common, or *bulb onions,* like white, yellow, or red, are best when sliced or chopped for use in stuffing or casseroles. Small onions, like *pearl onions,* are best for boiling or cooking with roasts and stews. They can also be prepared whole and served as a side dish.

Green onions, or *scallions,* are actually common onions that are pulled before they are mature. The slender, dark green leaves are attached to the thick white bulb. *Shallots* are shaped like small bulb onions. They separate into small cloves when broken apart. Their mild flavor makes them a great addition to meat dishes and sauces. *Leeks* resemble large green onions. They have the mildest flavor in the onion family, are best when baked or grilled, and are often used in stocks, sauces, and soups.

Exhibit 11.15
The purple onion is a variety of common, or bulb onion.

Tuber vegetables include potatoes, sweet potatoes, and yams. **Tubers** are enlarged, bulbous roots capable of generating a new plant. Tubers are actually fat, underground stems.

Potatoes are the world's most popular vegetable. Did you know that potatoes are

Onions have been a staple in people's diets since 2800 B.C. People have used them in religious ceremonies as symbols of fertility, and fed them to armies because they believed they possessed strength-giving powers.

served daily in over 60 percent of households in the United States? Potatoes are versatile and can be cooked many ways. The most common potatoes are the long russet, long white, round russet, round white, and round red.

A more unique but equally popular potato is the sweet potato. Native to the New World, the *sweet potato* has darker flesh than the white potato because of its higher sugar content. Its thick skin is not usually eaten. Sweet potatoes are best when boiled, baked, or puréed for soups. All potato varieties are a good source of vitamin A, vitamin C, iron, and thiamin.

Yams are often compared to sweet potatoes. However, the yam is not as sweet as the sweet potato. Its flesh ranges in color, from deep red to creamy white. Originally from Asia, yams are now grown in the Southern U.S.

Exhibit 11.16
Yams are a thick tuber that are often confused with the sweet potato.

Stem Vegetables

Stem vegetables include asparagus, celery, artichokes, and mushrooms. *Asparagus* was originally grown in Europe. Asparagus is best steamed while standing upright in a pot, with the tips on top. Asparagus is available fresh, canned, and frozen.

Like asparagus, *celery* was also originally grown in Europe. Green, leafy stalks of celery are familiar ingredients in salads, soups, stews, and as a garnish in tomato juice. In addition, its crispness and sturdy stalks make celery an excellent appetizer, either stuffed or served with dip.

Mushrooms come in many shapes, sizes, and colors. Though many varieties are perfectly safe to eat, there are some that can cause severe illness, or even death if eaten. Mushrooms should always be purchased from a reputable vendor, and should never be picked in the wild.

Artichokes are the immature flowers of a thistle plant brought to America by Italian and Spanish settlers. Young, tender globe artichokes can be cooked whole; more mature artichokes need to have the fuzzy center (known as the choke) removed first. Whole artichokes can be simmered, steamed, or microwaved. Often they are served with lemon juice, garlic butter, or hollandaise sauce. The artichoke heart may be cooked separately, then served in salads, puréed as a filling, or served as a side dish. Artichoke hearts are available fresh and canned.

Mushrooms are a family of fungi, many of which are edible. **Fungi** (FUN-ghee) are a large group of plants ranging from single-celled organisms to giant mushrooms. While both cultivated and wild mushrooms are available, it is important to purchase wild varieties from reliable vendors to avoid getting poisonous ones. The flavor of mushrooms ranges from delicate and fruity, to pungent and garlicky. Mushrooms are available fresh, frozen, canned, or dehydrated. They are served raw with dips and in salads, deep-fried, and cooked in a variety of sauces, soups, stews, and stir-fry recipes.

Artichokes are one of the oldest cultivated vegetables. Early French settlers brought artichoke seeds to the United States in the 17th century. Today, Castroville, California, is known as the artichoke capital of the world.

Review Your Learning 11.2

1. On a separate sheet of paper, match the vegetable on the left with the appropriate category on the right. Some letters will be used more than once.

Eggplant	a. Stem vegetable
Corn	b. Green leafy vegetable
Mushroom	c. Seed vegetable
Sweet potato	d. Fruit vegetable
Onion	e. Root vegetable
Mustard green	f. Flower vegetable
Broccoli	g. Tuber vegetable
Carrot	
Spinach	
Brussels sprout	

2. How are squash usually classified? Give some examples.

3. How are roots and tubers alike? How are they different? Give some examples of each.

4. Using a recipe from your family, explain how one of the vegetables discussed in this chapter is used.

SECTION 11.3

Purchasing and Storing Fruits and Vegetables

AFTER STUDYING SECTION 11.3, YOU SHOULD BE ABLE TO:

- List and explain the USDA quality grades for fresh fruits and vegetables.
- Demonstrate the procedures for properly storing ripe fruits, vegetables, roots, and tubers.
- Summarize ways to prevent fruits and vegetables from spoiling too quickly.

KEY TERMS

- **Ethylene (ETH-el-leen) gas**
- **Hydroponic (hi-droh-PON-ick) farming**
- **Quality grade**

How do you know when fruits and vegetables are fresh and of a high quality? Characteristics of freshness vary from one item to another, but there are some common traits. Fruits and vegetables should be plump and free of bruises, mold, brown or soft spots, and pest damage. Any attached leaves should be firm and not wilted. Overall, the color and texture should be appropriate to the particular type of fruit or vegetable.

QUALITY GRADES

The United States Department of Agriculture, or USDA, has developed quality grades for fresh fruits and vegetables, as well as for canned fruits and vegetables. **Quality grades** are like a rating system based on quality standards—the better the quality, the higher the quality grade assigned to it. USDA grades (from highest to lowest) for fresh fruits include *U.S. Extra Fancy, U.S. Fancy, U.S. No. 1, U.S. No. 2,* and *U.S. No. 3.*

Storing Fresh Fruits and Vegetables

- Produce must be delivered without any signs of spoilage, mold, or insects.
- Do not pinch, squeeze, or handle them unnecessarily.

While fresh fruits are graded before shipping, grading for fresh vegetables is voluntary. This means that produce growers and vendors are not required to give a grade to the food products. The major trading grade is *U.S. No. 1,* which means average quality. Lower graded items, particularly fruits, can be used in dishes such as baked pies, puddings, and cobblers where their appearance is not important.

Canned products rated *U.S. Grade A Fancy* have the highest quality, which means that their colors and flavors are excellent; the sizes and shapes are perfectly uniform. *U.S. Grade B Choice* are rated second best, which means that their overall colors and flavors are average. *U.S. Grade C Standard* means that the quality is poor. Some of the pieces may be bruised and mushy and have several imperfections.

Storing Produce

All produce must be properly stored. Roots and tubers should be stored dry and unpeeled in a cool, dark area. Other ripe fruits and vegetables (except for bananas) should be kept under refrigeration at temperatures of 40°F to 45°F (4.4°C to 7.2°C), with a relative humidity of 80 to 110 percent. Under the best circumstances, fruits should be stored separately in one refrigerator and vegetables stored in another.

Exhibit 11.17
Fresh produce is always given a quality food grade by the USDA.

Certain fruits (including apples, bananas, melons, and avocados) emit **ethylene** (ETH-el-leen) **gas,** which causes fruits to ripen. While this increases ripening in some unripe fruits, it also causes ripe fruits and vegetables to spoil. Ethylene-producing fruits should be stored in sealed containers if separate refrigeration or storage is not available.

Another reason to store fruits and vegetables separately is because some produce, such as onions or garlic, give off odors that taint the natural, delicate flavor of dairy items.

Most fruits and vegetables need to be kept dry because excess moisture causes produce to spoil quickly. For this reason, produce should not be peeled, washed, or trimmed until just before it is used. For example, outer leaves on lettuce should be left on the head, and carrots should be unpeeled. Leafy tops on green vegetables (beets, turnips, carrots, radishes) should be removed and either discarded or used immediately. The leaves on these green vegetables absorb nutrients from the root and increase moisture loss.

Fruits and vegetables that need to ripen should be stored at room temperatures of 65°F to 70°F (18.3°C to 21.1°C). Once produce is ripe, refrigerate it immediately or it will become overripe.

Even with proper storage, most foodservice operations *do not keep produce for more than four days.* Some vegetables and

Exhibit 11.18
Fresh produce should be stored appropriately to avoid spoiling or becoming overripe.

citrus fruits have a longer life, but most restaurants limit the storage of these items to three weeks.

Seasonal Availability of Produce

Fortunately, improved shipping methods and new ways of farming have made most produce available all year. The use of hydroponic farming is becoming more popular. In **hydroponic** (hi-dro-PON-ick) **farming,** vegetables are grown indoors year-round, under regulated temperatures and light in nutrient-enriched water. To reduce cost and promote freshness, some restaurants grow their own fresh herbs on the premises.

Some fruits and vegetables, such as bananas, apples, pears, grapes, spinach, potatoes, and broccoli are available all year; however, the quality and price vary with the season. Others, such as asparagus, peaches, plums, mangos, and berries, have a specific growing season. Knowing the growing season for a particular fruit or vegetable is important. During their growing seasons, the fruit or vegetable is plentiful, the quality is higher, and the prices are usually lower.

Review Your Learning 11.3

1. What are the different quality grades given to fresh fruit and canned produce by the USDA?
2. Why is it important for fruits and vegetables to be stored separately?
3. How long should most foodservice operations keep fresh produce?
4. What factors have allowed fresh produce to be available all year long?
5. How would you expect a lower graded fruit to be used in a foodservice operation?

SECTION 11.4

Cooking Fresh Fruit

AFTER STUDYING SECTION 11.4, YOU SHOULD BE ABLE TO:

- Match and cook fruits to appropriate methods.
- Explain how to prevent enzymatic browning of fruits.

While most fruits are eaten and served raw, some fruits can also be cooked. They can be served hot or cold, as part of the main entrée, as a snack, or as a dessert.

KEY TERMS

- **Coulis (cool-LEE)**
- **Enzymatic (en-zi-MAT-ick) browning**
- **Polyphenoloxidase (pol-lee-fen-il-OX-ee-days)**

Preparing Fruits

Preparing fruits for cooking involves washing them with water, and peeling, slicing, and cutting them. Some fruits, such as citrus fruits, melons, pineapples, and kiwi, keep their attractive appearance after they have been cut. However, there are other fruits (apples, pears, bananas, peaches, and others) that turn an unappetizing dark color when their flesh has been exposed to air.

A chemical process called **enzymatic** (en-zi-MAT-ick) **browning** occurs when oxygen in the air comes in contact with the flesh of cut fruit and turns it brown. This reaction occurs more quickly in fruits that contain the enzyme **polyphenoloxidase** (pol-lee-fen-il-OX-ee-days). The fruit, the enzyme, and the oxygen in the air combine to cause the darkening reaction. Enzymatic browning is a fruit's survival technique to protect it from the environment.

Exhibit 11.19
Coat fresh fruit with an acid to keep it from turning brown.

How much do you need?

Apples	**1 pound (3 or 4 medium) = 3 cups sliced**
Bananas	**1 pound (3 or 4 medium) = 1¾ cups mashed**
Berries	**1 quart = 3½ cups**
Dates	**1 pound = 2½ cups pitted**
Lemon	**1 whole = 1 to 3 tablespoons juice; 1 to 1½ teaspoons grated rind**
Lime	**1½ to 2 tablespoons juice**
Orange	**1 medium = 6 to 8 tablespoons juice; 2 to 3 tablespoons grated rind**
Peaches	**1 pound (4 medium) = 3 cups sliced**
Pears	**1 pound (4 medium) = 2 cups sliced**
Rhubarb	**1 pound = 2 cups cooked**
Strawberries	**1 quart = 4 cups sliced**

To keep cut fresh fruits from discoloring, coat them with some form of acid, such as lemon juice, as soon as they are cut.

Cooking Methods

It is always important to avoid overcooking fruits. Even minimal cooking can make fruits overly soft or mushy. When fruits are cooked with sugar, the sugar is absorbed slowly into the cells, firming the fruits. Acids, such as lemon juice, help fruits to retain their structure. Alkalis, such as baking soda, cause the cells to break down more quickly, making the fruits soft.

While every recipe and method is slightly different, most cooked fruits are done when they are tender and easily pierced with a fork. The following are just some of the methods used to cook fruit:

- Grilling and broiling
- Poaching
- Sautéing
- Baking
- Microwaving

When *grilling* or *broiling* fruits, the cooking must be done quickly to avoid breaking down the fruit's structure. Pineapples, grapefruits, bananas, and peaches are all good fruits to grill or broil. Cut the fruits into slices, chunks, or halves, and coat with sugar or honey to add flavor and carmelization. Place fruits to be grilled or broiled on an oiled sheet pan or broiling platter. Only thick fruit slices need to be turned or rotated to heat fully.

As explained in Exhibit 11.20, fruits that are *poached* are cooked in simmering liquid. In general, fruits to be poached should be firm enough to hold their shape during poaching. Some fruits that are suitable for poaching include plums, apples, peaches, and pears. Apples and pears can be cut in large pieces, but other small fruit should remain whole. Some famous poached fruit dishes include *Peach Melba* and *Pears Belle Hélène.* Poached fruits are also often used in other desserts as fillings or toppings.

Fruits have a rich, syrupy flavor when *sautéed* in butter, sugar, and spices. Some good fruits for sautéing are cherries, bananas, pears, and pineapples. When sautéing fruit, peel, core, and seed the fruit (remove all seeds) and cut into uniform sizes. Dessert fruits can be sautéed with sugar to create a carmelized glaze of syrup. They can be used to fill crêpes or as toppings for sponge cakes. Recipes for sautéed fruits that accompany main entrées add onions, shallots, or garlic to the mixture.

Fruit sauces can be made from a variety of fruits. Some of the most popular fruit sauces include applesauce, fresh berry **coulis** (cool-LEE), which is a sauce made from a purée of vegetables or

Exhibit 11.20
Poaching fruits.

- Prepare the fruit as necessary (seed, peel, etc.). The peel can be included with the fruit as it poaches to add flavor.
- Combine the fruit with enough poaching liquid to cover the fruit and bring it just to a simmer.
- Reduce the heat and gently poach the fruit until it is tender. Test the doneness by piercing the fruit with a sharp knife. There should be little or no resistance.
- Let the fruit cool in the poaching liquid, or serve immediately.

Exhibit 11.21
Apples are a good fruit for baking and for fruit sauces, such as applesauce.

fruit that can be served hot or cold, and compotes made by simmering dried fruits, such as apricots, currants, and raisins. Fresh berry sauces can also be used as a base for dessert soufflés, as flavoring for Bavarian creams, buttercreams, and other fillings and icings. Ideally, sauce should be made from fresh fruits, but a good quality sauce can be made by using unsweetened, frozen fruits.

Fruit sauces are made by first cooking the fruit in liquid, until the fruit has been broken down. A sweetener is then added, such as sugar, honey, or syrup. Once the sauce has cooled, spices and other flavorings are added to give it the finishing touch. Exhibit 11.22 details how to prepare fruit sauces.

Fruits can also be baked or prepared in a microwave oven. When *baking* fruits, choose firm fruits, such as apples, pears, and bananas, that are whole or in large pieces. Apples are the most popular baked fruit because they are easy to prepare. An apple well suited to baking is the *Rome Beauty*. Baked fruits, such as the baked apple, are a healthy and nutritious dessert.

Exhibit 11.22
Fruit sauces.

- Pare the fruit and cut into small pieces for faster cooking. *Alternative:* purée the fruit in a blender, food processor, food mill, or through a drum sieve.
- Add the appropriate amount of liquid and heat the purée in a saucepan until it is almost boiling. Lower the heat to a simmer, and cover the pan.
- Cook, stirring occasionally, until the fruit has broken down.
- Sweeten as desired with sugar, honey, or syrup.
- Add any additional spices or other flavorings, such as vanilla, once the sauce has cooled slightly.

When *microwaving* fruits, watch the cooking time carefully. It's easy to overcook fresh fruits because they are so tender. Always cover fruits when microwaving them, but leave a small opening for excess steam to escape. When cooking whole fruits, such as plums or pears in the microwave, puncture them with a fork in several places to keep them from bursting.

Exhibit 11.23
Baking apples.

- Core apples.
- Cut a thin strip of skin from around the middle of each apple to prevent them from splitting during baking.
- Fill each apple's core cavity with cinnamon, nutmeg, raisins, or dates for variety and flavor.
- Place the apples in 1/4 inch of hot water in a baking dish.
- Bake at 350°F (180°C) until tender, or about 45 to 60 minutes.

Review Your Learning 11.4

1. On a separate sheet of paper, match the fruit to its appropriate cooking method. Some fruits may be suitable to more than one cooking method.

Pineapples	a. Grilling and broiling
Apples	b. Poaching
Grapefruits	c. Sautéing
Bananas	d. Fruit sauce
Pears	e. Baking
Peaches	f. Microwaving
Raspberries	

2. Pick two of your favorite fruits and discuss the cooking method you would use to prepare them. Is there another cooking method you could use to prepare them?

3. What one new fruit would you like to try? Why? What cooking method would you use to prepare it?

4. What fruits experience *enzymatic browning* when they are cut and the flesh is exposed to air?

SECTION 11.5

Cooking Vegetables

AFTER STUDYING SECTION 11.5, YOU SHOULD BE ABLE TO:

- Match and cook vegetables to appropriate methods.

KEY TERMS

- **Anthocyanin (an-thoe-SIGH-ah-nin)**
- **Anthoxanthins (an-thoe-ZAN-thin)**
- **Carotenoid (car-AH-ten-oid)**
- **Chlorophyll (CLOR-o-fill)**
- **Glaze**
- **Pigment**
- **Purée (pure-RAY)**

Preparation Methods

Vegetables must be properly prepared before they are cooked by any method. Preliminary preparations include peeling, cleaning, and slicing. Exhibit 11.24 describes some important steps to take when washing fresh produce.

Vegetables should be prepared for cooking as close as possible to the actual cooking time. This will ensure the vegetables' freshness and contribute to the overall quality and flavor of the finished dish.

Ever wonder...?

Did you ever wonder what vegetables are made of? Vegetables consist of water, starch, and sugar. There are also four natural pigments, or colors, found in vegetables.

- **Anthocyanins (an-thoe-SIGH-ah-nin)—red and purple**
- **Anthoxanthins (an-thoe-ZAN-thin)—colorless or white**
- **Carotenoid (car-AH-ten-oid)—orange, yellow, red-orange**
- **Chlorophyll (CLOR-o-fill)—green**

Exhibit 11.24
Safety steps for washing fresh produce.

- Avoid washing fresh produce with soap or detergent. The produce can absorb the detergent and make people ill. In addition, the detergent may react with any pesticides and waxes on the produce, forming a combination that could be very harmful.
- Wash and rinse produce in cool, clear water several times, even if you're going to peel or pare it. Washing helps prevent chemicals and dirt from being transferred to the edible parts.
- Scrub thick-skinned produce, such as squash, and items that might have a lot of dirt, such as potatoes, with a thick brush. Avoid soaking the produce in water.

Other factors that are essential to successfully cooking vegetables are purchasing vegetables that are at the peak of quality, maintaining proper storage and handling standards, and selecting a cooking process that is best suited to the vegetable. Vegetables must be cooked in a way that retains their texture, flavor, color, and nutrients.

Working with knives requires special care and attention. Make sure that you have plenty of space around you, and cut away from your body. Only use knives that are sharp, never dull. It is also important to use knives that are appropriately sized to the food you are cutting; smaller items can be cut with a paring knife, while larger items may be cut using a butcher knife.

Exhibit 11.25 on the next page illustrates the different color changes in vegetables and shows whether cooking vegetables in acid or alkali is necessary to keep the natural color.

Cooking Methods

Maintaining the quality and flavor of the vegetable depends on both the type of vegetable and the cooking method used. Methods of cooking vegetables include almost all of the ones you learned in *Chaper 4: Kitchen Basics.*

- Boiling (blanching, parboiling)
- Steaming
- Microwaving
- Roasting and baking
- Sautéing and stir-frying
- Pan-frying
- Deep-frying
- Stewing and braising
- Puréeing

Appearance and texture are two tests of a vegetable's doneness. Green vegetables show a visible difference from one stage of doneness to another. White and orange vegetables show very little change in their color, so their texture must be checked.

Boiling is best for hard, starchy vegetables such as corn and potatoes. *Blanching,*

Exhibit 11.25
Vegetable color changes during cooking.

Color	Example of Vegetables	Cooked with Acid	Cooked with Alkali	Overcooked
White	Potatoes, turnips, cauliflower, onions, white cabbage	Yellow	Yellowish, gray	
Red	Beets, red cabbage (not tomatoes; pigment is like that in yellow vegetables)	Red	Blue/blue green	Greenish blue, faded
Green	Asparagus, green beans, lima beans, broccoli, Brussels sprouts, peas, spinach, okra, green peppers, artichokes	Olive Green	Bright green	Olive green
Yellow (and orange)	Carrots, tomatoes, rutabagas, sweet potatoes, squash, corn	Little change	Little change	Slightly faded

a form of cooking similar to boiling, is done by quickly and partially cooking a vegetable in hot water or oil. This cooking method makes the skins easy to remove; sets the color of vegetables to be served cold; eliminates or reduces strong flavors; and is the first step in other cooking methods. *Parboiling,* like blanching, partially cooks vegetables in boiling water.

Important nutrients in vegetables can be lost through overwashing, over-cooking, or being heavily processed. Vegetables start out with so much good stuff—it's important to preserve nutrients while cooking them.

Steaming is an excellent way to prepare vegetables for to-order service. Steaming is also the best method for retaining vitamins and minerals because they are cooked gently in a vapor, or steam bath, not in direct contact with water. Exhibit 11.26 shows the general steps for steaming vegetables.

When *microwaving* food, the friction of the vibrating food molecules generates heat, causing the food's natural liquids to steam the item. As discussed in Exhibit 11.27, vegetables should be cooked in a microwave-safe container with a small amount of liquid, and covered. The vegetable can also be left whole, with the skin or peel intact, and steamed with its own moisture.

Measuring Vegetables

Asparagus	1 pound = 3 cups chopped
Beans (string)	1 pound = 1 cup chopped
Beets	1 pound (5 medium) = 2½ cups chopped
Broccoli	1½ pounds = 6 cups chopped
Cabbage	1 pound = 4½ cups shredded
Carrots	1 pound = 3½ cups sliced or grated
Celery	1 pound = 4 cups chopped
Cucumbers	1 pound (2 medium) = 4 cups sliced
Eggplant	1 pound = 4 cups chopped (6 cups raw, cubed = 3 cups cooked)
Garlic	1 clove = 1 teaspoon chopped
Leeks	1 pound = 4 cups chopped (2 cups cooked)
Mushrooms	1 pound = 5 to 6 cups sliced = 2 cups cooked
Onions	1 pound = 4 cups sliced = 2 cups cooked
Parsnips	1 pound unpeeled = 1½ cups cooked and puréed
Peas	1 pound whole = 1 to 1½ cups shelled
Potatoes	1 pound (3 medium) sliced = 2 cups mashed
Pumpkin	1 pound = 4 cups chopped = 2 cups cooked and drained
Spinach	1 pound = ¾ to 1 cup cooked
Squash (summer)	1 pound = 4 cups grated = 2 cups salted and drained
Squash (winter)	2 pounds = 2½ cups cooked, puréed
Sweet potatoes	1 pound = 4 cups grated = 1 cup cooked, puréed
Swiss chard	1 pound = 5 to 6 cups packed leaves = 1 to 1½ cups cooked
Tomatoes	1 pound (3 or 4 medium) = 1½ cups seeded pulp
Turnips	1 pound = 4 cups chopped = 2 cups cooked, mashed

Exhibit 11.26
Steaming vegetables.

- Bring the liquid to a full boil and add the seasonings and aromatics.
- Add the vegetables to the steamer in a single layer.
- Steam the vegetable to the desired doneness.
- Serve the vegetables, or refresh and hold.

Exhibit 11.27
Microwaving vegetables.

- Place the vegetable in a suitable dish or plate and cover it.
- Place it in a microwave oven and cook it to the desired doneness.
- Serve the vegetable, or refresh and hold.

Roasting and *baking* are two very popular ways to cook vegetables. Vegetables should be cooked in a hot or moderate oven, and left whole or cut into large pieces with no additional liquid added. This cooking method is best suited to vegetables with thick skins, such as winter squash, potatoes, and eggplant, that protect the interior from drying or scorching. Exhibit 11.28 lists vegetables and the various cooking methods commonly used for each.

While thick-skinned vegetables are well suited for roasting, vegetables with little or no skin are best when *sautéed*. Sautéing gives vegetables a crisp texture. Some vegetables are suitable for sautéing from their raw state, such as mushrooms and onions. Denser vegetables, such as green beans and carrots, may be partially cooked before they are sautéed. Exhibit 11.31 details the proper steps to take when sautéing or stir-frying vegetables.

Exhibit 11.29
Roasting vegetables.

- Place the vegetable in a hot or moderate oven.
- Roast it to the desired doneness.
- Serve, hold, or use it in a secondary technique.

Warning!! All foods will be hot when removed from an oven, stove, or microwave. Be sure to let foods cool for the appropriate amount of time before serving them. Be careful, however; foods cooked in a microwave oven often heat unevenly. Even if the food item seems to have cooled completely, the center of the item may still be very hot.

Glazing is a finishing technique used to give vegetables as glossy appearance. A small amount of honey, sugar, or maple syrup is added to the vegetable, coating it and giving it a sheen as it reheats. For

Exhibit 11.28
Vegetable cooking guide.

Cooking Method	Appropriate for:
Baking	Carrots, eggplant, mushrooms, onions, potatoes, squash, tomatoes
Boiling	Dried beans and legumes, cabbage, carrots, corn on the cob, potatoes
Braising	Cabbage, celery, mushrooms, potatoes, squash, zucchini
Broiling	Eggplant, mushrooms, onions, tomatoes
Deep-frying	Brussels sprouts, carrots, cauliflower, eggplant, potatoes, squash, zucchini
Steaming	Artichokes, asparagus, green beans, beets, broccoli, Brussels sprouts, cabbage, carrots, cauliflower, celery, onions, potatoes

Exhibit 11.30
Stir-fried vegetables.

example, small pearl onions and baby carrots are often glazed.

Unlike previous cooking methods, *pan-fried* vegetables are often coated with breading, or batter. The amount of oil used in pan-frying is greater than that for sautéing. The batter-dipped vegetable is cooked in oil or butter until its exterior is lightly browned and crisp.

Like pan-frying, *deep-fried* vegetables are coated with breading or batter just before cooking. Instead of using a shallow pan, a deep-fryer or a large heavy pot is used. Slow-cooking vegetables, like broccoli and cauliflower, may be blanched before they are deep-fried to speed the cooking process.

Grilling is a popular method used to cook vegetables. Some vegetables can be grilled from the raw state, while others must be marinated. Marinated vegetables are soaked in oil, herbs, and spices. This gives them added flavor. The vegetable must be able to withstand the grill's intense heat. Some vegetables best suited for grilling are bell peppers, potatoes, zucchini, and onion.

Exhibit 11.31
Sautéing and stir-frying vegetables.

- Heat the pan; add the cooking medium and heat it.
- Add the vegetable.
- Sauté the vegetable, keeping it in motion.
- Add the aromatics, seasonings, or glaze and heat thoroughly.
- Serve the vegetable immediately.

Exhibit 11.32
Pan-frying vegetables.

- Heat the pan.
- Add the cooking oil and heat.
- Add the vegetable.
- Cook until its exterior is slightly browned and crisp.
- Blot it on absorbent paper toweling.
- Season and serve immediately.

Vegetable *stews* and *braises* are good ways to retain the vitamins and minerals that are transferred to the cooking liquid. In both cooking methods, vegetables are cooked in oil or stock and seasoned. Broth or another cooking liquid is then added, and the vegetables are cooked until tender. The liquid is then served as part of the dish. Stewed vegetables are cut into small pieces; braised vegetables are cut into large pieces or left whole.

Puréed vegetables can be served as individual dishes or may be used in other preparations, custards, and soufflés. As shown in Exhibit 11.36, the vegetable must be cooked until it is tender enough to purée easily by pushing it through a sieve or food mill, or by puréeing it in a vertical chopping machine or blender. Some vegetables, such as tomatoes, spinach, and cucumbers, can be puréed from the raw state.

Holding Vegetables

The best way to maintain overall quality is to cook vegetables rapidly and then serve them as soon as possible. Sometimes vegetables must be held for a time before being served, and there are several steps you can take to maintain their quality.

Exhibit 11.33
Deep-frying vegetables.

- Coat the vegetable with breading or batter.
- Heat the oil in a deep-fryer and add the vegetable.
- Fry the vegetable until it is evenly browned or golden.
- Remove from the oil and blot it on absorbent paper towels.
- Adjust the seasoning and serve the vegetable immediately.

Exhibit 11.34
Grilling vegetables.

- Heat the grill or broiler.
- Marinate the vegetable or brush it with oil.
- Grill or broil until the vegetable is tender and properly cooked through.
- Serve the vegetable immediately.

Exhibit 11.35
Stewing and braising vegetables.

- Heat the pan.
- Heat the oil or stock.
- Smother the vegetable with seasonings or aromatics.
- Add the liquid, bring it to a simmer, and cook the vegetable.
- Add the remaining vegetables and aromatics.
- Cook the stew or braise until the vegetables are tender.
- Adjust the seasoning and finish the dish according to the recipe.
- Serve the vegetable or hold.

Exhibit 11.36
Pureéing vegetables.

- Cook the vegetable until it is very tender.
- Drain it and remove any excess moisture.
- Purée the vegetable using a sieve.
- Adjust the seasoning, finish, and serve or use in a secondary preparation.

- Boiled or steamed vegetables can be refreshed in cold water; starchy vegetables should be well-drained and spread out to dry; baked or roasted vegetables should be held, uncovered, in a holding drawer; braised or stewed vegetables can be held in a steam table.
- Various methods of reheating vegetables include simmering them in stock or water; microwaving; or sautéing them in butter or cream.
- Avoid holding vegetables either in steam tables or directly in water for extended periods of time.

Review Your Learning 11.5

1. On a separate sheet of paper, match the vegetable to its appropriate cooking method. Some vegetables may be suitable to more than one cooking method.

Carrots	a. Baking
Eggplant	b. Boiling
Artichokes	c. Braising
Cabbage	d. Broiling
Potatoes	e. Deep-frying
Dried beans and legumes	f. Steaming
Brussels sprouts	
Tomatoes	

2. Pick two of your favorite vegetables and discuss the cooking method you would use to prepare them. Is there a different cooking method you could use to prepare them?

3. What one new vegetable would you like to try? What cooking method would you like to use to prepare it?

4. What are the safety steps you should know for washing vegetables?

5. If you have to hold vegetables before serving them, what should you do to maintain their quality?

Flashback

CHAPTER 11

SECTION 11.1: IDENTIFYING FRUITS

- Fruits are both delicious and nutritious because they are refreshing and are an excellent source of dietary fiber.
- The sweetness of fruits comes from **fructose,** a natural form of sugar.
- Fruits can be purchased fresh, frozen, canned, dried, or as preserves. Fruits are classified as *summer, winter,* or *tropical.*
- **Summer fruits** include berries, cherries, grapes, melons, peaches, nectarines, plums, and pears.
- Cherries, plums, peaches, nectarines, and apricots are called **drupes** because they have a central pit enclosing a single seed.
- *Melons* are categorized in two groups: sweet melons and watermelons.
- *Peaches* have a distinctive fuzzy skin and come in two categories: **freestone** and **clingstone.**
- *Plums* range in size from as small as an apricot to as large as a peach.
- Plums can either be dessert plums, or cooking plums.
- The most common types of *pear* are Bosc, d'Anjou, and Seckel.
- **Winter fruits** include citrus fruits and apples.
- Citrus fruits are characterized by thick skins with aromatic oils and segmented flesh.
- Citrus fruits are abundant in vitamin C and range in flavor from a sweet orange to a very tart, sour lemon.
- *Apples* are among the most commonly used and available fruits, and are either tart or sweet.
- **Tropical fruits** are named for the general climatic conditions under which they are grown and include bananas, figs, kiwis, mangos, papayas, pineapple, and coconut.
- *Bananas* are the most common of the tropical fruits. Unlike most fruits, bananas are picked almost green and allowed to ripen on the way from the plantation to the buyer.

- *Figs* are versatile fruit, often eaten raw and used in baking pies, cookies, and cakes.
- *Kiwis* have a fuzzy skin and bright green flesh whose taste can be compared to strawberries.
- *Mangos* have light yellow flesh and are spicy-sweet. They are an excellent addition to fruit salads, and go well with curry.
- *Papayas* have soft pink flesh and a central mass of black seeds. They are an excellent source of vitamin A and C.
- *Pineapple* is a very popular tropical fruit. It good when eaten raw, and is used in baking.
- *Coconuts* are native to Malaysia, and have bright white meat enclosed by a hard, brown hairy shell.

SECTION 11.2: IDENTIFYING VEGETABLES

- Fruits, vegetables, and herbs are popular with today's consumers who want to stay healthy and fit.
- It is important to select fruits and vegetables that are high in quality, fresh, and appropriate for the recipe or dish.
- Fruits and vegetables require extra care from selecting to receiving to storage to serving.
- The categories of vegetables discussed in this section are: **flower, fruit, green leafy, seed, root** and **tuber,** and **stem** vegetables. The edible part varies with each vegetable.
- **Flower vegetables** include broccoli, cauliflower, Brussels sprouts, and cabbage.
- **Fruit vegetables** include avocados, cucumbers, eggplants, peppers, squash, and tomatoes. With the exception of eggplant, these vegetables are most commonly served raw.
- **Green leafy vegetables** include various types of lettuce, mustard greens, spinach, and swiss chard.
- Green leafy vegetables are very high in vitamins A and C, iron, and magnesium.
- Common types of lettuce are *iceberg, romaine,* and *leaf.*
- **Seed vegetables** include corn, peas, and beans.
- They are most flavorful and sweet when they are eaten young and fresh.
- **Root vegetables** and **tubers** are grouped together because part, or all, of the plant is grown underground.
- Root vegetables include carrots, beets, radishes, turnips, and onion.

- Various types of onion are bulb, scallions, shallots, and leeks.
- Tubers are enlarged bulbous roots capable of generating a new plant.
- Tubers include potatoes, sweet potatoes, and yams.
- Yams are often compared to sweet potatoes.
- **Stem vegetables** include asparagus, celery, artichokes, and mushrooms.

SECTION 11.3: PURCHASING AND STORING FRUITS AND VEGETABLES

- The United States Department of Agriculture, or USDA, developed quality grades for fresh vegetables and fruits.
- All produce must be properly stored, with ripe fruits and vegetables (except for bananas, potatoes, and dry onions) kept under refrigeration at a temperature of 40°F to 45°F (4.4°C to 7.2°C), with a relative humidity of 80 to 110 percent.
- Fruits should be stored separately in one refrigerator and vegetables stored in another unit.
- Certain fruits and avocados emit **ethylene gas,** which causes them to ripen, promoting spoilage in ripe fruits and vegetables.
- Roots and tubers should be stored dry and unpeeled.
- Most roots and tubers will keep for several weeks if stored properly.
- Fruits and vegetables need to be kept dry. Excess moisture causes produce to spoil quickly.
- Produce should not be peeled, washed, or trimmed until just before it is used.
- Leafy tops on beets, turnips, carrots, and radishes should be removed and either discarded or used immediately. The leaves absorb nutrients from the root and increase the loss of moisture.
- Fruits and vegetables that need further ripening should be stored at room temperature 65°F to 70°F (18.3°C to 21.1°C).
- Once produce is ripe, refrigerate it immediately or it will become overripe.
- Even with proper storage, most foodservice operations do not keep produce for more than four days. Some vegetables and citrus fruits have

a longer life, but most restaurants limit the storage of these items to three weeks.

- Improved shipping methods and new ways of farming have made most produce available all year.
- **Hydroponic farming** makes it possible to grow vegetables indoors under regulated temperatures and light in nutrient-enriched water instead of soil.
- Some fruits and vegetables, such as bananas, apples, pears, grapes, spinach, potatoes, and broccoli, are available all year.
- Asparagus, peaches, plums, mangoes, and berries have a specific growing season. During this season, the fruit or vegetable is plentiful, the quality is higher, and the prices are usually lower.

SECTION 11.4: COOKING FRESH FRUIT

- Cooking fresh fruits adds variety to an operation's menu.
- Cooked fruits can be served hot or cold, as part of the main entrée, as a snack, or as a dessert.
- Always wash fresh fruit before using it raw or cooking it.
- Some fruits, such as apples, pears, bananas, and peaches, undergo **enzymatic browning** when the oxygen in the air comes in contact with the flesh of cut fruit.
- The enzyme **polyphenoloxidase** causes the darkening of the fruit to occur.
- When cooking fruits using any method, it is important to avoid overcooking fruits. Even minimal cooking can make fruits overly soft or mushy.
- In grilling or broiling fruits, the cooking must be done quickly to avoid breaking down the fruit's structure. Good fruits to grill or broil include pineapples, apples, grapefruits, bananas, and peaches.
- Fruits are cooked in a simmering liquid, and retain their natural shape as they cook.
- Fruits to be poached should be firm enough to hold their shape during poaching. Fruits that can be successfully poached include plums, apples, peaches, and pears.
- Fruits have a rich, syrupy flavor when sautéed in butter, sugar, and spices. Cherries, bananas, pears, and pineapples are good choices. They should

be peeled, cored, seeded, and cut into uniform sizes.

- Fruit sauces, such as applesauce, can be made from a variety of fruits.
- Fresh berry sauces also can be used as a base for flourless soufflés, as flavoring for Bavarian creams, buttercreams, and other fillings and frostings.
- Sauce should be made from fresh fruits, but a good quality sauce can be made by using unsweetened, frozen fruits also.
- Fruits can also be baked or microwaved.
- Choose firm fruits, such as apples, pears, and bananas, that are whole or in large pieces, for baking.
- Always cover fruits when microwaving them, but leave a small opening for excess steam to escape.
- Whole fruits, such as plums or pears, should be punctured with a fork in several places to keep them from bursting while in the microwave.

SECTION 11.5: COOKING VEGETABLES

- Vegetables consist of water, starch, and sugar.
- The four natural color **pigments** found in vegetables are **anthocyanins, anthoxanthins, carotenoids,** and **chlorophyll.**
- It's important to preserve as much natural color or pigment as possible when cooking vegetables.
- Purchase vegetables that are at the peak of quality, maintain proper storage and handling standards, and select a cooking process that is best suited to the vegetable.
- Vegetables must be properly prepared before they are cooked by any method.
- Preliminary preparations include removing seeds, peeling, cleaning, and slicing.
- Once any vegetable has been harvested, it begins to deteriorate. Vegetables must be cooked in a way that retains their nutritive value, best color, and freshest flavor.
- Cooking affects vegetables by changing their texture, flavor, color, and nutrients.
- Each vegetable cookery technique produces a different result. Methods such as sautéing, microwaving, and steaming are often used for cooking

vegetables that should have a crisp texture and bright color.

- Boiled vegetables are more moist and tender; baking vegetables makes them fluffy with a unique roasted flavor.
- Roasting and baking is best suited to vegetables with very thick skins, such as winter squash, potatoes, and eggplant.
- Small pearl onions and baby carrots are often **glazed**, or cooked with a small amount of sugar or honey.
- In pan-frying, vegetables are coated with breading, and cooked in oil or butter in a shallow pan.
- Deep-fried vegetables are also coated with batter, but are cooked in a large, deep pot filled with oil.
- Vegetables best suited for grilling are bell peppers, potatoes, zucchini, and onions.
- **Puréeing** vegetables involves chopping the vegetable into small pieces and pushing it through a sieve or food mill.
- The best way to keep vegetables' color and nutrients is to cook them rapidly and then serve them as soon as possible.
- Various methods of reheating vegetables include simmering them in stock or water; microwaving; or sautéing them in butter or cream.
- Appearance and texture are two tests of a vegetable's doneness.
- Green vegetables show a visible difference from one stage of doneness to another.
- White and orange vegetables show very little change in their color, so their texture must be checked.

Liz Kelly

Sales Associate
Catering Concepts
Washington, D.C.

Being a part of the foodservice industry is really challenging and a lot of hard work, but it is definitely rewarding! After I graduated from college with a Bachelor of Art degree in Political Science, I moved to Washington, D.C., and started working for the Hyatt on Capitol Hill as a catering assistant. Along with some administrative tasks, I was the liaison between our clients and the manager. I helped make sure all the catered events at the Hyatt ran smoothly.

My job as catering assistant introduced me to the world of catering, and I knew I wanted to pursue it further. Wanting more experience, I became one of four food and beverage managers at the Hyatt. In that job, I was responsible for all of the catering that the Hyatt provided for its many meeting rooms and ballrooms. I also managed the restaurant, the main bar, room service, hospitality suites, and helped manage the fine-dining restaurant. I also trained employees to give great service.

Working at the Hyatt on Capitol Hill gave me incredible experience in the industry and allowed me to be involved with so many aspects of catering. I knew that I wanted to work in off-site catering. I started working for one of the largest catering companies in the D.C. area.

Now, I'm responsible for planning and overseeing 10 to 15 catering events at a time, from small wedding receptions to events of up to 3,000 people. First, I meet with clients to discuss their needs. I really get to be involved in all aspects of the catering process. I create the menu, set up tastings for clients, choose the decor and setup for the room, and order all of the necessary equipment, from the salt and pepper shakers to the bain marie. There is a lot to remember, but it is really rewarding to see the event when everything has come together!

Catering is definitely what I love to do. The fast pace and changing day-to-day activities make this job really exciting. Though hectic and stressful at times, working with fun people and getting to meet new faces everyday make it all worthwhile!

CHAPTER 12

Controlling Foodservice Costs

12.1

SECTION 12.1

Cost Planning

AFTER STUDYING SECTION 12.1, YOU SHOULD BE ABLE TO:

- Analyze the relationship between cost and sales to determine food cost percentage.
- List the four steps in the process to control food costs.
- Calculate projected revenue, average cover, and find revenue level.
- Perform math computations to define cost/volume/profit relationships.

As you learned in *Chapter 10: Business Math,* strong math skills are important tools to have when working in many environments—especially in a foodservice operation. In order to have a successful business, a foodservice operation must have high business volume, efficient customer service, attractive decor, delicious food, and satisfied customers. But to guarantee profitability, the math skills discussed

KEY TERMS

- **Average cover**
- **Break-even point**
- **Budget**
- **Cost/volume/profit**
- **Fiscal year**
- **Fixed cost**
- **Food cost**
- **Food cost percentage**
- **Historical data**
- **Operating budget**
- **Profitability**
- **Reconcile**
- **Revenue**
- **Sales**
- **Variable cost**

in *Chapter 10: Business Math* and this chapter must be used to understand the relationship between cost and sales, and realistic planning and forecasting.

The Heart of the Matter

Controlling foodservice costs is a demanding process, at the heart of which are food cost and food sales. **Food cost** is found by adding all requisitions from the storeroom, as well as daily purchases. **Sales** result when an operation exchanges products and services for money.

Directly related to sales, **revenue** is the income from the sale of food items before expenses are subtracted. Revenue can be expressed in terms of total dollar sales; total dollar sales by category (beverage, seafood, steak, etc.); sales price; average dollar sales per customer, per server, and per seat; quantity of items sold; average number of items sold; and turnover.

By determining food cost and sales, managers can calculate the **food cost percentage** for each business day and record the information on a daily food cost sheet. The following formula can be used to compute the food cost percentage:

$$\frac{\text{Cost}}{\text{Sales}} = \text{Food cost percentage}$$

Exhibit12.1
Although it's essential, efficient customer service alone doesn't guarantee that a foodservice establishment will be profitable.

If an operation's daily food cost is \$190.80 and total sales are \$536.40, the food cost percentage is 35.6%:

$$\frac{\$190.80}{\$536.40} = 0.3557 = 35.6\%$$

The food cost percentage is useful to management in two ways: it provides a way to compare costs as they relate to sales for two or more periods, and it allows for meaningful comparison of two or more similar operations.

Give it a Try...

The foodservice manager at The Blue Bird Café projects monthly food costs to be \$21,500. If the desired food cost percentage is 24%, what should sales be?

Every operation will have a different food cost percentage goal. The trick is to match the goal to the actual percentage. Costs must also be matched with sales on a regular basis. Many foodservice operations gather cost information daily and compare these costs to sales information for the day to determine the daily cost percentage. Each cost percentage is then compared to those from previous periods to determine how well costs are being controlled. In general, comparisons are made for specific days of the week. For example, sales and costs from Friday of last week are compared to those for Friday of this week.

Along with tracking food cost and sales, managers should follow the basic four-step cost control process shown in Exhibit 12.2.

Cost control alone, however, will not guarantee **profitability**—having higher revenue than costs. Keeping careful and accurate records will give a realistic picture of how well the business is actually doing. Each sale must be accurately recorded and checked against production records to make sure that all quantities produced are accounted for. In addition, all prepared food that is served to guests must be recorded as sales, and any discrepancies should be reconciled. In this case, **reconcile** means to match sales checks from the kitchen to production records.

Exhibit 12.2
Four-step cost control process.

1. Create standards and standard operating procedures.
2. Train all employees to follow procedures.
3. Compare actual performance to standards.
4. Correct any changes.

What does it mean?

At a local restaurant, production records show that 22 steaks were prepared and served, but sales records show that only 18 were actually sold. What might have happened? *Here are some possibilities:*

- **A steak fell on the floor and was thrown away.**
- **A steak that was too well-done was returned by a customer and another new steak was cooked to replace it.**
- **A steak was thrown out because it had not been stored properly and was spoiled.**
- **One of the cooks cooked a steak for himself but did not pay for it.**

Can you see how all of these possibilities affect the operation's cost control?

Budgeting

The most common way to control business activities is through a budget. A **budget** is a realistic expression of management's goals and objectives expressed in

If, for example, an operation projects fixed costs for next year at $335,500 and variable costs at 29 percent of sales, you can use the cost/volume/profit formula to find the **break-even point,** which is the revenue level at which the operation neither earns a profit nor suffers a loss.

$$\frac{\$335{,}500 + 0}{100\% - 29\%} = \frac{\$335{,}500}{0.71} = \$472{,}535.21$$

The cost/volume/profit formula can also be used to find the revenue needed for an operation to earn a specific profit. For the same establishment to earn a profit of $50,000, for example, it needs $542,957.74 in revenue.

$$\frac{\$335{,}500 + 50{,}000}{100\% - 29\%} = \frac{\$385{,}500}{0.71} = \$542{,}957.74$$

Understanding the cost/volume/profit relationship is critical before you can create food cost and sales controls. Once desired levels of costs, sales, and volume have been determined, managers must work to maintain those levels.

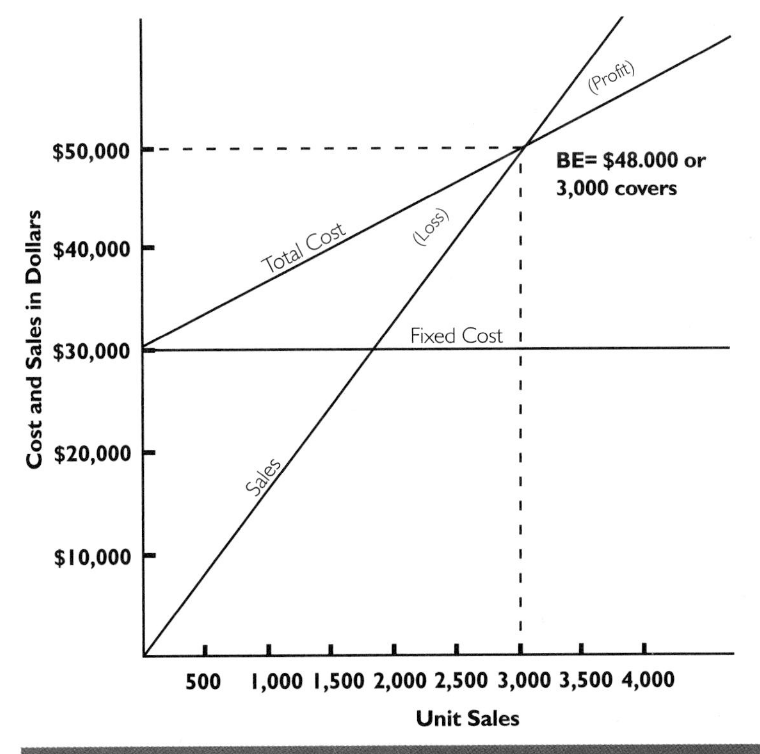

Exhibit 12.5
Break even (BE) occurs at the point at which sales equal total cost.

Reprinted with permission from *Principles of Food, Beverage, and Labor Cost Controls, Fifth Edition* by Paul R. Dittmer, and Gerald G. Griffin. Copyright ©1995 by Van Nostrand Reinhold.

Review Your Learning 12.1

1. If a restaurant's average daily food cost is $1,422 and its average daily sales total is $2,665, what is the operation's average daily food cost percentage?

   a. 19% b. 30% c. 41% d. 53%

2. On a separate sheet of paper, match each term on the left with its definition on the right.

   a. Operating budget
   b. Sales
   c. Revenue
   d. Break-even point
   e. Fixed cost
   f. Food cost percentage
   g. Budget
   h. Fiscal year
   i. Profitability
   j. Reconcile

   1. Food Cost ÷ Sales
   2. Income from the sale of food items
   3. Management's goals expressed in financial terms
   4. 365 days during which a business cycle takes place
   5. Result of exchanging products and services for money
   6. Salary of the chef
   7. Having higher revenue than costs
   8. Revenue = Costs
   9. Match sales checks from the kitchen to production records
   10. Forecast of sales activity and an estimate of costs that will be incurred in generating sales

3. Why is it more difficult to prepare a budget for a new business than for an existing establishment?

4. A restaurant has 98 seats and will be open for 340 days. It expects next year's customer turnover to be 2 and projects a check average of $11.25. What is the establishment's projected revenue for the year?

   a. $187,400

   b. $468,500

   c. $749,700

   d. $934,800

5. A foodservice operation projects next year's fixed costs to be $376,800 and variable costs to be 24% of sales.

   a. At what level of revenue will the operation break even?

   b. At what level of revenue will the operation earn a profit of $75,000?

12.2

SECTION 12.2

Controlling Sales

AFTER STUDYING SECTION 12.2, YOU SHOULD BE ABLE TO:

- Calculate the average sales per customer.
- Calculate total sales, including tax and tip.
- Balance cash register receipts and find actual receipts.

KEY TERMS

- **Average sale per customer**
- **Gratuity (gra-TOO-i-tee)**
- **Gross receipts**
- **Sales check**

The three goals of sales control are to sell products, earn revenue, and make a profit. To reach these goals, every foodservice operation must attract customers—and then give them what they want. While customer needs vary, all customers choose restaurants based on the following factors:

- Location
- Cleanliness
- Menu items
- Prices
- Decor
- Portion sizes
- Product quality
- Service

Focusing attention on these factors is the first step toward controlling and maximizing sales.

Standards and Standard Procedures

To control revenue, managers must establish standards and standard procedures. All food items sold, along with their prices, should be recorded, and daily revenues must be tracked.

One effective sales control procedure is the use of numbered guest checks. By recording sales and stamping numbered checks, cashiers can show that the checks have been paid.

Sales information is important when establishing standards and standard procedures. Finding the **average sale per customer** is one helpful way to develop sales information. The following equation shows how to calculate average sale per customer.

$$\frac{\text{Total dollar sales}}{\text{Total number of covers}} = \text{Average sale per customer}$$

For example, if an operation's sales total $38,520 for the month and 2,600 customers have been served, the average sale per customer is $14.82 *($38,520 ÷ 2,600)*.

Sales Checks and Tipping

The system that an operation uses to record customer sales must be efficient and understood by all employees. All customer sales are recorded on a sales check. A **sales check** contains lines, or spaces to itemize a customer's purchases. There are two basic ways to record sales: with blank checks and with printed checks. *Blank checks* contain blank lines to be filled in by servers. *Printed checks* list all of an operation's menu items, requiring servers to simply circle or mark customers' choices.

Every server must record sales and total each check completely and accurately. First, the items ordered by customers should be subtotaled. Then the sales tax must be added. Many operations have tax tables and charts showing appropriate tax for different totals, from which to take the tax amount; others use cash registers that automatically add the tax. You can also calculate the tax by hand using the state sales tax percentage. If, for example, a sales check subtotal is $51.68 and the state sales tax is 5%, the tax and total can be determined as follows:

$$\$51.68 \times 0.05 = \$2.58 + \$51.68 = \$54.26$$

In most American full-service operations, customers leave a **gratuity** (gra-TOO-i-tee), also called a *tip,* for servers equal to 15% to 20% of the sales check subtotal. Tips are calculated for check subtotals, not on the final amount

Give It a Try...

The Hot Dog Hut had a sales total of $14,000 and served 4,520 customers in November. Its neighbor, Café Renée, served 3,015 customers and had a November sales total of $36,580. What was the average sale per customer at each establishment? Do these figures surprise you? Why or why not?

Carlisle's

Date	Server	Table No.	No. Persons	No. 2370
1.				
2.				
3.				
4.				
5.				
6.				
7.				
8.				
9.				
10.				
11.				
12.			Subtotal	
			Tax	
			Total	
				No. 2370
Date	Guest Receipt	Persons	Amount of Check	

Carlisle's

Exhibit 12.6
Blank sales check.

Frank-n-Burger

Go	Stay						
No. of Items	1	2	3	4	5	W	WO
Hamburger	.70	1.40	2.10	2.80	3.50		
1/4 lb. Burger	.80	1.60	2.40	3.20	4.00		
Cheeseburger	.80	1.60	2.40	3.20	4.00		
Dbl. Chsburger	1.40	2.80	4.20	5.60	7.00		
Combo Meal	2.10	4.20	6.30	8.40	9.50		
Salad	.90	1.80	2.70	3.60	4.50		
Fries	.60	1.20	1.80	2.40	3.00		
Lg. Order Fries	.80	1.60	2.40	3.20	4.00		
Cola-Lrg.	.80	1.60	2.40	3.20	4.00		
Cola-Sm.	.70	1.40	2.10	2.80	3.50		
Orange-Lrg.	.80	1.60	2.40	3.20	4.00		
Orange-Sm.	.60	1.20	1.80	2.40	3.00		
Van. Shake	.80	1.60	2.40	3.20	4.00		
Choc. Shake	.80	1.60	2.40	3.20	4.00		
Coffee	.40	.80	1.20	1.60	2.00		
Milk	.40	.80	1.20	1.60	2.00		
Hot Choc.	.40	.80	1.20	1.60	2.00		

Subtotal________
Tax________
Total________

Exhibit 12.7
Printed sales check.

that includes tax. Some operations add the gratuity to the check automatically for large groups of customers. For example, a 15% tip can be found by using the following formula:

$$0.15 \times \text{Check subtotal} = 15\% \text{ Tip}$$

For the check subtotal of $51.68, for example, a 15% tip would be $7.75:

$$0.15 \times \$51.68 = \$7.75$$

When a tip is left, servers and managers can determine the percentage using a simple formula.

$$\frac{\text{Tip}}{\text{Check subtotal}} = \text{Percentage of check subtotal}$$

For instance, if a customer leaves a tip of $17.00 on a check subtotal of $84.79, the tip is 20% of the check's subtotal.

$$\frac{\$17.00}{\$84.79} = 0.2005 = 20\%$$

Let's try it!

Stuart was angry! "I know it was only my first day on the job," he said to Suzanne, "but I think that I deserve more than a 2% tip on a $35.63 sales check total!" Suzanne counted eight one-dollar bills on the table. What should she say to Stuart?

Balancing Cash Registers

At the end of each business day, recorded sales are balanced with the cash and credit card slips in the cash register to find actual receipts—or the actual money received. To do this, you first need to know the day's gross receipts. **Gross receipts** are all the recorded money received. The following formula can then be used to find actual receipts:

```
    Gross receipts
+   Change in drawer
-   Cash paidouts
    ----------------
    Actual receipts
```

Exhibit 12.8
A tip of 15% to 20% of the sales check subtotal is typical in American full-service restaurants.

If a register reads $841.96 in gross receipts, contains $25.00 in change, and has paid out $23.81, actual receipts will be $843.15.

```
   $841.96
+    25.00
   $866.96
-    23.81
   $843.15
```

Exhibit 12.9
Managers should balance recorded sales with cash and credit card slips in the cash register.

Balancing the cash register will help managers make sure that sales records are accurate.

Review Your Learning 12.2

1. A new French bistro is scheduled to open within the next six months. List the factors that customers consider when selecting a restaurant and explain how the bistro might need to prepare to respond to each of these factors.

2. A restaurant had total sales last month of $64,578 and served 2,966 customers. What was the operation's average sale per customer?

   a. $17.63
   b. $21.77
   c. $34.92
   d. $41.30

3. A guest check subtotal is $63.44. If sales tax is 6.7%, how much tax should be added? What would a 15% tip be on the sub-total?

4. A server at Miami Nights took the following order:

Soup	$3.95	Chicken teriyaki	$8.95
Dinner salad	$3.45	2 coffees	$1.05
Bacon burger	$6.95	Key lime pie	$1.05

   a. Subtotal the sales check.
   b. How much is an 8% sales tax on the subtotal?
   c. What is the check total once the tax is added?
   d. How much is a 15% tip on the total?
   e. If a customer leaves a tip of $2.75, what percentage has been left?

5. The Rockford Grill took in gross receipts of $1,096.57 for the day and paid out $16.03 in cash. At the close of the business day, $18.31 in change remains in the register. How much are actual receipts?

   a. $1,062.23
   b. $1,094.29
   c. $1,098.85
   d. $1,130.91

12.3

SECTION 12.3

Inventory Control

AFTER STUDYING SECTION 12.3, YOU SHOULD BE ABLE TO:

- Determine dollar value of inventory.
- Analyze five ways to determine closing inventory by performing math calculations.
- Determine daily and monthly food cost.

KEY TERMS

- **Book inventory**
- **Closing inventory**
- **First-in, first-out (FIFO)**
- **Inventory turnover**
- **Last-in, first-out (LIFO)**
- **Weighted average purchase price**

One important step in food cost and sales control is taking a physical inventory—or counting all items in stock. Taking physical inventory is usually done at the end of an accounting period, usually at the close of business on the last day of a calendar month. As you learned in *Chapter 10: Business Math,* taking physical inventory requires two employees to physically count and record the number of each item in the storeroom. Total values of each item are then calculated by multiplying the unit cost of the item by the number of items in inventory. For example, if there are 18 cans of peaches in inventory and each can costs $2.38, the total value of canned peaches is $42.84 *(18 × $2.38 = $42.84).*

Taking Inventory

After totals for each inventory item have been calculated, the **closing inventory,** or the total dollar value of the

FOODSERVICE OPERATION

Physical Inventory ________ 19______

Page 1

Classification	Item	Unit	Quantity	Unit Price	Total Cost

Total Page 1________

Exhibit 12.10
Sample physical inventory form.

inventory, can be calculated. There are five ways to determine the value of the closing inventory.

1. The *actual purchase price* method requires totaling the value of all remaining items in the closing inventory at the prices at which they were purchased.
2. The **first-in, first-out (FIFO)** method assumes that stock has been rotated during the month and that the items consumed were the first ones placed on the shelf. The items remaining, then, are those most recently purchased. The value of the closing inventory is calculated by using the prices at which the latest items were purchased.
3. The **weighted average purchase price** is determined by multiplying the number of items in the opening inventory and in each purchase by their individual purchase prices, adding these amounts to determine a total value for all inventory items, and then dividing by the total number of items involved.
4. The latest purchase price method involves simply multiplying the number of items remaining in inventory by the most recent price.
5. The **last-in, first-out (LIFO)** method uses the prices at which the earliest items were purchased. LIFO is usually used when management wants to maximize cost by minimizing the value of the closing inventory.

It's important to note that closing inventory values will usually differ slightly, depending on which method is used.

Food Cost Determination

Once a physical inventory has been taken, purchases have been totaled, and a closing inventory value has been determined, monthly food cost can be calculated using a simple formula.

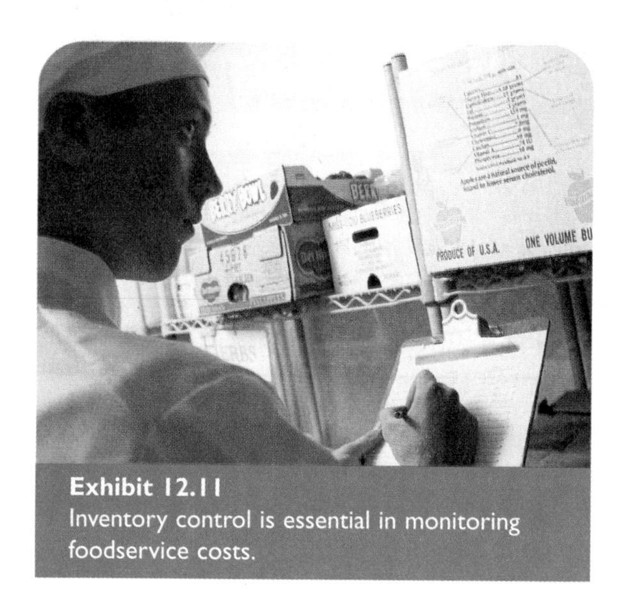

Exhibit 12.11
Inventory control is essential in monitoring foodservice costs.

Opening inventory (items on hand, first day of the month)
\+ Purchases (directs and stores)
Total available for sale
\- Closing inventory (items on hand, last day of the month)
Cost of food sold

For example, an operation begins the month with $4,050 in its food inventory, ends the month with $3,890 in inventory, and has receipts showing a total of $11,380 in purchases. The food cost for the month can then be calculated using the formula.

$4,050 Opening inventory
\+ 11,380 Purchases
15,430 Total available
\- 3,890 Closing inventory
$11,540 Monthly food cost

Keep in mind that adjustments to the monthly cost, such as account transfers, promotion expenses, employee meals, and complimentary items, must be made. Once all costs have been determined, a monthly cost report can be prepared. This report includes current figures, along with those from the previous month, under the categories of *food sales, net cost of items sold,* and *cost percentage.* These figures can help managers track the effectiveness of current procedures, as well as create goals for improving performance.

How About This?

For 32 oz jars of pickles at Bagels and More, records for the month indicate the following:

- **Opening inventory on the 1st of the month: 4 jars at $1.83 each**
- **Purchased on the 7th of the month: 10 jars at $2.57 each**
- **Purchased on the 16th of the month: 7 jars at $2.06 each**
- **Purchased on the 27th of the month: 3 jars at $2.75 each**

What is the weighted average purchase price?

Reviewing operating figures on a monthly basis might not be enough. If this is the case, daily cost calculations can be made. For food, the two categories of *directs* and *stores* form the basic parts of the daily food cost. As you learned in *Chapter 10: Business Math,* directs are charged to food cost immediately upon receipt, making it necessary to consult the receiving clerk's daily report to obtain the total of directs received on a given day. Stores, on the other hand, are charged to food cost as they are issued from inventory. Depending on an establishment's practices, additional figures, such as employee meals, must also be taken into account.

The daily cost of food can be calculated using a formula.

  Cost of directs
  (from the receiving clerk's daily report)
\+ Cost of stores
  (from requisitions and meat tags)
\+ Transfers from other departments or units to the food department
\- Transfers from the kitchen to other areas

  Cost of food sold
\- Cost of employee meals

  Daily food cost

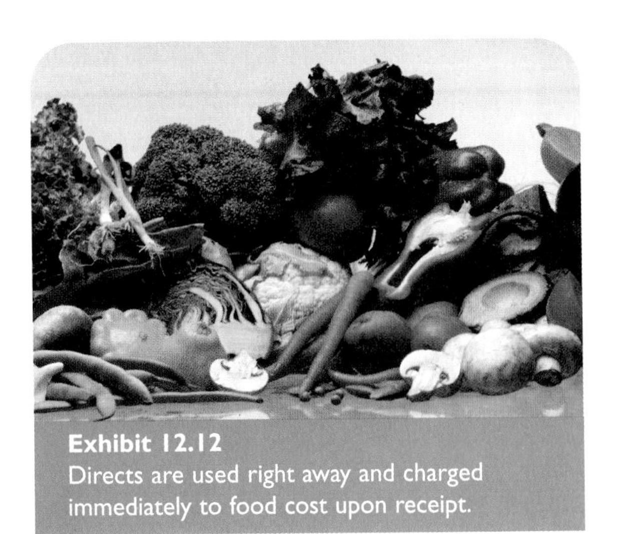

Exhibit 12.12
Directs are used right away and charged immediately to food cost upon receipt.

In addition to determining monthly and daily food cost, foodservice operations can be monitored by comparing *closing inventory,* or actual inventory, to book inventory. To calculate **book inventory** for any specific day, the closing inventory for the preceding day is added to stores purchased, and then any stores issued are subtracted. If this procedure is followed daily for a calendar month, the final figure will be the closing book value of the stores inventory for that month. Differences between book inventory and physical inventory could indicate that errors have been made in purchasing, receiving, storing, or issuing.

Inventory Turnover

There should always be appropriate amounts of food kept in inventory. To measure how often food has been ordered and used, managers can calculate the turnover of the inventory stock. Most restaurants keep a food supply that will last one or two weeks. Calculating **inventory turnover** is a two-step process. First you must determine the operation's average inventory, then calculate how many times the inventory has turned over.

$$\frac{\text{Opening inventory} + \text{Closing inventory}}{2} = \text{Average food inventory}$$

$$\frac{\text{Food cost for the month}}{\text{Average food inventory}} = \text{Inventory turnover}$$

If, for example, The Pasta Palace has an opening inventory of $5,000, a closing inventory of $6,500, and a food cost figure of $8,000 for the month, average inventory and inventory turnover is easy to determine.

$$\frac{\$5{,}000 + \$6{,}500}{2} = \$5{,}750$$

$$\frac{\$8{,}000}{\$5{,}750} = 1.39$$

If this rate stays constant over 12 months, The Pasta Palace's total inventory turnover for the year will be 16.68 times *(1.39 × 12)*, or once every 3.18 weeks *(52 weeks ÷ 16.68)*, which is substantially higher than the industry average of one or two weeks. At this point, the operation may want to re-examine its inventory levels and/or food cost.

Lets Try It...

The Ultimate Steakhouse's records for March 8 show the following:

Closing inventory for the preceding day:	**$12,848**
Stores purchased:	**$2,544**
Stores issued:	**$1,116**

What is the book inventory for the day?

Review Your Learning 12.3

1. On a separate sheet of paper, put the following inventory-related activities in their correct order by using the numbers 1 (first activity) through 7 (final activity).

   Total purchases

   Select valuation method

   Set goals for improving performance

   Take physical inventory

   Prepare monthly cost report

   Calculate closing inventory

   Compute monthly cost of food sold

2. Explain how to value closing inventory using each of the following methods:
   a. Actual purchase price method
   b. FIFO method
   c. Weighted average purchase price method
   d. Latest purchase price method
   e. LIFO

3. An operation opened in June with a food inventory of $6,220, closed with $5,650, and had purchases totaling $11,190. What was the cost of food sold?
   a. $4,680
   b. $6,440
   c. $10,620
   d. $11,760

4. The closing inventory for the preceding day is added to stores purchased and then any stores issued are subtracted to calculate:
   a. book inventory.
   b. daily food cost.
   c. amount transferred from other departments.
   d. cost of directs.

5. Boardwalk Burgers had an opening inventory of $3,500 for March and a closing inventory of $4,000. Its food cost for the month was $6,300.

   a. What was Boardwalk Burgers' average inventory for March?

   b. What was the operation's monthly inventory turnover?

   c. Does Boardwalk Burgers' inventory rate correspond to the industry average?

12.4

SECTION 12.4

Focusing on the Menu

AFTER STUDYING SECTION 12.4, YOU SHOULD BE ABLE TO:

- Determine standard portion cost.
- Determine selling prices using the food cost percentage method.
- Determine selling prices using the average check method.
- Determine selling prices using the contribution margin method.
- Determine selling prices using the straight mark-up pricing method.

KEY TERMS

- **Abstract**
- **Contribution margin**
- **Forecast**
- **Potential savings**

The menu is the primary sales tool in most foodservice operations. Since food costs influence what goes on the menu, foodservice managers must be aware of the factors that cause high food cost. These factors include:

- Improper purchasing.
- Inaccurate forecasting.
- Poor inventory control.
- Poor receiving procedures.
- Failure to follow standardized recipes.
- Poor production schedules.
- Lack of good selling and service.
- Improper selection of menu items.
- Employee theft.

Covering Costs

Whenever possible, the menu should reflect the overall cost of running the operation. That means the price of food should include all the costs needed to purchase, prepare, and serve it, along

Exhibit 12.13
Serving standard portion sizes helps to control costs.

with other costs, such as rent and labor. All costs need to be known, and controls must be established at every step in the operation.

One proven control is establishing standard portion sizes. As you'll recall from *Chapter 10: Business Math,* the standard portion size is the fixed amount of food served to a customer for a fixed selling price. Once standard portion size is known, managers can establish standard portion cost, or the dollar amount that a standard portion should cost. To determine the standard portion cost, the number of portions that a unit contains is divided by the unit's purchase price.

$$\frac{\text{Purchase price per unit}}{\text{Number of portions per unit}} = \text{Standard portion cost}$$

For example, if lettuce costs $42.00 per case and there are 160 heads of lettuce in a case, the standard portion cost is $0.26 *($42.00 ÷ 160).*

In addition to reflecting food cost, the menu also determines the number of employees needed at a given time. Labor cost is controlled by forecasting, or estimating, based on realistic goals and standards, how many customers are expected for meal times and how many employees are needed to meet their needs. Complicated menu preparations require skilled labor. When more preparation time is needed to produce food items, labor costs will be higher.

Menu Pricing

After a menu has been planned, each individual item has to be priced. Prices greatly influence customers' impressions of an operation. Therefore, menu planners take great care in pricing menu items.

> **Give It a Try...**
>
> **Tomato juice costs $38.00 per case, and there are 250 single-portion cans of tomato juice in a case. What is the standard portion cost?**

To price the menu, managers must determine what customers are willing to pay and examine competitors' prices, cost-to-sales ratios, and contribution margins. A **contribution margin** is the portion of dollars that a particular menu item contributes to overall profits.

Foodservice operations can use any one or a combination of methods to price the menu.

Food cost percentage method—The food cost percentage is the key to effective pricing. As you learned in Section 12.1, this percentage is equal to food cost divided by food sales. If an operation projects monthly food cost to be $18,000 and monthly food sales to be $62,000, the food cost percentage will be 29% *($18,000 ÷ $62,000)*. Based on this figure, managers can price all food items on the menu. If an item costs $1.12, its selling price can be determined using this pricing formula.

$$\frac{\text{Item cost}}{\text{Food cost percentage}} = \text{Price}$$

$$\frac{\$1.12}{0.29} = 3.862, \text{ or } \$3.86$$

Such a selling price would usually be rounded up, in this case to $3.90.

Average check method—To calculate the average check, total revenue is divided by the number of seats, average seat turnover, and days open in one year. The average check gives managers an idea of the price range of items on the menu. This range, along with an approximate food cost percentage, can then be used to determine each item's selling price. External factors, such as competition, should also be considered.

Timko's Fun-Drink-Eatery, owned and operated by Bennett Enterprises, Inc., Perrysburg, Ohio.

Exhibit 12.14
There are several methods that foodservice operators can use to price the menu.

Contribution margin method—Knowing the portion costs for each item sold, foodservice operators can determine the average contribution margin needed to cover overhead and yield a desired profit at an expected level of sales volume. Let's consider the following example in which 30,000 customers we're served.

$	100,000 Gross food sale
-	40,000 Cost of food sold
	60,000 Gross profit (total contribution margins)
-	50,000 Overhead costs
$	10,000 Profit

Each customer in the example above spent an average of $3.33 *($100,000 ÷ 30,000)* and contributed an average of $2.00 *([$50,000 + $10,000] ÷ 30,000)* to overhead and profit. Using the contribution margin method, the restaurant would price each menu item at $2.00 above cost. If sales volume matched forecasts, the minimum acceptable dollar amount would be met, provided that costs were kept strictly under control in all areas.

Straight mark-up pricing method—In straight mark-up pricing, managers multiply raw food cost by a predetermined fraction. For example, if an operation pricing a menu item with a raw food cost of $0.63 uses a straight two-thirds mark-up, the menu price will be calculated as follows:

$$0.63 \times \tfrac{2}{3} = 0.42$$

$$0.42 + 0.63 = \$1.05$$

Managers must choose the pricing method or variation of methods that best suits their operation.

The Importance of Forecasting

In order to control menu costs, managers must forecast sales of menu items, control portions, and carefully select food items that meet the operation's cost and operating needs. As you'll remember from *Chapter 10: Business Math, forecasting* is a procedure in which data are used to predict what is likely to happen in the future. This guesswork is often a major factor in successful menu planning. Once forecasting has been done, managers can establish standard portion sizes and corresponding standard portion costs.

Comparing actual costs to standard costs allows foodservice operators to monitor the success of an establishment. When these costs are compared, managers have a clear picture of any problems that may exist in the daily operation.

One way to examine actual and standard costs is through daily comparison. To use this method, managers must analyze the menu precost and abstract form. This form is divided into two sections—the **forecast,** before sales have taken place, and the **abstract,** after sales have taken place. At the close of a business day or after a meal period, the forecasted sales figures are compared to actual sales.

The difference between actual and standard costs is called **potential savings.** Potential savings can be recorded as dollars and/or percentages of sales. The difference between actual and standard costs may be caused by overproduction, overpurchasing, or a failure to follow standardized recipes.

Used properly, forecasting enables a manager to track the popularity of existing menu items and to predict those that might prove popular in the future. This information is especially helpful when the menu is being revised.

Cost Control: What the Future Holds

Managers in the 21st century can expect to assume a greater responsibility for managing costs and expenses, as well as sales and revenues. This is especially true since a manager's salary and benefits are directly linked to efficiently managed income and expenses. Managers will also need to have a good understanding of financial statements and be more involved in budgeting and forecasting.

Date Monday 11/1/99

Menu Item	Number Forecast	Forecast			Total Cost	Total Sales	Number Sold	Forecast			Total Cost	Total Sales
		Cost	S.P.	F.C.%				Cost	S.P.	F.C.%		
A	80	2.05	5.95	34.5	164.00	476.00	75	2.05	5.95	34.5	153.75	446.25
B	65	2.45	6.95	35.3	159.25	451.75	60	2.45	6.95	35.3	137.00	417.00
C	10	4.30	12.95	33.2	43.00	129.50	6	4.30	12.95	33.2	25.80	77.70
D	165	2.60	7.95	32.7	429.00	1,311.75	159	2.60	7.95	32.7	413.40	1,264.05
				33.6	795.25	2,369.00				33.6	739.95	2,205.00

Exhibit 12.15
Sample menu precost and abstract form.

Review Your Learning 12.4

1. What are the causes of high food cost?

2. If apples cost $37 per case and there are 85 portions in each case, what is the standard portion cost for apples?

   a. $0.44 c. $1.39

   b. $0.48 d. $2.30

3. Indicate which menu pricing method you would use if you had only the following information. Then calculate the price for the menu item indicated.

   a. Food cost is to be increased by 1/3.
   Menu item—Chicken Parmesan at a cost of $4.87.

   b. Gross food sale = $210,000; cost of food sold = $120,000; overhead costs = $60,000; number of customers served = 30,000.
   Menu item—Onion rings at a cost of $1.17.

   c. Monthly food cost = $16,000; monthly food sales = $56,000.
   Menu item—Rice pudding at a cost of $0.64.

4. Which of the following gives managers an idea of the price range of items on the menu?

   a. Standard portion cost.

   b. Total revenue.

   c. Average check.

   d. Contribution margin.

5. On a separate sheet of paper, fill in the missing figures for the menu precost and abstract form shown below.

Date: Friday, June 14

Menu Item	Number Forecast	Cost	Forecast Sales	FC Price	Total Cost %	Total Sales
Hamburger	60	2.65	7.95	___	______	______
Pizza	47	4.40	11.95	___	______	______
Burrito	82	2.10	6.95	___	______	______
Hot Dog	58	2.55	7.95	___	______	______

Menu Item	Number Sold	Cost	Forecast Sales Price	FC %	Total Cost	Total Sales
Hamburger	51	______	______	___	______	______
Pizza	55	______	______	___	______	______
Burrito	88	______	______	___	______	______
Hot Dog	31	______	______	___	______	______

Flashback

CHAPTER 12

SECTION 12.1: COST PLANNING

- Understanding the relationship between cost and sales, along with realistic planning and forecasting, is essential to the profitability of all food operations.
- **Food cost** is found by adding all requisitions from the storeroom, as well as daily purchases. **Sales** result when an operation exchanges products and services for money. **Revenue** is the income from the sale of food items before expenses are deducted.
- By determining food cost and sales, managers can calculate the **food cost percentage** for each business day. The formula for computing the food cost percentage is *Cost ÷ Sales = Food cost percentage.*
- Managers should follow the basic, four-step cost control process: (1) Establish standards and standard operating procedures; (2) Train all employees to follow established procedures; (3) Monitor performance and compare actual performance to standards; and (4) Take appropriate action to correct deviations or changes.
- Cost control alone will not guarantee **profitability**—having higher revenue than cost.
- Measures must be taken to make sure that all sales result in appropriate income to the business. Each sale must be accurately recorded and checked against production records. All portions that have left the kitchen must be recorded as sales, and any discrepancies should be **reconciled.**
- A **budget** is a realistic expression of management's goals and objectives expressed in financial terms.
- An **operating budget** is a forecast of sales activity and an estimate of costs that will be incurred in generating sales. Once an acceptable budget is approved for an upcoming period, it is compared to the establishment's operating performance at regular intervals as the **fiscal year** progresses.
- Creating a budget for a new business is more difficult than preparing one

for an existing establishment because **historical data** is not available. Managers must use a combination of known facts, comparable industry averages, and formulas to determine anticipated costs and revenue.

- When projecting foodservice revenue with a formula, a variety of factors may come into play, including number of seats, estimated turnover, estimated average check, and number of days in the year that the operation will be open.
- Good cost-to-sales relationships do not automatically result in profits, and lower cost percentages are not always more desirable than higher ones.
- Foodservice managers often calculate an **average cover** to help them determine the number of sales dollars and customers required to meet a financial goal. The formula to find the average cover is: *Total variable cost for the period ÷ Total number of customers during the period = Average cover.*
- **Variable costs** are expenses that are directly affected by changes in sales volume, while **fixed costs** do not change with business volume.
- Relationships exist among sales, cost of sales, cost of labor, cost of overhead, and profit. This is known as the **cost/volume/profit** relationship and can be expressed with the formula *(Fixed costs + Profit desired) ÷ (100%Variable cost percentage) = Revenue level.*
- The cost/volume/profit formula can be used to determine the **break-even point,** which is the revenue level at which an operation neither earns a profit nor suffers a loss. The formula also allows you to calculate the level of revenue needed for an operation to earn a specific profit.

SECTION 12.2: CONTROLLING SALES

- The three goals of sales control are to sell products, earn revenue, and make a profit.
- All customers select restaurants based on location, cleanliness, menu items, prices, decor, portion sizes, product quality, and/or service.
- To control revenue, managers must establish standards and standard procedures. All food items sold, along with their corresponding prices, should be recorded, and daily revenues must be tracked. Numbered guest checks can also be used.

- One helpful formula for developing accurate sales information determines the **average sale per customer** for each meal: *Total dollar sales ÷ Total number of covers = Average sale per customer.*
- A **sales check** contains lines, or spaces, to itemize customers' purchases.
- There are two basic ways to record sales. Blank sales checks contain blank lines to be filled in by servers. Printed checks list all of an operation's menu items, requiring servers to simply circle or mark customers' choices.
- Every server must record sales and total each check completely and accurately. First, the items ordered by customers should be subtotaled. Then the sales tax must be added. Many operations have tax tables from which to take the tax amount; others use cash registers that add the tax on automatically. You can also calculate the tax by hand using the state sales tax percentage.
- In most American full-service operations, customers leave a **gratuity,** or tip, for servers equal to 15% to 20% of the sales check total. A 15% tip can be determined by using the formula *0.15 × Check total = Tip.*
- When a tip is left, servers and managers can determine the percentage as follows: *Tip ÷ Check total = Percentage of check total.*
- At the end of each business day, employees should balance recorded sales with the cash and credit card slips in the cash register. The following formula can be used: *Gross receipts (all recorded money received) + Change in drawer - Cash paidouts = Actual receipts.*

SECTION 12.3: INVENTORY CONTROL

- A physical inventory of all items in stock is typically done at the close of business on the last day of a calendar month. Total values of each item are calculated by multiplying the unit cost of the item by the number of items in inventory.
- After totals have been added, the **closing inventory,** or the total dollar value of the inventory, can be calculated. There are five ways to determine the value of the closing inventory.

1. The actual purchase price method requires totaling the value of all remaining items in the closing inventory at the prices at which they were bought.
2. The **first-in, first-out (FIFO)** method assumes that stock has been rotated during the month and that the items consumed were the first ones placed on the shelf. Items remaining in inventory are multiplied by the price of the latest items.
3. The weighted average purchase price is determined by multiplying the number of items in the opening inventory and in each purchase by their individual purchase prices, adding these amounts to determine a total value for all inventory items, and then dividing by the total number of items involved.
4. The latest purchase price method involves simply multiplying the number of items remaining in inventory by the most recent price.
5. The **last-in, first-out (LIFO)** method uses the earliest prices at which items were purchased. LIFO is usually used when management wants to maximize cost by minimizing the value of the closing inventory.

- Monthly food cost can be calculated with the following formula:

  Opening inventory (items on hand, first day of the month)
  \+ *Purchases*
  ___
  Total available for sale
  \- *Closing inventory (food on hand, last day of the month)*
  ___
  Cost of food sold

- For food, the two categories of **directs** and **stores** form the basic parts of the daily food cost.
- The following formula can be used to calculate daily food cost:

  Cost of directs (from the receiving clerk's daily report)
  \+ *Cost of stores (from requisitions and meat tags)*
  \+ *Transfers from other departments or units to the food department*
  \- *Transfers from the kitchen to other areas*
  ___
  Cost of food sold
  \- *Cost of employee meals*
  ___
  Daily food cost

- Managers can monitor operations by comparing closing inventory, or actual inventory, to book inventory. To calculate **book inventory** for any specific day, the closing inventory for the preceding day is added to stores purchased, and then any stores issued are subtracted.
- To measure how often food has been ordered and used, managers can calculate the frequency of turnover of the inventory stock. Most restaurants keep a food supply that will last one or two weeks.
- The following formulas are used to calculate monthly **inventory turnover:** *(Opening inventory + Closing inventory) ÷ 2 = Average inventory; Food cost for the month ÷ Average food inventory = Inventory turnover.*

SECTION 12.4: FOCUSING ON THE MENU

- The menu is the primary sales tool in most foodservice operations.
- Managers must be aware of the factors that cause high food cost.
- The menu should reflect the overall cost of running the operation. One proven control is the establishment of **standard portion size,** the fixed quantity served to a customer for a fixed selling price, and **standard portion cost,** the dollar amount that a standard portion should cost. To determine the standard portion cost, the following formula is used: *Purchase price per unit ÷ Number of portions per unit = Standard portion cost.*
- In addition to reflecting food cost, the menu will largely determine the number of employees needed at a given time.
- To price the menu, managers must determine what customers are willing to pay and examine competitors' prices, cost-to-sales ratios, and contribution margins. A **contribution margin** is the portion of dollars a particular menu item contributes to overall profits.
- With the food cost percentage method, menu items are priced by dividing the item cost by the food cost percentage.
- To calculate the average check in an establishment, total revenue is divided by the number of seats, average seat turnover, and days open in one year.

  The average check gives managers an idea of the price range of items on the menu.

- Knowing the portion costs for each item sold, foodservice operators can determine the average contribution margin needed to cover overhead and yield a desired profit at an expected level of sales volume.
- In straight mark-up pricing, managers multiply raw food cost by a predetermined fraction.
- **Forecasting** is a procedure in which data is used to predict what is likely to happen in the future. This guesswork is often a major factor in successful menu planning.
- One way to examine actual and standard costs is through daily comparison. To use this method, managers must analyze the menu precost and abstract form. This form is divided into two sections—the **forecast,** before sales have taken place, and the **abstract,** after sales have take place. At the close of a business day or after a meal period, the forecasted sales figures are compared to actual sales.
- The difference between actual and standard costs is called **potential savings.** Potential savings may be caused by overproduction, overpurchasing, or a failure to follow standardized recipes.
- Managers in the 21st century can expect to assume a greater responsibility for managing costs and expenses, as well as sales and revenues. They will also need to have a good understanding of financial statements and be more involved in budgeting and forecasting.

Glossary
OF KEY TERMS

A

Abstract
Part of the menu precost and abstract form on which data is recorded after sales have taken place

Accident
Unplanned, undesirable event that can cause major property damage, injuries or fatalities, lost time from work, and disruptions of work

Accompaniment
Side dishes to a main dish

Accompaniment salad
Salad that balances and complements the rest of the meal; light and flavorful, but not too rich

Acid
Contained in foods such as citrus, vinegar, and wine that have a sour taste; when used in cooking, it affects the pigment of certain vegetables and fruits; acids have a pH less than seven

Alkaline
Found in baking soda or any other substance with a pH level greater than seven; when used in cooking, it affects the pigment of certain vegetables

Amino (uh-MEAN-oh) acid
Building blocks of proteins; of the 22 amino acids, 9 are essential amino acids

Anthocyanin (an-thoe-SIGH-ah-nin)
Red or purple pigment in vegetables and fruits

Anthoxanthin (an-thoe-ZAN-thin)
Colorless or white pigment in vegetables and fruits

Appetizer salad
Attractive salad served as a first course to stimulate the appetite

Application form
Form that asks basic information about the applicant that must be completed in order to apply to colleges, trade schools,

or for a job

Arson
Deliberate and malicious burning of property

Arugula (ah-ROO-guh-luh)
Bitter, aromatic salad green with a peppery mustard flavor

As purchased (AP) amount
Amount or weight of food before trimming

Average cover
Total variable cost for a period of time divided by total number of customers during that period

Average cover formula
Formula used to calculate the number of customers served; total dollar sales for a period of time divided by the number of customers served

Average sales per customer
Total dollar sales divided by total number of covers

B

Babaganoush (bah-bah-ghan-OOSH)
Middle Eastern eggplant dip

Back-of-the-house
Areas of the foodservice operation, like the kitchen, storage area, or pantry, where employees don't see customers on a regular basis; includes all positions in areas outside of public space; the team of individuals who perform all the food production tasks for an operation

Bacteria
Single-celled organisms that are invisible and often cause disease

Bain marie (bayn muh-REE)
Hot-water bath used to hold hot foods

Bake
Cook food in a closed oven without liquid

Bake pan
Shallow rectangular pan used to bake foods

Balance scale
Scale used in the bake shop to weigh dry ingredients

Barbecue
Cook food on a grill while basting with a marinade or sauce

Base
Part of a salad, also called the *underliner*

Baste
Moisten food during cooking with pan drippings, sauce, or other liquid; also refers to method in which food, such as an egg, is fried and then steamed in a covered pan

Bench scraper
Used to cut and separate dough and scrape extra dough and flour from tables

Blanch
Cooking an item briefly in boiling water or hot fat before finishing or storing it

Body
Main ingredient of a salad

Boil
Cook food submerged in a liquid that has reached the boiling point

Boning knife
Six-inch knife used to separate raw meat from the bone

Book inventory
Value of inventory determined by adding the closing inventory from the preceding day to stores purchased and then subtracting any stores issued

Borrow
Take 10 ones from the column immediately to the left in order to subtract a larger digit from a smaller one

Bound salad
Salad mixed with a heavy dressing, such as mayonnaise, used to hold the ingredients together

Braise
Cooking method in which food is browned, then covered and simmered with a small amount of liquid until food is tender

Brazing pan
High-sided, flat-bottomed cooking pan used to braise, stew, and brown meats

Break-even point
Revenue level at which an operation neither earns a profit nor suffers a loss

Broil
Cook food by placing it below a very hot heat source

Budget
Realistic expression of management's goals and objectives expressed in financial terms

Butcher knife
Used to fabricate raw meat

C

Calorie
Measurement of the energy released by some nutrients

Can opener
Machine used to open cans; can be small and hand-held or large and attached to work tables

Canapé (CAN-uh-pay)
Tiny open-faced sandwich served as an hors d'oeuvre

Caramelize
Brown fruit or vegetables with a small amount of sugar in the presence of heat

Carbohydrate
Nutrient used mainly for energy

Carcinogenic
Substance that can cause cancer

Cardiopulmonary resuscitation (CPR) (CAR-dee-oh-PULL-man-air-ee ree-SUHS-i-TAY-shun)
First-aid technique that tries to restore breathing and heartbeat to persons who show no signs of breathing or pulse

Career
Profession or work in a certain field

Career ladder
Series of jobs through which a person can advance in a career

Carotenoid (car-AH-ten-oid)
Orange, yellow, red-orange, or red pigment in vegetables and fruits

Cast iron skillet
Heavy, thick pan made of cast iron; used for frying foods

Celsius (SELL-see-us)
Metric temperature measure

Centi-
Metric prefix equaling one one-hundredth

Charbroiler
Used to broil foods with a result similar to a charcoal broiler

Chef's knife
All-purpose knife used to chop, slice, and mince all types of foods

Chef's salad
Main course salad containing mixed greens, raw vegetables, and strips of meat and cheese

Chemical leaveners
Ingredients, such as baking soda or baking powder, used to leaven (raise) baked goods quickly

China cap
Cone-shaped strainer used to strain soups, stocks, and other liquids

Chinois (chee-no-AH)
Very fine-meshed china cap, used to strain very small solid ingredients

Chlorophyll (CLOR-oh-fill)
Green pigment in vegetables and fruits

Cholesterol
White, waxy substance found in foods derived from animals products; helps the body carry out its many processes

Circular dishwasher
Dishwasher that circulates dishes through two or three tanks

Clam knife
Short, blunt knife used to shuck, or open clams

Clarify
Purify a hot liquid by removing solids and impurities; process used to make clarified butter

Classical French garnish
Accompaniments to a main entrée

Clean
Free of visible soil such as dirt, dust, or food waste

Cleaver
Heavy, rectangular knife used to chop a variety of foods

Clingstone
Type of peach whose flesh sticks to the pit

Closed question
Question that can be answered with a simple *yes* or *no* or with a brief, factual statement

Closing inventory
Total dollar value of the remaining inventory after totals for each inventory item have been calculated

Club sandwich
Three slices of toast filled with sliced meat or poultry, bacon, lettuce, and tomato

Coffee maker
Machine used to make coffee; quantities range from a few cups to several gallons

Colander (CAH-len-der)
Strainer that stands on metal feet used to drain liquid from cooked pasta and vegetables

College application
Form designed by colleges that asks basic personal information about applicant's background and education

Combination cooking
Cooking method that involves both moist and dry heat

Combination salad
Combination of different ingredients or different kinds of salads

Comment cards
Quick surveys that customers complete telling how satisfied they were with their food and service; should be kept short and simple

Comp (complimentary)
To not charge for

Complement
To add to the flavor or appearance of food

Complete protein
Protein that contains all the essential amino acids in the right amounts

Condiment
Cooked or prepared flavorings

Consommé (CON-suh-may)
Rich, flavorful broth or stock that has been clarified

Contamination
Unintended presence of harmful substances or micro-organisms in food or water

Contribution margin
Portion of dollars a particular menu item contributes to overall profits

Convection oven
Oven with a fan that circulates hot air

Conventional (standard) oven
Standard type of oven with the heat source located on the floor of the oven

Conversion factor
Number determined by dividing a desired recipe yield by the original yield in order to convert recipe ingredient amounts

Conveyor (con-VAY-er) oven
Oven in which food is moved back and forth on a conveyor belt inside the oven

Cook's fork
Long fork with two pointed tines used to test the doneness of braised meats and vegetables, lifting items to the plate, and for steadying items being cut

Cooked salad
Main course salad that contains cooked foods as the main ingredients

Cooking loss test
Control method used to determine the standard portion cost of meat items that experience weight loss during the cooking process

Corrosive
Eats away or dissolves material

Cost
Money spent to make something or to provide a service

Cost control
Ongoing process of regulating costs and standards

Cost/volume/profit
Relationship among cost, volume, and profit expressed as a mathematical formula

Coulis (coo-LEE)
Vegetable sauce made from a purée of vegetables or fruit that can be served hot or cold

Countertop broiler
Small broiler that sits on top of a work table; used primarily in quick-service restaurants

Cover
Customer served

Cover letter
Letter sent with a resume to a potential employer

Cream
Fatty component of milk; can be classified as heavy (whipping) or light

Crêpe (crape or crepp)
Thin pour batter that has been cooked on a slightly greased griddle; also called Swedish pancake

Critical control point
Point where specific action can be taken to eliminate, prevent, or minimize a hazard from happening

Cross multiply
Method used to multiply fractions; multiply the numerator of one fraction by the denominator of the other

Cross-contamination
Transfer of harmful microorganisms to foods by human hands, utensils, equipment, or directly from another food

Crudité (croo-dee-TAY)
French term for raw vegetables served as a relish

Customary unit
Standard unit of measurement, most commonly used in the United States

Customer service
Employee and manager attitudes, skills, and policies that allow an operation to meet its customers' needs and wants

D

Deci-
Metric prefix equaling one-tenth

Deck oven
Type of conventional oven in which two to four shelves, or decks, are stacked on top of each other

Deep-fat fryer
Used to cook foods in hot oil or fat

Deep-fry
Cook breaded or batter-coated food by immersing it completely in hot fat or oil

Denominator
Bottom portion of a fraction

Depreciation (dey-PREE-she-AY-shun)
Decline in value of an asset over time

Desired yield
Number of servings needed

Dessert salad
Salad that is sweet and contains fruits, sweetened gelatin, nuts, cream, or whipped cream

Dialect
Variation of a language spoken by a particular group of people

Dietary Guidelines for Americans
General dietary recommendations for healthy Americans aged two or older

Dip
Thick sauces served hot or cold to accompany other foods

Directly variable cost
Cost that varies directly with sales volume; every change in sales volume results in a corresponding change in cost

Directs
Food items purchased for immediate use and charged immediately to cost

Discrimination
Making a decision based on prejudice

Diversity
Refers to the great variety of people and their backgrounds, experiences, opinions, religions, ages, talents, and abilities

Dividend
Number placed inside the long division sign

Divisor
Number placed outside the long division sign

Dollop (DOLL-up)
Small scoop or spoonful

Double boiler
One pot fitted into another to gently cook delicate foods, such as cream and chocolate, over simmering or boiling water

Dough arm
Mixer attachment used to mix heavy, thick doughs

Drupe (droop)
Fruit that has a central pit enclosing a single seed, such as cherry, peach, apricot

Dry lab
When someone enters temperatures in a record book without actually measuring the temperature of the food item

Dry-heat cooking
Cooking method in which food is cooked either by direct application of heat or by indirect heat without the use of moisture

Dupe (doop)
Duplicate of guest check

E

Edible portion (EP) amount
Amount or weight of food after trimming

Employee manual
Written booklet containing general information about employment, includ-

ing company policies, rules and procedures, employee benefits, and other topics related to the company

Employee turnover
Ratio of employees who leave to total employees

Emulsified (uh-MUL-si-fide) vinaigrette dressing
Salad dressing with added egg yolks, which make the dressing thicker, coating ingredients more heavily

Entrepreneur (ON-trah-prah-NOOR)
Person who owns and runs his or her own business

Entry-level job
Job that requires very little or no previous experience

Enzymatic (en-zi-MAT-ick) browning
Chemical reaction that causes certain fruits to turn dark once the inside flesh is exposed to air

Escarole (ESS-kuh-role)
Type of salad green

Essential amino acid
Amino acid that must be provided by food because it cannot be produced by the body; nine of the 22 amino acids are essential amino acids

Essential fatty acid
Necessary for healthy skin, healthy cells, and other bodily functions

Ethylene (eth-el-LEEN) gas
Natural agent in fruits that causes them to ripen

Etiquette (EH-tah-kit)
Proper behavior; good manners

F

Fat
Nutrient that supplies essential fatty acids, which are necessary for healthy skin, healthy cells, and other bodily functions.

Fat-soluble vitamin
Vitamins that mix only with fat (vitamins A, D, E, and K)

Feedback
Comments about or corrections to an action or process

Fiber
Found only in plant foods; part of plants that cannot be digested by humans; not absorbed in the intestines and therefore eliminated

First aid
Treatment given to an injured person until more complete treatment can be provided by emergency service or other health care providers

First in, first out (FIFO)
Stock rotation and storage principle of using older items before new ones

Fiscal year
Twelve-month period during which a business cycle takes place

Fixed cost
Expense that does not change with sales volume

Fixed equipment
Permanent equipment that cannot be moved for cleaning

Flat beater
Mixer attachment used to mix, mash, and cream soft foods

Flat-top burner
Type of range; a thick slate of cast iron steel that covers the heat source; provides even and consistent heat

Flight (rackless) dishwasher
Dishwasher that prewashes, washes, and rinses dishes

Flow of food
Route food takes on its way to being served, from receiving to serving

Flowchart
Chart that follows a menu item from the point when the ingredients are received to the moment the item is served to the customer

Flower vegetable
Vegetable in which the flower and the attached stem of the plant are eaten.

Focus group
Group of customers called together regularly to provide feedback on ways to improve customer service

Food chopper
Used to chop vegetables, meats, and other foods using a rotating blade and bowl

Food cost
Cost found by adding all requisitions from the storeroom to daily purchases

Food cost percentage
Food cost divided by sales

Food Guide Pyramid
Model visual guide designed by the U.S. Department of Agriculture to help plan healthy meals

Food mill
Used to purée foods to different consistencies

Food warmer
Used to hold hot foods for service

Foodborne illness
Illness that is carried or transmitted to people by food

Foodborne outbreak
Incident of foodborne illness that involves two or more people that eat the same food

Foodservice management
Coordination of people, resources, products, and facilities related to the design, preparation, and presentation of food outside the home

Forecast
Procedure in which data is used to predict what is likely to occur in the future; part of the menu precost and abstract form on which data is recorded before sales have taken place

Forecasting
Procedure in which data is used to predict what is likely to happen in the future

Freestone
Type of peach thats flesh separates easily from the pit

French toast
Sliced bread dipped in an egg-and-milk mixture and lightly fried

Front-of-the-house
All areas or departments whose employees meet and talk directly to guests; includes positions such as host/hostess, cashier, bar staff, wait staff, and bus persons

Fructose (FROOK-tose)
Natural form of sugar found in fruits and vegetables

Fruit
Organ that develops from the ovary of a flowering plant and contains one or more seeds

Fruit salad
Salad with fruits as the main ingredient

Fruit vegetables
Vegetables that develop from the ovary of a flowering plant and contain one or more seeds

Fungi (FUN-ghee)
Large groups of plants ranging from single-celled organisms to giant mushrooms

G

Garnish
Decorative, edible items added to ornament or enhance the appearance of the main food item

Gelatin
Jelly-like substance that can be used as a thickener and stabilizer; can be made from prepared mixes with sugar and color added

General safety audit
Safety inspection of an operation's facilities, equipment, employee practices, and management practices

Glaze
Finish in which a small amount of honey, sugar, or maple syrup is added to the vegetable, coating it and giving it a sheen as it heats

Glucose
Type of simple sugar; the body's primary energy source and the only energy source for the brain and nervous system

Gram
Metric weight measure

Grater
Used to grate hard cheeses, vegetables, potatoes, and other foods

Gratuity (gra-TOO-i-tee)
Money charged or left as a tip for service

Green leafy vegetable
Vegetables with broad leaves that range from dark green to pale green

Griddle
Flat, heated surface on which foods are directly cooked

Grill
Cook food on a rack above a heat source

Gross receipts
All recorded money received

Group training
Best method to use for large numbers of employees when demonstration and practice at a work station or with equipment are not necessary

Guacamole (gwah-kuh-MOE-lee)
Traditional Mexican dip that used avocados as the main ingredient

H

Hash
Mixture of chopped meats, potatoes, and onions

Hash browns
Grated or chopped potatoes pan-fried to a crispy brown

Hazard
Biological, chemical, or physical properties that might make food unsafe

Hazard Analysis Critical Control Point (HACCP)
Food safety system that highlights potentially hazardous foods and how they should be handled

Hazard Communication Standard (HCS)
OSHA requirement that operators notify all their employees about chemical hazards on the job, and train them to use chemicals safely; also called *Haz-Com* and *Right-to-Know*

Health hazard
Condition that causes long- or short-term injuries or illnesses; can include chemicals that are toxic (poisonous), carcinogenic (cause cancer), irritating, or corrosive (cause a material to be eaten away or dissolved)

Heat detector
Device that detects fires where there is no smoke; activated by a significant increase of temperature associated with fire

Heimlich maneuver (HIME-lick mah-NOO-ver)
Procedure that removes food or other obstacles from a choking person's airway

Herbs (urbs)
Leaves, stems, or flowers of an aromatic plant; available in either fresh or dried form

Historical data
Past information including sales, customer counts, costs, etc.

Home fries
Thickly-sliced or large-diced potatoes lightly pan-fried

Homogenization (huh-MAH-juh-ni-ZAY-shun)
Treatment that distributes milkfat uniformly throughout milk

Hormone
Special messengers that regulate many different body functions

Hors d'oeuvres (or DERVS)
Small, bite-sized finger foods that have a spicy or savory flavor; used often as an appetizer

Hotel broiler
Used to broil large amounts of food quickly

Hotel pan
Used for baking, roasting, or poaching meats or vegetables

Human resources
People who work for an operation and help it achieve its service goals

Hummus
Middle Eastern dip made of chick peas

Hydroponic (high-dro-PAHN-ick) farming
Technique that involves growing vegetables in nutrient-enriched water rather than in soil

I

Ice machine
Machine that makes ice in cubes, flakes, chips, and crushed ice

Incomplete protein
Protein that lacks one or more of the essential amino acids

Insulin
Hormone that controls blood sugar levels

Integrated Pest Management (IPM)
System to prevent, control, or eliminate pest infestation in foodservice establishments

Internal customer
Employees and coworkers who depend on one another to do a good job

Inventory turnover
Food cost for the month divided by average food inventory

Invoice
Bill from a vendor or supplier

Issue
Distribute food items from inventory storage

J

Job application
Form designed for employers that asks basic personal information about background

Job interview
Meeting with a potential employer in which qualifications for a job are discussed

K

Kilo-
Metric prefix equaling 1,000

L

Ladle
Long-handled spoon used to portion out liquids

Last-in, first-out (LIFO)
Valuation method that uses the earliest prices at which items were purchased

Legume (lay-GOOM)
Food group that includes protein-rich beans, peas, and other pod-growing plants

Liability
Legal responsibility that one party has to another, enforceable by law in court

Liaison
Mixture of egg yolks and cream

Liter
Metric volume measure

Long-term goal
Operation goal that covers a two- to five-year period or longer

Lowest common denominator
Smallest number that all denominators can be divided into evenly

M

Macronutrient
Nutrients that the body needs in a relatively large quantity; examples are carbohydrates, fat, and proteins; macronutrients provide fuel for energy

Main course salad
Salad large enough to serve as a full meal, usually containing protein ingredients

Margarine
Manufactured food product that looks and tastes like butter, but contains no milk products

Marinate
Method used to soak food in a mixture of herbs, spices, and liquid to tenderize and add flavor to the food

Master cleaning schedule
Schedule or chart showing a cleaning program; lists what is to be cleaned, who is to clean it, how it is to be cleaned, and how often

Material resources
Equipment and materials used to operate a business

Material Safety Data Sheet (MSDS)
Informational sheet given to operators by chemical suppliers or manufacturers listing hazards and necessary precautions for safe use and storage

Mayonnaise (MAY-uh-naze)
Most stable emulsified dressing

Measuring cup
Used to measure liquid and dry ingredients

Measuring spoon
Used to measure small amounts of spices or liquids

Meter
Metric length measure

Metric system
Measurement system based on multiples of ten

Metric unit
Standard unit of measurement used in many parts of the world; based on multiples of ten; used also by scientists and health professionals

Micronutrient
Nutrients that the body needs in relatively small amounts; examples include vitamins, water, and minerals

Microorganism
Form of life that can be seen only with the aid of a microscope, such as bacteria, molds, parasites, viruses, and fungi

Microwave oven
Oven used mainly to reheat and thaw foods by heating the food's molecules with microwaves

Milli-
Metric prefix equaling one one-thousandth

Mineral
Substances classified as major or trace according to the amounts needed by the body

Mise en place **(meez ahn PLAHS)**
Literally, in French, "to put in place;" the preparation and assembly of ingredients, pans, utensils, and equipment or serving pieces needed for a particular dish or service

Mission statement
Description of an operation's philosophy of doing business

Mixer
Used to mix and process large amounts of food with specialized attachments

Moist-heat cooking
Cooking method in which food is cooked in a hot liquid or steam

Mold
Highly-adaptable organisms that grow quickly and can cause serious infections and allergies; can also produce illness-causing toxins

Multidecker sandwich
More than two slices of bread or roll filled with several ingredients

Mystery shopper
Person hired to visit an operation and report on his or her experiences and impressions of the operation

N

Near miss
Event in which property damage or injury are narrowly avoided

Networking
Contacting people who can provide information about job openings

Nonperishable
Food with a relatively long shelf life (compared to perishable items)

Numerator
Upper portion of a fraction

Nutrient
Chemicals in food that the body needs in order to work properly

O

Occupational Safety and Health Administration (OSHA)
Federal agency that creates and enforces safety-related standards and regulations in the workplace

Offset spatula **(SPACH-e-la)**
Utensil used to turn and flip foods on a griddle or broiler

Omelet
Slightly beaten egg dish usually with a filling

On-the-job training
Appropriate for teaching skills that are easily shown and practiced; allows

employees to demonstrate skills and reinforce what they have been taught

Open burner
Grate-style burner that supplies direct heat to the item being cooked

Open-ended question
Question that requires a more in-depth answer than *yes* or *no* and encourages job applicants to talk about themselves

Open-faced sandwich
Single slice of bread or roll topped with hot or cold fillings and toppings

Operating budget
Forecast of sales activity and an estimate of costs that will be incurred in generating sales

Operational plan
Statement outlining the goals of an organization and plans for reaching the goals

Organization chart
Chart that shows job positions according to function and indicates reporting relationships

Orientation
Process that helps new employees learn about the operation, various procedures and policies, and introduces them to their coworkers

Osteoporosis (AHS-tee-oh-purr-OH-sis)
Condition in which the bones gradually lose their minerals, becoming weak and fragile

Overhead costs
All fixed costs associated with operating an establishment

Oxidation
Chemical process that causes fats to spoil

Oyster knife
Short, blunt knife used to shuck, or open, oysters

P

Pancake
Medium-weight pour batter that has been pan-fried on an open greased griddle

Pan-fry
Cook food in hot fat or oil over medium heat

Parasite
Organism that needs to live inside a host to survive; one example is trichinella spiralis, commonly known as roundworms

Parboil
Cooking food slightly before braising, grilling, or gratining

Paring knife
Small knife used to trim and pare vegetables and fruits

Parissienne (pah-REE-see-en) scoop
Used to cut out ball shapes from soft fruits and vegetables

Pasteurization (pass-cher-i-ZAY-shun)
Heat treatment that destroys harmful bacteria in milk and eggs

Pastry bag
Bag made of canvas, plastic, or nylon used to pipe out frostings, creams, and puréed foods

Pastry brush
Used to apply egg wash and other liquids to baked goods

Pastry knife
Used to mix shortening into dough

Peak hours
Times when an establishment is very busy

Percent
Number of parts per 100

Perforated spoon
Serving spoon with holes

Performance evaluation form
Form used to evaluate an employee's performance

Perishable
Food with a relatively short shelf life

Perpetual inventory
Inventory tracing through the use of continuous records of requisitions

pH
Measure of acidity or alkalinity on a scale from 0 to 14.0

pH level
Measure used to indicate the acidity or alkalinity of a food

Physical hazard
Materials that are flammable, explosive, highly reactive to air or water, or stored under pressure that could cause damage to property and immediate injury

Physical inventory
Actual number of units of goods in storage

Pie server
Used to lift out and serve individual pieces of pie

Pigment
Substance that gives a food its color

Pizza cutter
Used to cut pizza and rolled-out dough

Plating
Arranging the presentation of food items on the serving plate or dish

Poach
Cook food completely submerged in liquid below the boiling point at temperatures of 180°F to 185°F (82.2°C to 85°C)

Polyphenoloxidase (PAHL-lee-fen-il-OX-ee-days)
Enzyme in some fruits that causes cut fruit to turn brown once the inside flesh is exposed to air

Popularity index
Percentage of total portion sales represented by each item

Portfolio
Collection of samples that highlight your interests, talents, contributions, and studies; important item to bring to job interviews

Portion inventory and reconciliation
Control method that compares portion inventory and the number of portions consumed

Portion scale
Scale used to measure ingredients, from 1/4 oz to 1 lb

Potable water
Water that is safe for drinking

Potential savings
Difference between actual and standard costs

Potentially hazardous foods
Foods that are most often the cause of foodborne illness outbreaks, usually moist, high-protein foods

Potwashing machine
Dishwasher large enough to wash large pots and pans

Prejudice
Biased judgment or opinion not based on fact

Premises
Property including restaurant and surrounding areas

Prime cost
Total cost of food sold, payroll, payroll taxes, and employee benefits

Production sheet
Form used to determine production quantities; lists each menu item and the portion of each expected to be sold

Profit
Dollar amount left when revenues are greater than costs

Profitability
Having higher revenue than costs

Profiterole (pro-FEET-uh-roll)
Tiny, unsweetened cream puff shell

Protein
Nutrient used mainly to build and repair body tissue

Pullman loaves
Loaves of sliced white bread used to make sandwiches

Pulper extractor
Waste disposal system that removes moisture and water from waste and reduces it to a paper-like consistency

Purchase specification
Form that lists food items to be purchased and the desired characteristics of each

Purée
Method used to process food into a smooth pulp

Q

Quality grade
Grading standards developed for fresh and canned fruits and vegetables by the USDA

Quiche (keshe)
Egg custard baked in a pastry shell

Quick bread
Bread made with chemical leaveners that work more quickly than yeast; including muffins, scones, and biscuits

R

Radicchio (rah-DEE-key-oh)
Type of salad green

Ramekin (RAM-uh-kin)
Small ceramic, oven-proof dish

Range
Cooking unit with open heat sources

Reach-in refrigerator/ freezer
Smaller than a walk-in refrigerator or freezer; usually has one, two, or three internal compartments with full-sized or half doors

Receiving table
Table where employees check, weigh, and inspect delivered items

Recommended Dietary Allowance (RDA)
Daily nutrient standards developed by the National Academy of Sciences that cover the average needs of various population groups

Reconcile
Match sales checks from the kitchen to production records

Reduce
Decrease the volume of liquid by simmering or boiling

References
People who know an applicant well and can provide information about that person—his or her character, work ability, or academic standing; needed for job application forms

Requisition
Form used to record items taken from inventory

Résumé (RE-zoo-may)
Written summary of past experience, skills, and achievements related to the job being sought

Revenue
Income from the sale of product before expenses are deducted

Ring-top burner
Range with different sized rings or plates that can be added or removed to allow more or less heat to cook the food item

Risk
Chance that a condition or set of conditions will lead to a foodservice hazard

Roast
Cook food using indirect heat in a closed environment; requires a longer cooking time than baking

Roasting pan
Shallow pan used to roast and bake foods such as meats and poultry

Role play
Training exercise in which employees act out the parts of the job function they have learned

Root vegetable
Vegetable that has a single root that extends into the ground and provides nutrients to the part of the plant that exists above ground

Rotary oven
Oven with 3-5 circular shelves on which food cooks as the shelves move around a central rod

Rotisserie (roe-TIS-er-ee)
Cooks food on a rotating spit in front of a heat source

Rubber spatula (SPACH-e-la)
Used to fold ingredients together and scrape the sides of bowls

S

Salad
Single food or a mix of different foods accompanied by or held together with a dressing

Salad dressing
Liquids or semi-liquids used to flavor salad

Salamander
Small broiler used primarily for browning or glazing the top of food

Sales
Income resulting from an establishment exchanging products and services for money

Sales check
Form on which a server records items ordered by customers

Sales history
Written record of the number of portions of each item sold every time that item appeared on the menu

Salsa
Mexican dip containing peppers and tomato sauce

Sandwich spreader
Short, stubby spatula used to spread sandwich ingredients and condiments

Sanitarian
Representative of a public health department who is professionally trained in sanitation and public health

Sanitary
Free of harmful levels of disease-causing microorganisms and other harmful contaminants

Sauce pot
Used to prepare sauces, soups, and other liquids

Saucepan
Small pan with a single long handle used for general cooking on ranges

Sauté(saw-TAY)
Cook food quickly in a small amount of fat or oil over high heat

Sauté(saw-TAY) pan
Either a slope-sided or straight-sided pan used to sauté and pan-fry a variety of foods

Scale
Equipment used to weigh ingredients

Scoop
Short-handled measuring utensil used to portion soft foods such as ice cream, butter, and sour cream

Seed vegetable
Vegetable in which the seed, and/or pod of the plant is eaten

Semivariable cost
Cost that has both a fixed and a variable component

Separate course salad
Light salad that "cleanses the palate" after a rich dinner and before dessert

Serrated slicer
Knife with a long, thin, serrated blade used to slice breads and cakes

Service encounter
Customer contact with an operation's employees

Service guarantee
Operation's guarantee of customer service satisfaction

Service plan
Organized, systematic method of handling customer service

Shallow poach
Cook food partially submerged in a liquid below the boiling point at temperatures between 160° and 180°F (71.1° and 82.2°C)

Sharpening stone
Used to sharpen knives

Sheet pan
Shallow pan used to bake cookies, rolls, and cakes

Shirr
Cooking method in which food, such as an egg, is cooked in a shallow, buttered dish

Short-term goal
Operation goal that covers periods of time, such as one day, one month, or one year

Shuck
Term used to describe opening a mollusk

Sieve (siv)
Used to sift flour and other dry ingredients

Simmer
Cook food completely submerged in liquid below the boiling point at temperatures of 185° to 205°F (85° to 96.1°C)

Single-tank conveyor (con-VAYer) dishwasher
Dishwasher in which dishes are sent through one tank on a conveyor

Single-tank door dishwasher
Dishwasher in which dishes are sent through one tank through a door

Skimmer
Used to take the foam off of stocks and soups

Slicer (knife)
Used to slice cooked meats

Slicer (machine)
Machine used to slice foods using a circular blade

Slotted spoon
Serving spoon with long openings that allows liquid to drain while holding solid food items on the spoon

Slow-roasting oven
Roasts meats slowly at low temperatures to reduce shrinkage, maintain moisture, and brown the surfaces of meats

Smoke detector
Device designed to detect fire in its early stages; requires an air flow to detect a fire

Solid spoon
Serving spoon without holes used to spoon out both liquid and solid ingredients

Soufflé (soo-FLAY)
Light, fluffy baked egg dish consisting of a base (such as a heavy white sauce) mixed with egg yolks and flavoring ingredients into which beaten egg whites are folded just before baking

Spices
Bark, roots, seeds, buds, or berries of an aromatic plant; most often used in their dried form; can be purchased whole or ground

Spit
Stick or post on which meat is placed and cooked in a rotisserie oven

Standard employee hours
Number of employee work hours required in both variable-cost and fixed-cost categories to perform forecasted work

Standard portion cost
Dollar amount that a standard portion should cost, given the standard ingredients and procedures for its production

Standard portion size
Fixed quantity served to a customer for a fixed selling price

Standardized recipe
Detailed instructions describing the way a particular foodservice operation prepares a particular dish

Starch
Complex carbohydrate found in foods such as potatoes, corn, rice, grits, pasta, oatmeal, and cornmeal

Steak knife
Used to cut cooked cuts of meat

Steam
Cook food over, but not directly in, boiling liquid in a covered pot

Steam table
Used to hold hot foods for service

Steamer
Steams food using a set of stacked pots; the lower pot holds boiling water; the upper pot has perforated bottom that allows the steam to enter through and cook the food in the pot above

Steam-jacketed kettle
Free standing or tabletop kettle used to heat liquid foods like soups and stews quickly and evenly

Stem vegetable
Vegetable in which the fibrous plant stem is eaten

Stereotype
Assumption that all members of a group fit the same pattern

Stew
Sear bite-sized pieces of food, then

cover them in liquid and simmer in a covered pot

Stir-fry
Cook food quickly in a small amount of fat or oil over high heat while constantly stirring

Stock pot
Large pot used to prepare stocks

Stores
Food items purchased and kept in inventory for future use; charged to cost when issued from inventory

Straight spatula (SPACH-e-la)
Flexible, round-tipped spatula used to ice cakes, spread fillings and glazes, and level dry ingredients when measuring

Strainer
Used to strain pasta, vegetables, and other larger foods cooked in liquid

Summer fruit
Fruit thats natural growing season occurs during the summer months

T

Tahini (tuh-HEE-nee)
Sesame seed paste

Tea sandwich
Small, cold sandwiches usually served on bread or toast, trimmed of crusts, and cut into shapes

Temperature danger zone
Temperature range between 40° and 140°F (4.4° and 60°C) within which most microorganisms grow and reproduce

Tempura (tehm-POO-rah)
Japanese breaded and deep-fried vegetables

Tilting fry pan
Used to grill, steam, braise, sauté, and stew all types of food

Tongs
Scissor-like utensil used to pick up and handle all kinds of food items

Tourné (TOUR-nay)
Knife used for cutting curved surfaces onto vegetables

Toxic
Poisonous

Toxic metal contamination
Contamination that occurs when high-acid foods are prepared with utensils or stored in containers made of metals such as copper, brass, or galvanized zinc

Toxin
Poison

Trade school application
Form designed by trade schools that asks basic personal information about background and education

Trash compactor
Waste disposal system that reduces dry waste by smashing it down, or making it more compact

Tropical fruit
Fruit that originates in tropical locations

Tuber
Fleshy root or stem of a plant, such as a potato, that is able to grow into a new plant

U

Underliner
Part of the salad also called the base

USDA
The United States Department of Agriculture; responsible for developing quality grades for fresh and canned vegetables and fruits

Utility cart
Used to transport food and supplies to storage areas

Utility knife
All-purpose knife used to cut fruits and vegetables

V

Variable cost
Expense directly affected by changes in sales volume

Vegetable
Herbaceous (herb-like) plant that can be partially or wholly eaten; has little or no woody tissue

Vegetable peeler
Used to peel potatoes, carrots, and other vegetables

Vegetable salad
Salad with vegetables as the main ingredients

Vertical cutter mixer (VCM)
Used to cut, mix, and blend foods quickly with a rotating blade

Vinaigrette (vin-uh-GRETT)
Classic French salad dressing made with oil and vinegar and optional herbs, spices, and flavorings

Virgin olive oil
Oil made from the first pressing of olives

Virus
Small, simple microorganisms that need living cells to grow and multiply; are transported by food and water and cause foodborne illness even when present in small numbers

Vitamin
Compounds found in many types of foods that help carbohydrates, proteins, fats, and minerals work properly

Void sheet
Form used to record the number of portions rejected by customers; lists the server, the reason the item was returned, and the sales volume of the menu item

Volume
Amount of space an ingredient takes up; type of measurement

Volume measure
Similar to liquid measuring cups, but bigger; usually in customary sizes 1 pint, 1 quart, 1/2 gallon, and 1 gallon

W

Waffle
Medium-weight pour batter that is cooked and formed in a specially designed waffle maker or iron

Walk-in refrigerator/freezer
Large refrigerator or freezer that is large enough to walk into

Water activity (a_w)
Moisture or water content in food

Water-soluble vitamin
Vitamins that mix only with water (vitamins B and C)

Weighted average purchase price
Price determined by multiplying the number of items in the opening inventory and in each purchase by their individual purchase prices, adding these amounts, and then dividing by the total number of items involved

Wing whip
Mixer attachment used to whip, mash, and cream heavy foods

Winter fruit
Fruit thats natural growing season occurs in the winter months

Wire whip
Used to mix, beat, and stir ingredients; also a mixer attachment used to add air to light foods, such as egg whites and frosting

Word-of-mouth advertising
Advertising that results from customers sharing their opinions of a restaurant with their friends and acquaintances

Workers' compensation
State-administered program designed to help employees who are injured in accidents that occurred at work, or who become sick because of job-related reasons

Y

Yeast
Fungi that require sugar and moisture for survival; can spoil food

Yield
Number of servings or portions a recipe makes

Yield percentage
Percent of an entire purchase that is available for portioning after all in-house processing has been done

Zester
Used to shred small pieces of outer peel from citrus fruits such as oranges, lemons, and limes

Index
OF KEY TERMS

B

F

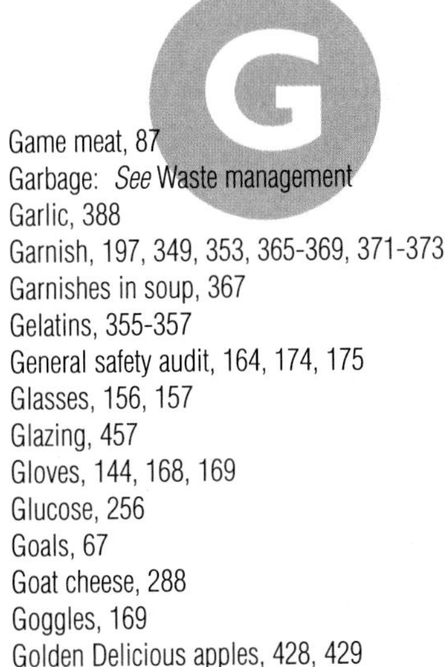

H

I

N

O